Atrocities on Trial

Historical Perspectives on the Politics of Prosecuting War Crimes

Edited by

PATRICIA HEBERER

and

JÜRGEN MATTHÄUS

Foreword by

MICHAEL R. MARRUS

Published in association with the United States Holocaust Memorial Museum

UNIVERSITY OF NEBRASKA PRESS · LINCOLN AND LONDON

Published in association with the United States
Holocaust Memorial Museum, 100 Raoul Wallenberg
Place Southwest, Washington DC 20024-2126

© 2008 by the Board of Regents
of the University of Nebraska
All rights reserved
Manufactured in the United States of America
∞
Library of Congress Cataloging-in-Publication Data
Atrocities on trial : historical perspectives on the
politics of prosecuting war crimes / edited by Patricia
Heberer and Jürgen Matthäus ; foreword by Michael
R. Marrus.
p.   cm.
Includes bibliographical references and index.
ISBN 978-0-8032-1084-4 (pbk. : alk. paper)
1. War crime trials—Germany. 2. War crime trials.
I. Heberer, Patricia. II. Matthäus, Jürgen, 1959–
KZ1176.A87 2008
341.6'90943—dc22
2007036395
Set in Minion by Bob Reitz.
Designed by R. W. Boeche.

Contents

Tables

Foreword

MICHAEL R. MARRUS

Who could deny, as Hannah Arendt contended in the *Postscript* to her famous work on the Eichmann Trial, "the inadequacy of the prevailing legal system and of current juridical concepts to deal with the facts of administrative massacres organized by the state apparatus"?[1] Certainly not the authors presented in this collection, whose work is so diligently assembled by my colleagues Patricia Heberer and Jürgen Matthäus. I draw evidence from virtually all of our authors of how difficult it was to bring the Holocaust into the courtroom in a way that seems commensurate with that catastrophe—not only in the immediate aftermath of the Second World War, but extending forward, even to our own time.

Despite this inadequacy, Arendt insisted on the urgent need to bring legal judgment to bear, and to do so precisely because the crimes in question were beyond the reach of conventional legal thinking and processes. Her case depended partly on the gravity of the offenses that were at the limits of human experience. Arendt insisted on the unprecedented character of the crimes of Nazism, and in particular those against the Jewish people. She wrote of "unheard-of atrocities, the blotting out of whole peoples, the 'clearance' of whole regions of their native population, that is, not only crimes that 'no conception of military necessity could sustain' but crimes that were in fact independent of the war and that announced a policy of systematic murder be continued in time of peace."[2]

Arendt's case for judicial proceedings also depended upon what she believed to be the continuing threat of totalitarian dictatorships. Awesome in scale and significance, the crimes of Nazism were in her view harbingers of a new dark age. It was "hardly deniable that similar crimes may be committed in the future," she observed. And so however ill-prepared the machinery and however undeveloped the conceptual apparatus, trials had to go forward. "It is essentially for this reason: that the unprecedented, once it has appeared, may become a precedent for the future, that all trials touching upon 'crimes against humanity' must be judged according to a standard that is today still an 'ideal.' If genocide is an actual possibility of the future, then no people on earth—least of all, of course, Jewish people, in Israel or elsewhere—can feel reasonably sure of its continued existence without the help and the protection of international law."[3]

How were the trials to help and protect? In her quarrel with the Israeli prosecutors of Adolf Eichmann, Arendt insisted that "the purpose of a trial is to render justice, and nothing else." The "something else," of course, was a message about history. This is not to say that Arendt opposed wider objectives. Doing justice, she implied, would fortify the commitment to doing right internationally and might undermine patterns of complicity that enabled crimes against humanity. Her animus, it became clear, was not so much against the storytelling elements of the Israeli prosecutors' case, but rather against the particular story they wanted to tell of Jewish suffering throughout the ages. Arendt was as keen as any of the participants to see her own understanding of Eichmann's crimes set the tone for the proceedings. But she had her own story to tell, having to do with the rise of totalitarianism in the modern era, with its great proclivity to commit crimes against all of humanity.

Notwithstanding her famous injunction about justice-seeking, Arendt sought what Lawrence Douglas has called a didactic trial, and in this she joined most of those responsible for putting Holocaust-related atrocities into the courtroom.[4] Providing explanations, indeed, seems to have been inseparable from justice-seeking in almost all war crimes prosecutions, as our authors frequently make clear. From the very first postwar trials of Nazi war crimes, prosecutors committed themselves to account for the stunning atrocities committed by the Nazi regime. And those who judged, even when they exercised judicial restraint in rendering their decisions, were conscious of the gravity of their choices, not only for the accused but also for those who sought to comprehend the significance of the crimes that had been committed. "It is our deep obligation to all the peoples of the world to show why and how these things happened," declared American prosecutor Telford Taylor, giving voice to this aspiration at the beginning of the Nuremberg Doctors' Trial.[5]

The chapters that follow recount, in varying ways, how contemporaries pursued their combined quest for justice and historical explanation with inadequate means. Reading through the contributions to this book sharpens one's appreciation of the legal and conceptual inadequacies to which Arendt referred, seen particularly from the vantage point of the prosecutors and other decision makers who framed the proceedings against the accused. Let me try to summarize what was missing from the standpoint both of justice and history. First, no one pretended that even the major perpetrators could all be found and brought before the bar. Many did not survive; many managed to escape, some with the help of powerful parties; and some slipped into an occupation zone where priorities were on cases other than those brought before the bar. As for perpetrators of lesser standing, whose involvement enabled the machinery of destruction, they were not always known and were certainly too numerous to bring to trial at the time. And sometimes too, it must be said, the energy or the will to do so was simply missing.

Second, it was not always clear that authorities had proper jurisdiction over the cases brought before them. Decision makers often divided on such issues because the crimes were unprecedented and the law was unclear, because the victorious powers could not always agree among themselves, because the standing of successor regimes was disputed or uncertain, and because different claims of jurisdiction were sometimes vigorously challenged. Third, the course of the trials was determined by the indictments of the accused, and these were shaped by any number of considerations—and not always a sober assessment of the historical record. Sometimes politics drove the proceedings, as with concerns, for example, that crimes against Allied military personnel be given precedence over crimes against German civilians. Sometimes prosecutors framed indictments with a view to securing convictions most easily, rather than venturing into legally uncertain territory. And sometimes prosecutors simply did not fully grasp the scope and character of the crimes that had been committed.

Fourth, the evidence was not always available or was imperfectly understood. Sometimes evidence had been destroyed or was difficult to find, but more often the occupation authorities found themselves swamped by evidence of massive criminality, without either the capacity or the means properly to assess it. And finally, although dedicated investigators and legally trained personnel poured into newly liberated zones seeking to discover wrongdoing, assemble cases, and conduct trials, experience and ability were sometimes inadequate to the task, and home governments did not always follow through with the necessary support or commitment to realize their objectives.

In consequence, the results were mixed, and understandably our authors provide different assessments about how well they did. Several essays end with allusions to the present, prompting my own question. Those in charge of prosecuting Nazi war crimes worked in unfamiliar territory, contending, for better or worse, with the historical conditions described in this book. Partly because of the historical research presented in this volume, we now know better. How well will our contemporaries do with similar challenges?

Notes

1. Hannah Arendt, *Eichmann in Jerusalem: A Report on the Banality of Evil*, rev. and enlarged ed. (New York: Penguin Books, 1997), p. 294.
2. Arendt, *Eichmann in Jerusalem*, p. 257. See my essay, "Eichmann in Jerusalem: Justice and History," in *Hannah Arendt in Jerusalem*, ed. Steven E. Aschheim (Berkeley: University of California Press, 2001), pp. 205–13.
3. Arendt, *Eichmann in Jerusalem*, p. 273.
4. Lawrence Douglas, *The Memory of Judgment: Making Law and History in the Trials of the Holocaust* (New Haven CT: Yale University Press, 2001).
5. *Trials of War Criminals before the Nuremberg Military Tribunals under Control Council Law No. 10*, Nuremberg, October 1946–April 1949 (Washington DC: U.S. G.P.O, 1949–1953), available online at http://www.ushmm.org/research/doctors/charges.htm, last visited 25 April 2006.

Introduction
War Crimes Trials and the Historian
PATRICIA HEBERER AND JÜRGEN MATTHÄUS

Confronted with new genocides and new issues of adjudicating state-sponsored crime across the globe, the international community looks to the past in its quest for a safer and more humane future. The specter of German atrocities committed during the Second World War appears both haunting and revealing. Much has been written on the history of trials against perpetrators of atrocities since 1945. The best-known chapter in this story is the effort of the International Military Tribunal (IMT) at Nuremberg to punish the top National Socialist leaders for waging aggressive war and perpetrating war crimes and crimes against humanity, including the implementation of what later became known as the Holocaust. Yet, in its historical and current implications, the issue transcends the Nuremberg case.

Despite the widespread desire to derive lessons from history, key questions relating to the origins and adjudication of extreme violence remain unanswered and have become the subject of considerable debate, both in our understanding of past trials of Nazi offenders and in our efforts to apply the principles of those prosecutions to present cases. What was originally perceived as a "war crime," an "act of atrocity," and a "crime against humanity," and how have these concepts and their application changed over time? How do the victors and the vanquished deal with mass violence and its universal, transnational, as well as societal, ramifications? In which contexts do investigations and trials take place, and how do these contexts influence their outcome? What is the relationship between historical reality, public perception, and their judicial treatment? Who are the perpetrators and what image—as a group as well as individuals—is portrayed of them in the course of the judicial process? How do historians, with the benefit of hindsight, judge the efforts by prosecutors and courts?

This book offers less clear-cut answers to these questions than it does evidence for the diversity and multifaceted nature of the subject matter in its historicity. The volume focuses on the murder of the European Jews—a crucial crime not only in itself, but also for our general understanding of the interrelation between atrocities and adjudication. The prosecution of Nazi offenders has continued with varying intensity for the past five decades, as has the attempt at coming to terms with the question of where to draw the line between legitimate and illegitimate violence in times of war. Although the number of court cases related to the Second World War has declined over the years, public interest in punishing crimes against humanity has increased due to the growing perception that they form less an aberration than a potentiality in the history of modern societies. If this book contributes to a better understanding of these crimes in their historical contexts, it will have achieved its goal.

War Crimes

Definitions of "war crimes" and their manifestations remain problematic. In public as well as in scholarly discourse, the term's connotations range from state-sponsored violence, atrocities, violations of the rules of war, military aggression, and crimes against humanity to genocide.[1] Since 1945 the changed understanding of the Holocaust corroborates the fact that the application of these terms to any specific historical set of events depends on the quality and scope of violence as much as on contemporary perceptions and interests. Today, reference to "Nazi crimes" can include legalized expropriation and state-sanctioned robbery suffered by Jews during the Third Reich; yet during the war, there was not even a word to properly describe the murder of the European Jews by Germany and its allies, other than the bizarre euphemism coined by the perpetrators—"Final Solution of the Jewish question." It was at least partly this terminological void that prompted Raphael Lemkin to devise the concept of genocide as a heuristic prerequisite for the understanding of this most troubling of all political phenomena.[2]

The mass atrocities that occurred throughout the twentieth century, and continue to occur, point to the inherent quandary of dealing with a subject that seems to transcend the limits of historiographical analysis. It is indeed understandable and tempting to give in to the desire to remove crimes of these proportions from history—for example, by pointing to innate, quasi-anthropological factors as the origins for hatred and aggression. The trials and investigations presented here indicate both the potential and the danger of judicial investigation for comprehending state-sponsored crime. This duality manifests itself in various forms: on the one hand, prosecutors, judges, and even the defendants and their counsel proceeded along the lines of logic in their dealing with the settings, circumstances, and suspects of acts of atrocity. In the process, historical data—perpetrator documents, witness statements, and additional evidence—were accumulated; these often turn out to be invaluable to those particularly interested in the historical setting. The murder of the European Jews is no exception: since the IMT, investigations and trials have collected, as well as generated, massive amounts of material that no individual scholar can ever hope to read, much less comprehend. No study that aims for new empirical insights into the Holocaust can ignore these sources.

On the other hand, due to their raison d'être of establishing personal guilt in the context of a specific legal framework, these same proceedings tend to isolate the crimes at hand and to stress the importance of individual over other, group-related or societal factors. It goes without saying that each person is responsible for his or her actions, and that the last bulwark against participation in genocide is the existence of moral or analogous inhibitions. Yet, the more that judicial proceedings focus on perpetrator motivation, the less likely they are to get us closer to historical reality. Not only will the individual impulse for a deed more often than not remain shrouded in the mysteries of the past; this past itself also gets more blurry if we move away from the victims' experiences and the broader setting and root causes that facilitated the transformation of murder into genocide.

"Victors' justice," a term especially popular in postwar Germany, implies the imposition of an alien, largely inappropriate, and unfair legal procedure against the vanquished. In view of the cases presented here, it is obvious that if this kind of justice ever existed, it offered the only chance for legal retribution. The total defeat of Nazi Germany and the Allied seizure of its governmental records were crucial for conducting postwar trials according to due process, either in terms of military, international, or criminal legal standards. These trials formed the basis for the perception of the true scope and quality of German crimes. As exemplified by the Nuremberg precedent, the work of prosecutors and courts reflects the legal as well as the broader environment within which they operate. In the aftermath of the Second World War, nations and governments were grappling with the effects of mass death, political disintegration, social crisis, and, in many cases, the legacy of collaboration. In one way or another, all these factors had an impact on the trials, producing what might appear from our current perspective as a streamlined, simplified, or distorted approach toward historical reality.[3]

Trials and History

Whoever wishes to perceive the phenomenon of war crimes and their adjudication based on historiographical findings must be aware that he or she stands on shifting ground. Nothing better attests to this fact than the interrelation between the Holocaust and its judicial treatment after 1945. According to conventional wisdom, especially the proceedings under Allied authority in the city of the Nazi Party rallies had a crucial and, for that matter, largely positive effect on the understanding of the Nazi system in general and of the Holocaust in particular. Michael Marrus has defined the IMT despite its shortcomings as "a turning point" in the public perception of the Holocaust as it "presented the first comprehensive definition and documentation to a non-Jewish audience of the persecution and massacre of European Jewry during World War II."[4] Other scholars have interpreted Nuremberg and its long-term impact similarly, first as it established the notion that the "Final Solution of the Jewish question" had been a deliberate aim of German politics until its culmination in the mass production of death in Auschwitz; and second by amassing an immense amount of incriminating material on the scope and quality of the murder of the European Jews.[5]

Recent scholarship has not refuted the claim that the IMT and subsequent Allied trials were of crucial importance for the postwar perception of Nazi crimes, yet its overall balance regarding their contribution to the proper understanding of the Holocaust is much more negative. Reconstructing the political framework of Holocaust-related trials in the first decade after the war, the British historian Donald Bloxham argues that "there was a fundamental dissonance between the *national* cleavage of the various trial programs in existence and the *international* nature of Nazi criminality in terms of both the locus of the crimes and the profile of the victims."[6] Consequently, the murder of the European

Jews as a specific topic of judicial investigation is basically absent from the record, trials such as the one against former *Einsatzgruppen* members in Nuremberg and a few other isolated cases notwithstanding.[7] According to Bloxham, as the Western Allies' official reactions to the unfolding "Final Solution" were "characterized by a reluctance to recognize the specificity of Jewish suffering . . . , so too the prosecution of Axis criminality was based on wrongly applied principles of liberal universalism which refused to give appropriate weight to the particular anti-Semitic thrust of Nazi racism."[8]

This assessment ties in with other shortcomings as perceived by current historiography. Even sympathetic commentators such as Michael Marrus have criticized judges and prosecutors for making "mistakes in detail and in wider conception" and for leaving "much work to be done in order to understand what we have come to call the Holocaust."[9] Other critics share Donald Bloxham's interpretation that the effects of Nuremberg included the "depiction of the Holocaust as a by-product of a monolithical German-Nazi conspiracy for European domination through war" and the "removal of the question of individual motivation to murder by subordinating it totally to meta-historical forces."[10] The prosecution, it seems in this perspective, got it all wrong when it comes to the proper understanding of such key aspects as decision making in the Third Reich, the German concentration camp system, the murder of approximately two million Polish Jews during "*Aktion Reinhard*," and the exploitation of Jewish forced labor. Where they got it right, they did not go far enough beyond the immediate surroundings of those sitting in the dock.[11]

The revision of conventional wisdom about Nuremberg that has taken place in recent years is to a large extent the result of the changing perception of both the Holocaust and the underlying Nuremberg principles in the sense of their growing disconnect since the time of the proceedings. In the decades after Nuremberg and in conjunction with shifting trends in historiography, politics, and public opinion, the Holocaust came to be regarded not only as the defining element of the Nazi era but also as the archetypical evil.[12] The interpretation of the "Final Solution" fostered at Nuremberg as a blueprint conceived by top Nazi leaders around Hitler and executed by the lower echelons in the field remained strong in historiography until the 1990s saw an increased interest in the murderous events themselves. In the course of a series of case studies on the Holocaust in Eastern Europe, historians came to place greater emphasis on shared responsibilities within German society, on local initiative as distinguished from top-level intervention. As a result, the proceedings in Nuremberg appeared to have led scholars into a blind alley cut off from properly perceiving historic reality.

By highlighting the shortcomings of the IMT and other Allied proceedings in dealing with the Holocaust, current historiography helps debunk the persistent myth of the German nation taken hostage by a small band of Nazi criminals. Yet at the same time, scholars run the risk of applying ahistorical categories to the work of jurists and thus blaming the past for omissions and faults visible only from the vantage point of the present. What the current focus on the failures of Nuremberg tends either to ignore or to criticize are basically two aspects: first, the achievements of Allied adjudication in broadening the concept of legal culpability to more than the few individuals in the dock, most notably by defining "criminal organizations" such as the SS and the Gestapo, without applying blanket assumptions about guilt by association; and second, the prime interest of the Nuremberg prosecutors in the future development of international law to confront the constant threats of aggressive war and state-sponsored mass violence.

Interpretations

Neither Nuremberg nor any other trial immediately after the Second World War was designed as a primarily historical enterprise to document the murder of European Jews outside the context of other German crimes. For the lawyers presenting the case for the prosecution, legal considerations and concerns about the future prevailed. In his final report on the proceedings, Telford Taylor, Chief of Counsel for War Crimes, points to the "major contribution which the Nürnberg trials have made to the preservation of peace and the establishment of world order under the rule of law." In the chapter of his report entitled "Significance and Influence of the Trials," only implicit mention is made of the Holocaust (regarding the "'Aryanization' of Jewish property"); in an earlier chapter (on "The Charges"), Taylor refers to "the crimes the average man would think of as most characteristic of the Nazis," namely the persecution and extermination of "national, political, racial, religious, or other groups" that "cover the vast and terrible world of the Nürnberg laws, yellow arm bands, 'Aryanization,' concentration camps, medical experiments, extermination squads, and so on."[13]

Taylor and the other Nuremberg prosecutors were not historians—even if they came to be regarded as such due to their later activities and writings[14]— but had an active interest in contemporary politics as a means to counteract the imminent threat of the world relapsing into a condition of lawlessness and mass violence. While Taylor was clearly aware that "the documents and testimony of the Nuremberg record can be of the greatest value showing the Germans the truth about the recent past," he focused less on historical events than on preventing their recurrence in the future by establishing the mechanisms for a working system of international penal law.[15]

Recent historiography's critical interpretation of the Nuremberg proceedings is based on the notion that Taylor and his colleagues interpreted the murder of the Jews and indeed Nazi policy at large as a top-down process driven by the mechanics of order and compliance in combination with Hitler's ability to implant his blueprint for the Nazi millennium into the entire German state apparatus, if not into German society. This approach is generally referred to as "intentionalism," one of the two main camps in historiography from the late 1960s until well into the 1990s.[16] Supporters of the opposing interpretation, "functionalism," might get a sense of achievement out of their rivals' failing scholarly appeal, would it not come at a time when especially among German historians functionalism is criticized for its reluctance to address the issues of perpetration and Holocaust memory.[17]

From a broader perspective, one could turn this criticism around and ask what intentionalism, or for that matter any other historiographical school, has done to give a voice to survivors and their memory. Indeed, with notable exceptions such as Joseph Wulf, Leon Poliakov, and a few others, even Jewish scholars tended to rely heavily on documentation generated by perpetrators, most notably the massive body of sources entered into the Nuremberg evidence, in their efforts to identify the process character of the Holocaust, its agents, and driving forces.[18] The most influential and to this day authoritative monographs study on the Holocaust—Raul Hilberg's *Destruction of the European Jews*—attests to the crucial insights that can be gained from a thorough study of the massive mountain of documentation left by the Third Reich.

After 1945, judicial proceedings had used mainly survivor testimony, if only marginally. While the Eichmann Trial brought about a sea change in the direction of firmly integrating live Holocaust memory into judicial proceedings, the Jerusalem court relied on survivor testimony less to attest to Eichmann's criminal record than to present the history of the Holocaust in general. Especially the national setting of subsequent trials has highlighted the problem of political utilization. Having no trials is as much a political statement as is conducting them in the public limelight; yet it is the latter that draws the most criticism. Hannah Arendt went as far as branding the Jerusalem proceedings a "show trial," an interpretation Lawrence Douglas has criticized for its formalistic nature;[19] still, the borderline between rendering justice based on specific charges and providing a forum for the public perception of monstrous crimes remains elusive.

With its broad definition of what legal proceedings should or can be about, the Eichmann Trial also changed the role of the defense lawyer. Instead of grounding their case on the conviction that the claim of the accused to innocence is correct, defense attorneys have increasingly criticized extra-legal influences on trials and the containment of perpetration, allegedly out of political expediency, to the person in the dock. Similarly, many lawyers and others active in the legal support of prominent politicians brought before a judge for having committed war and related crimes—Slobodan Milosevic, Saddam Hussein—attempt to transcend what prosecutors wrote in the indictment and to use court proceedings for what from their perspective looks like setting the historical record straight.

Perspectives

While the IMT and other prominent trials dominated the historian's perception of German crimes during the Nazi era, mainstream historiography ignored for a long time the later, more recent investigations and court proceedings against persons involved in one way or another in the implementation of the "Final Solution." In West Germany alone, more than 100,000 investigations into Nazi-related crimes carried out until 1992 led to roughly 6,500 guilty verdicts of which 85 percent related to lesser crimes or crimes committed prior to the outbreak of war.[20] With the exception of a few internationally recognized trials, the significance of cases against the large number of unknown but crucially important agents of genocide, including those who had not been former members of "criminal organizations" as defined at Nuremberg, remained unexplored by historians until fairly recently.

There are two principal reasons for this. First, public opinion in general and professional historians in particular in the countries where the trials were held took little notice of them.[21] Second, the legacy of Nuremberg, as perceived by most historians, implied that it would make more sense for the understanding of the "Final Solution" and its driving forces to investigate Hitler's *Weltanschauung*, high-level policy, and decision-making processes than to bother with the details of what appeared as the implementation of a preconceived grand design. Seen from this perspective, trials against the executors of the "Final Solution"—especially those posted on the eastern borders of the German wartime empire—seemed to be largely a forensic and much less an analytical enterprise, with few if any scholarly implications.

In recent years this situation has changed markedly, although there are still large numbers of cases—for example, the British war crimes program or early postwar proceedings at German courts[22]—that remain to be thoroughly researched. There is a wave of interest taken by international scholarship not only in the documentation collected in the course of post-Nuremberg trials and investigations but also in the history of these later and less well-known trials themselves. This broadening of the source base has led to some important modifications in our understanding of the Holocaust, especially in regard to perpetration. The image of the agents of genocide now incorporates institutions such as the German Army, the "ordinary men" of the German order police, or the health and labor administrations that before received little or no attention. Though often highly specialized, these studies have linked perpetration to other, ostensibly less destructive aspects of Nazi rule, such as race and resettlement policy, and have shown the many structural links between the persecution of Jews and other victims groups. A whole new subfield focuses on studying perpetrators, particularly on their motivation at the time of the crime. This is not surprising given the obvious desire to know why those who committed the murder of the European Jews did what they did; another reason is the heavy reliance of this new area of research on postwar judicial sources, especially testimony produced for trial purposes.[23]

The interest historians currently display in the often graphic evidence generated by prosecutors and courts will no doubt generate further insights into the machinery of mass murder; yet it is not without problems. While the question of perpetrator motivation clearly played a role at court, especially in West German proceedings, the judicial record is extremely difficult to use for historical purposes, as are all postwar statements coming from the perpetrators themselves. Generally, the rule applies that the reliability of perpetrator testimony is greatest the further it is removed from the issue of personal guilt and the more it can be scrutinized against the background of other sources, such as witness testimonies, diaries, letters, or other wartime writings, rare as they usually are. Consequently, affidavits by the accused, created in the course of judicial investigations, should only be used with caution; they are a most problematic source to gauge personal motivation of perpetrators at the time of the crimes.

It is the task of historians to raise questions about the role of war crimes trials for our understanding of the past; at the same time, however, historical findings and the role of their originators cannot avoid becoming objects of critical reflection. As can be seen from the many trials that took place after 1945 to which historians paid little or no attention, lawyers displayed a greater and earlier interest in the historicity of the Holocaust than did the professional keepers of memory. Despite all progress and occasional claims to the contrary, there is no reason to believe that Holocaust historiography has reached its peak of insight. The broad and persistent interest taken in the "Holocaust in the courtroom" should not deflect our attention from the fact that the historical dimension—that is, the potential to document the murder of the European Jews—is just one and, given our limited ability to learn from the past in a positive sense, probably not the most important aspect of war crimes trials.

Instead of perceiving war crimes trials as mere tools to foster our understanding of the events under investigation, historians should place greater emphasis on analyzing the legal and political contexts of these trials. While innovative in historiographical terms, some aspects of the current criticism of Nuremberg have rather positivistic connotations by feeding into the skepticism vis-à-vis international mechanisms of adjudicating war crimes and by supporting the notion that in punishing these crimes political expediency often overrides legal principles. This seems especially problematic at a time when national attempts at punishment pose grave questions as to their moral legitimacy and judicial viability, be it as a result of extraterritorial incarceration, military justice, or the rulings of civilian courts, and when the definitions of war and its systems of rules are undergoing significant changes.

On the part of those involved in the prosecution, Nuremberg was as much an exercise in setting the historical record straight as it was a means to establish the mechanism for enforcing the rules of law in a future international setting. Telford Taylor wrote at the height of the Vietnam War in view of the atrocities committed by American troops: "As the principal sponsor, organizer, and executant of the Nuremberg trials, the United States is more deeply committed to their principles than any other nation."[24] With the benefit of hindsight and in view of the ongoing refusal by the U.S. government to subject its own citizens to an international criminal court, it seems that Taylor's analysis was overly optimistic. It may well be that, over time, the accuracy of Taylor's analysis will be measured by the outcome of the still ongoing American debate about the desirability of subjecting its own citizens to the jurisdiction of a permanent international criminal court.

Topics

Based on a wide range of archival sources, many of which have become available to researchers only since the early 1990s, this book provides both case studies and in-depth analyses on the historical and contemporary dimensions of applying the rules of law to state-sponsored crimes. Instead of aiming at an inevitably elusive comprehensiveness and finality, the contributions to this anthology present insights into the complexity of the issues involved that make it difficult to arrive at simple answers and all-encompassing generalizations. The balance may fall short in terms of justice being done to such a topic; yet, what holds the book together is the awareness that justice is, like historiography, an exercise in approximation. Beyond preserving the evidence of the crimes committed, it is part of the historian's task to do justice to the attempts by lawyers, judges, and the wider legal, political, and societal framework in coming to terms with war crimes in their deadly and destructive manifestations.

Part 1 of this volume explores precedents set in the adjudication of German war crimes in the twentieth century, both in the historical setting of the Weimar Republic and again in the very earliest months of Allied occupation of Germany following World War II. Articles in this segment examine the notion of what a war crime is and how the unprecedented scope of the Holocaust has altered and transformed this notion. In "The Lessons of Leipzig: Punishing German War Criminals after the First World War," volume co-editor Jürgen Matthäus shows how the failure of an Allied proposal to set up an international court in the wake of the Great War left adjudication of the crimes of the Kaiser's Germany to fledgling Weimar courts. With one degree of separation from "victors' justice," the German Supreme Court in Leipzig (*Reichsgericht*) largely failed to grapple with the issues of legitimate war crimes in a direct or impartial way. A stillborn effort at effective justice, Matthäus argues, these trials represented an unfinished prologue to later efforts at Nuremberg following yet another destructive European war.

In "Early Postwar Justice in the American Zone: The 'Hadamar Murder Factory' Trial," co-editor Patricia Heberer assays the expansion of the definition of "war crimes" in the face of extraordinary Nazi German criminality. In trying the personnel of the Hadamar "euthanasia" (T4) facility in October 1945, American prosecutors stepped beyond the traditional interpretations of "war crimes" in order to conduct the first mass atrocity trial in the U.S. zone of occupation. Their endeavors tested the reach of international law before the legal concept of "crimes against humanity," set down by the IMT at Nuremberg, greased the wheels of postwar justice. In "U.S. Army War Crimes Trials in Germany, 1945–1947," Lisa Yavnai further elucidates this trend, examining the work of U.S. military commissions in adjudicating classical violations of international law and Nazi atrocities in the American zone. In what was the largest-scale prosecution of military, civilian, and state-sponsored war crimes in history, Yavnai shows how essentially unprepared American prosecutors and officials struggled to bring Nazi perpetrators to book. She illustrates how particularly the American system of formulating "parent" cases for concentration camp settings in the U.S. zone became an valuable legacy for later generations of prosecutors and historians with important legal, political, and historical ramifications.

Part 2 of this volume, "Allied Courts and German Crimes in the Context of Nuremberg," puts the complex of trials following the International Military Tribunal—its successor Nuremberg cases and contemporary national and Allied zonal trials—at center stage. Here, not only the will to do justice but also the political agendas and expediencies associated with the Cold War brought their part to bear upon the development of these proceedings. Jonathan Friedman explores the difficulties and conflicts involved in American efforts to bring "major war criminals"[25] to justice in "Law and Politics in the Subsequent Nuremberg Trials, 1946–1949." After attempts to mount additional trials under quadripartite Allied auspices foundered with the conclusion of the IMT, prosecutors in the American zone forged on alone with twelve subsequent Nuremberg proceedings, focusing their aim on disparate professional groups and organizations that had taken part in Nazi criminality. Friedman examines the confluence of legal and geopolitical interests in shaping this network of trials. Following this, we examine one of the successor proceedings; in "The Nuremberg Doctors' Trial and the Limitations of Context," Michael R. Marrus shows how the first of these twelve subsequent trials held under American auspices at Nuremberg proved to be a missed opportunity to define the principal crimes of German physicians during the Third Reich. An overemphasis on the grisly aspects of medical experimentation, an underestimation of the scope of the deadly "euthanasia" program, and complete silence with regard to the Nazis' ambitious compulsory sterilization policy gave a distorted view of medical crimes perpetrated in the name of National Socialism. Prosecutors' narrowly legalistic approach and a lack of comprehension of both the degree and breadth of medicalized killing ended in a significant failure to lay bare the responsibility of the wider German medical community in the Holocaust and other Nazi offenses.

Next, Ulf Schmidt connects the dots between this so-called Doctors' Trial and efforts of other postwar powers to adjudicate similar crimes. In "'The Scars of Ravensbrück': Medical Experiments and British War Crimes Policy, 1945–1950," Schmidt examines the jostling of British, American, and Polish authorities to bring the same criminals to trial. In doing so, he delineates the contours of a British postwar proceeding long overshadowed by its more famous Nuremberg contemporary, while portraying a German medical establishment complicit in the most horrific aspects of human medical experimentation. Finally, Jonathan Friedman returns with an essay exploring a series of cases trying personnel of the infamous Sachsenhausen concentration camp under three separate political jurisdictions. In "The Sachsenhausen Trials: War Crimes Prosecution in the Soviet Occupation Zone and in West and East Germany," Friedman notes how the influences of the Cold War and the political structures and agendas of each of the adjudicating powers left its different mark upon the same complex of crimes. How the Soviet Union, East Germany, and the German Federal Republic adjudged perpetrators against the backdrop of Sachsenhausen has just as much to say about the political orientation, national identity, and geopolitical raison d'être of each entity as it has about the crimes themselves.

Part 3 of this anthology, "Postwar Society and the Nazi Past," goes further with the suggestion that a state trying crimes that have both national and universal significance often, in doing so, casts a reflection of its own public consciousness. Was—and is—it possible for the countries most intrinsically involved in the crimes of the Holocaust—here Germany and Austria—to adjudge these crimes in a way that serves both justice and their own national reconstruction? How does a nation deal with its own criminal past, and does its historical conceptualization of this past change over time? In "'No Ordinary Criminal': Georg Heuser, Other Mass Murderers, and West German Justice," Jürgen Matthäus examines the career of Heuser, whose bloody role in the murder of Jews as a leader in the command of the Security Police and SD (KdS) in Minsk did not prevent him from becoming chief of the criminal police in the state of Rhineland-Westphalia in 1956. In so doing, Matthäus shows that by the time more systematic mechanisms for prosecution were in place in the Federal Republic and there was the will to use them, many agents of Nazi criminality had eased their way back into positions of relative security and respectability in postwar society.

In a similar vein, Rebecca Wittmann's "Tainted Law: The West German Judiciary and the Prosecution of Nazi War Criminals" highlights the difficulties imposed by both societal constraints and the German legal structure in prosecuting Nazi criminals in the German context. Focusing upon the Frankfurt Auschwitz Trial, the abortive investigations of the *Reichssicherheitshauptamt* (RSHA) infrastructure, and the Majdanek proceedings held in Düsseldorf in the 1970s, Wittmann shows that the prosecutors' narrow interpretation of the law and the German penal code's own statutes governing homicide and other capital offenses proved unwieldy tools in trying crimes of such an unprecedented magnitude. Generational change in the 1960s ushered in not only a fresh soci-etal perspective on the Nazi past, but also a new generation of jurists and pros-ecutors; still these developments proved inadequate to provide a framework for a more rigorous and efficacious determination of justice for the perpetrators of the Holocaust and related crimes.

Despite its ambiguous record, West Germany's efforts at postwar war crimes adjudication compares favorably with the example of its wartime partner, Aus-tria. In "Justice in Austrian Courts? The Case of Josef W. and Austria's Difficult Relationship with Its Past," Patricia Heberer explores how Austria's self-styled postwar national identity as "first victim of Nazi aggression" allowed that na-tion to ignore the extensive involvement of native Austrians in the crimes of the Holocaust. For while West German courts realized nearly seven hundred trials of accused Nazi perpetrators between 1955 and 1978, Austrian jurisprudence generated only twenty-eight similar proceedings within roughly the same time-frame. The example of gas van driver Josef W.—acquitted of murder in 1970 despite his full confession on the stand—emblemizes Austria's continuing in-ability and unwillingness to deal with its National Socialist past in a significant way.

The final installment of this volume, part 4, examines the legal, political, and ethical implications of past and present instances of jurisprudence involving war crimes and crimes against humanity. It explores the legacy of Nuremberg and its "progeny" both in terms of historical significance and in its modern-day applications. In "Crimes-against-Humanity Trials in France and Their Histori-cal and Legal Contexts: A Retrospective Look," Richard J. Golsan utilizes re-cent French court cases to question whether legal proceedings genuinely serve a historical purpose and fulfill our duty to remember. Reflecting on the Barbie, Touvier, Bousquet, and Papon cases of the late 1980s and 1990s, Golsan ob-serves France's amnesia—and later obsession—with the *les années noires*, the "dark years" of its Vichy past. His examples also serve vividly to demonstrate the manner in which latter-day jurisprudence can blur legal and ethical lines and obscure the historical record.

Next, Donald Bloxham considers more closely the ambiguous legacy of the International Military Tribunal. In "Milestones and Mythologies: The Impact of Nuremberg," Bloxham ponders whether that first international court of its kind was truly efficacious in meting out justice, in bearing witness to what was later known as the Holocaust, or indeed in serving as a deterrent to future state-sponsored programs of mass murder. Nuremberg did not inspire social change in either the victor or the vanquished, Bloxham argues, but social change—and the advent of modern day-genocides in Rwanda and Darfur—have changed the way we look at Nuremberg. John K. Roth has the last word. In "Prosecution, Condemnation, and Punishment: Ethical Implications of Atrocities on Trial," Roth surveys the ethical ramifications of prosecuting and punishing humans guilty of inhuman crimes. Punishment of the perpetrators of the Holocaust is not equal to complete justice for those who suffered, nor can it restore "the losses that do not go away," for Shoah victims and their families; yet there is no choice other than to pursue legal proceedings for such crimes, Roth argues, agreeing with Nuremberg prosecutor Justice Robert H. Jackson that "'civilization cannot tolerate their being ignored because it cannot survive their being repeated.'" Roth explores the ethics inherent in the Sixth Commandment, "Thou shalt not murder," musing that until its moral imperative is examined and observed in the individual conscience and in political and societal infrastructures, "humankind is just civilized enough not to succumb completely to atrocity but not to keep it in check either."

This work would not have possible without the help and support of many individuals. The editors would like to thank Paul Shapiro for breathing life into a long-dormant project, Benton Arnovitz and Peter Black for taking it under their wings in a phase of transition, and, especially, our contributors for their patience, cooperation, and warm collegiality in the face of one of history's many bleak subjects.

This project was initiated under the direction of the late Sybil Milton (1941–2000), Senior Historian of the United States Holocaust Memorial Museum from 1993 to 1997. This volume is dedicated to her memory.

Notes

1. For an overview of the existing literature, see Donald Bloxham, "From Streicher to Sawoniuk: The Holocaust in the Courtroom," in *The Historiography of the Holocaust*, ed. Dan Stone, pp. 397–419 (Houndmills/Basingstoke: Palgrave Macmillan, 2004); A. Dirk Moses, "The Holocaust and Genocide," in Stone, *Historiography of the Holocaust*, pp. 533–55, as well as the literature offered in the bibliography of this volume.

2. See Raphael Lemkin, *Axis Rule in Occupied Europe: Laws of Occupation, Analysis of Government, Proposals for Redress* (Washington DC: Carnegie Endowment for International Peace, 1944). On Lemkin and his impact on genocide studies, see Samuel Totten and Steven L. Jacobs, eds., *Pioneers of Genocide Studies* (New Brunswick NJ: Transaction, 2002).

3. On the interrelation between postwar trials and representation, see Lawrence Douglas, *The Memory of Judgment: Making Law and History in the Trials of the Holocaust* (New Haven: Yale University Press, 2001); Mark Osiel, *Mass Atrocity, Collective Memory, and the Law* (New Brunswick NJ: Transaction, 1997).

4. Michael Marrus, "The Holocaust at Nuremberg," *Yad Vashem Studies* 26 (1998): 5–41 (esp. 5–6); see also Jacob Robinson and Henry Sachs, *The Holocaust: The Nuremberg Evidence* (Jerusalem: Yad Vashem, 1976).

5. Donald Bloxham, *Genocide on Trial: War Crimes Trials and the Formation of Holocaust History and Memory* (Oxford: Oxford University Press, 2001), pp. 1–3. Joseph E. Persico in his *Nuremberg: Infamy on Trial* (New York: Penguin Books, 1994), p. 441, argues that "the one indisputable good to come of the trial is that, to any sentient person, it documented beyond question Nazi Germany's crimes" and that it proved regarding the Holocaust "that it all happened."

6. Bloxham, "Holocaust in the Courtroom," p. 399 (emphases in the original); see also his contribution in this volume.

7. *Trials of War Criminals before the Nuernberg Military Tribunals under Control Council Law No. 10*, vol. 4 (Washington DC: Government Printing Office, n.d.), Case 9: The *Einsatzgruppen* Case.

8. Bloxham, "Holocaust in the Courtroom," p. 401.

9. Marrus, "Nuremberg," p. 41; see also his "The Nuremberg Doctors' Trial in Historical Context" in this volume.

10. Bloxham, *Genocide on Trial*, p. 12.

11. See Bloxham, *Genocide on Trial*, p. 219; Hilary Earl, "Scales of Justice: History, Testimony, and the *Einsatzgruppen* Trial at Nuremberg," in *Lessons and Legacies*, vol. 6: *New Currents in Holocaust Research*, ed. Jeffry M. Diefendorf (Evanston IL: Northwestern University Press, 2004), pp. 325–51.

12. See John K. Roth, *Ethics during and after the Holocaust: In the Shadow of Birkenau* (Houndmills/Basingstoke: Palgrave Macmillan, 2005); Richard J. Bernstein, *Radical Evil: A Philosophical Interrogation* (Cambridge: Polity Press, 2002).

13. Telford Taylor, "Final Report to the Secretary of the Army on the Nuernberg War Crimes Trials under Control Council Law No. 10," Washington DC, 15 August 1949, pp. 64–71, 107–12 (quotes: 64, 112).

14. From among those involved with the Nuremberg proceedings, memoirs or similar accounts were written by Robert H. Jackson, Telford Taylor, Benjamin Ferencz, Whitney Harris, Drexel Sprecher, Robert M. W. Kempner, and Michael Musmanno.

15. Taylor, "Final Report", p. 112. See also Telford Taylor, *The Anatomy of the Nuremberg Trials: A Personal Memoir* (Boston: Little, Brown, 1992), p. 641, where he stresses that "the laws of war do not apply only to the suspected criminals of the vanquished nations."

16. For a summary of the debate, see Christopher R. Browning, "Beyond 'Intentionalism' and 'Functionalism': The Decision for the Final Solution Reconsidered," in Christopher R. Browning, *The Path to Genocide: Essays on Launching the Final Solution* (Cambridge: Cambridge University Press, 1992), pp. 88–101.

17. Nicolas Berg, *Der Holocaust und die westdeutschen Historiker: Erforschung und Erinnerung* (Göttingen: Wallstein Verlag, 2003); for an apt criticism of this book see Ian Kershaw, "Beware the Moral Highground," *Times Literary Supplement*, 10 October 2003.

18. See Dan Michman, *Holocaust Historiography: A Jewish Perspective: Conceptualizations, Terminology, Approaches, and Fundamental Issues* (London: Vallentine Mitchell, 2003).

19. Douglas, *Memory of Judgment*, pp. 110–12.

20. For the broader context see Rebecca Wittmann, *Beyond Justice: The Auschwitz Trial* (Cambridge MS: Harvard University Press, 2005), and her contribution to this volume.

21. See, e.g., Jürgen Wilke et al., *Holocaust und NS-Prozesse: Die Presseberichterstattung in Israel und Deutschland zwischen Aneignung und Abwehr* (Cologne: Böhlau, 1995).

22. The United Kingdom National Archive (former Public Record Office) in London holds records on c. 300 cases investigated between 1945 and 1950 that never made it to court. (We thank Stephen Tyas for this information.) The United States Holocaust Memorial Museum (USHMM) has microfilmed extensive collections of East German court cases against Nazi criminals at various German archives; these are available at the USHMM archive (see www.ushmm.org).

23. See, e.g., Alan E. Steinweis and Daniel E. Rogers, eds., *The Impact of Nazism: New Perspectives on the Third Reich and Its Legacy* (Lincoln: University of Nebraska Press, 2003); Diefendorf, *Lessons and Legacies* vol. 5; Jürgen Matthäus, "Historiography and the Perpetrators of the Holocaust," in Stone, *Historiography of the Holocaust*, pp. 197–215.

24. Telford Taylor, *Nuremberg and Vietnam: An American Tragedy* (Chicago: Quadrangle Books, 1970), p. 14. Earlier in the book, Taylor quotes Robert H. Jackson's opening words at the Nuremberg tribunal: that despite its focus on German crimes, "if it is to serve any useful purpose it must condemn aggression by any other nations," including those sitting in judgment at the IMT (pp. 11–12). While rejecting the use of "Nuremberg" as a label without historical precedent (p. 16), Taylor directly compares depictions of German atrocities committed against Jews in Eastern Europe and civilians in Greece with American actions in Vietnam (pp. 124–25, 138–39).

25. The Moscow Declaration of 1943 defined alleged perpetrators as "lesser war criminals," whose crimes were limited to a distinct locality, and "major war criminals," whose crimes had no specific geographical jurisdiction.

I

Precedents in Punishment

The Lessons of Leipzig
Punishing German War Criminals
after the First World War
JÜRGEN MATTHÄUS

One of the key twentieth-century events that prompted debates on war crimes and their adjudication was the experience of the First World War, with its unprecedented level of destructiveness. In the wake of the collapse of Imperial Germany in 1918, Allied leaders considered and then abandoned plans to prosecute German war criminals. Trials were eventually held in 1921 under German auspices at the German Supreme Court (Reichsgericht) in Leipzig, based on Allied allegations. According to traditional interpretations, this attempt at trying German war criminals proved abortive to the point that, in the Allied discussions during the Second World War, "the fiasco of the Leipzig trials" was regarded as an ideal example of how *not* to proceed.[1] In recent years, however, scholarship has embraced a new approach that echoes the assessment by Ernest Pollock, expert on international law, member of the British mission at the Leipzig court, and a prominent spokesman for legal reform at the Versailles peace conference.[2] In 1921 Pollock predicted that, in view of their unprecedented nature, "the effect of the [Leipzig] convictions will stand for ever."[3] He was right; the ongoing struggle by the victors and the vanquished with the issue of war crimes points to problems in coming to grips with these types of crimes that transcend the post–World War One setting.

The Inter-Allied Debate at the End of the War

The trials at the Leipzig Reichsgericht in 1921 marked a late phase in the Allies' attempt at addressing atrocities committed by Germans during the First World War. By the end of 1918, public discourse in Allied countries had defined specific incidents as typical of German brutality: in Britain, the execution of nurse Edith Cavell and Captain Charles Fryatt assumed emblematic value, while in the United States it was the sinking of the *Lusitania*. Belgium and France had less of a need for symbolic events since their people, cities, and landscape displayed the deep scars of an all-too destructive war. Russia and the Balkans, on the other hand, though heavily affected by Germany's military might, played no significant role in the perception of the victorious Western powers.[4]

The intensity of the debate in the Allied countries stood in marked contrast to the practical measures adopted in preparation for the peace conference. "Winning the war" had absorbed the energies of the Allies, while many of the questions relating to postwar policymaking remained unresolved. When their leaders gathered in Paris, they delegated the war crimes issue to a special body, the Commission on the Responsibilities for the War and Its Conduct.[5] Comprising fifteen men from ten countries and headed by U.S. Secretary of State Robert Lansing, the commission convened for the first time on 3 February 1919 at the French Department of the Interior to deliberate about a range of tasks around the core problem of the responsibility for war crimes.[6]

In order to proceed quickly, the commission divided itself into three groups with specific, though overlapping tasks. Sub-Commission no. 1 ("Sub-Commission on Criminal Acts") was "to discover and collect the evidence necessary to establish the facts relating to culpable conduct" regarding the inception and waging of the war. Sub-Commission no. 2 ("Sub-Commission on the Responsibility for the War"), presided over by Ernest Pollock, had to "prepare a report indicating the individual or individuals who are in its opinion guilty and the Court before which prosecutions should proceed," while Sub-Commission no. 3 chaired by Robert Lansing dealt with the "responsibility for violations of the laws and customs of war."[7] The commissions' reports were passed on to the Council of Four, which used them to formulate Articles 227 to 230 in Part VII ("Penalties") of the Versailles Treaty, closely followed (in Part VIII "Reparation") by the momentous war-guilt Article 231.[8]

Article 227 dealt specifically with the ex-Kaiser, providing for his public arraignment for supreme offenses "against international morality and the sanctity of treaties." An international tribunal was to be established "guided by the highest motives of international policy, with a view to vindicating the solemn obligations of international undertakings and the validity of international morality." As the Kaiser had removed himself from the scene by escaping to the Netherlands, the Allies pledged themselves to seek his surrender from the government at The Hague. Articles 228 to 230 dealt with other "persons accused of having committed acts in violation of the laws and customs of war" so they could be tried and punished according to military law after they had been handed over to the Allies "notwithstanding any proceedings or prosecution before a tribunal in Germany or in the territory of her allies." Germany was also obliged to surrender "documents and information of every kind" relevant for investigative and judicial purposes.[9]

Already the meetings of the Commission on the Responsibilities for the War and Its Conduct foreshadowed the problems that impacted on the trials at Leipzig. In the first days of inter-Allied talks in Paris, it became evident that different interests, attitudes, and approaches had to be reconciled. Focusing on how to establish a stable world order, the American delegation was highly skeptical of unprecedented judicial attempts at punishing war crimes.[10] France and Belgium, the two countries most affected by German military operations on the Western Front, expected quick material compensation and guarantees toward their future security—an aim that the issue of responsibility for the war and war crimes could help achieve. Among the leading Allied politicians, British prime minister David Lloyd George pushed hardest for an international war crimes tribunal.

The application of legal sanctions confronted the Allies with a number of practical problems, some of which were reflected in the agenda of the subcommissions. First, since the armistice was concluded before the Allies conquered much German territory, not only the Kaiser but also less senior German suspects remained outside the Allies' sphere of jurisdiction, while only a few suspected war criminals could be found among German POWs. Second, together with the majority of potential perpetrators, the Allies lacked the necessary evidence to substantiate allegations before a court. Britain, as it turned out at the first meeting of the Commission on the Responsibilities for the War and Its Conduct, was the only country that had prepared a preliminary list of the "principal offenders."[11] Lack of consensus triggered intense debate and occasional clashes among Allied delegates on the commission. Few of the basic arguments later brought forward in preparation for the International Military Tribunal at Nuremberg remained unmentioned; yet in Paris it was the Americans—the advocates of a new world order based on collective security—who resisted the changes in international law and practice sought by some European delegates.

In view of the problems involved, Ernest Pollock moved at the second meeting of the "Commission on the Responsibilities" that the Peace Conference be asked "to make it a condition of the next renewal of the Armistice, that the enemy shall hand over, for detention and trial, to any authority appointed by the Allied powers and the United States all persons whose names are notified to the enemy from time to time and also all documents which may be specified."[12] This proposal was of crucial importance for getting hold of war crimes suspects *prior to* the signing of the peace treaty and thus for carrying out trials under Allied jurisdiction. While delegates of other nations favored Pollock's initiative, chairman Robert Lansing nipped it in the bud by ruling "that this resolution exceeded the province of the Commission."[13]

Pollock also called for the creation of "an International Tribunal . . . composed of representatives of the Chief Allied States and the United States" that was to pass a sentence on the basis of "the principles of the Law of Nations as they result from the usages established among civilized peoples, from the laws of humanity, and the dictates of public conscience." The procedure to be followed by the tribunal allowed for representation by counsel, cross-examination of witnesses, public judgment, and trial in absentia. In its closing argument, the British memorandum stressed that the Allies should insist on proceeding quickly to facilitate an early sitting of the tribunal so that "stern justice be meted out to the offenders," and a "salutary example may then be set for all time."[14]

A heated debate ensued about the basic assumptions of Pollock's argument. Lansing objected "to the creation of a new tribunal, of a new law, a new penalty, which would be *ex post facto* in nature and thus contrary to an express clause of the Constitution of the United States and in conflict with the law and practice of civilized communities." The American representatives declared themselves "unwilling to be a party to the creation of an international tribunal before which, and under circumstances which could not be foreseen, the head of a State—in their case the President of the United States—could be haled as an ordinary individual." Despite pressure from Lloyd George and French Prime Minister Georges Clemenceau, President Woodrow Wilson upheld the American opposition toward creating an international court.[15]

In late April 1919, after the Allied leaders had basically agreed upon the "Penalties" clauses of the peace treaty,[16] Wilson convinced the other members of the

Council of Four that the proposal to keep in detention German POWs who were suspected of having committed war crimes meant "practically to take hostages." According to Wilson, if there was a precedent for such action, one would have to go back some hundreds of years in history.[17] By interpreting Pollock's idea of direct Allied control over potential war criminals as a retrogressive and illegitimate step, the U.S. administration turned it on its head before it was finally abandoned by leading Allied politicians. Having decided not to establish an international tribunal, the Allies left only two possibilities for war crimes trials to take place: according to Article 228, either the suspects were to be handed over to them, or Germany itself would initiate judicial proceedings. Instead of, as Pollock had argued, "the jurisdiction [being] secured by the terms imposed by the Victors in the war over the vanquished,"[18] the Allies based their hope for justice being done on Germany's willingness to cooperate. By this time, however, this expectation already seemed unfounded.

The Debate in Germany

Even before the Allies' conditions for concluding the Versailles Treaty became known, the German government had insisted that to hand over those of their countrymen accused by the victors of being war criminals would be totally unacceptable and threaten the very existence of postwar Germany. As the Western powers attempted but failed to secure from the Netherlands the extradition of the former Kaiser, political attention shifted to the question of how to try less prominent perpetrators living in Germany. When, in May 1919, former Imperial chancellor Theobald von Bethmann-Hollweg asked the Foreign Office for assistance in offering himself to the Allies to be tried in lieu of Wilhelm von Hohenzollern, officials of the new republic reiterated that "the Reich government will . . . in general decline to hand over a German to a court assembled by the enemy powers," as this would violate commonly accepted legal principles and existing German law.[19]

In the mind of Germany's military elite, extraditing suspected war criminals was one of those elements of the peace treaty that called for massive and, if need be, violent resistance to Allied demands.[20] Despite its defeat and the German revolution of 1918, the army had lost neither its prestige as a bastion of national honor nor its close links to the centers of state power.[21] The German war experience had been too traumatic for the general public to understand why, in addition to the human, material, and territorial losses inflicted on it, the Reich should bear the blame of having started the war, followed expansionist aims, and violated traditional rules of warfare. As soon as the Allies began drawing up lists of alleged German war criminals, politicians and military men in the Reich demanded a "counter-list" (*Gegenliste*) of Allied war crimes that, although never officially published, threatened further to alienate the Western powers.[22]

In August 1919 the constitutional convention of the young German republic (*Verfassunggebende Deutsche Nationalversammlung*) decided to establish a commission that would deal with questions of war guilt and the conduct of the war. In line with the prevailing attitude of the population at large, most of the parliamentarians of the Nationalversammlung and later the Reichstag favored a quid pro quo approach that gave allegations of Allied misconduct a higher priority than those directed against Germans. The final report of the commission, published in 1927, condemned the Allied demand to hand over suspected war criminals as an unprecedented breach of most elementary legal concepts.[23] Even liberal-minded men like the sociologist Max Weber were convinced that trials against German officers lacked any judicial foundation and merely reflected the political interests of "vengeful enemies" (*rachsüchtige Feinde*).[24]

After the signing of the peace treaty, German resistance against its "paragraphs of shame" (*Schmachparagraphen*) including "war guilt" Article 231 remained firm despite a rapidly changing political landscape. At the same time, in America as well as in Britain, popular support for taking decisive action eroded while France and Belgium insisted on the implementation of the "penalty" articles of the Versailles Treaty, if only to claim in case of German default that further sanctions were necessary. Attempts at compiling lists of suspects to be handed over by Germany for trial added to the inter-Allied controversy and reinforced German opposition. In the absence of any prospect for trials under international authority and in view of the diversity of Allied opinion, the German offer to proceed along the only alternative path left—that is, to try before the highest German court a comparatively small number of accused chosen from the roughly thousand cases on the Allied list—seemed to lead out of the impasse.[25]

The Kapp Putsch in March 1920 followed by the landslide election victory of the right in June confirmed the frailty of the Weimar Republic. In early May the Allies accepted the German proposal to have forty-five cases, selected by Britain, France, and Belgium, tried by the Reichsgericht. While the trials were to be held under the full legal responsibility of the Germans, the three Allied powers agreed to send missions to follow the court proceedings. Under the leadership of Solicitor-General Ernest Pollock, the British were best prepared: by late October 1920 they provided the Reichsgericht with a printed volume containing evidence for the (initially six, later reduced to four) British cases.[26] After several months of preparations and a purely German "test case" against three soldiers who were found guilty of plunder committed in the last weeks of the war in Belgium, the court was ready.[27]

On 23 May 1921 Dr. Heinrich Schmidt, chief justice (*Senatspräsident*) of the Second Criminal Senate, opened proceedings for the first case at Leipzig amidst the background of severe political turmoil over Upper Silesia and a number of other issues closely related to the peace treaty. The cases presented by the state prosecuting attorney (*Oberreichsanwalt*), Dr. Ludwig Ebermayer, on the basis of Allied evidence were handled with breathtaking speed. Some of the suspects could not be traced; others, such as U-boat commander Helmut Patzig, charged by the British with sinking a hospital ship and its lifeboats, had escaped the Reich. By 4 June 1921 the four British cases had been closed, resulting in one acquittal and three sentences between six and ten months' imprisonment. If the British had reason to complain, the Belgians and French were outraged: their cases tried until early July led to only one conviction and five acquittals followed by a massive wave of public consternation at home. An inter-Allied commission reviewing the German trials in January 1922 concluded that it was useless to proceed with further cases and that the remaining accused should be handed over to the Allies—a demand the Germans once again vigorously rejected. While the Reichsgericht continued until the early 1930s to lay and dismiss charges against alleged war criminals, the Allies remained divided on the issue. Great Britain, Japan, and Italy put the matter to rest. Belgium and France, on the other hand, pressed on until the mid-1920s by holding courts-martial of war criminals in absentia, as well as by demanding political sanctions against Germany.[28]

The verdicts leave no doubt that the Leipzig court's attempt at professional impartiality found its limitation where political interest and national honor were at stake. In the majority of cases, bias in favor of the defendants was hidden behind legal formalities: while the carefully selected four British cases were handled with great care, the less substantiated Belgian and French charges encountered fierce German resistance, even from state prosecutors and judges, and collapsed altogether with the withdrawal of the two missions after the first acquittals. Seniority also mattered: the higher the rank of the accused, the less likely it was that the court would pass a guilty verdict. In the case of General Karl Stenger, who allegedly had ordered the execution of French POWs, his mere word sufficed to convince the state prosecutor and the judges of his innocence, while one of his subordinates who claimed to have followed the general's orders received a prison sentence.[29] Observers outside Germany minced no words in criticizing the Leipzig proceedings as a "travesty of justice," a "judicial farce," and—in the case of the *New York Times*—a "great moral show . . . where the German Supreme Court is making of a few privates and minor officers scapegoats for the army and the nation."[30]

For different reasons, German press coverage of the trials was just as critical. As the war crimes issue offered an ideal focal point for national identification in a time of intense inner-German turmoil, only a few newspapers, such as the Berlin-based *Vossische Zeitung*, aimed at a factual report of the proceedings. Conservative and provincial dailies branded the whole enterprise as unprecedented, unjustifiable, and immoral, a parody of justice based on national self-abuse and the overwhelming power of the victors. The actual allegations receded into the background. Whether the accused was a criminal or not, the *Braunschweiger Neueste Nachrichten* wrote in an editorial at the start of the first trial, "this is not the question to be considered here. Rather, the question is how low Germany has sunk."[31]

This paper and others slandered the German left for contributing to "the haze of lies and contempt" spread by Allied propaganda.[32] In fact, there was little evidence for this allegation. According to dailies associated with the Social Democratic Party, the trials offered a chance to highlight the corruption of the old system, a fault that had been visible in its treatment of the lower classes.[33] However, the Social Democratic left did not differ appreciably from right-wing critics in commenting on the international aspects of the Leipzig trials. The *Bremer Volkszeitung* stated that the charges brought by the Allies were "careless distortions and clearly aimed at inciting the indignation of the cultivated peoples." Not only did the claim "that the entire German army is an army of 'huns'" serve political purposes, but German judges also participated in a "comedy" and provided the enemy countries with "subterfuges to again agitate against Germany."[34] While deploring the undeniable degeneration of warfare and morality, the paper called for closure: "Whatever might follow, these war criminals' trials remain a tragedy. Again and again they incite passion and evoke the most terrible pictures of the world war in the memory of the peoples, while only a beneficent forgetfulness [*ein wohltuendes Vergessen*] could prepare real peace."[35]

Exceptional Ruling: The Dithmar/Boldt Case

The case against two German navy lieutenants, Ludwig Dithmar and John Boldt, who had served aboard the submarine *U-86*, had special features that highlight the political and legal dimensions of the Leipzig experiment. The initial impulse for the investigation had come from the British, who accused First Lieutenant Helmut Patzig, the commander of *U-86* during the war, of having torpedoed the hospital ship *Llandovery Castle* off the Irish coast on 27 June 1918. However, the actual charges against Dithmar and Boldt were of German making. Both had been interrogated and had refused to give evidence on the grounds that they had pledged their word to Patzig not to disclose anything about the events of that night. After sinking the hospital ship outside the no-sail zone (unilaterally declared by the German admiralty), the U-boat commander, according to the testimony of surviving crew members, turned its deck gun against the life boats, inflicting a total loss of 234 lives. Dithmar and Boldt were implicated in these actions as being the only officers consulted by Patzig, now at large, even though they may not have been directly involved in the killing.[36]

The case was too visible for German prosecutors to ignore. Yet, given the turmoil in the Reich on the one hand and the international situation on the other, it was clear that political considerations were as important as the legal evidence. In order to avoid further antagonizing the British, whose criticism of Leipzig had been—compared to the French and Belgian reaction—fairly mild, and whose political support at the time of the French occupation of the Rhineland and the crisis over Upper Silesia seemed crucial, the German state prosecutor cooperated closely with the law officers of the Crown in preparing the charges. The team of well-trained and highly efficient legal experts around Ernest Pollock had less than three weeks to find witnesses; twelve of them testified at the trial.

After the French delegation had left Leipzig to protest the acquittal of General Stenger and after yet another acquittal of generals accused by the French, matters went, according to the London *Times*, "from bad to worse." Nevertheless, the British mission took its place in the courtroom, leaving no doubt that the Allies were not united in their judgment of the trials. In Germany, the case raised the highly contentious question of how to reconcile the traumatic past, based on a military tradition firmly rooted in the Kaiserreich's imperialist grand designs, with the democratic present and visions of future national revival. In mid-July 1921 amidst protests from officer associations and other right-wing German groups, the Reichsgericht opened proceedings against officers Dithmar and Boldt.[37]

State prosecutor (*Oberreichsanwalt*) Ebermayer, who had been promoted only weeks before,[38] charged the defendants with violating paragraph 211 of the German penal code (*Strafgesetzbuch*), relating to complicity in murder, and paragraph 47 of the Military Penal Code (*Militärstrafgesetzbuch*), on the execution of an illegal order. At the opening Dithmar again refused to make any statement, while Boldt stressed that he had acted solely on the basis of an order from Patzig, one that at the time he did not regard as unlawful. Patzig received eloquent praise from both of the accused for his performance as a U-boat commander fighting "the inhumanity of the British hunger blockade," although Boldt admitted that his superior might on occasion have "played the wrong note in selecting his means of action."[39]

In the course of the trial, the prosecution probed into what had happened after the *Llandovery Castle* had been struck by the U-boat's torpedo. The evidence spoke a clear, though foreign, language: while the accused remained silent, the testimony of a number of British survivors left little doubt that the German commander, having found no evidence for his suspicion that the hospital ship was carrying military personnel or equipment, had tried to get rid of undesirable witnesses, sinking two of the three lifeboats; the boats and their passengers were never seen again. Dithmar and Boldt, it turned out, had been involved in both the decision to sink the lifeboats and its implementation.

As the evidence at hand left no reasonable doubt about the role of the accused, the defense tried to resurrect familiar features of wartime propaganda. A number of witnesses were presented in order to prove that the nature of German submarine warfare was a reaction toward the Allies' abuse of hospital ships for military purposes. After behind-the-scenes protests by the British delegation, the court ruled that statements referring to alleged breaches of the rules of warfare by the Allies were irrelevant.[40] Attempts at playing to the gallery and to the wider German public did not stop there. From the display of their war decorations to their behavior during the trial, the accused as well as their supporters showed considerable contempt for the highest court of the Weimar Republic in its half-hearted endeavor to come to terms with the war's ugly legacy. On the part of the German observers, the "electric atmosphere" at court, as Claud Mullins describes it,[41] resulted from the disturbing clash between historic reality reflected in the evidence and the deeply held national myth of Germany being victimized by the Allies.

Tension and contradictions transcended into the prosecution's case. In his final plea, delivered on July 15, *Oberreichsanwalt* Ebermayer had a hard time reconciling professional impartiality with his nationalism. Starting with the confession that "hardly ever in my almost forty years as public prosecutor and judge, has doing my official duty been as difficult as today," Ebermayer set out to explain his understanding of the case: the lifeboats of the *Llandovery Castle* were shot at by *U-86* after Patzig, the commander, had consulted Dithmar and Boldt; the sinking of two of these boats, and the likely but not certain killing of its passengers constituted a crime. This being the case, Dithmar and Boldt—in the absence of Patzig, the main culprit—had to be held partly responsible. The adequate punishment for both would be, according to Ebermayer, four years' imprisonment (*Zuchthaus*).[42]

While the prosecution stressed legal aspects of the case, the defense voiced the sentiments of German nationalists and all others whose political blindfolds prevented them from acknowledging the historical facts: "In this room, between files and inkstands, after more than three years an event is to be assessed which had taken place on a dark night of the war in the Atlantic Ocean, at a time when, as it is often put, all was at stake; [today] are the actions of men to be reconstructed who [then] could any time expect to drown in the depths of the sea.... If the two officers are sentenced today, they could only be sentenced as a result of their faith in their commander, as a result of their faith and comradeship towards each other."[43]

The prosecution too had stressed the patriotism of the defendants;[44] yet their lawyers as well as some military experts went much further by arguing that in wartime any action that assists the final victory of one's country is legitimate as long as it is not dominated by selfish considerations.[45] Among nationalists, the famous phrase "*Not kennt kein Gebot*" (loosely translated: in times of emergency there is no law), coined in the early days of the war by Chancellor Theobald von Bethmann-Hollweg to sanction the German disregard of Belgium's treaty rights, carried much more weight than any argument in favor of applying the rules of law to the field of war.

Senatspräsident Schmidt turned out to be unimpressed both by Ebermayer's attempt at toning down the political implications of the case and by nationalists who regarded war as a concept outside the sphere of law. Schmidt rebuked the defense for addressing the British mission and tried whenever possible to avoid issues that could antagonize the law officers of the Crown or British public opinion in general—such as the nature of British warfare at sea or the "hunger blockade." "Had the trial of General Stenger been conducted in the same manner," the London *Times* remarked fittingly, "there would have been no reason for the French to leave."[46]

Already in the Stenger case, Schmidt had ruled that wartime killings are punishable if they are performed under circumstances not sanctioned and legitimized by the practice of international law and the customs of war ("*durch völkerrechtliche Maßnahmen und durch Kriegsübung nicht gedeckt und nicht gerechtfertigt*").[47] In the U-boat case the court handed down a sentence of four years' imprisonment to both defendants for having aided and abetted manslaughter; in addition, Dithmar was ordered to be dismissed from the navy while Boldt lost the right to wear his officer's uniform.[48] The verdict attests to the court's attempt to rise above the confines of national narrowmindedness:

> *The killing of enemies in war is in accordance with the will of the
> State that makes war (whose laws as to the legality or illegality on
> the question of killing are decisive) only in so far as such killing is in
> accordance with the conditions and limitations imposed by the Law
> of Nations. . . . The rule of international law, which is here involved,
> is simple and is universally known. No possible doubt can exist with
> regard to the question of its applicability. The Court must in this in-
> stance affirm Patzig's guilt of killing contrary to international law.*[49]

Following Patzig's order, Dithmar and Boldt had acted as accessories, but
not under duress, as it must have been "perfectly clear to the accused that killing defenseless people in the life boats could be nothing else but a breach of
law." While in the court's mind, "the habit of obedience to military authority"
presented a mitigating circumstance, the killing of the shipwrecked amounted
to nothing but "an act in the highest degree contrary to ethical principles." The
presiding judge's own sentiment found expression in his statement that "the
deed throws a dark shadow on the German fleet, and especially on the submarine weapon which did so much in the fight for the Fatherland."[50]

The Aftermath

Did the Leipzig court's ruling in the Dithmar/Boldt case have the potential to
establish principles of international law in dealing with German war crimes?
Schmidt's judgment pointed in this direction; yet for the verdict against the
two navy officers to have a positive effect within Germany, further action by
German prosecutors as well as a greater willingness among the German public
to question familiar stereotypes, especially in regard to the image, role, and
responsibility of the military, would have been necessary. Instead, the army's
tradition and leadership, most notably in the figure of Field Marshall Paul
von Hindenburg, remained a focal point of national identification while the
Reichsgericht continued to treat war crimes cases primarily as a means to refute
claims that Germany had not fulfilled its treaty obligations.

The Leipzig court's record speaks volumes. After the trials of 1921, the prosecutors made hardly any effort to hide their nationalistic bias: the accused did
not have to be present and could easily escape the force of law. Of the 861 cases

dealt with by the Reichsgericht until 1927, only 13 ended with a verdict.[51] The disinclination by German courts to prosecute war criminals attests to the same prejudice that dominated the German judiciary's handling of political violence and that did so much to prepare Hitler's coming to power.[52] Lieutenant General August Keim, an ultra pan-Germanist even before the war and accused by Belgian authorities of war crimes, wrote in his memoirs: "I repeatedly received from the Supreme Court in Leipzig a few written questions which I left unanswered. Then, on orders of the solicitor-general, the district court sent me a subpoena. I went but refused to make any deposition whatsoever, with the motivation that otherwise I would indirectly admit the enemies' right to bring me before their tribunal, which I refuse under all circumstances." He got away with it; in mid-1923, the Reichsgericht notified Keim that his case had been dismissed.[53]

At the same time, German nationalists intensified their efforts to revoke even the feeble impact of Leipzig by gaining the release of those few officers who had been sentenced to term imprisonment. Schmidt's intention to use punishment to cleanse the war record of the German navy was not appreciated outside the courtroom, where different ideas prevailed about what constituted national shame: the headline of a Leipzig paper on the occasion of the sentencing of Dithmar and Boldt read "Four Years' Imprisonment for U-boat Heroes [*Ubootshelden*]"—a judgment the London *Times* regarded with some justification as typical of the attitude of the German press and people.[54] As the Berlin-based "Association of Former Sailors" stated on behalf of their brothers in arms: "With the hour of passing the judgment [against Lieutenants Dithmar and Boldt], all comrades stood firm in their wish and desire to help."[55]

The issue mobilized and galvanized the German right. On behalf of Dithmar and Boldt, the Reichsgericht received, usually via the office of the Reich president, petitions from officers' associations, right-wing political groups, and individuals asking for an early release or the revocation (in part or in full) of the sentence. Displaying a large swastika on their letter, the *Deutschvölkische Jugend* Bremerhaven asked to have the "U-boat heroes" transferred to a more honorable place of detention. The staff of the Technical University in Aachen claimed that both officers had been motivated by the desire to help their people.[56] Some petitions struck a personal note: the president of the Prussian Diet, who personally knew Boldt, wrote to *Reichspräsident* Friedrich Ebert to have the former officer released from jail as the prisoner was "completely broken," while Boldt's father, a retired army surgeon, claimed that his son was suffering from a hereditary nervous disorder.[57]

Not all former soldiers identified unequivocally with the convicted war criminals. The Lützower *Offiziersverein* in Aachen admitted in its plea for transferring Dithmar and Boldt to a penitentiary that both, while acting on the basis of "honorable motives," had "*objectively* violated the penal code as well as the rules of warfare."[58] In their efforts to have the sentences repealed or altered, right-wing activists received support from large sections of the press as well as, in a more indirect and clandestine way, from German law enforcement agencies. By early 1922 two other convicted war criminals had already been released because of bad health or family hardship.[59]

Help for Dithmar and Boldt came from outside as well as from within a justice system that had no interest in transforming the verdict in the case into a lasting precedent. Less than half a year after the verdict in the *Llandovery Castle* case, *Oberreichsanwalt* Ebermayer notified the Reich Ministry of Justice in a letter marked "top secret" that he had overheard during the trial a member of the British mission, probably Claud Mullins, say "that after some time the question of pardon might be approached"; for the immediate future, Ebermayer recommended dropping the "purely honor-related sentences" (*reine Ehrenstrafen*) of dismissal from military service and prohibition of wearing an officer's uniform.[60] Shortly afterward, the issue was resolved without Ebermayer's intervention: on 17 November 1921 Boldt escaped from Fuhlsbüttel prison; in late January 1922 Dithmar bolted from Naumburg prison. Despite high rewards, printed posters, and police investigations, both remained at large.

The two convicted war criminals had been assisted in their escape by members of the Organisation Consul (OC), a group associated with the militant right-wing. By late August 1921 they had already attempted to free their fellow officers from the prison in Leipzig. More importantly, the OC was involved in assassination attempts on Weimar political figures such as Matthias Erzberger (killed in August 1921), Walther Rathenau (killed in June 1922), Philipp Scheidemann, and Maximilian Harden (assassination attempts in June and July 1922).[61] After Boldt's escape, the Reich Ministry of Justice had advised the *Oberreichs-*

anwalt in Leipzig to take "appropriate measures" in order to prevent the escape of other convicted war criminals.[62] Upon investigation, Dithmar's conditions of imprisonment in Naumburg, although very favorable, showed nothing suspicious or irregular until he too escaped.[63]

Out of jail, the two former U-boat officers spent most of their time abroad, Dithmar in Spain, Boldt in Colombia. From this safe distance, in mid-1926 they applied to the Reichsgericht for retrial. Although their application was denied, the court decided to withdraw the arrest warrant and to postpone the execution of the sentence.[64] Despite the clear verdict in the case, even the German parliamentary commission investigating war-related crimes expressed serious doubts about the legal culpability of the defendants.[65] On 4 May 1928 in closed session the Reichsgericht repealed the verdict of 1921 and notified both men about their right to receive compensation from the Reich Treasury.[66] After intense negotiations, Boldt received 50,000 Marks, while Dithmar was rewarded with 20,000 Marks and a three-month reinstatement as a navy officer. In early 1931 the case against Patzig, the commander of *U-86*, was closed after his deeds had been reinterpreted as a "political crime" for which a "general amnesty" had been enacted.[67]

At that time, those responsible for the judgment of 1921 were no longer involved in any way in the matter. Dr. Ludwig Ebermayer had retired in mid-1926, and Dr. Heinrich Schmidt had died in April 1927. Their roles in the Leipzig trials, however, were not forgotten. Commenting on Ebermayer's retirement, a right-wing newspaper stated that his dealing with war criminals "will remain an eternal disgrace of our highest jurisdiction."[68] On his death, Schmidt, who in early 1923 had been promoted to president of the State Court for the Protection of the Republic (*Staatsgerichtshof zum Schutz der Republik*), received an obituary from the Reichsgericht president, who commended him for succeeding "in making the representatives of the enemy countries—as far as those were able at all to come to an objective judgment—feel respect for the German judiciary."[69]

In the context of the history of twentieth-century trials regarding German war crimes, what is interesting about the Leipzig proceedings is not that they failed. No realistic observer at the time expected anything else given the inter-Allied debates preceding these trials as well as the German attitude toward them. For the Allies, leaving the matter to the Germans, even if they dropped it, seemed to be the lesser evil compared to establishing an international court— an idea ruled out already in 1919 by American politicians—or to enforcing the extradition clause of the Versailles Treaty regarded by the British as a highly dangerous approach threatening the political stability of central Europe.

The educational effect of the Leipzig trials on German society, which Ernest Pollock hoped for, was negligible, if not counterproductive. Unbroken identification with militaristic tradition dovetailed with widespread denial of German war crimes and of the Allies' right to bring charges against their former foe. Those sentenced at Leipzig were usually referred to as "*Kriegsverurteilte*" or, as in the case of Dithmar and Boldt, as national heroes. The judgment against the two navy officers—based on the most thorough investigation German prosecutors carried out into crimes committed during the First World War—came to be regarded by the German right as an all-time low in national morale and by significant parts of the general public as a disgrace, adding fuel to the attempts at undermining the fragile basis of Weimar democracy. Elements of this distorted, yet unchallenged, perception survived the Second World War and clearly contributed as much to the prevailing German unwillingness to confront crimes committed during the Nazi era as did the continuity of German elites, including officers and jurists.

Despite their major shortcomings, the Leipzig trials occupy a place in legal history.[70] Among several factors that contributed to their failure, what seems to have been of central importance was the growing discrepancy between the Allies' willingness to enforce the relevant terms of the peace treaty on the one hand and the active resistance of a militarily vanquished and politically deeply shaken Germany on the other. The problem of legal culpability was brought into sharper focus as a result of the fact that it was not the Reich but one of its allies—the Ottoman Empire—that had committed the most hideous crime of the First World War: the genocide of the Armenians. Over time, as Turkish perpetrators escaped under the very eyes of the Allies, and as the Kaiser lived out his life sawing wood in the tranquility of rural Holland, the effort of enforcing the trial and punishment of comparatively minor German figures appeared to be a futile endeavor even to those who had once favored drastic legal action. At the end of the Second World War, the adjudication of German perpetrators depended not only on the willingness of the Allies to confront war crimes and organized mass murder, but also on the unconditional surrender of Germany, the occupation of the country, and Allied access to its records.

Notes

1. For contemporary accounts, see *German War Trials: Report of Proceedings before the Supreme Court in Leipzig* (London: Parliamentary Papers [Commons, Cmd. 1450], 1921); Claud Mullins, *The Leipzig Trials: An Account of the War Criminals' Trials and a Study of German Mentality* (London: H.F. & G. Witherby, 1921). Later studies include James F. Willis, *Prologue to Nuremberg: The Politics and Diplomacy of Punishing War Criminals of the First World War* (Westport CT: Greenwood Press, 1982); David A. Foltz, "The War Crimes Issue at the Paris Peace Conference, 1919–1920" (Ph.D. diss., American University, 1978); and Gordon W. Bailey, "Dry Run for the Hangman: The Versailles-Leipzig Fiasco, 1919–1921, Feeble Foreshadow of Nuremberg" (Ph.D. diss., University of Maryland, 1971). For an early post–World War II reference to the Leipzig precedent, see *History of the United Nations War Crimes Commission and the Development of the Laws of War Compiled by the UN War Crimes Commission* (London: HM Stationery Office, 1948), p. 111.
2. See John Horne and Alan Kramer, *German Atrocities, 1914: A History of Denial* (New Haven: Yale University Press, 2001); Gerd Hankel, *Die Leipziger Prozesse: Deutsche Kriegsverbrechen und ihre strafrechtliche Verfolgung nach dem Ersten Weltkrieg* (Hamburg: Hamburger Edition, 2003); Arieh J. Kochavi, *Prelude to Nuremberg: Allied War Crimes Policy and the Question of Punishment* (Chapel Hill: University of North Carolina Press, 1998); and Tony Millett, "The Leipzig Trials: Lessons or Warning?" (M.A. thesis, King's College London, Department of War Studies, 2002). I would like to thank Tony Millett for providing me with a copy of his thesis.
3. Quoted from Mullins, *Leipzig Trials*, p. 14.
4. For the lead-up to the Leipzig trials, see Horne and Kramer, *German Atrocities*; Alan Kramer, "Versailles, deutsche Kriegsverbrechen und das Auslieferungsbegehren der Alliierten 1919/20," in *Kriegsverbrechen im 20. Jahrhundert*, ed. Wolfram Wette and Gerd R. Ueberschär, eds., pp. 72-84 (Darmstadt: Wissenschaftliche Buchgesellschaft, 2001); Willis, *Prologue*; Bailey, "Dry Run."
5. See Willis, *Prologue*, chapter 3; Mullins, *Leipzig*, pp. 5–14; Arthur Walworth, *Wilson and His Peacemakers: American Diplomacy at the Paris Peace Conference, 1919* (New York: W.W. Norton, 1986).
6. Robert Lansing (1864–1928), Secretary of State from mid-1915 to February 1920. Another member of the American delegation was John Foster Dulles, who helped shape U.S. policy toward Germany after 1945 (see Walworth, *Wilson*, pp. 21–43). See Annex III to the minutes of the meeting of the Commission on the Responsibilities for the War and Its Conduct, held 7 February 1919, National Archives and Records Administration, College Park MD (hereafter NARA) M820 (Records of the U.S. Delegation at the Paris Peace Conference), roll 140, frame 623 (181.1201/2).
7. Program: Organization of the Sub-Commissions of the Commission on the Responsibilities for the War and Its Conduct, minutes, meeting of the Commission on the Responsibilities for the War and Its Conduct, held 7 February 1919, NARA M820, roll 140, frames 616–18 (181.1201/2).

8. See Willis, *Prologue*, pp. 68–80; Proceedings of the First and Second Meeting of the Commission on the Responsibilities for the War and Its Conduct, 3 and 7 February 1919, NARA M820, frames 373–81 (181.1201/1), 603–19 (181.1201/2).

9. See Willis, *Prologue*, pp. 177–78; Foltz, "War Crimes Issue"; *The Treaty of Versailles and After: Annotations of the Text of the Treaty* (Washington DC: U.S. Government Printing Office, 1947), pp. 371–80.

10. Walworth, *Wilson*, pp. 213–16.

11. Minutes of the meeting held 3 February 1919, NARA M 820, roll 140, frame 379 (181.1201/1).

12. Minutes of the meeting of the Commission on the Responsibilities for the War and its Conduct held on 7 February, 1919, NARA M820, Roll 140, frame 611 (181.1201/2). See also Memorandum presented by the British Solicitor-General, NARA M820, Annex II to the minutes, Roll 140, frames 620–21.

13. NARA M820, Roll 140, frames 611–15.

14. Memorandum submitted by the British delegates to the Commission of the Responsibilities for the War and Its Conduct, NARA M820, roll 140, frames 624–37 (181.1201/2).

15. Memorandum of reservations presented by the American representatives to the report on the Commission on Responsibilities for the War and Its Conduct, 4 April 1919, NARA M820, roll 142, frames 467–95 (181.1202/7); see also Kramer, "Versailles," pp. 76–78.

16. Draft clauses prepared by the Drafting Committee of the Peace Conference, 26 April 1919, NARA M820, roll 348, frames 262–63 (185.118/64).

17. Excerpt from the minutes of a meeting of the Council of Four, 29 April 1919, NARA M820, roll 348, frame 278 (185.118/67).

18. Memorandum submitted by the British delegates to the Commission of the Responsibilities for the War and Its Conduct, NARA M820, roll 140, frames 630–37 (181.1201/2).

19. German Foreign Office to Bethmann-Hollweg, 20 May 1919, NARA T-120 (German Foreign Office files), roll 2404, frames E213588–90. See also Hankel, *Leipziger Prozesse*, pp. 41–57. For the German attitude in general, see Klaus Schwabe, *Deutsche Revolution und Wilson-Frieden: Die amerikanische und deutsche Friedensstrategie zwischen Ideologie und Machtpolitik 1918/19* (Düsseldorf: Droste, 1971).

20. See the discussions between leading German politicians and army officers immediately prior to the signing of the peace treaty, in Horst Mühleisen, "Dokumentation: Annehmen oder Ablehnen? Das Kabinett Scheidemann, die Oberste Heeresleitung und der Vertrag von Versailles im Juni 1919," in *Vierteljahrshefte für Zeitgeschichte* 35 (1987): 419–81.

21. See Hans Mommsen, *The Rise and Fall of Weimar Democracy* (Chapel Hill: University of North Carolina Press, 1996), pp. 109–10, 202–3; Harold J. Gordon, *The Reichswehr and the German Republic, 1919-1926* (Princeton: Princeton University Press, 1957).

22. See Willis, *Prologue*, pp. 82–86; "Akten betr. Rechtsverletzungen im Kriege und das Verfahren gegen die Angeschuldigten," NARA T-120, roll 1567, frames 684971–685259.

23. Expert opinion by Professor Christian Meurer, in *Völkerrecht im Weltkrieg (Das Werk des Untersuchungsausschusses der Verfassunggebenden Deutschen Nationalversammlung und des Deutschen Reichstags 1919–1928, 3. Reihe)*, vol. 3, pt. 1 (Berlin: DVA, 1927), pp. 57–58.

24. Max Weber to General Erich Ludendorff, 14 May 1919, NARA T-120, roll 2404, frames E213579–82. In this letter Weber pleaded with Ludendorff to turn himself, together with other leading men of the *Kaiserreich*, over to the Allies in order to prove the absurdity of the allegations.

25. Kramer, "Versailles," pp. 79–81.

26. *German War Trials*, p. 5.

27. Hankel, *Leipziger Prozesse*, pp. 63–73; also for other aspects of the trials and their public perception in Germany.

28. See Hankel, *Leipziger Prozesse*, pp. 472–500; Mullins, *Leipzig Trials*, chapters 3–5; Willis, *Prologue*, pp. 126–47.

29. See Bundesarchiv Lichterfelde (subsequently BA) R 3003 (Akten des Oberreichsanwalts am Reichsgericht Leipzig) aJ95/21 vol. 8, verdict in the case of Stenger/Crusius, 29 June–1 July 1921.

30. Willis, *Prologue*, pp. 135–36, 139; "Plain truth at Leipsic [sic]," *New York Times*, 3 June 1921, p. 14. See also *New York Times*, 7 June 1921, p. 19, and 8 July 1921, pp. 1–2; *Times* (London), 9 July 1921, p. 9, and 12 July 1921, p. 9.

31. "Das Recht," *Braunschweiger Neueste Nachrichten*, 28 May 1921, p. 1.

32. "Das Recht," *Braunschweiger Neueste Nachrichten*, 28 May 1921; Willis, *Prologue*, pp. 131–32.

33. *Bremer Volksblatt*, 29 April 1921, p. 2, and 27 May 1921, p. 2.

34. "Das Ausland zu dem Freispruch in Leipzig," *Bremer Volksblatt*, 8 July 1921, p. 1; "Protest der Entente gegen das Reichsgericht," *Bremer Volksblatt*, 9 July 1921, p. 1; "Schiffer rühmt die Justizkomödie," *Bremer Volksblatt*, 14 July 1921, p. 2.

35. "Verurteilung im Ubootsgreuel-Prozeß," *Bremer Volksblatt* , 18 July 1921, p. 1.

36. On the Dithmar/Boldt case, see also Hankel, *Leipziger Prozesse*, pp. 452-64; Mullins, *Leipzig Trials*, pp. 107-34; Willis, *Prologue*, pp. 137–38.

37. See *Times* (London), 11 July 1921, p. 9; *New York Times*, 11 July 1921, p. 3.

38. See BA R 3002 (Reichsgericht-Personalia), file Dr. Ludwig Ebermayer.

39. BA R 3003 aJ95/21 vol. 7: "Stenographischer Bericht über die vom 12. bis 16. Juli 1921 vor dem Reichsgericht stattgehabte Verhandlung gegen die Oberleutnants Dithmar und Boldt," pp. 1–188 (12 July 1921).

40. Mullins, *Leipzig Trials*, pp. 121–22.

41. Mullins, *Leipzig Trials*, p. 134.

42. BA R 3003 aJ95/21 vol. 7, pp. 555–79; Willis, *Prologue*, pp. 137–38; Mullins, *Leipzig Trials*, pp. 125–26. In the German legal system, "*Zuchthaus*" is a milder form of imprisonment that—unlike "*Gefängnis*"—was not automatically connected with the loss of civic rights.

43. BA R 3003 aJ95/21 vol. 7, pp. 582–99 (defense attorney von Zwehl).

44. BA R 3003 aJ95/21 vol. 7, pp. 623–42 (Reichsanwalt Dr. Feisenberg).

45. BA R 3003 aJ95/21 vol. 7, 13/14 July 1921 (Admiral von Adolf Trotha).

46. "Warnings to Torpedoed Officers," *Times* (London), 16 July 1921, p. 9.

47. BA R 3003 aJ95/21, vol. 8, p. 1385 (verdict in the French case of Stenger/Crusius).

48. BA R 3003 aJ95/21, vol. 7, pp. 658–68 (verdict).

49. Judgment in the case of Lieutenants Dithmar and Boldt, 16 July 1921, quoted from *German War Trials*, p. 55.

50. *German War Trials*, pp. 55–57.

51. *Völkerrecht im Weltkrieg*, vol. 3, pt. 1, p. 58.

52. For Hitler's high-treason case following his 1923 Putsch, his light sentencing, and early release, see Ian Kershaw, *Hitler, 1889–1936: Hubris* (New York: W.W. Norton, 1999), pp. 212–19, 235–39.

53. August Keim, *Erlebtes und Erstrebtes* (Hannover: Letsch, 1925), p. 253, quoted in Hans Ernest Fried, *The Guilt of the German Army* (New York: Macmillan, 1942), p. 38.

54. "Blot on Navy: German Officers Sentenced," *Times* (London), 18 July 1921, p. 10.

55. Letter by Verein ehemaliger Matrosen, 6 November 1921, BA R 3003 aJ95/21, vol. 3: "Gnadengesuche," pp. 54–56.

56. Letter Deutschvölkische Jugend Bremerhaven to Reichspräsident Ebert, 3 August 1921, BA R 3003 aJ95/21, vol. 3, fol. 8; petition by Technische Hochschule Aachen, 5 November 1921; BA R 3003 aJ95/21, vol. 3, p. 40.

57. Letter of the Präsident des Preußischen Landtags to Reichspräsident Ebert, 8 October 1921, BA R 3003 aJ95/21, vol. 3, p. 12; letter Generaloberarzt a.D. Dr. Boldt to Chef der Marineleitung, 8 August 1921, BA R 3003 aJ95/21, vol. 3, p. 9.

58. Letter Lützower Offiziersverein to Reichspräsident Ebert, 21 July 1921; BA R 3003 aJ95/21, vol. 3, pp. 4–5 (emphasis in the original).

59. See Willis, *Prologue*, p. 141.

60. Ebermayer to Reichsjustizministerium, 15 November 1921, Streng Geheim, BA R 3003 aJ95/21 vol. 1, p. 28; memo Ebermayer, 15 November 1921; BA R 3003 aJ95/21, vol. 3, pp. 88–89.

61. Letter by Sächsisches Justizministerium to Oberreichsanwalt, 6 March 1922; BA R 3003 aJ95/21, vol. 1, pp. 157–59; secret letter by Staatsanwaltschaft Leipzig to Oberreichsanwalt, 26 August 1921; BA R 3003 aJ95/21, vol. 1, p. 14; file note by Ebermayer, 30 November 1922; BA R 3003 aJ95/21, vol. 6, fol. 31; interrogation Tillessen, 21 December 1922, BA R 3003 aJ95/21, p. 34; verdict by the Schöffengericht Leipzig vs. Tillessen, 10 July 1923, BA R 3003 |aJ95/21, pp. 56–58. Ebermayer was the prosecutor in the Rathenau murder case; see Martin Sabrow, *Der Rathenaumord: Rekonstruktion einer Verschwörung gegen die Republik von Weimar* (Munich: Oldenbourg, 1994), pp. 129–30. On the escape of Dithmar and Boldt, see also Hankel, *Leipziger Prozesse*, pp. 464–70.

62. Letter by Radbruch (Reichsjustizministerium) to Ebermayer, 16 December 1921, BA R 3003 aJ95/21, vol. 1, p. 59.

63. In contrast to standard prison practice, Dithmar was allowed to receive weekly visits from his wife, to wear his own clothes, smoke, and read newspapers and books; in addition, he was relieved from the duty to clean his prison cell (cable by Gefängnisvorsteher Naumburg to Oberreichsanwalt, 9 December 1921; BA R 3003 aJ95/21, vol. 1, p. 55).

64. Circular by Oberreichsanwalt to the police administrations in Germany, 20 July 1926; BA R 3003 aJ95/21, vol. 4, p. 1.

65. *Völkerrecht im Weltkrieg*, vol. 2, pp. 480, 492.

66. Verdict by Reichsgericht, 4 May 1928, BA R 3003 aJ95/21, vol. 2, fol. 1-3; vol. 5, pp. 1–3.

67. BA R 3003 aJ95/21, vol. 2, pp. 4-220; vol. 5, pp. 4–99; see also Hankel, *Leipziger Prozesse*, pp. 500–506.

68. *Das deutsche Tageblatt*, no. 104, 5 May 1926, BA R 3002, personal file Ebermayer, pp. 7-8. Ebermayer died in June 1933. The last item in his personal file relates to a rumor, spread in the Nazi press in 1939, that he had been of Jewish descent (BA R 3002, personal file Ebermayer, p. 36).

69. *Leipziger Neueste Nachrichten*, 3 May 1927, BA R 3002, personal file Schmidt, p. 116.

70. See, e.g., the reference to the Dithmar/Boldt judgment in the *Peleus* Trial by the British Military Court at Hamburg, 17–20 October 1945, Case no. 1 in United Nations War Crimes Commission, *Law Reports of Trials of War Criminals* (London: HM Stationery Office, 1947), pp. 19–20.

Early Postwar Justice in the American Zone
The "Hadamar Murder Factory" Trial

PATRICIA HEBERER

On the morning of 8 October 1945, seven German civilians—six men and a woman—faced an American military tribunal in a Wiesbaden district court-house in the case of the *United States v. Alfons Klein et al.*[1] The proceedings, which lasted seven days, received wide publicity in the American press as the first mass atrocity trial held in U.S.-occupied Germany but were quickly over-shadowed by larger events occurring as the trial began. On 8 October 1945, the International Military Tribunal (IMT), assembling for the first time in Berlin, prepared to hand down indictments for twenty-four major Nazi war crimi-nals, to be tried that next month at Nuremberg.[2] In Rome, German general Anton Doestler stood accused of ordering the execution of fifteen captured American servicemen, while in Paris, the collaboration trial of Vichy premier Pierre Laval drew to a close; in proceedings much criticized for their arbitrary nature, a French court condemned Laval to death on 9 October. By 8 October, the first trial of Japanese war criminals—that of General Tomoyuki Yamashita, the "Tiger of Malaya," was underway in Manila. In Japan itself, American au-thorities reported that their equipment could detect "no dangerous rays now at Nagasaki."[3] Closer to events in Wiesbaden, commandant Josef Kramer, the "Beast of Belsen," had taken the stand in his own defense in Lüneburg, where British occupation officials had charged him and forty-five SS personnel with administration of the concentration camp Bergen-Belsen. And in the American zone, General George S. Patton's unfortunate remarks to the press comparing Nazis and anti-Nazis with American Republicans and Democrats had led to his ouster as military governor of Bavaria.[4]

Amidst such events, the Klein case was "second page" news. Alfons Klein and his fellow defendants had served as staff members of a state sanatorium for the mentally ill in Hadamar, Germany, some thirty miles north of Frankfurt. Officials of the United States War Crimes Branch had charged the seven with violation of international law in the murder of some 476 individuals within the institution's wards. The dead, Soviet and Polish forced laborers, had been transferred to the Hadamar facility beginning in July 1944, ostensibly for treatment of tuberculosis, a common malady among forced labor populations in Germany.[5] Within hours of their arrival, these "patients" had been murdered by lethal overdoses of morphine-scopolamine or Veronal and buried in mass graves in the institution's cemetery.

Despite the lurid headlines it received in the press, the "Hadamar Murder Factory" trial failed to capture the attention of the American public.[6] Many prominent legal scholars at the time noted the trial's original aspects: that the charge leveled was that of war crimes, although both the accused and their victims had been civilians, and that the crimes had been committed before American military authorities had occupied the territory in question, a fact that challenged U.S. jurisdiction in the case.[7] But the crimes at Hadamar—the killing of ailing laborers in their hospital beds—seemed to pale beside the murderous excesses perpetrated against American POWs and Asian civilians in the Far East or the horrors that U.S. troops encountered as they liberated Nazi concentration camps. Only the careful American reader that autumn could guess that Hadamar had had a bloody history long before that summer of 1944 when *Ostarbeiter* (Eastern workers) arrived at the facility: from January 1941 until March 1945, the *Landesheilanstalt* Hadamar (the Hadamar state sanatorium) had been a major site of the infamous Nazi "euthanasia" program, a mass murder campaign targeting Germany's institutionalized mentally and physically disabled.

The Nazi "Euthanasia" Program

The "euthanasia" program implemented by the National Socialist government beginning in the autumn of 1939 constituted one of many radical measures that aimed to restore the "racial integrity" of the German nation.[8] Nazi eugenics policies began in 1933 with legislation mandating the compulsory sterilization of Germans suffering from certain "hereditary" disorders and ended with the systematic murder of Jews, "Gypsies" (Roma and Sinti), and other groups considered racially undesirable.[9] An integral component of this eugenics strategy was the elimination of what some racial hygienists of the interwar period had begun to term "life unworthy of life" ("*lebensunwertes Leben*"): those who because of mental retardation, severe physical deformity, or incurable mental illness might be regarded as "human ballast," whose institutional care represented both a genetic and financial burden on German society and the state.[10] In the fall months of 1939, Adolf Hitler signed a document on his personal stationery formally authorizing Philipp Bouhler, the director of his private chancellery (the *Führer* chancellery) and Karl Brandt, his attending physician, to spearhead a "euthanasia" killing operation.[11] At the same time, Bouhler and Brandt initiated a child "euthanasia" program, through which at least 5,000 physically and mentally disabled children were murdered during the war years through starvation or lethal overdose of medication. By 1940 an adult killing campaign paralleled the murder of disabled German infants, toddlers, and juveniles. Codenamed Operation T4, the effort took its epithet from the street address of its central coordinating office at Berlin's Tiergartenstrasse 4. Beginning in January of that year, patients selected for the "euthanasia" program were transferred to one of six killing centers throughout Germany and Austria: Brandenburg on the Havel, near Berlin; Grafeneck in southwestern Germany; Bernburg and Sonnenstein/Pirna, both in Saxony; Hartheim, near Linz on the Danube; and Hadamar in Hessen-Nassau.[12] Within hours of their arrival at such a facility, transports of victims were gassed with carbon monoxide in specially designed gas chambers and cremated in nearby crematory ovens.

Because the program was a clandestine one, elaborate efforts were undertaken to conceal its deadly designs. Although, in every case, official records were falsified to indicate that the victims had died of natural causes, the "euthanasia" program quickly became an open secret. Fearing public unrest at a critical point in the war effort, Adolf Hitler himself gave orders on 24 August 1941 to halt the T4 operation. According to T4's own internal calculations, 70,273 institutionalized mentally and physically disabled persons perished at the six "euthanasia" gassing facilities between January 1940 and August 1941.[13] Yet Hitler's order for the termination of the action did not mean an actual end to the killing. The child "euthanasia" effort continued throughout the "euthanasia pause." More significantly, a drive to reinitiate the adult "euthanasia" program crystallized in the summer of 1942 into a second murder phase. More decentralized than the initial gassing action, the renewed campaign continued to select, transport, and process its victims, while local authorities determined the pace of the killings. Employing drug overdoses and starvation—already used successfully in child "euthanasia"—as a more covert means of killing, T4 resumed at a broad range of institutions throughout the Reich and continued to claim victims until the arrival of Allied troops in the spring of 1945. In all, historians estimate that 200,000 institutionalized mentally and physically disabled persons were murdered as a result of Operation T4 and its corollaries between 1939 and 1945.[14]

Hadamar was the last of six "euthanasia" killing centers established during T4's gassing phase and, in light of postwar publicity, the most notorious. After the Hadamar facility began killing operations in January 1941—at a time when most other T4 installations had already been in operation for a year—the staff succeeded in murdering 10,072 German patients in eight short months. Hadamar lay dormant during the "euthanasia" pause from August 1941 until the summer of 1942.[15] Killing began again at Hadamar in early August 1942, and the institution's inauguration of a new period of decentralized "euthanasia" heralded Hadamar's ascendancy as the longest-running T4 center.[16] The site's history reveals a terrible truth: that as the killing process expanded in its second phase, it spiraled outward to include a new and ever-widening circle of victims. Besides the institutionalized mentally and physically disabled—still T4's principal victims—afflicted Wehrmacht soldiers,[17] temporarily disoriented bombing victims, Jewish *Mischling* children who had become wards of the state,[18] and tubercular Soviet and Polish forced laborers were murdered at the facility. In all, Hadamar claimed 15,000 lives. Killing continued there until the arrival of Allied forces.

The "Hadamar Murder Factory"

On 26 March 1945, troops of the U.S. First Army's 2nd Infantry Division entered the town of Hadamar. Receiving disturbing reports from local residents that thousands of persons had been murdered in the sanatorium above the town, Captain Alton H. Jung decided to investigate. American officials conducted their first visit of the Hadamar facility on 29 March. Although a visit to the basement morgue yielded only five bodies, further investigation uncovered 481 mass graves in the institution's cemetery; a death register containing the name of Hadamar victims was discovered in the wine cellar.[19] Convinced that the team's findings represented the worst fears of local townspeople, Captain Jung alerted the United States War Crimes Branch (USWCB), then quartered in Paris.

Created under the auspices of the Judge Advocate General's Office of the U.S. Army in autumn 1944, the USWCB in both European and Asian theaters of war had the task of aiding in the collection of evidence and in the apprehension of suspected Axis war criminals. After the liberation of France, the USWCB, European Theater, settled its head office in the French capital; in July 1945, the branch moved to American occupation headquarters in Wiesbaden, Germany. At approximately the same time, the Combined Chiefs of Staff authorized the Supreme Headquarters of the Allied Expeditionary Force (SHAEF) to try war crimes under the auspices of the commanding general of the European theater.[20] Colonel Claude B. Mickelwait, a Regular Army man and an able lawyer, became the first deputy theater Judge Advocate, to be succeeded in time by Colonel Clio E. Straight. Under Mickelwait, a Trial Section established within the War Crimes Branch was tasked with the assignment of preparing charges for the adjudication of alleged war criminals in the American zone. Trials conducted by the USWCB began in July 1945 with the so-called Darmstadt Trial. By the end of January 1946, 33 proceedings had been held throughout the zone, involving 110 accused and resulting in 97 convictions.[21]

The case of the "Hadamar Murder Factory" was the first mass atrocity trial to be conducted in the American zone and among the first proceedings to be tried there by an American military tribunal. Having received confirmation from U.S. War Crimes Investigating Team #6822 of the existence of a prima facie case against Hadamar personnel still to be named, Colonel Mickelwait began to seek a suitable individual to serve as Trial Judge Advocate, the term applied to the chief prosecutor in American military courts.[22] Several options presented themselves, but in the end Mickelwait chose a formerly obscure corporate lawyer from Houston, Texas, named Leon Jaworski. Destined to gain fame in the Nixon era as Watergate special prosecutor, then Colonel Jaworski was no stranger to the War Crimes Branch or to the prosecution of war criminals. In 1944 he had headed the Investigations and Examinations Divisions of the USWCB. When the branch moved to Wiesbaden, Jaworski became chief of the War Crimes Trial Section in the American sector.[23] That summer Jaworski had already scored a ringing success in the zone's first war crimes trial; in the above-mentioned Darmstadt proceedings he had successfully prosecuted ten German civilians in the beating deaths of six downed American fliers.[24]

As War Crimes Investigating Team #6822 continued to accumulate evidence for trial, Jaworski and his team of legal experts began to prepare the prosecution of the Hadamar case, or United Nations War Crimes Commission Case no. 4, as it was known at this stage. Originally American authorities had been eager to try Hadamar staff personnel for the murders of the 15,000 mentally ill and disabled patients killed at the institution. Here, though, the prosecution team encountered a setback when on 28 July they were advised that it would be impossible to prosecute the Hadamar defendants for the murders of the German patients. As these crimes had been carried out by German citizens against their fellow nationals, they could not be considered a violation of international law; and as the Hadamar trial preceded, the December 1945 promulgation of Control Council Law No. 10, which allowed the more elastic charge of "crimes against humanity," an American military tribunal would have no jurisdiction to try such a case.[25] Only one option remained for American prosecutors. An American military court *was* empowered to investigate and adjudicate crimes against Allied servicemen or civilians, and among the Hadamar dead there had been 476 Soviet and Polish forced laborers. These, then, were the victims upon which Jaworski and his team would build their case.

Ostarbeiter *Caught in the Web of Destruction: The Example of Hadamar*

The German conquest of Poland and the invasion of the Soviet Union brought a massive influx of civilian laborers to Germany from the East, most of them forcibly deported from their homelands to augment the Reich's critical labor shortage in agriculture, manufacturing, and the armaments industries. By 1944, 7.5 million foreign laborers, including prisoners-of-war, remained on German soil, among them 2.2 million Soviet and 1.65 million Polish civilians.[26] Laboring and subsisting under deplorable conditions, these Eastern workers) fell victim in large number to serious illness, injury, or debilitating psychiatric disorders. Overcrowded and unheated barracks, unsanitary living conditions, and inadequate nourishment and medical care made the highly contagious disease tuberculosis the leading cause of affliction and death among Eastern workers.[27]

Before mid-1943, those foreign laborers incapacitated by illness or exhaustion for more than three weeks were simply sent back to their countries of origin.[28] Yet, by the summer of that year, the successful advance of the Red Army and the pressing need for all available resources in support of retreating German lines began to make such deportations impossible. It is most likely that an initial order to halt "repatriation" came in June 1943, with a decree from Plenipotentiary for Labor Allocation Fritz Sauckel ordering that "mentally ill" Soviet and Polish forced laborers who were unable to work be placed in German mental health facilities. On 6 September 1944, a Reich Interior Ministry decree reinforced this measure. Thereafter, physically incapacitated *Ostarbeiter* were transferred to so-called *Krankenlager* (infirmary camps), often little more than fenced enclosures where forced laborers were incarcerated, and often perished, under the most primitive conditions. On the instruction of local labor offices (*Arbeitsämter*), mentally ill Eastern workers were concentrated in a series of specially designated custodial institutions, thus inhibiting long-term stays of Eastern workers in German psychiatric facilities.[29]

Hadamar figured as one of the collection points for Eastern workers, functioning for the *Gaue* of Hessen-Nassau and Kurhessen.[30] The killing of "mentally ill Eastern workers" here and at other specially designated facilities operated within the parameters of a ministerial decree and required the coordination of responsible agencies through the T4 Central Office.[31] Nevertheless, most Eastern workers killed at Hadamar did not suffer from mental disorders but rather from tuberculosis, contracted in the crowded forced labor camps of Hessen-Nassau. There is strong evidence to indicate that Hadamar was the only institution at which tubercular Soviets and Poles were murdered within the context of T4 operations.[32] In this case, tubercular Eastern workers killed at Hadamar were transferred exclusively upon the initiative of the Hessian labor offices, and it is clear that the impetus for their murders issued not from a central directive from Berlin but from a local public health imperative. Protecting the German population—and as far as economically feasible, the Reich's forced labor force—from the contagious disease tuberculosis represented a priority for regional labor and public health officials.

According to his testimony in the 1945 Wiesbaden trial, Alfons Klein, as director of the Hadamar facility, had discussed the possibility of the transfer of tubercular Eastern workers with the administrator of state hospitals in the Hessen-Nassau region, Fritz Bernotat, and with Jakob Sprenger, *Gauleiter* of Hessen-Nassau. Two weeks after Klein's discussions with his superiors, Bernotat visited Hadamar in order to relay to his subordinate "that these incurable Eastern workers should be brought to Hadamar and that they should die there" in exactly the same manner as the German patients.[33] The *Gau* Labor Office informed Hessian labor offices under its jurisdiction concerning plans for the ailing Eastern workers, and transports organized by these agencies, carrying only tubercular forced laborers from infirmary camps in the area, began to arrive at Hadamar in earnest in late 1944. Klein instructed his staff to kill the Eastern workers upon their arrival; and thus 476 civilian forced laborers from the "East" shared the fate of Hadamar's nearly 15,000 German victims.

Prosecuting the Hadamar Seven

It was clear in July 1945 that Jaworski would have to concentrate solely upon the deaths of the Soviet and Polish nationals in order to make a case against Hadamar personnel. A shift in focus in the nature of the crimes at Hadamar signaled a redefinition of the circle of perpetrators whom the prosecution could indict for the killings. Limiting the trial to the murders of the "Eastern workers" meant that some suspects who were heavily implicated in the killing of German patients would have to be released as suspects,[34] while other Hadamar personnel not originally listed among the accused, such as chief female nurse Irmgard Huber, would have to be taken into custody. Prosecutors were certain from the outset that the elderly chief physician Adolf Wahlmann, who had overseen the deaths of the *Ostarbeiter*, would figure as one of the accused. Hadamar's administrative head, Alfons Klein, who had transmitted the order to murder the forced laborers from local administrators to his staff, became the lead defendant. Also included on the charge sheet were male nurses Heinrich Ruoff and Karl Willig, who admitted to the actual killings of the Eastern workers, and head female nurse Irmgard Huber, who was responsible for dispensing the deadly quantities of morphine and scopolamine from the pharmacy under her control. Finally, the prosecution added to the roster Hadamar clerk Adolf Merkle, who had falsified the death records of the tubercular Soviets and Poles, and handyman Philipp Blum, who had supervised the interment of Hadamar victims, including the dead workers.[35] The indictment, served on 25 September 1945, charged these Hadamar personnel with violation of international law in that they,

> *acting jointly and in pursuance of common intent, and acting for and on behalf of the then German Reich, did, from on or about 1 July 1944 to on or about 1 April 1945, at Hadamar, Germany, willfully, deliberately, and wrongfully aid, abet, and participate in the killings of human beings of Polish and Russian nationality, their exact name and number being unknown but aggregating in excess of 400, and who were then and there confined by the then German Reich as an exercise of belligerent control.[36]*

Two names were missing from the indictment. American officials had hoped from the outset of the case to name Fritz Bernotat, administrator for state mental health facilities in the Nassau region, and Jakob Sprenger, *Gauleiter* of Hessen-Nassau, as chief defendants in the proceedings. It was Sprenger who had instructed Hadamar administrator Alfons Klein to accept the tubercular "Eastern workers" from local labor offices in July 1944, and Bernotat who had ordered their deaths. Blind in one eye and partially disabled since World War I, Bernotat had for years promoted the "euthanasia" of "useless eaters" in the medical facilities under his control with extraordinary zeal and ruthlessness. American authorities scoured the German countryside for Sprenger and Bernotat throughout the summer. Bernotat continued to elude them. For Sprenger, too, they would search in vain. The *Gauleiter* and his wife were found dead in a coppice of forest near Kitzbühl, Austria, on 24 August 1945; they had swallowed poison.[37]

On the morning of 8 October 1945, U.S. military commission members Colonel John Dicks, Colonel Trevor Swett, Colonel David Waystaff Jr., Colonel Daniel Stevenson, Colonel Daniel A. Richards, and Lieutenant Colonel James C. Dobbins assembled at the former district court building in Wiesbaden to hear the case of *U.S. v. Alfons Klein et al.* Trial Judge Advocate Leon Jaworski had specifically requested that he might prosecute the case before a military commission rather than before a newly defined U.S. Military Government court; the proceedings would have been the first effort for the latter body, a fact that Jaworski was convinced would entail considerable confusion and delay.[38] The trial lasted seven days. With the preponderance of evidence on Jaworski's side, his prosecution strategies were relatively straightforward and reworked themes that he had used so successfully to try war crimes offenses in the Darmstadt case a few months earlier. His arguments emphasized the assembly-line nature of the killings at the Hadamar "murder factory" and stressed that each of the defendants had played an integral role in the killing process. Citing as an example Title 18, Section 550 of the U.S. Penal Code, which several years earlier had eliminated distinctions between accomplices and accessories before and after the fact in American federal law, Jaworski argued that each of the Hadamar defendants had been a principle in "a production line of death"[39]:

> Not a single one of these accused could do all of the things that were necessary in order to have the entire scheme of things in operation. . . . For instance, the accused Klein, the administrative head, couldn't make the arrangements and receive those people and very well attend to undressing them and make arrangement for their death chamber and at the same time go up there and use the needle that did the dirty work, and then also turn around and haul the bodies out and bury [them] and falsify . . . the death certificates. No, when you do the business on a wholesale production basis, . . . it means that you have to have several people doing different things . . . in order to produce the results, and you cannot draw a distinction between the man that may have initially conceived the idea of killing them and those who participated in the commission of those offenses.[40]

Parallel to his "assembly line" argumentation, Jaworski had two further considerations. The first was to show that the Soviet and Polish workers discussed in the indictment had not suffered from mental illness. In doing so, he hoped to avoid discussion of the murder of German patients and the Hitler authorization for the killings—which might be construed as a state directive—and to waylay defense attempts to apply the authorization to the deported "Eastern workers."[41] Likewise, he hoped to show that the Soviets and Poles did not exhibit advanced or incurable stages of tuberculosis upon their arrival at Hadamar and that no effort had been made there to examine or treat them for their illnesses. For this, Jaworski relied heavily upon the testimony of USWCB pathologist Major Hermann Bolker, who had conducted autopsies upon the bodies of selected "Eastern workers" buried in the Hadamar institution's cemetery. Summarizing from the autopsies upon six remains, Bolker was able to show that none of the individuals he examined suffered from advanced stages of tuberculosis, nor had they died from the illness from which they had suffered.[42] Bolker further testified that he had discovered no equipment on the premises employed to treat tubercular patients (e.g., no X-ray or pneumothorax machine), and that the only two drugs uncovered in the Hadamar pharmacy had been morphine and scopolamine, hardly treatments the psychiatrist Wahlmann would have prescribed to persons with tuberculosis, particularly as morphine "depresses [the] centers for breathing and heart action in the brain," and thus was never prescribed to patients suffering from lung ailments.[43] Bolker's testimony represented, for all practical purposes, the close of Jaworski's case, and in its entirety proved the most damning evidence against the Hadamar defendants.

Perhaps the most significant aspect of the 1945 Hadamar trial was the degree to which it tested Allied military tribunals' efforts to prosecute civilians of foreign governments under international law. In common practice, an occupying power was authorized to try alleged war criminals for offenses against its own military or civilian personnel, if those offenses occurred at the time in which the occupying country maintained *de facto* control over the area in question.[44] As American prosecutors began to prepare the Hadamar case, a controversy ensued among occupation officials as to whether the United States held jurisdiction in the proceedings, since none of the victims of the Hadamar institution had been American nationals and since American forces had not occupied Hadamar or its environs at the time when the crimes had taken place.[45] Likewise, legal scholars pondered how the U.S. Army Judge Advocate General's office might pursue arraignment of the seven Hadamar defendants on the charge of war crimes, when neither the victims nor the perpetrators had belonged to the armed forces and when the offenses occurred hundreds of miles from frontline activity. Appointed American chief defense counsel Lieutenant Colonel Juan Sedillo used these arguments as a major line of defense, disputing American jurisdiction in the case.[46] All charges should be dropped, Sedillo argued, on the grounds that "there is no rule of law existing under International Law such as the specification alleges the accused of violating."[47] Sedillo mustered traditional American military policy and War Department memoranda in defense of the Hadamar accused. Citing a confidential dispatch to Headquarters, European Theater of Operations, "Establishment of War Crimes Branches," dated 24 February 1945, he showed that USWCB policy itself dictated that "action by members of the United States forces in cases involving . . . nationals of other United Nations will normally be limited to cooperation with the appropriate [national] agencies investigating such matters."[48] Thanks to the early efforts of USWCB legal experts, Jaworski could parry Sedillo's arguments with a comprehensive memorandum on the issue of American jurisdiction, penned by Captain Charles H. Taylor of the Prosecution Subsection. It had already been suggested that the military commission was within its rights to note "that hundreds of thousands of Soviet and Polish citizens from occupied territories had been compulsorily deported to Germany for work," that the German government had viewed deportation and application of foreign forced laborers as measures necessary to their war effort, and that as such the murder of those deported aliens represented a war crime.[49] In his "Has the Commission Jurisdiction to Hear and Determine the Hadamar Case?" Taylor supported this interpretation and bolstered the commission's claims of competence with articles of the 1907 Hague Convention on the Rules of Land Warfare. Taylor further cited the Judge Advocate General of the U.S. Army, who in 1943 wrote: "An offense against the laws of war is a violation of the laws of nations, and is a matter of general interest and concern. Whether committed by their forces or those of the enemy, all civilized belligerents have an interest in the punishment of offenses against the laws of war."[50] Pursuant to this statement, Taylor suggested that, in the case of Hadamar, "custody of the accused is sufficient basis for jurisdiction, at least where, as here, the victims were nationals of our war allies."[51]

In the end, the commission held with the prosecution, upholding its charges based on the "general doctrine recently expounded and called 'universality of jurisdiction over war crimes,' which has the support of the United Nations War Crimes Commission and according to which every independent state, has, under International Law, jurisdiction to punish not only pirates, but also war criminals in its custody, regardless of the nationality of the victim or of the place where the offense was committed, particularly where for some reason the criminal would otherwise go unpunished."[52]

In the late evening of 15 October 1945, the six-man tribunal convicted all seven Hadamar accused of violation of international law in the murders of the 476 Soviets and Poles. At 9:45 p.m., commission president Colonel Dicks pronounced the sentence of death by hanging for chief defendant Alfons Klein and the male nurses Heinrich Ruoff and Karl Willig. Dr. Adolf Wahlmann, because of his advanced age and poor physical health, was spared the death penalty, instead receiving a life sentence at hard labor. For Adolf Merkle and Philipp Blum, the commission decreed prison terms at hard labor for periods of thirty-five and thirty years, respectively. Irmgard Huber received the mildest sentence—that of twenty-five years at hard labor. By 7 March 1946, the sentences had been approved by commanding general of the Seventh U.S. Army and by Theater Commander General Dwight D. Eisenhower.[53] On 14 March, Klein, Ruoff, and Willig went to the gallows. American authorities transferred the remaining prisoners—Wahlmann, Merkle, Blum, and Huber—from the district jail in Wiesbaden, where they had remained interned since proceedings began, to Bruchsal Prison, near Karlsruhe, to serve out the remainders of their sentences.

The Hadamar Case in German Jurisprudence

Although they had escaped the "supreme penalty," trouble for Dr. Wahlmann and Nurse Huber was just beginning. On 30 October 1945, as a step toward democratization, the Allied occupying powers issued Control Council Law No. 4, which extended the authority of German courts to all punishable acts except those perpetrated by German citizens against Allied nationals or their property. Two months later, the quadripartite Allied Control Council cemented its commitment to involve German justice in the adjudication of war crimes and crimes against humanity. On 20 December 1945 it promulgated Control Council Law No. 10, which authorized German courts of law to pass sentence on crimes committed by German citizens against other German nationals, or against stateless persons.[54] Following the example set at the 1945 American Hadamar trial, occupation forces left "euthanasia" offenses—generally a German-on-German crime—to newly reconstructed German tribunals.[55] In February 1946 the Frankfurt public prosecutor's office initiated proceedings against personnel of the *Landesheilanstalt* Hadamar for the murders of nearly 15,000 German patients killed at the facility between 1941 and 1945.[56] Former chief physician Adolf Wahlmann and Hans Bodo Gorgass, a young physician who had gassed thousands of patients at Hadamar in the course of the year 1941, figured as chief defendants, while head female nurse Irmgard Huber appeared third on the list of the accused. Many Hadamar personnel who had served as witnesses in the 1945 American trial would now sit in the dock as defendants.[57]

The 1947 Hadamar trial before Frankfurt's *Strafkammer* IV lasted thirteen days. The proceedings, adjudged by a panel of three German jurists, differed from the American trial in several important respects. More clearly than in the Wiesbaden proceedings, the scope of the Frankfurt trial embraced the full breadth of crimes committed at Hadamar, while the defendants in the dock represented a broader range of perpetrators, encompassing physicians, nursing staff, technical workers, and bureaucratic personnel. Unaided by those rules of procedure that had provided the American military commission considerable latitude, the German jurists were forced to work within the confines of the newly reinstated German penal code, which disallowed charges of conspiracy and which set strict guidelines for the sentence of murder.[58] Finally, the unique aspects of "euthanasia" crimes prepared unforeseen difficulties for German justice, in a way in which the much broader conceptualization of war crimes—the charge that the American tribunal imposed—did not. As a generation of German prosecutors would discover, mass murder carried out in an institutional setting proved much harder to litigate than killings perpetrated in the concentration and extermination camps of Nazi Europe.[59] Unlike the "Final Solution" and related crimes, a written "*Führer* decree," signed by Hitler himself, had authorized the T4 killing action. Credible testimony and circumstantial evidence suggested that many perpetrators believed in the existence of a secret "euthanasia" law, a fact that made intent more difficult to prove, particularly in the German legal context.[60] Moreover, there was much about the nature of the T4 murders that failed to resonate with jurists or later with German lay juries. To the uninitiated, "euthanasia" crimes appeared less "brutal" than the murders of Jews on the killing fields of the Soviet Union or in the extermination centers of the "Final Solution." This was particularly true of the second killing phase, in which victims were murdered by overdose or lethal injection. Severely mentally and physically disabled individuals proved less sympathetic victims than concentration camp prisoners or political detainees; often public support rested more squarely with physicians and caregivers—"solid citizens" who practiced universally respected professions—who put T4 "patients" "to sleep." While the 1945 American commission convicted all in the dock, its German counterpart sentenced only eleven of the original twenty-five accused. Chief defendants Wahlmann and Gorgass earned death sentences for their roles in the murders, while members of the Hadamar nursing staff drew sentences ranging from two and a half to eight years. While the majority of medical personnel—who had carried out the actual task of killing—received prison terms, all bureaucratic and technical staff were acquitted.[61]

Conclusion

Both trials quickly sank into obscurity beneath the long shadow of Nuremberg. If the 1945 Wiesbaden hearing is remembered at all, it is in the writings of legal scholars who recall it as America's first significant effort to punish Nazi criminals or who remark upon the legal maneuvers of its prosecutors, fettered by international law in those brief months before the charge of "crimes against humanity" greased the wheels of postwar justice. But seen in a judicious light, the 1945 Hadamar proceedings hold a special place in the prosecution of National Socialist crimes, representing the first in a chain of "euthanasia" trials that continue to the present day. The proceedings against the now late Austrian physician Heinrich Gross at Am Spiegelgrund may have signaled the last of these proceedings.[62] To be sure, the swift, certain justice reflected in the sentencing by the American military commission remained an unequaled standard in subsequent "euthanasia" cases. In the immediate postwar, perpetrators could expect conviction and rigorous sentencing. In March 1946 a female physician and nurse were condemned to death by a Berlin-Moabit court for murders committed at the Pomeranian "euthanasia" facility Meseritz-Obrawalde; the women were executed the following January.[63] Likewise, in December 1946 a court of the *Landgericht* Frankfurt sentenced the infamous Fritz Mennecke to death and his colleague, Dr. Walter Schmidt, to life-long incarceration, for murders at Hadamar's sister facility, Eichberg.[64] In January 1947 the same Frankfurt court decreed the death penalty for three persons accused of killings at the Hessian institution Kalmenhof. This trend of death sentences for medical perpetrators in positions of authority continued with the convictions of Adolf Wahlmann and Hans Bodo Gorgass in the Frankfurt trial of Hadamar offenders. In the end neither man was ultimately executed for his crimes. In 1949, as Drs. Gorgass and Wahlmann awaited the outcome of the appeals process to confirm their sentences, the new Federal Republic of Germany promulgated its constitution (*Grundgesetz*), whose Article 102 forbade capital punishment. In July 1949, in accordance with the instructions of the *Ministerpräsident* of Hessen, the state's attorney attached to the *Landgericht* Frankfurt commuted the physicians' death sentences to life imprisonment. In September 1951 the U.S. Army Reviewing Authority, bowing to cold war pressures with a wave of amnesties, suggested a reduction of Wahlmann's sentence, citing his advanced age, failing health, and excellent conduct in captivity. With a further decrease in his German sentence, the aged physician was released to the custody of his daughter in December 1952. Hans Bodo Gorgass was also paroled; by the time of his release in January 1958, not one surviving member of the Hadamar staff convicted in either the 1945 or 1947 trials remained in confinement.

Even so, the 1947 Hadamar proceedings were the last "euthanasia" trial in the future Federal Republic to draw such stiff sentences.[65] Cold war exigencies encouraged a comprehensive clemency policy for Nazi crimes. At the same time, a growing West German determination to pass into its new democratic future by suppressing its past blunted West German prosecution efforts so effectively that the wheels of justice ground to a virtual standstill throughout the 1950s.[66] With each passing year the war became a more distant memory, and sympathy for the victims of the Nazi "euthanasia" program began to erode into empathy for the accused. Jurists once stunned by the merciless actions of T4 perpetrators began to speak with compassion of the untenable circumstances under which doctors, nurses, and bureaucrats labored in the years of the Nazi dictatorship. In the end there seemed to be no perpetrators, only victims. At the last large-scale "euthanasia" trial, the 1949 hearings against T4 personnel active at facilities in the former state of Württemberg, 27 persons were listed in preliminary proceedings, including 19 personnel of the Grafeneck facility, where 10,000 persons perished. In the end, only 8 individuals were indicted and 3 convicted; the harshest sentence amounted to five years' imprisonment.[67] In the same year a court of the *Landgericht* Hamburg decided to acquit 19 accused for the murders of 56 children at the pediatric hospital Rothenburgsort, since the bench was "not of the opinion that the destruction of completely mentally dead individuals and of 'empty husks of humanity' [*leerer Menschenhülsen*] is absolutely and *a priori* immoral."[68]

The two Hadamar proceedings, and especially the 1945 Wiesbaden trial, were an abject lesson that tough sentencing for the victims of Nazi criminality had been a real possibility only in the immediate postwar years. Throughout the 1950s and 1960s, "euthanasia" perpetrators "large" and "small" could succeed in reintegrating into German society, re-establishing themselves in positions of influence and authority without significant exposure to litigation and without perceptible blemish to their professional reputations. Indeed, in postwar inquiries, members of the medical profession protected and preserved the reputations of T4 physicians, psychiatrists, and caretakers, cloaking their crimes and ensuring their full rehabilitation in postwar society. In truth, those very professions that had worked to power the machinery of the T4 killing apparatus and to guarantee its deadly efficiency—the medical community, public health officials, and the judiciary—closed ranks to protect their own, so that those former T4 personnel who succeeded in lying low in the early postwar years might escape prosecution altogether. And those perpetrators—whether jurists, bureaucrats, or public health officials—who had carefully organized and implemented the "euthanasia" program, but whose links to T4 required time-consuming investigation and tenacious prosecution *could* literally get away with murder. Hadamar taught that lesson too. At the time of preparations for the Hadamar trial in 1945, American military authorities had also attempted to bring proceedings against the president of the *Gau* Labor Office Rhein-Main, Ernst Kretschmann, and his chief physician, Hans Welcker. Both men had been instrumental in transferring tubercular Eastern workers to their deaths at Hadamar when it was clear that the ailing laborers could no longer work and when it was no longer feasible to repatriate them. Establishing definitively that Kretschmann and Welcker knew transport to Hadamar meant a death sentence proved difficult, and the proceedings foundered.[69] They were never prosecuted. And Fritz Bernotat, the partially disabled administrator who facilitated the deaths of the *Ostarbeiter* and whose ruthless energy and ambition shaped Hadamar into a killing center that claimed 15,000 lives? Bernotat lived under an assumed name until his death in 1951. He died a free man.

Notes

1. Records pertaining to the 1945 Hadamar Trial appear in National Archives Microfilm Publication M1078, *United States of America v. Alfons Klein et al.*, Case Files 12–449 and 000–12–31, 3 rolls, which combines pertinent documents of Record Group 338, Records of United States Army Commands, 1942–, Operational, Historical, and Administrative Records of the Judge Advocate General for War Crimes, United States Forces, European Theater; and Record Group 153, Office of the Judge Advocate General of the United States Army; National Archives and Records Administration (hereafter NARA), College Park, Maryland. (Noted hereafter as Hadamar Case.)

2. Of the twenty-four Nazi officials indicted by the IMT, only twenty-one actually stood trial. German industrialist Gustav Krupp had been included in the original indictment but was elderly and in failing health, and in preliminary hearings it was decided to exclude him from the proceedings. Nazi Party secretary Martin Bormann was tried and convicted in absentia, and Robert Ley committed suicide on the eve of the trial.

3. "No Dangerous Rays Now at Nagasaki," *Saint Louis Post Dispatch* (8 October 1945), p. A5.

4. To members of the Associated Press, Patton is reported to have said of the American denazification effort: "Nazis and anti-Nazis: why, it's only the ins and outs, just like Republicans and Democrats back home." Patton had already been compromised for his support of German politician Friedrich Schaffer, who, in his capacity as head of the new Bavarian parliament, had appointed some twenty former Nazis to positions of power.

5. See Matthais Hamann, "Die Morde an polnischen und sowjetischen Zwangsarbeitern in deutschen Anstalten," in Götz Aly et al., *Aussonderung und Tod: Die klinische Hinrichtung der Unbrauchbaren [Beiträge zur nationalsozialistischen Gesundheits- und Sozialpolitik*, vol. 1] (Berlin: Rotbuch Verlag, 1985), pp. 121–87. For a discussion of foreign forced laborers in Nazi Germany in a broader context, see also Ulrich Herbert, *Hitler's Foreign Workers: Enforced Foreign Labor in Germany under the Third Reich*, trans. William Templer (Cambridge: Cambridge University Press, 1997).

6. The case was so called in Colonel Clio E. Straight's "Report of the Deputy Judge Advocate for War Crimes, European Command, June 1944–July 1948," 29 June 1948, Telford Taylor Papers (unpublished).

7. See Maximilian Koessler, "Euthanasia in the Hadamar Sanatorium and International Law," *Journal of Criminal Law, Criminology and Police Science*, 43 (March–April 1953): 735–55.

8. For an in-depth exploration of the "euthanasia" (T4) program, see, inter alia, Ernst Klee, *"Euthanasie" im NS-Staat: Die "Vernichtung lebensunwerten Lebens,"* 2nd ed. (Frankfurt am Main: Fischer Taschenbuch Verlag, 1985); Götz Aly, ed., *Aktion T4, 1939–1945: Die "Euthanasie"-Zentrale in der Tiergartenstrasse 4* (Berlin: Edition Hentrich, 1989); Henry Friedlander, *The Origins of Nazi Genocide: From Euthanasia to the Final Solution* (Chapel Hill: University of North Carolina Press, 1995); Heinz Faulstich, *Hungersterben in der Psychiatrie, 1914–1949: Mit einer Topographie der NS-Psychiatrie* (Freiburg im Breisgau: Lambertus-Verlag, 1998); and Winfried Süß, *Der "Völkskörper" im Krieg: Gesundheitspolitik, Gesundheitsverhältnisse und Krankenmord im nationalsozialistischen Deutschland, 1939–1945* (Munich: Oldenbourg Verlag, 2003).

9. As set out in the 1933 Law for the Prevention of Progeny with Hereditary Diseases (*Gesetz zur Verhütung erbkranken Nachwuchses*). The seminal work concerning Nazi compulsory sterilization policy remains Gisela Bock's *Zwangssterilisation im National-*

sozialismus: Studien zur Rassenpolitik und Frauenpolitik (Opladen: Westdeutscher Verlag, 1986).

10. Alfred Hoche und Rudolf Binding, *Die Freigabe der Vernichtung lebensunwerten Lebens* (Leipzig: Verlag von Felix Meiner, 1920). Fueling much debate in the 1920s and 1930s with their treatise, Binding and Hoche argued not only for the legalization of classical euthanasia (including assisted suicide) for terminally ill patients but also for state intervention in ending the lives of individuals who lived "ballast existences"—including the grievously maimed and severely mentally and physically disabled living in institutions. Their term for these individuals, "life unworthy of life," was adopted by the planners of the "euthanasia" program.

11. "*Reichsleiter* Bouhler and Dr. med. Brandt are charged with the responsibility for expanding the authority of physicians to be designated by name, to the end that patients considered incurable in the best available human judgment, after critical evaluation of their state of health, may be granted a merciful death [*Gnadentod*]." The text was backdated to 1 September 1939, to suggest it was a war-related measure.

12. Only four killing centers operated at any one time during this period.

13. "*Die Zahl der Vergasten, 'verteilt auf die einzelnen Anstalten' für die Monate der Jahre 1940/1941"(Hartheim Statistics)*, reprinted in Ernst Klee, *Dokumente zur Euthanasie* (Frankfurt/Main: Fischer Taschenbuch Verlag, 1985), p. 233.

14. Gerhard Baader, Johannes Cramer, and Bettina Winter, "*Verlegt nach Hadamar": Die Geschichte einer NS-"Euthanasie"-Anstalt: Historische Schriftenreihe des Landeswohlfahrtsverbandes Hessen*, Kataloge Band 2 (Kassel: Eigenverlag des LWV Hessen, 1994), p. 24.

15. See Patricia Heberer, "'*Exitus Heute in Hadamar'*: The Hadamar Facility and 'Euthanasia' in Nazi Germany" (Ph.D. diss., University of Maryland at College Park, 2001), pp. 338f.

16. The Hartheim facility near Linz actually surpassed Hadamar as a killing center, functioning from May 1940 until December 1944, but its primary role as a gassing installation that murdered concentration camp prisoners for the program 14f13 ("Invalid Operation") throughout T4's second killing phase complicates its history as a "pure" "euthanasia" site. For a history of the Hartheim T4 center, see Wolfgang Neugebauer, *Tötungsanstalt Hartheim* (Linz: Oberösterreichisches Landesarchiv/Lern- und Gedenkort Schloss Hartheim, 2005). Concerning the understudied murder program 14f13, see Walter Grode, *Die "Sonderbehandlung 14f13" in den Konzentrationslagern des Dritten Reiches: Ein Beitrag zur Dynamik faschistischer Vernichtungspolitik* (Frankfurt am Main/Bern/New York: Peter Lang, 1987).

17. In most cases, these men had suffered extensive head injuries, or their front-line experiences had triggered psychiatric disorders. A handful of foreign *Waffen-SS* soldiers were also murdered at the facility.

18. Suzanne Scholz and Reinhard Singer, "Die Kinder in Hadamar," in *Psychiatrie im Faschismus: Die Anstalt Hadamar, 1933–1945*, ed. Dorothee Roer and Dieter Henkel, pp. 214–36 (Bonn: Psychiatrie-Verlag, 1986).

19. John Thompson, "Twenty Thousand Slain in Nazi House of Shudders," *New York Times Herald*, 10 April 1945, p. A4.

20. On 14 July 1945, SHAEF was dissolved, and U.S. Forces, European Theater (USFET) took over as theater headquarters for all U.S. military commands in Europe.

21. Leon Jaworski, *After Fifteen Years* (Houston: Gulf, 1961), p. 61. For a comprehensive ex-

amination of U.S. military commission proceedings in the American zone during the time of U.S. occupation, see the contribution of Lisa Yavnai in this volume.

22. Fulton C. Vowell to Commanding General, First U.S. Army, 16 April 1945, Hadamar Case, Reel I.

23. Jaworski, *After Fifteen Years*, pp. 65–101.

24. Also known as the Rüsselsheim Death March Case; see NARA, Record Group 549 (Records of the U.S. Army, Europe [USAREUR]), War Crimes Cases Files—Cases Tried, Case 12–1497, *U.S. v. Josef Hartgen, et al.*, Boxes 167–170.

25. Robert W. Mapes, War Crimes Branch, to Lt. Col. Mize, War Crimes Branch, 28 July 1945, Hadamar Case, Reel I.

26. Hamann, "Die Morde," p. 122.

27. Holker Kaufmann and Klaus Schulmeyer, "Die polnischen und sowjetischen Zwangsarbeiter in Hadamar," in *Psychiatrie im Faschismus: Die Anstalt Hadamar, 1933–1945*, ed. Dorothee Roer and Dieter Henkel (Bonn: Psychiatrie-Verlag, 1986), p. 264.

28. Hamann, "Die Morde," p. 122.

29. Bundesarchiv Berlin-Lichterfelde, RG 1501 (Reichsministerium des Innern), Akte 3763, Runderlass des Reichsministers des Innern, betr. geisteskranke Ostarbeiter und Polen, 6 September 1944; see also Kaufmann and Schulmeyer, "Die polnischen und sowjetischen Zwangsarbeiter," pp. 262–63.

30. The other institutions designated in the ministerial decree included the *Heil- und Pflegeanstalt* Tiegenhof for East Prussia, Danzig, West Prussia, and the Wartheland; the *Heil- und Pflegeanstalt* Lüben for Upper Silesia, Lower Silesia, and the Sudetenland; the *Heil- und Pflegeanstalt* Landsberg on the Warthe for Pomerania, Mecklenburg, the *Kurmark*, and Berlin; the *Heil- und Pflegeanstalt* Schleswig for Schleswig-Holstein and the city-state of Hamburg; the *Heil- und Pflegeanstalt* Lüneburg for the city-state of Bremen, Braunschweig, and the regions of Weser-Ems, Hanover-South, and Hanover-East; the *Heil- und Pflegeanstalt* Bonn for Lippe, Westphalia, and the *Rheinprovinz*; the *Heil- und Pflegeanstalt* Schussenried for Baden, Württemberg, the province of Hohenzollern, and the *Westmark*; the *Heil- und Pflegeanstalt* Kaufbeuren for Bavaria; the *Heil- und Pflegeanstalt* Pfaffenrode for Thuringia, Saxony, and Saxon-Anhalt, and the *Heil- und Pflegeanstalt* Mauer-Öhling for the Alpine and Danubian provinces.

31. Polish and Soviet foreign laborers diagnosed with psychiatric disorders perished at a number of German institutions. Although lack of thoroughgoing research on the topic makes aggregate figures difficult to ascertain, at least 58 "Eastern workers" died at Kaufbeuren, 143 at Meseritz-Obrawalde, 18 in Eglfing-Haar, and 27 at Eichberg (including three workers from former Yugoslav territories, individuals who were not normally included in the rubric of "Eastern workers"). An unknown number of *Ostarbeiter* were also murdered at Mauer-Öhling, Tiegenhof, Pfaffenrode, and the Hessian institutions of Haina and Merxhausen.

32. Kaufmann and Schulmeyer, "Die polnischen und sowjetischen Zwangsarbeiter," pp. 269–71.

33. Alfons Klein, quoted in Earl Kintner, ed., *Trial of Alfons Klein, Adolf Wahlmann, Heinrich Ruoff, Karl Willig, Adolf Merkle, Irmgard Huber, and Philipp Blum (The Hadamar Trial)* [War Crimes Trial Series, ed. by David Maxwell Fyfe] (Edinburgh: William Hodge, 1949), p. 89.

34. Mapes to Mize, Reel I.

35. Blum figured on the investigative unit's original suspect list, as witnesses had implicated

him in administering lethal overdoses of medication to "Eastern workers" on at least one occasion, but this was never proven.

36. Willard B. Cowles, "Trials of War Criminals (Non-Nuremberg)," *American Journal of International Law* 42 (April 1948): 311.

37. *News of Germany, Information Control Division*, USFET, No. 18 (25 August 1945), p. 1, Hadamar Case, Reel I.

38. Col. Leon Jaworski, Trial Judge Advocate, to Colonel Claude Mickelwait, Theater Judge Advocate General, 13 September 1945, Hadamar Case, Reel I.

39. Col. Leon Jaworski, Closing Arguments of the Prosecution, 15 October 1945, Trial transcript, p. 372, Hadamar Case, Reel II.

40. Jaworski, Closing Arguments, p. 372, Reel II.

41. Mapes to Mize, Reel I.

42. Testimony of Hermann Bolker, 9 October 1945, Trial transcript, pp. 116–17, Hadamar Case, Reel II.

43. Testimony of Bolker, pp. 118–19.

44. Cowles, "Trials of War Criminals," p. 312.

45. Cowles, "Trials of War Criminals," p. 312.

46. In addition to any German defense counsel requested by the accused in U.S. military commission trials, defendants charged with capital crimes (which might warrant the death penalty) were automatically assigned a U.S. military counsel to head the defense team.

47. Juan Sedillo, Defense Pleas for Abandonment of the Proceedings, n.d., Hadamar Case, Reel I.

48. War Department memorandum to Headquarters, European Theater of Operations, "Establishment of War Crimes Branches," 24 February 1945, cited by Juan Sedillo, Defense Pleas for Abandonment, Hadamar Case, Reel I.

49. Cowles, "Trials of War Criminals," p. 312.

50. Judge Advocate General of the U.S. Army, quoted by Charles Taylor, "Has the Commission Jurisdiction to Hear and Determine the Hadamar Case?" n.d., Hadamar Case, Reel I.

51. Taylor, "Has the Commission Jurisdiction?" Reel I.

52. U.S. Military Commission, *U.S. v. Alfons Klein et al.*, quoted in Cowles, "Trials of War Criminals," p. 313.

53. *U.S. v. Alfons Klein, et al.*, Memorandum of Brigadier General Edward C. Betts, Theater Judge Advocate, "Confirmation of Sentences," n.d., p. 2, Hadamar Case, Reel III.

54. This authorization was dependent upon approval of the zonal occupying authorities who required German courts to petition in order to obtain jurisdiction; see Adalbert Rückerl, "Nazi War Crimes," in *Leo Baeck Institute Yearbook* 29 (1984), p. 622.

55. By 1958 German courts had adjudicated some 16 "euthanasia" trials, with several proceedings against high-ranking T4 perpetrators continuing into the 1960s and 1970s. Other trials involving German-on-German offenses tried in the years before 1950 included the deportation of German Jews and "Gypsies" (Roma and Sinti) and the denunciation of German Jews and other political or ideological opponents of the National Socialist regime to Gestapo or police officials.

56. Hessisches Hauptstaatsarchiv Wiesbaden (HHStAW) 461/32061–7, LG Frankfurt/Main, *Verfahren gegen Adolf Wahlmann, et al.*, 4a Kls 7/47 (4a Js 3/46), Protokoll der Öffentlichen Sitzung der 4, Strafkammer des Landgerichtes Frankfurt am Main (hereafter *Verfahren gegen Adolf Wahlmann, et al.*).

57. Other defendants in the case included nurses Lydia Thomas, Margarete Borkowski, Isabella Weimer, Agnes Schrankel, and Christel Zielke; orderlies Paul Reuter, Benedikt Härtle, Paul Hild, Wilhelm Lückoff, and Erich Moos; handymen Fritz Schirwing and Hubert Gomerski, and administrative personnel Judith Thomas, Maximilian Lindner, Paula Siegert, Johanna Schrettinger, Hildegard Rützel, Elfriede Häfner, Elisabeth Utry, Ingeborg Seidel, Margot Schmidt, and Lina Gerst.

58. Because of its designation as a military commission, the tribunal proceeded under the recognized rules of procedure and evidence governing U.S. courts-martial. In accordance with Military Government policy, however, the commission had leave to make such rules as they deemed necessary in order to assure a fair and impartial trial. In particular, commission members were instructed to accept any testimony that "would seem probable to a reasonable man." In practice, this regulation effectively allowed the admission of hearsay evidence, generally inadmissible in standard American jurisprudence, while permitting the commission to dismiss any evidence that might find irrelevant. See Manual 27–5, *Military Government and Civil Affairs*, p. 3, Hadamar Case, Reel I. Concerning the constraints that the German penal code imposed on West German war crimes trials, see the contribution of Rebecca Wittmann in this volume.

59. Susanna Benzler and Joachim Berels, "Justiz und Staatsverbrechen: Über den juristischen Umgang mit der NS-'Euthanasie,'" in *NS-"Euthanasie" vor Gericht: Fritz Bauer und die Grenzen juristischer Bewältigung*, ed. Hanno Loewy and Bettina Winter, eds. (Frankfurt am Main: Campus Verlag, 1996), p. 29.

60. The testimony of T4 medical director Werner Heyde in the 1947 Hadamar proceedings that he and T4 coordinator Viktor Brack had circulated copies of an unsigned draft of a "euthanasia" law to German jurists at a debriefing of leading justice officials (the *Haus der Flieger* Conference) in April 1941 helped to confirm the testimony of those defendants who claimed they had seen copies of legislation that T4 administrators had described as an unpublished law that could be made public only at war's end. See *Verfahren gegen Adolf Wahlmann, et al.*, Testimony of Werner Heyde, 11 March 1947, p. 339; Testimony of Hans Bodo Gorgass, 24 February 1947, pp. 31–32; Testimony of Maximilian Lindner, 3 March 1947, p. 122.

61. *Verfahren gegen Adolf Wahlmann, et al.*, Verdict, p. 4. Among the acquitted was Hubert Gomerski, later convicted by a German court for crimes at the notorious Sobibor extermination camp.

62. See Marianne Enigl, "'Ich bin nicht verhandlungsfähig': Der NS-Arzt Heinrich Gross über sein Verfahren wegen Mordverdacht," *Profil* 46 (November 1998), pp. 60–63; and Marianne Enigl, "Fluch der bösen Tat: Kommt die Anklage wegen neunfachen Mordes gegen den früheren NS-'Euthanasie'-Arzt Heinrich Gross zu spät?" *Profil* 16 (19 April 1999), pp. 52–54. Gross, a psychiatrist interested in gathering brain material from mentally ill patients for his research in brain pathology, handpicked children for killing at Am Spiegelgrund, a pediatric ward attached to the Viennese psychiatric facility then known as Am Steinhof. Gross was tried by an Austrian court in 1947 for manslaughter, but his conviction was overturned on a technicality. The discovery of his brain preparations in a building of the University of Vienna in the late 1990s led to an indictment for murder in 1999. In March 2000, proceedings against him were delayed on grounds of incompetence (*Verhandlungsunfähigkeit*), although the elderly Gross appeared lucid in interviews outside the court setting. Gross died in December 2005. For a broader discussion of Heinrich Gross and proceedings against him, see "Justice in Austrian Courts?

The Case of Josef W. and Austria's Difficult Relationship with Its Past" by Patricia Heberer in this volume.

63. Willi Dressen, "NS-'Euthanasie'-Prozesse in der Bundesrepublik Deutschland im Wandel der Zeit," in Loewy and Winter, NS-"*Euthanasie*" *vor Gericht*, pp. 36–38.

64. Mennecke had worked steadily as a medical "expert" for the "euthanasia" and 14f13 programs (the latter extended the T4 killing process to ill and exhausted concentration camp inmates) and had participated in the murder of patients at the Eichberg "euthanasia" facility in Hessen-Nassau. He died under mysterious circumstances while awaiting confirmation of his sentence. Schmidt's sentence was commuted in 1953, apparently as a result of local public pressure.

65. Ernst Klee, *Was sie taten—was sie wurden: Ärzte, Juristen und andere Beteiligte am Kranken-und Judenmord* (Frankfurt am Main: Fischer Taschenbuch Verlag, 1986), pp. 189–95.

66. Dick de Mildt, *In the Name of the People: Perpetrators of Genocide in the Reflection of Their Post-War Prosecution in West Germany: The "Euthanasia" and "Aktion Reinhard" Cases* (The Hague: Martinus Nijhoff, 1996), p. 82.

67. This sentence was meted out to Dr. Otto Mauthe, compiler of reports for mental health affairs in Württemberg. Because the court ruled that he was "an opponent of National Socialism and had participated only out of weakness," Mauthe was paroled for the rest of his sentence.

68. Klee, *Was sie taten*, p. 211.

69. Hamann, "Die Morde," p. 176.

U.S. Army War Crimes Trials in Germany, 1945–1947

LISA YAVNAI

In the aftermath of World War II, the United States embarked on the largest-scale war crimes prosecution program in its history. Between 1945 and 1949 it prosecuted 1,885 war criminals in the American zone of occupation in Germany.[1] The trials took place under three separate jurisdictions: the International Military Tribunal (IMT) at Nuremberg, the Subsequent Nuremberg Trials, and the U.S. Army Trials at Dachau. Each jurisdiction dealt with different types of accused. The IMT, convened under the London Charter by the United States, Great Britain, the Soviet Union, and France, prosecuted twenty-four of the highest-ranking Nazi military and political leaders for crimes against peace, crimes against humanity, and war crimes.[2] The Subsequent Nuremberg Trials, established by the American Military Governor for Germany in accordance with Control Council Law No. 10, prosecuted 185 leaders of the Third Reich ministries, the military, industrial concerns, the SS, and the legal and medical professions for the same crimes.[3] The U.S. Army trials at Dachau, established in accordance with the Moscow Declaration and Joint Chiefs of Staff directives, prosecuted lower-ranking war criminals for violations of the laws of war. The purpose of these trials, as part of the U.S. occupation's goals for Germany, was to punish the perpetrators, educate the public about the crimes of the Nazi regime, and help democratize the Germans.

The U.S. Army, as implementer of the government's war crimes punishment policy in Europe, was the most active entity in bringing war criminals to justice. Between 1945 and 1947, the Army prosecuted 1,676 lesser war criminals in 462 trials.[4] The majority of trials took place at the site of the former Dachau concentration camp, near Munich. The accused included military and state officials, concentration camp personnel, and civilians accused of violations of the laws of war. Through an overview of these trials, this essay explores the role of the U.S. Army in bringing war criminals to justice in Germany. It examines the

Army's efforts to investigate war crimes in the field, the types of courts it established for the prosecution of suspected war criminals, the categories of cases prosecuted, and their legal, political, and historical significance.

War Crimes Investigations

The U.S. government's policy on war crimes punishment evolved from a reluctant condemnation of Nazi atrocities into an organized preparation campaign for the prosecution of lesser war criminals. The Moscow Declaration on German Atrocities, signed on 1 November 1943 by the United States, Great Britain, and the Soviet Union, formed the legal foundation of the U.S. commitment to the prosecution of war criminals. It stated that upon Germany's surrender the Allies would prosecute two groups of Nazi offenders. The first group included lesser war criminals who committed crimes in specific geographic locations. These perpetrators would be prosecuted by the countries in which their crimes took place "according to the laws of these liberated countries."[5] The second group of perpetrators consisted of major war criminals, the policymakers, and those whose crimes "had no particular geographic location." The Allies would punish these offenders according to a joint policy, agreed upon later.[6] From a legal perspective, the declaration asserted the right of the United States and its allies to prosecute enemy nationals for violations of the rules of war in accordance with established international law. The United States supported the prosecution of lesser war criminals in national or military courts based on its own military laws and experience in conducting similar trials in other occupied territories. It considered this type of prosecution a military necessity, part of preserving the safety of its troops and administering occupied areas.

In contrast to the punishment of the major war criminals, which remained an open question until the end of the war, the punishment of lesser war criminals gained support and rare agreement from the relevant branches of the U.S. government. In May 1944, one month before the D-Day invasion, Secretary of War Henry L. Stimson designated the Army's Judge Advocate General's office to coordinate and implement U.S. war crimes punishment policy.[7] The State and Navy departments concurred that the Army would be in the best position to implement this policy in the field by collecting evidence and preparing cases for trial.[8] By that time, at least twenty-five other U.S. government agencies independently accumulated fragmented information about enemy perpetrators and their crimes.[9] However, without a central agency to collect and analyze this information, it was of little value.

On 25 September 1945, in response to a long-standing request by the United Nations War Crimes Commission (UNWCC) and in order to address logistical concerns, Stimson created one central agency to handle all activities related to the punishment of war crimes. Stating that "one of the momentous tasks still remaining is the speedy but just punishment of war criminals," Stimson established a National War Crimes Office in Washington DC, under the direction of Brigadier General John M. Weir.[10] The purpose of the office was to collect from every available source all evidence of war crimes, process the evidence, arrange for the apprehension and prompt trial of persons against whom a prima facie case was established, and ensure the execution of the sentences imposed.[11]

The U.S. government recognized the importance of war crimes investigations in the field, particularly in regard to collecting evidence against the lesser war criminals. Initially, after the D-Day invasion the Supreme Headquarters, Allied Expeditionary Force (SHAEF) handled all reports of war crimes committed against Allied nationals.[12] A standing court of inquiry investigated select cases involving American and British victims.[13] In addition, SHAEF forces apprehended, "so far as the exigencies of the situation permit," all war criminals including: (1) those on a list of suspects furnished by the Combined Chiefs of Staff; (2) members of Nazi groups designated by the Supreme Commander; and (3) specific individuals on whom the Supreme Commander had "evidence of responsibility for flagrant violation of the laws and customs of war in friendly or enemy territory prior to occupation or liberation by Allied Forces."[14] SHAEF issued a ban on the prosecution of these suspects during active combat for fear of reprisals against Allied prisoners of war by the Axis powers.[15] However, it did permit army commanders to set up military tribunals for the prosecution of individuals charged with violations of the laws of war that posed an immediate threat to the security or effectiveness of SHAEF forces.[16]

In the winter of 1945 SHAEF transferred the responsibility for coordinating war crimes investigations directly to the U.S. and British armies. The changing conditions in the field, including an increase in reports of mass atrocities against civilian populations, required a more elaborate investigative mechanism. For this purpose, the National War Crimes Office established a U.S. War Crimes Branch in the European Theater under the direction of Colonel Claude B. Mickelwait, Deputy Judge Advocate for War Crimes, in the headquarters of the European Theater Judge Advocate, Brigadier General Edward C. Betts.[17] As one of its first acts and in an effort to help control the quality of investigations, the U.S. War Crimes Branch in Europe created nineteen professionally trained war crimes investigation teams (WCITS).[18] Each team had authorization for two legal officers, a medical officer, a forensic evidence expert, a warrant officer, a court reporter, a stenographer, a photographer, an interpreter, and two drivers.[19] The U.S. War Crimes Branch in Europe assigned eight WCITS to 12th Army Group headquarters; three to 6th Army Group headquarters; six to the base sections, Communications Zone; and two to headquarters command, European Theater of Operations. The purpose of these WCITS was to assist the war crimes offices with their field assignments.[20]

The positioning of the war crimes investigators and professional WCITS in the field required careful planning. The Seventh U.S. Army, for example, conducted a preliminary study of its military zone, geographically positioning its war crimes investigators in a manner that would ensure maximum coverage of the area. The investigation teams selected their own temporary bases in accordance with accessibility to other information agencies, the scene of the alleged crimes, and the available communication facilities.[21] Other numbered U.S. armies followed similar planning.

With these resources in place, Mickelwait directed war crimes personnel to focus on investigating crimes against American nationals and mass atrocities.[22] The investigation into crimes against Americans received first priority, as the Army viewed such investigations as a military necessity. These cases usually involved American airmen shot down over Germany. The victims had either been beaten to death by civilians or executed by local Nazi officials.[23] Although months had elapsed since the crimes had taken place, the majority of eyewitnesses and accused were still living in the same area. Despite the availability of witnesses, however, the local population proved especially hostile and uncooperative, to the point that investigators had to exhume the bodies of victims in order to determine their identity and nationality.[24] Still, the Army managed to investigate cases involving over 1,200 American victims, including not only downed flyers but also soldiers killed after surrendering to German forces as prisoners of war.

The second type of investigations, the mass atrocities, initially received low investigative priority. The Army did not anticipate uncovering mass atrocities against civilians inside Germany and therefore did not prepare for such large-scale investigations. In addition, most of the crimes involved other Allied nationals as victims. In accordance with the Moscow Declaration, the Army expected to prosecute only cases dealing with American victims. However, with the liberation of concentration camps by the U.S. Army in the spring of 1945 and the ensuing public and political pressure to bring those responsible to justice, the priority of the mass atrocities cases increased. Most of the investigations in this category took place in the first weeks after Germany's surrender.[25]

Much like the American soldiers who liberated the camps, war crimes investigators were often unprepared for what they found. Already understaffed, working with few resources and under extremely difficult conditions in the field, investigators had to exercise creativity in order to complete their mission. For Benjamin Ferencz, a Third U.S. Army war crimes investigator, this meant recruiting the help of former inmates. Arriving with only one other investigator at Flossenbürg concentration camp shortly after liberation, Ferencz immediately realized he would need help:

> *I took over two large offices for our headquarters. . . . Some of the inmates had hidden the books with the names and statistics of the prisoners, and those were now brought out and I put a crew to work tabulating the data. I had two long-time French inmates, as well as one Polish journalist start writing a complete history of the camp. To another I assigned the job of compiling the names of all known SS men who were ever in the camp. A Dr. was gathering statements from persons in the hospital, and I went to work furiously gathering statements from others whom I started calling to the office.*[26]

American war crimes investigators who entered Mauthausen, Dachau, Buchenwald, and Nordhausen concentration camps had similar experiences.[27] By the fall of 1945, the US War Crimes Branch in the European Theater had completed the gathering of evidence for most of the mass atrocities cases.[28]

U.S. war crimes investigators gathered evidence against suspected war criminals in at least 3,887 cases.[29] On 19 June 1945, the Combined Chiefs of Staff lifted the ban on war crimes prosecutions by authorizing theater commanders to prosecute suspects "other than those who held high political, civil or military positions."[30] In accordance with the Moscow Declaration and the Yalta and Potsdam agreements, each occupying power would prosecute lesser war criminals who had committed crimes against its nationals or in its zone of occupation in Germany. The U.S. Army became responsible, through the U.S. War Crimes Branch in the European Theater, for prosecuting war crimes suspects in the American zone of occupation.

Military Courts

On 25 August 1945 General Dwight D. Eisenhower, commander of U.S. Forces in Europe, authorized the Third and Seventh U.S. armies, which governed the Eastern and Western military districts, respectively, of the American Zone of Occupation in Germany, to appoint military government courts. The purpose of these courts was to protect the occupation forces, enforce the laws and usages of war, and advance "political, military and administrative objectives" as set forth by the occupation government.[31] The courts had authority to handle the prosecution of violations of the laws of war, laws of nations, and laws of occupied territory.[32] Military government courts had to conduct their work with "a view to the attainment" of these objectives "to the fullest extent possible."[33] The three-tiered U.S. Military Government court system, first used in Italy, included General, Intermediate and Summary courts.[34] The basic difference between the courts was in their composition and sentencing powers.[35]

The Military Government courts handling war crimes had, "to the greatest practicable extent," to adopt fair, simple and expeditious procedures designed to accomplish "substantial justice without technicality."[36] The implication of this directive was that the procedure adopted by war crimes courts had to be flexible enough to streamline cases, yet provide a fair process in which the rights of the accused would be protected. The Army did not have time to create new procedures, so it therefore had to rely on existing rules and regulations that could be adopted by military courts dealing with war crimes cases.[37]

In order to determine which cases to prosecute, the U.S. War Crimes Branch in the European Theater began reviewing investigation reports.[38] The reviewing staff Judge Advocates determined whether the alleged crimes constituted war crimes and confirmed that either the victims were Americans or that the crimes took place in the American zone of occupation in Germany.[39] Officers then evaluated the sufficiency of evidence, the location of the main suspects, their competency to stand trial, the availability of witnesses, and whether further investigation was necessary.[40] Based on these parameters the reviewing officers then determined whether cases should be referred to trial or closed administratively. Of the 3,887 war crimes cases investigated, the Deputy Judge Advocate for War Crimes closed 3,029 cases for a variety of reasons, including the minor nature of the offenses, inability to obtain evidence, or inability to apprehend the accused.[41] The Army consolidated the remaining 858 cases into 462 trials.[42]

Once cases were approved for trial, the Deputy Judge Advocate for War Crimes appointed a court and assigned staff Judge Advocates as prosecutors and defense counsel in each case. The accused received the charges against them prior to the trial in order to facilitate their preparation for trial. The charges focused exclusively on violations of the laws and usages of war in accordance with established international law. This was in contrast to the charges of crimes against peace and crimes against humanity used in the IMT and subsequent Nuremberg proceedings.

The U.S. Army's trials of war criminals, which began in June 1945 and ended in December 1947, took place for the most part in specially appointed military government courts located in Ludwigsburg, Darmstadt, Munich, Augsburg, Ahrweiler, Heidelberg, Freising, and Wiesbaden in Germany, as well as in Salzburg, Austria.[43] Some of the leading considerations for determining the locations of prosecution included proximity to sites where the crimes occurred and availability of adequate facilities to accommodate the court and its assigned army personnel, witnesses, accused, and spectators.[44] The majority of the Army's war crimes trials, and all trials conducted after June 1946, took place on the site of the former Dachau concentration camp, about ten miles northwest of Munich.[45] The site was chosen by the Army for several reasons. First, in accordance with the Moscow Declaration, the Allies agreed to bring war criminals back to the locations of their crimes for trial. Some of the perpetrators in U.S. custody served at Dachau. Prosecuting these perpetrators at the site of their crimes addressed this obligation. Second, the site offered excellent facilities, accommodating three courtrooms with working plumbing and heating, offices for war crimes staff, and holding blocks for the accused. Finally, the site was in close proximity to Landsberg prison, where convicted war criminals could be incarcerated. The U.S. Army trials of war criminals became known as the "Dachau Trials" for the location where most of them took place, rather than because of the type of perpetrators prosecuted there.

Crimes against Americans

As soon as the Combined Chiefs of Staff (ccs) lifted the ban on war crimes prosecutions in June 1945, the U.S. Army began prosecuting cases involving American victims, mostly members of the U.S. Army Air Force. The decision to begin with these cases reflected priorities outlined in the Moscow Declaration but also resulted from practical considerations. Investigators were still gathering evidence on mass atrocities that had only recently been uncovered. The investigations into cases involving American victims, however, had been ongoing since the summer of 1944. The speedy prosecution of these cases was important for the protection of American troops in Germany and the advancement of U.S. occupation goals. As a result, for the first six months of its war crimes trials program, the Army prosecuted almost exclusively cases involving crimes against American victims.[46] By December 1947 it had conducted 226 trials of 646 accused, who had committed war crimes against approximately 1,244 known American victims.[47] The courts acquitted 113 defendants and sentenced 199 to death, 93 to life in prison, and 248 to prison terms ranging from two months to thirty years.[48]

Most of the accused, among them fifteen women, were German or Austrian nationals, with the exception of four Hungarians, two Czechs, two Romanians, and one Dutch national. Their ages ranged between eighteen and seventy-two years. They included three main groups of accused: German civilians, police and Nazi Party officials, and German military personnel who committed crimes against American soldiers on the battlefield.[49]

The first group of perpetrators, German civilians, was accused of mistreating downed flyers who surrendered: instead of treating the captives as prisoners of war, medical treatment was often withheld, and some prisoners were beaten, lynched, or otherwise executed. The accused were ordinary citizens who were not members of the Nazi Party. They ranged from housewives and bakers to farmers and shopkeepers. In court they argued that the trauma they had suffered from heavy bombardment by the Allies in the last months of the war, their loss of life and property, and subjugation to relentless Nazi propaganda influenced them to seek revenge. As even the prosecution noted in some cases, it was unlikely that the accused would have committed similar crimes outside of a mob setting. The revenge, though legitimized by the Nazi regime, did not stem from Nazi ideology, nor was it specifically directed against Americans. Rather, as the evidence suggested, it was a spontaneous response against those perceived to be responsible for the suffering of the local German population.[50]

The accused in the second group consisted of perpetrators who had committed crimes against downed flyers and included local police and Nazi officials from the Gestapo, SD (the intelligence service of the SS), *Gendarmerie*, *Landwacht*, and *Landesschützen*; a *Wehrkreis* leader and staff members of SS—General Ernst Kaltenbrunner's Reich Security Main Office (RSHA); local Nazi Party officials ranging from cell leaders (*Zellenleiter*) to *Gauleiter*; as well as members of the SA (or storm troopers), *Allgemeine* SS and Hitler Youth. These cases demonstrated the eagerness of the perpetrators to do their share in defending the home front. Toward that end they issued, circulated, and executed orders that resulted in the mistreatment and death of downed flyers. In contrast to crimes committed by civilians in the first group, the crimes committed by these accused were less spontaneous. Nevertheless, they did illustrate the panic that existed in the ranks of local police and party officials as a result of the constant Allied bombardment.

Perpetrators in the third group of accused who committed crimes against American soldiers included German military personnel from the Wehrmacht, Waffen SS, Luftwaffe, Navy, Volkssturm, and special commando forces. The vast majority of these defendants participated in the killing of downed flyers while on furlough or when on assignment to the home front. In a handful of cases, however, the crimes took place on the front lines, and the victims were infantry personnel rather than downed flyers. These crimes represented traditional violations of the laws of war, especially violations of the Geneva Conventions relating to prisoners of war. The evidence presented demonstrated the chaos that existed on the battlefield, especially during the Ardennes offensive. It also illustrated the tension between perceived military necessity and acceptable warfare practices. Finally, the evidence highlighted the strong loyalty and comradeship that existed between the defendants, even after the war ended.

In the cases involving American victims, the prosecution established through testimony and documentary evidence that the Nazi leadership had a secret official policy against Allied downed flyers—a policy that it disseminated through police and Nazi Party ranks both verbally and in writing. Developed by Himmler and Bormann as early as 1940, this policy encouraged on-the-spot killing of all enemy commando and sabotage forces.[51] It included a systematic propaganda program to incite the German civilian population to lynch law and open mob violence against captured enemy flyers.[52] It also advocated withholding of military and police protection to enemy flyers captured by civilians;[53] severe punishment of all Germans who treated captured enemy flyers humanely and sympathetically; denial of POW status to captured enemy flyers; the turning over to the SD for execution of all captured enemy flyers who escaped death through lynch law or mob violence;[54] and the immediate segregation and classification of all captured enemy flyers as criminal perpetrators in order to circumvent the Geneva Convention before their execution. The Army further argued that this policy was disseminated through all echelons of the military, police, and party channels of the Nazi government.[55] Beyond its legal significance, presenting this historical context provided a helpful tool for educating the public about the war crimes charged, the motives of the perpetrators, and reactions of civilians and military personnel to the trauma they had suffered during the war.

The prosecution of war crimes against American soldiers was based on established international law. These crimes represented traditional violations of the laws of war against military personnel, crimes that the Army had experience prosecuting in the past. These cases shed light on the fate of American soldiers in the custody of the Third Reich, provide a glimpse into the life of German civilians during the war, and illustrate the effects of Nazi orders and propaganda on the motivation of the perpetrators. The knowledge and experience gained by the Army from the prosecution of these cases formed the basis for its later prosecution of mass atrocities.

Mass Atrocities Cases

On 4 April 1945, elements of the U.S. Army's 4th Armored Division and the 89th Infantry Division ("Rolling W") overran Ohrdruf, a small concentration camp near the town of Gotha, Germany. Established in 1944 to supply slave labor for railway construction, the camp held 11,000 inmates at its highest capacity. One of approximately 120 satellite camps of the Buchenwald concentration camp, Ohrdruf was the first concentration camp liberated by American forces in Germany. The evidence of mass atrocities uncovered by the American liberators was so shocking that on 12 April 1945, Generals Dwight D. Eisenhower, George S. Patton, and Omar Bradley visited the camp to see the evidence personally. After viewing mass graves and speaking with former inmates who described the torture they had to endure, General Eisenhower famously declared that every GI should visit the camp to be reminded why the United States was fighting the war, and that German civilians should be forced to go to see the camp to witness personally the crimes of their government.[56]

American forces went on to liberate dozens of camps and sites of mass atrocities in Germany and Austria.[57] While the Joint Chiefs of Staff authorized the United States to prosecute war crimes committed within its zone of occupation, the Army did not initially give priority to the prosecution of mass atrocities cases. It was more interested in prosecuting cases involving Americans rather than other Allied victims. This attitude changed, however, after the British Army prosecuted the Bergen-Belsen case in September 1945. The ensuing publicity, which renewed public interest in bringing war criminals to justice, and pressure from other Allied governments through the UNWCC to prosecute these cases contributed to this change in attitude.[58] Consequently, beginning in November 1945 and through December 1947, the U.S. Army prosecuted 1,030 perpetrators in 232 mass atrocities trials. The cases centered on violations of the laws of war committed in six Nazi concentration camp rings including Dachau, Mauthausen, Buchenwald, Mühldorf, Flossenbürg and Nordhausen, as well as at the Hadamar "euthanasia" facility.[59]

In order to effectively handle the massive amount of mass atrocities evidence collected, and the approximately 15,000 suspected war criminals in its custody, the Army had to devise a prosecutorial strategy that would allow swift and effective trials. It did so by adopting two crucial elements: the common design charge, which addressed the problem of the large number of accused, and the parent case system, which addressed the problem of large amounts of evidence that included in excess of eighteen tons of documentary and other evidence gathered by war crimes investigators. The common design charge allowed the army to prosecute groups of perpetrators, as many as sixty-one accused in one trial, for violations of the laws of war. The characteristics of the charge were similar to conspiracy, except that a previously conceived plan was not an essential element. On the principle of vicarious liability, the mere participation in an unlawful act that resulted in a homicide was sufficient grounds for conviction. It did not require proof of prior agreement between the defendants to commit the crime, nor did it require direct proof that each defendant caused the death of the victim.[60] The common design charge was used in the majority of the mass atrocities cases and in some of the cases involving crimes against Americans.

The parent case system provided the army with a method of presenting mass atrocities evidence in a coherent and cost-effective manner. In accordance with this strategy, the army prosecuted one main case for each concentration camp liberated by the U.S. Army. The evidence about the criminal nature of that camp was presented in the main case, and the court made official findings of fact based on the evidence. In subsequent proceedings dealing with perpetrators from related subcamps, prosecutors did not present the same evidence again. Instead, they asked the court to take judicial notice of the findings of fact rendered in the parent case. This strategy required the army to make a complete presentation of the evidence only once, thereby conserving resources that could be diverted to the prosecution of additional trials. It also helped to speed the trials against hundreds of accused.[61]

The Army selected the accused for trial in a process that involved several steps. First, it administered the *Fragebogen* to all suspected war criminals in its custody. These detailed background questionnaires required suspects to provide their name, age, nationality, marital status, education, civilian address, and occupation, followed by wartime information, including ranks, positions held, locations stationed, and memberships in Nazi organizations, including corresponding dates. After this initial identification, prosecutors invited concentration camp survivors to select from "line-ups" of suspected perpetrators those who should be brought to trial. Survivors had an opportunity to provide a statement about the conduct of the selected perpetrators in the camp. According to the accused themselves, witnesses made a distinction between suspects they considered "good" and those they considered "bad." Willy Hertha, a thirty-two-year-old German who became an SS technical sergeant and worked as a detail leader at Dachau, explained that after his identification by a witness he had to step forward from the line. An American official then asked the witness whether Hertha should be separated as a candidate for trial. The witness said no. Hertha recalled that the witness "was very decent, and three or four other Poles . . . who were standing behind the first Pole and who were elderly people called out several times: 'Good man. Good man.'"[62] Because each concentration camp functioned with the help of dozens, if not hundreds, of personnel, prosecutors selected suspects who had held key positions in the camps, who represented the camp's main offices, and who were most likely to be convicted based on the available evidence.[63] The *Fragebogen*, line-ups, and processing of evidence were the three main components in this selection process.

In some cases, suspects in American custody not selected for prosecution by the United States were selected for prosecution by other Allied governments. The Joint Chiefs of Staff directed General Eisenhower, as commander-in-chief of U.S. forces, to "promptly comply" with extradition requests by other Allied nations for war crimes suspects in their custody. The directive only prohibited the extradition of high-ranking government and military officials who would possibly face trial by international tribunals. All other suspects accused of war crimes were eligible for extradition and had to be prosecuted within six months of delivery. Otherwise, the suspects were to be returned to the original detaining power.[64] In accordance with this directive, in the first nineteen months after the end of the war the United States handled 8,116 extradition requests from sixteen countries. Of the 3,914 requests granted, the U.S. Army extradited 37 percent of the suspects to France, 30 percent to Poland, 15 percent to the United Kingdom, 9 percent to Yugoslavia, and the rest to the other Allied nations.[65]

The 1,030 perpetrators eventually selected by the U.S. Army for trial in its mass atrocities cases were a diverse group. While nearly 80 percent were Germans or ethnic Germans, other accused perpetrators were Austrian, Czech,

Dutch, Hungarian, Latvian, Polish, Romanian, Ukrainian, and Yugoslav nationals. Their ages ranged between twenty-one and seventy-four years. In civilian life they had worked as doctors, businessmen, accountants, architects, carpenters, electricians, locksmiths, barbers, merchants, painters, civil servants, farmers, and laborers, among other occupations. During the war these accused, including only three women, had been members of the Nazi Party, Allgemeine SS, SA, Waffen-SS, Wehrmacht, Navy, or Luftwaffe, and were privileged concentration camp prisoners including kapos and block elders. The courts found 885 defendants guilty of war crimes. It sentenced 233 to death, 106 to life in prison, and the rest to prison sentences ranging from one to twenty years.[66]

Eighty-five percent of the accused in the mass atrocities cases were members of the Wehrmacht, Luftwaffe, or Waffen-SS. The military status of the accused was a central element in their trials. The courts tried to determine whether accused were volunteers or draftees, and whether they had actively tried to avoid service in the camps. In 1941 Hitler issued an order stating that concentration camp personnel could be relieved of their camp duties if they volunteered to fight on the front lines. In light of this decree, the Dachau courts generally considered accused who did not ask for a transfer and who remained on camp duty in the last months of the war as volunteers.[67] This determination was important in ascertaining the level of culpability of each of the accused. The common design charge required prosecutors to show that the accused were aware of, and took an active part in, the practice of cruelties and abuses against foreign nationals in violation of the laws of war. This charge did not require prosecutors to prove the accused had a motive to commit the crime. However, for the Dachau courts the level of culpability of accused who volunteered for service in the camps was higher than that of draftees who tried to transfer out of the concentration camp to a different assignment.

Perhaps the most controversial perpetrators put on trial were the 9 percent of defendants who were political, criminal, Jewish, or homosexual concentration camp inmates. These accused held functionary positions at the camps, thereby helping in its administration. Selected by the SS, these prisoners served as camp, block, or room elders, work detail kapos, orderlies, male nurses, and clerks. In exchange for complete obedience to the SS, they received more food, warmer clothing, and better sleeping accommodations. Such amenities, unattainable to the regular prisoner population, increased the likelihood of survival significantly. Being a privileged inmate often meant the difference between life and death. In most cases, the privileged inmates became the instruments through which the SS imposed a regime of terror over the general camp population. While they viewed themselves as victims of the Nazis, other prisoners regarded these camp functionaries as Nazi collaborators. In the days following the liberation of the camps, many former prisoners expressed their anger toward their tormentors by killing kapos. By that time most of the camps' SS personnel had already fled, leaving behind their perceived accomplices. As Allied soldiers stood by, former inmates beat, hanged, and otherwise mistreated the most brutal kapos. By some accounts, after liberation inmates killed in excess of fifty kapos at Ebensee concentration camp alone.[68] As American investigator Ferencz later noted, war crimes prosecutors had to determine whether to apply the values and standards of a civilized world to people who had been tormented for years. Prompted by witness testimonies, however, prosecutors eventually selected some of the most brutal kapos in their custody for trial, alongside SS personnel. Other kapos served as witnesses at the Dachau trials, proving that neither the survivors nor the prosecutors considered all kapos as perpetrators.[69]

The accused in the Dachau cases raised six types of defenses. They argued that they executed legal orders, followed superior orders, suffered duress, were victims of mistaken identity, were the target of revenge by witnesses, or simply had not committed the crimes with which they were charged. The defense of superior orders was the one most argued by defendants at the Dachau trials. The Dachau courts held that in accordance with the Army's *Rules of Land Warfare*, superior orders did not absolve military personnel from responsibility for committing war crimes.[70] However, the fact that the accused had committed war crimes pursuant to an order of a superior or government sanction was taken into consideration in the mitigation of punishment.[71] An accused who sought relief on such grounds assumed the burden of establishing (a) that he had received an order from a superior directing him to commit the wrongful act; (b) that he had not known, or as a reasonably prudent person could not have known, that the act ordered was illegal or contrary to universally accepted standards of human conduct; and (c) that he acted at least to some extent under immediate compulsion. The degree to which the sentence was mitigated depended on "the character and extent of the immediate compulsion under which he acted."[72]

Because the Army had to prosecute crimes of unprecedented scale and nature within the narrow legal framework of violations of the laws of war, it could not present a coherent historical account of the mass atrocities it prosecuted. Often, relevant historical information lay outside the legal scope of the court and would therefore not be introduced. Specifically, prosecutors could not present evidence on the Holocaust because genocide was not yet a recognized crime under international law, and persecution based on religion was a crime against humanity but not a violation of the laws of war.[73] As Donald Bloxham notes, even the IMT, which had the necessary legal framework to prosecute crimes against the Jews, had done so in a very limited manner.[74]

Dachau prosecutors therefore focused on historical evidence relating to the daily life at the camps. Through witness testimonies supported by documentary evidence, prosecutors illustrated the various forms of mistreatment, malnutrition, hard labor, executions, disease, and gassing that caused the deaths of many inmates. While this evidence helped achieve convictions, it forfeited an opportunity to educate the public about Nazi policy against specific victim groups.

Outcome

The U.S. Army trials at Dachau concluded on 31 December 1947. Several political and practical considerations contributed to the decision to end the trials. From the political perspective, the change in U.S. occupation goals for Germany in light of the emerging cold war, the desire for political stability, as well as plans to establish a democratic German government, were decisive factors. On a practical level, the continued expenditure of resources on the prosecution and incarceration of the accused, diminished public interest in the trials, difficulty in identifying and locating witnesses, and criticism about specific methods of prosecution also contributed to the decision to end the Dachau trials.

Criticism of the Dachau trials began with the Malmédy case, in which the U.S. Army prosecuted seventy-three Waffen SS soldiers for killing American prisoners of war during the Battle of the Bulge. The accused claimed they signed false confessions under duress following questionable interrogation tactics by U.S. Army personnel. In time, the allegations of misconduct spread to other trials and included complaints about the amount of time detainees were held in confinement without reason; insufficient time between services of charges and trial; delayed designation of defense counsel; use of professional witnesses; intimidation of witnesses and accused by threats, such as surrender to Eastern powers for trial, beatings, promises of favor, and prolonged interrogations; inaccurate statements presented to witnesses and accused for signature; inclusion of broad evidence; and poor interpreters in court.[75] In the Malmédy case, for example, the secretary of the Army and a subcommittee of the Armed Forces Committee of the U.S. Senate conducted investigations into these and other allegations.

Official investigations into the allegations of procedural misconduct did not find substantial wrongdoing on the part of the Army. However, the ensuing public discourse developed into a campaign by various German and American political, religious, patriotic, social welfare, and other pressure groups and organizations to win the release of convicted war criminals from Landsberg prison. The German public viewed crimes against downed flyers or American prisoners of war on the battlefield as part of the suffering of war. They identified with the accused civilians and considered the convicted Waffen-SS "good German soldiers" who did what they had to do for their country. The concentration camp personnel were the only group of accused considered as criminals. Despite differences in perception of the accused, pressure groups advocated the release of all war criminals by discrediting the conduct of the army and calling for the restitution of German military honor.

Several prominent German and American clerics became instrumental in the campaign to release the war criminals. On the Catholic side, Johann Neuhäusler, auxiliary bishop of Munich and an inmate at Dachau between 1941 and 1945 was a leading figure together with Cardinal Josef Frings of Cologne, chairman of the Bishop's Conference in Fulda, among others. On the Protestant side, Theophil Wurm of Stuttgart and council chairman of the German Protestant Church, state bishop (*Landesbischof*) Hans Meiser of Bavaria, and church president Martin Niemöller of Wiesbaden were some of the active clerics.[76] In the United States, Catholic bishop Aloisius Muench from North Dakota, Vatican nuncio to Germany, was in close contact with American occupation authorities, other religious leaders, and the convicted war criminals themselves regarding this issue. The Catholic clergy in particular focused on the theme of love and mercy instead of vengeance.[77] They ignored the fact that the accused were not all soldiers, but included Nazi Party functionaries, SS members, and civilians accused of murder.[78]

Pressure on the U.S. Military Government for Germany eventually resulted in the appointment of a Clemency Petititions and War Crimes Modification Board in 1949 to examine and make recommendations on clemency and the release of the accused at Landsberg prison. While the Dachau convicted war criminals did not have an opportunity to appeal their sentences in accordance with military procedure, the Army staff Judge Advocates automatically reviewed each case for procedural errors and appropriateness of the imposed sentence. Nevertheless, by October 1951 the Clemency Petitions and War Crimes Modification Board considered 512 cases and made recommendations that resulted in the reduction of many sentences.

On 26 May 1952 the United States, France, Great Britain, and Germany signed the Bonn Conventions, terminating the occupation of Germany. During the negotiations leading up to the agreement, war crimes prisoners became a political issue, with the German representatives attempting to gain concessions in favor of the prisoners by bargaining on other issues.[79] The Germans refused to recognize the legality of the war crimes conventions and considered the convicted war criminals as "prisoners of war." The Federal Republic of Germany argued that the convicted war criminals had not violated existing German law during the war, and therefore their convictions were ex post facto in nature. Nevertheless, in the Bonn Conventions the FRG agreed to take custody of the prisoners and enforce the execution of the sentences in the future. In the meantime, however, the U.S. high commissioner for Germany and the commander in chief, USAREUR (the U.S. Army Europe), issued a joint directive on 31 August 1953 establishing a Mixed Parole and Clemency Board, composed of three American members and two German members, to consider applications for parole and clemency. By then, however, the Army already had executed 261 accused. Nevertheless, as a result of this program the last Dachau defendants were released from Landsberg prison in December 1957.[80]

Conclusion

With the prosecution of the Dachau trials, IMT, and Subsequent Nuremberg Proceedings, the United States emerged as the political and moral leader of the effort to punish Nazi war criminals in Germany.[81] The Dachau trials constituted the earliest, longest, and largest-scale American effort to bring war criminals to justice as part of this endeavor. The trials advanced the concept that enemy soldiers or civilians could be held individually accountable for war crimes, irrespective of the overall responsibility of their governments. Following the orders of their superiors or government did not absolve these individuals from personal liability for violations of the laws and usages of war. The Dachau trials therefore served as general reminder that all perpetrators, regardless of their rank or position, could be punished for their crimes.

The significance of the Dachau trials should be considered not only from the legal perspective, but also from the political and historical contexts. As demonstrated in this essay, the role of the Dachau trials extended beyond their immediate legal purpose of punishment. Through a systematic judicial response to Nazi crimes, the trials served a broad political agenda designed to advance U.S. occupation goals in Germany. The Dachau trials functioned as one of the pillars in the American effort to reorient the Germans. Together with the denazification courts and formal education programs, the trials helped to delegitimize the Third Reich by establishing the existence of past wrongs; clarifying some of the crimes perpetrated by the Nazi regime; allowing a process in which investigation and public presentation of related evidence could take place; and creating a forum in which such crimes could be denounced. These factors were particularly important to a society coming to grips with its past.[82]

From a historical perspective, the Dachau trials provided the earliest glimpse into the identity of "ordinary" war criminals, the experience of the Nazi concentration camps, and the attitudes of the German population toward captured American prisoners of war. The evidence gathered by war crimes investigators offered some of the most timely witness testimonies collected during the war and shortly after liberation. Yet the limitations on the type of crimes that the Dachau courts could prosecute resulted in a presentation of evidence that was often narrow, limited in scope, or detached from its historical context. Nevertheless, the Dachau trials provided a starting point in which the history and criminality of the Nazi regime could be discussed in the immediate aftermath of war. Their importance, therefore, rested in their timing rather than the completeness of evidence or historical narrative.

Notes

1. The United States also participated with Australia, Canada, China, France, Great Britain, India, the Netherlands, New Zealand, the Philippines, and the Soviet Union in the prosecution of 28 war criminals in Tokyo by the International Military Tribunal for the Far East. See Bernard Röling and C. F. Rüter, eds., *The Tokyo Judgment: The International Military Tribunal for the Far East (I.M.T.F.E.), April 29, 1946–November 12, 1948* (Amsterdam: APA University Press, 1977).

2. The trial took place between 20 November 1945 and 1 October 1946. Of the 22 accused actually prosecuted, the tribunal acquitted three accused and sentenced 12 to death, three to life imprisonment, and four to prison sentences.

3. The twelve trials took place between December 1946 and April 1949. Of the 177 defendants actually prosecuted, the courts acquitted 35 accused, sentenced 24 to death, 20 to life imprisonment, and 98 to prison terms. See the contribution by Jonathan Friedman, "Law and Politics in the Subsequent Nuremberg Trials, 1946–1949," in this volume.

4. The term "lesser war criminals" is used in accordance with the Moscow Declaration to distinguish the accused from the major war criminals prosecuted at Nuremberg. The term does not refer to the severity of the crimes committed.

5. Declaration on German Atrocities (Moscow Declaration), 1 November 1943, National Archives and Records Administration (hereafter NARA), RG 549, Cases tried, Box 298.

6. Declaration on German Atrocities, 1 November 1943, NARA, RG 549, Cases tried, Box 298.

7. Stimson to Hull, 3 May 1944, NARA, RG 153, Judge Advocate General of the Army (hereafter JAG) Law Library, Box 57; *A History of the War Crimes Office, 25 September–30 June 1945*, p. 2, NARA, RG 153, JAG Law Library, Box 57.

8. Acting Secretary to Stimson, 23 February 1944, NARA, RG 153, JAG Law Library, Box 57; Stimson to Hull, 3 May 1944, NARA, RG 153, JAG Law Library, Box 57.

9. *A History of the War Crimes Office*, pp. 16-19, NARA, RG 153, JAG Law Library, Box 57.

10. Stimson to Cramer, 25 September 1944, NARA, RG 153, General Records, Box 1.

11. *A History of the War Crimes Office*, p. 6, NARA, RG 153, JAG Law Library, Box 57.

12. *Report of the Deputy Judge Advocate for War Crimes*, p. 14, NARA, RG 549, General Admin., Box 13.

13. *Law Order and Security, Occupation Forces in Europe Series, 1945-1946*, p. 3, NARA, RG 549, General Admin., Box 13.

14. *War Crimes and Punishment of War Criminals, Study No. 86*, p. 7, NARA, RG 549, General Admin., Box 14; Ulio to Commanding General, European Theater of Operations, 12 August 1944, NARA, RG 153, General Records, Box 21.

15. *War Crimes and Punishment of War Criminals*, p. 9.

16. *War Crimes and Punishment of War Criminals*, p. 7.

17. "War Criminals," 28 November 1944, NARA, RG 549, General Admin., Box 1.

18. Lovett to Commanding Generals, 24 February 1945, NARA, RG 153, War Crimes Branch, JAG Law Library, Box 57.

19. *War Crimes and Punishment of War Criminals*, p. 8.

20. *Report of the Deputy Judge Advocate for War Crimes*, pp. 21-25, NARA, RG 549, General Admin., Box 13.

21. *A History of the Judge Advocate War Crimes Branch of Headquarters, Seventh United States Army*, p. 13, NARA, RG 549, General Admin., Box 16.

22. *Law Order and Security: Occupation Forces in Europe Series, 1945–46*, p. 13, NARA, RG 549, General Admin., Box 1.

23. *Law Order and Security*, p. 14.

24. Ferencz to Trudy, 4 April 1945, United States Holocaust Memorial Museum Archive (hereafter USHMM) RG 12.001.03*01, Benjamin Ferencz Papers.

25. *History of the Judge Advocate War Crimes Branch*, p. 14.

26. Ferencz to Trudy, 29 April 1945, USHMM, RG 12.001.03*01, Benjamin Ferencz Papers.

27. Cohen to Commanding General, 12th Army Group, 17 June 1945, NARA, RG 549, Cases Tried, Box 345.

28. *History of the Judge Advocate War Crimes Branch*, p. 16.

29. *Report by the Deputy Judge Advocate for War Crimes*, p. 160, appendix 18, NARA, RG 549, General Admin., Box 13.

30. Telford Taylor, *Final Report to the Secretary of War on the Nuremberg War Crimes Trials under Control Law no. 10* (Washington DC, 1949), pp. 3–4.

31. Eisenhower to Commanding Generals, 25 August 1945, NARA, RG 338, General Admin., Box 13.

32. Section 5–351, Title 5, *Legal and Penal Administration of Military Government Regulations, Headquarters, United States Forces, European Theater, 30 November 1945*. Reprinted in Report by Deputy Judge Advocate for War Crimes, p. 52, NARA, RG 338, General Admin., Box 13.

33. *Guide to Procedure: Technical Manual for Legal and Prison Officers*, 2nd ed., June 1945, in Holger Lessing, *Der Erste Dachauer Prozeß* (1945/6), pp. 349–56 (Baden Baden: Nomos, 1993).

34. Eli E. Nobleman, *American Military Government Courts in Germany: Their Role in the Democratization of the German People*, Training Packet no. 52 (1950), pp. 42–47.

35. General Military Government courts could impose any lawful sentence including death and had at least five members; Intermediate Courts, which had at least three members, could impose sentences of up to ten years imprisonment and up to $10,000 in fines; Summary Courts, which included at least one member, could impose imprisonment of up to one year and a fine up to $1,000. See Ordinance no. 2, Military Government Germany, Military Government Courts, September 1944. Reprinted in Lessing, *Der erste Dachauer Prozeß*, pp. 328–33. Nobleman, *American Military Government Courts*, p. 52.

36. J.C.S. 1023/10, 8 July 1945 Directive on the Identification and Apprehension of Persons Suspected of War Crimes or Other Offenses and Trial of Certain Offenders, RG 549 General Admin., Box 1.

37. Existing rules included *Guide to Procedure*; Title 5 of the *Legal and Penal Administration of Military Government Regulations*; and the *Manual for Trial of War Crimes and Related Cases*. Report by the Deputy Judge Advocate for War Crimes, p. 53. Lessing, *Der erste Dachauer Prozeß*, pp. 349–56.

38. *Report by the Deputy Judge Advocate for War Crimes*, p. 33.

39. See Inter-Office Memo, War Crimes Branch, 26 November 1945, Records of U.S. Army Commands, 1942—War Crimes Cases Not Tried, USHMM, RG 06.005.05M, Reel 8.

40. "Closing of Various Cases at Dachau," 18 November 1947, signed Major Paul T. Scott, Chief of Evidence Section, Records of U.S. Army Commands, 1942—War Crimes Cases Not Tried, USHMM RG 06.005.05M, Reels 1–7.

41. Conference with Straight, 28 October 1947, NARA, RG 549, General Admin., Box 1; Russ to Martin, 1 November 1955, NARA, RG 549, General Admin., Box 12.

42. Lisa Yavnai, "Military Justice: The US Army War Crimes Trials in Germany, 1944–1947" (Ph.D. diss., London School of Economics and Political Science, 2007).

43. Yavnai, "Military Justice," Annex trials chart.

44. Leon Jaworski, *After Fifteen Years* (Houston: Gulf, 1961), p. 75.

45. In June 1946 the Third U.S. Army became exclusively responsible for the prosecution of war crimes trials. The site of the Dachau concentration camp was under its control.

46. Yavnai, "Military Justice," Annex trials chart.

47. *Report by the Deputy Judge Advocate for War Crimes*, pp. 49–50.

48. Yavnai, "Military Justice," Annex trials chart.

49. Yavnai, "Military Justice," Annex trials chart.

50. See, for example, Case 12–1497, *United States v. Joseph Hartgen et al.*

51. The Führer order no. 003830/42 g.Kdos. OKW/WFSt, 18 October 1942, NARA, RG 549, Cases Tried, Box 260.

52. See, for example, an editorial by Goebbels on the subject; the piece appeared on 29 May 1944 in the *Völkischer Beobachter*. The article denounced Allied flyers as terrorists who murdered defenseless women and children. It stated that the terrorist flyers were not entitled to any protection from Wehrmacht or police if aroused German population took retaliatory measures. NARA, RG 549, Cases Tried, Box 251.

53. Himmler, Order RF/48/16/43 g, 10 August 1943, NARA, RG 549, Cases Tried, Box 260.

54. Keitel to the Supreme Commander of the Air Force, 14 June 1944, NARA, RG 549, Cases Tried, Box 260.

55. See, for example, *United States v. Jürgen Stroop et al.*, Case 12–2000 etc., NARA, RG 549, Cases Tried, Box 214.

56. United States Holocaust Memorial Museum, *Liberation, 1945* (Washington DC: United States Holocaust Memorial Council, 1995), p. 17.

57. The U.S. Army liberated Ohrdruf, Buchenwald, Dachau, Dora, Ebensee, Flossenbürg, Gunskirchen, Gusen, Kaufering, and Mauthausen concentration camps, among others. Abraham J. Edelheit and Hershel Edelheit, *History of the Holocaust: A Handbook and Dictionary* (Boulder CO: Westview Press, 1994), pp. 333–34.

58. Hodgson to Secretary of State, "Trial of German Concentration Camp Cases," 1 March 1946, NARA, RG 153, War Crimes Branch, General Records, Box 3.

59. Yavnai, "Military Justice," Annex trials chart. For an exploration of the Hadamar "euthanasia" facility and the 1945 American trial of its personnel, see "Early Postwar Justice in the American Zone: The 'Hadamar Murder Factory' Trial" by Patricia Heberer in this volume.

60. *Report of the Deputy Judge Advocate for War Crimes*, p. 62.

61. Maximilian Koessler, "American War Crimes Trials in Europe," *Georgetown Law Journal* 39:1 (1950): 18–112; Dachau (40 accused, 15 November–13 December 1945); Mauthausen (61 defendants, 29 March–13 May 1946); Flossenbürg (45 defendants, 12 June 1946–22 January 1947); Mühldorf (14 defendants, 1 April–13 May 1947); Buchenwald (31 defendants, 11 April–14 August 1947); and Nordhausen (19 defendants, 7 August–30 December 1947).

62. Court transcript pp. 145–46, case 000-50-2-15, NARA, RG 549, Cases Tried, Box 295.

63. See, for example, *U.S. vs. Martin Gottfried Weiss et al.*, Case no. 000–5–2, NARA, RG 549, Cased Tried, Box 285.

64. J.C.S. 1023/10, 8 July 1945.

65. Deputy Judge Advocate for War Crimes, SOP No. 14, "Subject: Extradition by Other Governments," 1 November 1946, NARA, RG 549, General Admin., Box 10.

66. Yavnai, "Military Justice," Annex trials chart.

67. Denson to Counsel section, Status of Personnel in Concentration Camps, Flossenbürg Concentration Camp Case, 15 November 1946, NARA, RG 549, Cases Tried, Box 296.

68. Ebensee was a subcamp of Mauthausen concentration camp; United States Holocaust Memorial Museum, *Liberation 1945*, p. 83.

69. Ferencz letter to Trudy, 29 April 1945, USHMM, RG 12.001.03*01, Benjamin B. Ferencz Papers.

70. *Rules of Land Warfare*, paragraph 347.1, as amended on 15 November 1944.

71. *Report by the Deputy Judge Advocate for War Crimes*, p. 16.

72. *Report by the Deputy Judge Advocate for War Crimes*, p. 64.

73. "Genocide," a term coined by Raphael Lemkin, became officially recognized as a war crime in 1948.

74. Bloxham, *Genocide on Trial*, p. 11.

75. Conference at Munich on 6 and 7 September 1947 with Colonel Straight respecting alleged irregularities in the operation at Dachau and other matters, 17 September 1947, NARA, RG 549, General Admin., Box 1.

76. Norbert Frei, *Adenauer's Germany and the Nazi Past: The Politics of Amnesty and Integration* (New York: Columbia University Press, 2002), p. 98.

77. Suzanne Brown-Fleming, *The Holocaust and Catholic Conscience: Cardinal Aloisius Muench and the Guilt Question in Germany* (Notre Dame: University of Notre Dame Press, in association with the United States Holocaust Memorial Museum, 2006), p. 6.

78. Frei, *Adenauer's Germany and the Nazi Past*, p. 102.

79. Concerning the subject of West German public opinion regarding immediate postwar justice and its lack of efficacy in democratization efforts, see Donald Bloxham, "Milestones and Mythologies: The Impact of Nuremberg," in this volume.

80. Yavnai, "Military Justice," Annex trials chart.

81. Frei, *Adenauer's Germany and the Nazi Past*, p. 103.

82. Ruti G. Teitel, *Transitional Justice* (Oxford: Oxford University Press, 2000), p. 49.

II

*Allied Courts and German Crimes
in the Context of Nuremberg*

Law and Politics in the
Subsequent Nuremberg Trials, 1946–1949

JONATHAN FRIEDMAN

Historians have written volumes on the International Military Tribunal of Major War Criminals held at Nuremberg between November 1945 and October 1946, commonly referred to as the IMT. Yet scholars have not paid adequate attention to the twelve subsequent proceedings conducted in that city by the U.S. Army between 1946 and 1947. In these trials U.S. officials prosecuted the second tier of Germany's elite, 185 individuals in all, including members of the SS, civil service, officer corps, military and industrial spheres, and the medical profession. The opening of Allied documents, coupled with a shift in historiography toward the immediate postwar period, has sparked interest in these cases and their importance in the broader scope of contemporary European history and international war crimes prosecutions. This essay explores the functions of the twelve tribunals and assesses their place in the overall context of American denazification policy and the emerging cold war. The obvious question begged by this line of inquiry is: to what extent did the post-IMT trials dispense justice effectively, and by effectively I mean proportionate to the crimes committed?

The Road to Nuremberg

Before the end of the Second World War, the major Allied powers fighting against Nazi Germany (the United States, Great Britain, and the Soviet Union) resolved to bring suspected war criminals to justice. Under the terms of the Moscow Declaration of November 1943, the three Allies announced that anyone participating in war crimes would be tried by the courts of those countries on whose territory the infractions had occurred.[1] The Moscow agreement excluded major war criminals whose acts could not be limited to any defined geographical area. Ultimately, these were to be tried and punished in accordance with a subsequent joint decision, adopted on 8 August 1945 as the "London Agreement on the Punishment of the Major War Criminals of the European

Axis." This declaration, signed by twenty-three states, provided for the establishment of the International Military Tribunal made up of judges from the United States, Great Britain, the Soviet Union, and France.[2] It was the IMT that went on to pronounce judgment at Nuremberg on twenty-four of the leading personalities within the Nazi hierarchy.

The IMT was the principal of three institutions vested with jurisdiction over war crimes in the U.S. occupation zone. The second was the Judge Advocate General (JAG) of the U.S. Army. In January 1944 a War Crimes Office was established within JAG, and after the war, it tried cases involving atrocities in concentration camps that the U.S. Army had liberated, the murder and mistreatment of American soldiers, and other crimes in the area comprising the U.S. zone of occupation (the states of Bavaria, Baden-Württemberg, and Hessen).[3] The subsequent U.S. Military Tribunals at Nuremberg, affiliated not with JAG but with the institution that administered the occupation, the Office of Military Government, U.S. Zone (OMGUS), came to constitute the third jurisdiction over war crimes in the American zone.

The legal foundations for the latter jurisdiction came on 20 December 1945, one month after the formal opening of the IMT. On that date the Allied Control Council overseeing Germany's occupation passed Control Council Law No. 10 to establish a uniform legal basis for the prosecution of Nazi war criminals.[4] The law permitted each major ally to try war crimes in its respective zone and even allowed German courts, at the discretion of each zonal military authority, to deal with cases involving crimes committed by the Nazi state against other German nationals or stateless persons.[5] Article II recognized as punishable four distinct crimes—crimes against peace, war crimes, crimes against humanity, and membership in organizations declared criminal by the IMT (the SS, for instance). Individuals involved in these acts were liable for ordering, abetting, or consenting to commit such a crime, and those found guilty might be punished with death, life imprisonment, hard labor, fine, forfeiture of property, restitution or deprivation of civil rights.[6]

By making it possible for American officials to try war crimes on their own, Control Council Law No. 10 obviated the need for a second International Military Tribunal. Even without the law, however, a subsequent Allied tribunal might not have been convened as it lacked support from some of the major figures, including chief American prosecutor Supreme Court Justice Robert Jackson, who disliked the methods of his Soviet counterparts. Colonel Telford Taylor, also a major figure on the U.S. prosecution team who went on to direct the successor trials at Nuremberg, was one of the few advocates of a second international trial. In a series of meetings in May 1946, Taylor met with representatives from Great Britain, the Soviet Union, and France and made arrangements for a hearing that would be smaller than the IMT. The defendants were to include Alfried Krupp, the head of the Krupp steel concern; Hermann Schmitz and Georg von Schnitzler, executives from the chemical conglomerate I.G. Farben; Kurt von Schroeder, the Cologne banker at whose home Hitler and Franz von Papen had reached the fateful January 1933 understanding with President Paul von Hindenburg; and Hermann Röchling, the director of a coal and steel enterprise in the Saar.[7] Nevertheless, in January 1947, three months after the IMT rulings, the U.S. government rejected the official appeal (coming from French authorities) for a second Allied tribunal.[8]

Preparations for additional trials in the American zone were initially the task of the Subsequent Proceedings Division of Jackson's organization, the Office of Chief of Counsel for the Prosecution of Axis Criminality. At the end of March 1946 Jackson named Taylor as his successor, charging him with the responsibility of administering the next series of prosecutions.[9] As an incentive to head up this body, Taylor was offered the rank of brigadier general.[10] But that proved insufficient enticement. Taylor had been in the United States for several weeks trying to recruit jurists for the subsequent trials and was having little luck signing up lawyers. He informed Jackson that if the Army lifted its ban on spouses, not only would he gladly return, but he could persuade other litigators to join him. Over Jackson's objections, the Army removed the spousal ban and authorized Taylor to return to Nuremberg with his wife. In the long run, this inducement did little to bolster the general's confidence in his legal staff; as late as September 1946 he remained unsatisfied with the quality of many of the lawyers assigned to him: "With few exceptions, the lawyers recruited have been poor. I do not refer to Pomerantz and Robbins. . . . Most of the rest, however, are utterly vacuous political hacks. They are of no earthly use to us and if they aren't very unhappy already they are going to be very shortly."[11]

Taylor's concern about the quality of the judges presiding over the tribunals matched his trepidation over the competence of his lawyers. In the same memo in which he lambasted his prosecutors, Taylor told Jackson that "it is quite bad enough to have such persons visited upon us as lawyers, but it would be fatal in the case of the judges. I think that no judge should be sent over here without the personal approval of yourself or Judge Patterson."[12] In fact, one of the U.S. trial lawyers whom Taylor had praised, A. Pomerantz, quit in protest over what he saw as obstacles placed in the way of his prosecution of the I.G. Farben case and because of the "character of the judges."[13]

Taylor's anxiety regarding the adjudication of the trials was not unfounded. Following the IMT trial, U.S. Supreme Court Chief Justice Harlan F. Stone had prohibited Supreme Court justices from serving on any subsequent war crimes tribunal. In so doing, he sought to avoid a repeat of the situation during Jackson's absence, in which the Court often found itself deadlocked on major decisions.[14] His successor, Fred Vinson, extended the ban to federal judges. That left state judges and attorneys, in many respects more appealing choices because of their status as Washington outsiders and their projection of "homespun" wisdom and impartiality. However, none of the thirty-two judges who were selected by OMGUS to serve on the twelve tribunals had extensive experience in international law or military law.[15] Twenty-five were or had been state court judges, and fourteen had served on state supreme courts. The others included trial judges and a law school dean (Paul Hebert of Louisiana State University Law School).

Even during the course of the trials, administrative uncertainties remained. In October 1946, when Taylor filed the first indictments against Karl Brandt and other Nazi doctors, he still had not determined the exact number of defendants he wished to prosecute and the number of cases he wanted to try. Initially estimating that a hundred individuals would be indicted, he increased his projection to between two and five hundred as he became more familiar with the government, military, and economic structure of the Third Reich.[16] The discovery of *Einsatzgruppen* records by American prosecutor Benjamin Ferencz prompted Taylor to consider an additional trial of twenty-two officials from the mobile killing squads.[17] As late as May 1947, eight months after the trials had begun, Taylor planned to conduct sixteen hearings, down from an original goal of eighteen.[18] One of these cases involved the leaders of the Dresdner Bank, who, for bureaucratic reasons, were able to escape trial.[19]

In the end, 185 persons were indicted in twelve separate cases; 8 suspects were not tried because of illnesses or death. The hearings fell into the following categories: cases involving medical abuses (the Brandt or Medical case and the case against Field Marshal Erhard Milch); cases against SS officials (the Pohl case, dealing with leaders of the SS Economic-Administrative Main Office or WVHA, the *Einsatzgruppen* case, and the case against the Race and Resettlement Main Office, or RuSHA); cases involving industrialists (the Flick, I.G. Farben, and Krupp cases); cases against cabinet or other government officials (the Justice and Ministries cases); and cases against military leaders (the Hostage and High Command, or OKW, cases). According to Taylor, the figures of 185 individuals and twelve trials arose out of "circumstances as they developed" and a simple desire to try fewer cases as quickly as possible.[20]

Procedures and Issues at Nuremberg

Contrary to what many German critics alleged, the Nuremberg tribunals were characterized by a sense of fairness and impartiality.[21] Indeed, both the IMT and the subsequent trials adopted numerous safeguards from Anglo-American legal tradition, including the right to counsel, the presumption of innocence, and the rule that conviction is dependent upon proof of the crime beyond a reasonable doubt.[22] Following the completion of trials, the U.S. Military Governor reviewed each decision, although there was no appellate court in this process. Defendants also had the right to petition the U.S. Supreme Court for a review of their cases.[23]

Some of the judges maintained that these safeguards were not merely hallmarks of the Anglo-American system of jurisprudence but were vital to the integrity of the trials.[24] Nearly two hundred German attorneys, many themselves the subject of denazification proceedings, served as defense lawyers at Nuremberg, and they went on to conduct nearly two-thirds of the sessions.[25] Approaching the tribunals with caution at first, they soon realized that they could adopt a bold and intransigent attitude without risking any unpleasant consequences. In an essay on the tribunals, Telford Taylor mentions that Dr. Otto Kranzbühler, counsel for Admiral Karl Dönitz before the IMT and then for Alfried Krupp, went so far as to charge Germany's conquerors with hypocrisy, arguing that it was inappropriate for the United States to stage war crimes proceedings when it had, he argued, also committed crimes against humanity with its incendiary and atomic bombings.[26]

One of the more legitimate complaints of the defense concerned the lack of access to evidence held by the prosecution. In the course of the trials American prosecutors chose from the millions of captured records available to them about 18,000 documents to be presented as evidence to the tribunals, of which approximately 2,500 were affidavits. The defense was more reactive, as it could only await specific indictments. Of the 23,000 defense exhibits, half were sworn statements. In a number of instances, however, defense documentation proved deficient both in quality and quantity. Ernst Biberstein, a Protestant minister who became a Gestapo official and chief of an *Einsatzkommando*, offered in his defense only three documents, one of which was a dictionary definition of the term "execution." Max Kiefer, an official in the WVHA, was tried in the Pohl Case for complicity in the administration of concentration camps. He presented in his defense only two affidavits and received a sentence of life imprisonment.[27]

It was generally true that SS defendants had greater difficulty in obtaining documents for their defense than non-SS prisoners. In the Medical and *Einsatzgruppen* cases, the tribunals limited defense access to evidence held by the prosecution, while in the Hostages and OKW Cases, the defense was permitted to procure war diaries of the German Army from the German Military Document Section in the Pentagon. The defense obtained greater access to prosecution documents in the Justice, Farben, and Ministries cases as well. In the Justice case, the prosecution furnished the defense German-language copies of their exhibits before these were submitted into evidence. Altogether, the tribunal received 1,452 pieces of evidence from the defense.[28] In the Ministries case, the wealth of documentation held by the defense prompted the *prosecution* to request access to it, a petition that the tribunal denied.

A final factor influencing evidentiary claims was the disposition of the judges. Justices from the U.S. East, who presided over the initial cases, including Robert Toms, Fitzroy Phillips, Michael Musmanno, and John Speight (on the Milch and Pohl cases), were more liberal toward the prosecution. By contrast, later judges, primarily from the West and Midwest, such as Charles Wennerstrum (Hostages), Curtis Shake (I.G. Farben), and William Christianson (Flick and Ministries), put the defense in a more advantageous position.[29]

While access to documents often proved difficult for the defense, the prosecution encountered similar obstacles. Finding incriminating evidence against Alfried Krupp, for example, involved plumbing deep into mines, searching through remote houses in the Harz Mountains, and digging up canisters of microfilm in thick forest. A few key pieces of evidence in the Farben Case were discovered in a bathroom cupboard, hidden there by the personal assistant of one of the defendants, Otto Ambros, the mastermind behind the development of I.G. Auschwitz. (Ambros had apparently destroyed hundreds of documents but had hidden a handful whose destruction even he could not countenance. He also had the protection of French authorities who only reluctantly agreed to turn him over to the Americans to stand trial).[30]

One of the major legal hurdles that the prosecution had to overcome was the charge that the tribunals violated the ex post facto tradition of not trying individuals for acts that were not illegal when they were committed. German defense attorneys consistently argued that there were no precedents in international law criminalizing the various deeds committed by the Nazis, and their prosecution amounted to a dispensation of retroactive justice. The Latin phrase to which they referred was *nullem crimen sine lege, nulla poena sine lege* (no crime without law, no punishment without law). Some American legal theorists also doubted the legality of the charges, believing that Nuremberg opened the door to an arbitrary selection of offenses and an arbitrary selection of offenders. Federal judge Charles Wyzanski felt this way early on but came to support the trials as a lesser evil, arguing that it would be worse not to agree on an international code of conduct and not to criminalize behavior universally regarded as a violation of international treaties and standards.[31]

Despite conceding that international law had not heretofore codified specific war crimes, the tribunals contended that Control Council Law No. 10 had broad precedents. In fact, many of the offenses with which the defendants were charged violated existing codes of German criminal law.[32] In the OKW and Hostage Cases,[33] the tribunals argued that the crimes specified in the Nuremberg Charter and Law No. 10 merely restated Articles 43, 46, 47, and 50 of Section III and 23h of Section II of the 1907 Hague regulations on warfare, to which Germany had been a signatory.[34] Article 46 specifically stated that during wartime, "family honor and rights, the lives of persons, and private property, as well as religious convictions and practice, must be respected."[35] The preamble to the declarations of both the first Hague Convention in 1899 and the fourth Hague Convention in 1907 also decreed that wars should be governed at all levels by civilized "laws of humanity."[36] Moreover, the tribunals pointed out that Germany had signed the Geneva Convention of 1929, which dealt with the protection of prisoners of war, and had been a party to the Kellogg-Briand Pact of the previous year, which had outlawed aggressive wars.[37] In contrast to the rulings in the OKW and Hostage cases, the tribunal of the *Einsatzgruppen* case declared that the trials not only accorded with existing international law but made a major contribution to it.[38] (For example, the so-called Nuremberg Code, a set of ten principles dealing with human experimentation, was a direct result of the decision in the Medical case.[39])

The contention by the defense that the jurisdiction of Allied tribunals violated German sovereignty also met with a vigorous response. Two of the three judges in the Justice case argued that the legitimacy of the tribunals was based on the legitimacy of the Allied defeat of Germany:

> *It is this fact of the complete disintegration of the government in Germany, followed by unconditional surrender and by occupation of the territory, which explains and justifies the assumption and exercise of supreme governmental power by the Allies. The same fact distinguishes the present occupation of Germany from the type of occupation which occurs when, in the course of actual warfare, an invading army enters and occupies the territory of another state, whose government is still in existence and is in receipt of international recognition, and whose armies, with those of its allies, are still in the field. In the latter case, the occupying power is subject to the limitations imposed upon it by the Hague Convention and by the laws and customs of war. In the former case (the occupation of Germany) the Allied Powers were not subject to those limitations. By reason of the complete breakdown of government, industry, agriculture, and supply, they were under an imperative humanitarian duty of far wider scope to reorganize government and industry and to foster local democratic governmental agencies throughout the territory.[40]*

Judge Mallory Blair, from Texas, offered a much different opinion:

> *Under the foregoing rules of military operation [for the United States,*
> *the Basic Field Manual on Rules of Land Warfare issued in 1940 by*
> *the Judge Advocate General], there is no rule which would, because of*
> *the unconditional surrender of the German armed forces, transfer the*
> *sovereignty of Germany to the Allied occupants, or to either of them,*
> *in their respective zones of occupation. It may here be pointed out*
> *that the report of 1919 by the Commission on the Responsibility of the*
> *Authors of War and Enforcement of Penalties lists among other war*
> *crimes in violation of international law or of the laws and customs of*
> *land warfare, "the usurpation of sovereignty during military occupa-*
> *tion."*[41]

However, the position of the vast majority of the justices on the issue of jurisdiction was typified by the ruling in the Hostages case: "Such crimes [such as mass murder] are . . . war crimes because they were committed under the authority or orders of the belligerent who, in ordering or permitting them, violated the rules of warfare. Such crimes are punishable by the country where the crime was committed or by the belligerent into whose hands the criminals have fallen, the jurisdiction being concurrent."[42]

Related to the overall issue of jurisdiction were the problems of dealing with prewar atrocities, specifically, membership in a criminal organization, conspiracy, crimes against peace, and crimes against humanity (i.e., crimes committed by the Nazi government against its own civilians before the outbreak of war in 1939). Unlike the Nuremberg Charter regulating the IMT, Control Council Law No. 10 did not include a reference to crimes committed before the war; moreover, it did not require that crimes against humanity be "in execution of or in connection with any crime within the jurisdiction of the Tribunal."[43] As a result, prosecutors in many of the tribunals broadened the scope of their allegations.

With respect to the membership charge, no effort was made to handle cases involving simple affiliation with a criminal organization. These cases were to be dealt with by local, denazification courts, the so-called *Spruchkammern*. Defendants selected for trial on other charges and who happened to be members of an organization declared criminal by the IMT were indicted accordingly, but no defendant was ever tried at Nuremberg for the crime of membership alone.[44] Meanwhile, the prosecution in seven cases brought a charge of conspiracy against the defendants, but in each case the justices threw it out, arguing that neither the Charter of the IMT nor Control Council Law No. 10 defined conspiracy to commit a war crime or a crime against humanity as a separate infraction.[45]

As for crimes against peace, the tribunals adopted the guiding principle that in order to establish individual criminal liability, the prosecution had to demonstrate the intentional commission of a criminal act or the wanton failure to fulfill a legal duty.[46] Liability was limited to those at the policy level who knowingly participated in the preparation, planning, initiation, and waging of aggressive war. Therefore, Carl Krauch of I.G. Farben was acquitted of the charge of crimes against peace because the tribunal believed that, despite Krauch's involvement in rearming the Reich, he lacked the criminal intent to prepare Germany for such an offensive: "The evidence is clear that Krauch did not participate in the planning of aggressive wars. The plans were made by and within a closely guarded circle. The meetings were secret. The information exchanged was confidential. Krauch was far beneath the membership in that circle. No opportunity was afforded to him to participate in the planning, either in a general way or with regard to any of the specific wars charged in Count One."[47] In the Ministries case, however, the tribunal convicted defendant Paul Körner of preparing for a war of aggression, concluding that, as the coordinator of the Reich's Four Year Plan, he was directly involved in Germany's rearmament.[48]

In the Krupp case the charges were peculiar because the prosecution claimed that, while Krupp's executives may not have been part of the "Nazi conspiracy" to start a war, they engaged in a separate conspiracy of their own. Prosecutors alleged that Gustav Krupp and his associates had been plotting since 1919 to undo the disarmament clauses of the Versailles Treaty. In rejecting this argument, the justices pointed out that Alfried, not his ailing father Gustav, was on trial and that only three of the defendants in the case had been connected with the firm at the time of the alleged conspiracy. (Alfried was not one of them.) The justices further contended that none of the three occupied a sufficiently important position to justify charging them with the responsibility for a decision taken at the end of 1920.[49]

In considering the "euthanasia" charges against Karl Brandt, the Medical case tribunal focused narrowly on crimes against non-German nationals committed during the war.[50] However, the tribunal in the Justice case noted that Control Law No. 10, through its omissions, did not prohibit the subsequent hearings from assuming jurisdiction over Nazi crimes against the German people.[51] Crimes against German nationals were investigated in the trial of Erhard Milch as well, but the tribunal determined that the prosecution had not produced sufficient evidence to justify convictions.[52]

Count Four in the Ministries case, the charge of atrocities against German nationals between 1933 and 1939, was more problematic because it involved crimes committed by the Nazi state against its own citizens during peacetime. In their decision, the justices dismissed the count with the belief that crimes against humanity perpetrated by a government against its own nationals were not crimes according to international law: "Such arguments and observations rather serve to emphasize the urgent need of comprehensive legislation by the family of nations, with respect to individual human rights. Such steps as have been taken in this direction since the late war may need to be further advanced and implemented. This, however, involves functions beyond the province of this Tribunal."[53]

Even more disturbing was the dismissal of Count Four in the Flick case because the charge implicated Flick only in the takeover of Jewish businesses before 1939, an act, the tribunal asserted, that was not declared criminal by either the IMT or Control Council Law No. 10.[54] In their excessively strict interpretation of both decrees, the judges ignored clauses that stated that crimes against humanity include "other inhumane acts committed against any civilian population or persecutions on political, racial, or religious grounds whether or not in violation of the domestic laws of the country where perpetrated."[55]

Establishing criminal liability proved easier to establish in the charges of war crimes and wartime crimes against humanity. The tribunals insisted that inhumane acts such as murder, deportation, enslavement, and persecution on the basis of racial and religious grounds shocked the conscience of every decent human being, ruling that those who participated in such conduct could not claim that they did not realize the illegality of their actions.[56] The tribunals also held defendants liable for the independent actions of those under their command in cases where the panel determined that the defendants should have been aware of their subordinates' actions. Günther Joel, a defendant in the Justice case, was found guilty because, as the attorney general of the court of appeals in Hamm, he supervised the prosecutors who handled the so-called Night and Fog concentration camp cases.[57] Similarly, the justices in the Pohl case convicted Karl Mummenthey, the administrator of the SS commercial enterprises that supplied concentration camp labor, despite his contention that he knew nothing of his subordinates' activities.[58] And even though the tribunal in the Flick case acquitted Friedrich Flick of the charge of "Aryanizing" Jewish businesses, it did find him guilty of war crimes and crimes against humanity because of his membership in Heinrich Himmler's "Circle of Friends," an organization that worked closely with the SS. The tribunal determined that Flick must have known of the Circle's activities and declared that it was immaterial whether their monetary contributions were spent on salaries or for lethal gas.[59]

Not all of the tribunals attributed knowledge to defendants without direct evidence. In convicting Milch on the charge of exploiting slave labor, the tribunal in Case 2 consistently required that the prosecution submit more than presumptions of the field marshal's knowledge of what was taking place: "It must be established that he, himself, participated in the slave labor enterprises, or knowing that such illegal practices were being committed, he having the power to do so, made no effort to curb or halt them."[60]

The tribunal in the Farben case, in a two-to-one vote, acquitted defendants charged with supplying Zyklon-B to the concentration camps and providing vaccines used in medical experimentation. In direct contrast to the decision in the Flick case, the two judges wrote that Farben's executives may not have known of the criminal purposes to which Zyklon-B and the vaccines were put.[61]

Those, too, with authority and who possessed actual knowledge of criminal activity committed by subordinates were deemed criminally negligent if they failed to prevent such action. Karl Brandt, Hitler's former attending physician, was convicted for this reason, among others.[62] By the same token, those who knew of illegal activity but who lacked authority over those actions were not held accountable: the Ministries Tribunal acquitted Otto von Erdmannsdorff, chief of the Political Division of the Foreign Office under Joachim von Ribbentrop, not because he lacked knowledge of crimes but because of his relative lack of power and influence.[63]

Some defense strategies were unsuccessful, among them the claim that the laws of war had been rendered irrelevant by the new concept of total war and the invocation of the *Tu Quoque* doctrine to implicate the Soviet Union, as a signatory to the 1939 Molotov-Ribbentrop Pact, in war crimes. The tribunals also rejected the contention that the defendants were only following orders. In the Hostage case, for example, the judges stated clearly that "army regulations are not a competent source of international law when a fundamental rule of justice is concerned . . . [hence] superior order is not a defense to an international law crime."[64] Although officially barred as a factor in determining guilt or innocence, the claim was permitted as a mitigating factor in sentencing. However, the tribunal in the *Einsatzgruppen* case maintained that this was a privilege bestowed by the Allies and that Article 47 of the German Military Penal Code actually took a harsher position on the defense of superior orders than did Control Council Law No. 10: "Under the German code, the subordinate may be convicted even if no crime was actually committed. It is sufficient if the order aims at the commission of a crime or offense. The German code makes the obeying subordinate responsible even for any 'civil' or 'general offenses,' i.e., for comparatively insignificant breaches of law which are not contemplated in the Allied law. Nor does the German code, as contrasted to the Allied law, mention the defense of superior orders as a possible mitigating circumstance."[65]

One of the more successful defense tactics was the allegation that many of the defendants acted out of "necessity," a claim linked to superior orders as it presupposed the commission of an act out of undue pressure and a lack of choice. In essence, the defendants insisted that refusal to comply with orders from above exposed them to imprisonment and even death.[66] Still, only the invocation of *Befehlsnotstand*, the pressure stemming from superior orders, and not *Putativnotstand*, behavior based on presumptive duress, proved effective in court. With respect to the latter contention, some of the defendants in the *Einsatzgruppen* case argued that in executing Soviet Jews they acted in self-defense to save Germany—the alleged third party—from the threat that Jews posed to it. The justices quickly dispensed with this "argument," however, declaring that the defendants did not succor Germany from any real or assumed danger by killing Jews but executed them simply because they were Jewish.[67]

By contrast, the industrialists in the Flick and Farben cases benefited from the defense of necessity. Flick insisted that the SS had forced him to accept slave laborers, despite proof that he had initiated negotiations with the SS for the supply of Soviet POWs to help manufacture railway cars. The judges considered this to be an isolated incident, and although they convicted Flick of exploiting slave labor, they imposed a light seven-year sentence, noting that "the Reich, with its hordes of enforcement officials and secret police, was always present, ready to go into instant action and to mete out savage and immediate punishment against anyone doing anything that could be construed as obstructing or hindering the carrying out of government regulations."[68] Judge Curtis Shake, who presided in the Farben case, held that the criterion for guilt was whether the defendants had used their own initiative in procuring slave labor. Citing the Flick precedent, the Farben judges concurred that the defendants did not have control over the forced labor program and that it was dictated by the Nazi state. Yet in pretrial hearings later denied in court by the defendants and ignored by the judges, several Farben directors admitted that they had voluntarily chosen to build a factory at Auschwitz because the cheap labor guaranteed higher profits.[69]

In contrast to the Flick and Farben precedents, two of the three justices in the Krupp case found Alfried Krupp and many of his associates guilty of spoliation and utilizing slave labor—despite acquitting the defendants of conspiracy. Ruling against Krupp, presiding judge H. C. Anderson maintained: "If we may assume that as a result of opposition to Reich policies Krupp would have lost control of his plant and the officials their positions, it is difficult to conclude that the law of necessity justified a choice favorable to themselves and against the unfortunate victims who had no choice . . . the officials of the Krupp firm well knew that any expansion of its facilities and activities would require the employment of forced labor, brought from occupied territories, prisoners of war and concentration camp inmates."[70]

In the end, of the 177 defendants tried in the subsequent Nuremberg proceedings, 142 received convictions. Twenty-five were sentenced to death, 7 in the Medical case, 4 in the Pohl case, and 14 in the *Einsatzgruppen* case. In a supplemental ruling the tribunal in the Pohl case reduced SS Major General Georg Loerner's sentence to life imprisonment. As Military Governor, General Lucius Clay did the same for Major General Karl Sommer. The remaining 23 death sentences were upheld upon review. In 1948 the 7 defendants in the

Medical case were executed, following the U.S. Supreme Court's rejection of a petition for habeas corpus filed on their behalf.[71] (The fate of the other death row inmates would be determined later.) Of the 118 defendants convicted but not condemned to death, 20 were given life sentences. The rest received terms ranging from five to twenty-five years. Seventy-five percent of the defendants received sentences ranging from seven to twenty years, and the average sentence was approximately ten years in length.[72]

After a short review Clay modified the sentences in only three of the twelve cases. He reduced the term of imprisonment for I.G. Farben executive Paul Häflinger from two years to time served and, as mentioned above, commuted the sentence of WVHA division deputy chief Karl Sommer from death to life imprisonment.[73] In the Krupp case, Clay confirmed the confiscation of Alfried Krupp's estate but decreed that his property was to be transferred to the commander of the occupation zone in which it was located rather than to the Allied Control Council.[74]

Defense counsel seeking a review of the last case to finish, Case 11 or the Ministries case, benefited from an administrative change in American occupation policies. On 6 June 1949 the office of the U.S. High Commissioner for Germany (HICOG) was established, officially ending the Military Government of the U.S. Zone of Germany. Thereafter, the responsibility for the execution and review of sentences fell to the new civilian High Commissioner, former Assistant Secretary of War John J. McCloy, who took a more lenient position toward the defendants. All of this occurred before the Ministries tribunal was able to rule on defense motions filed in April, alleging errors of fact and law in the final judgment. In December 1949 the often divided justices reduced Foreign Office State Secretary Ernst von Weizsäcker's and Undersecretary Ernst Woermann's sentences for waging aggressive war from seven years to five. The tribunal also set aside State Secretary Steengracht von Moyland's conviction for murdering POWs.[75] In January 1951 High Commissioner McCloy reduced an additional eight sentences, three of them to time served.[76]

Clearly, not everyone was pleased with the tribunals' findings. Telford Taylor, for one, believed that the judgments were too mild:

> It was apparent to anyone connected with the entire series of trials under Law No. 10 that the sentences became progressively lighter as time

went on. Defendants such as Darré, Dietrich, and Stuckart in the Ministries Case who, although convicted under two or more counts of the indictment of serious crimes, received very light sentences in April 1949, would surely have been much more severely punished in 1946 or 1947. No doubt a number of factors played a part in this trend towards leniency, including waning interest on the part of the general public and the shift in the focus of public attention resulting from international events and circumstances.[77]

Howard Watson Ambruster, writing for the left-wing American journal the *Nation*, called the decision in the Farben case "appalling" and reproached the court for "[failing] in its duty to render justice, strengthen international law, and destroy the seeds of future wars."[78] Allegations of judicial leniency were strengthened by the seemingly concessionary written opinions of some of the later justices such as Daniel O'Connell (from the RuSHA case) and H. C. Anderson (the presiding judge on the Krupp case). Judge O'Connell argued that his tribunal failed to consider necessity as a mitigating factor in sentencing six of the defendants (Greifelt, Creutz, Lorenz, Brückner, Hofmann, and Hildebrandt).[79] And although Judge Anderson concurred in the length of Alfried Krupp's prison sentence, he dissented from the order confiscating Krupp's property. He also disagreed with the sentences imposed on all of the other defendants in the case.[80] Taylor's claim that the later trials brought lighter sentences was not axiomatic, however, as revealed by the death sentences in Case 9, the *Einsatzgruppen* case. It would have been more accurate to suggest that SS officials involved in executions stood more of a chance of facing severe penalties than did industrialists or desk perpetrators (so-called *Schreibtischtäter*).

Perhaps the most infamous dissent came from the chief justice in the Hostage case, Judge Charles Wennerstrum, formerly of the State Supreme Court of Iowa. Hours before leaving Nuremberg, Wennerstrum gave an interview to the *Chicago Tribune* in which he denounced the American prosecutors for failing "to maintain objectivity aloof from vindictiveness, aloof from personal ambitions for convictions." He further contended that the lack of an appeals process left him with the feeling that justice had been denied. Last, he accused the prosecution of laying down no important precedent that "might help the world avoid future wars."[81] In a response printed on the same page as Wennerstrum's interview, General Taylor dismissed the judge's charges as baseless and subversive to the interests and policies of the United States.[82] Other judges agreed with Taylor. Judge Walter Beals, who presided in the Medical case, expressed surprise at Wennerstrum's outburst, while James Brand, the presiding judge in the Justice case, said that his charges bordered on libel.[83] What made the postmortem assault on the Hostages Tribunal all the more disturbing was the fact that Wennerstrum had helped to pen its judgment.

The impact of this controversy had hardly subsided when an account of a pretrial interrogation appeared to confirm the worst of Wennerstrum's allegations.[84] Defense counsel in the Justice case advanced the argument that Dr. Friedrich Gaus, one of the witnesses for the prosecution in the Justice case, had agreed to testify against his former colleagues after being held in solitary confinement for four weeks with threats that he would be handed over to the Soviets. Charles La Follette, the chief trial prosecutor, dismissed this accusation as rumor, insisting (dubiously) that more Germans than Americans had criticized the *leniency* of the tribunal's rulings.[85]

Politics, Public Opinion, and the Trials

German public opinion was generally ill disposed to the tribunals,[86] while the immediate response of the American public to the decisions ranged from support to indifference. American newspapers, by and large, were sympathetic, but there was a ground swell of hostility in Congress, where the focus had already shifted to the exigencies of the cold war.[87] From the first trial session in October 1946 to the last review in December 1949, the world had witnessed an escalating series of confrontations between the Western Allies and the Soviet Union, among them the Communist incursion into southeastern Europe and central Asia before 1947, which inspired the Truman Doctrine; the Communist coup in Czechoslovakia in March 1948; the promulgation of the Marshall Plan one month later; the Berlin Blockade in the summer of that year; the founding of the North Atlantic Treaty Organization on 4 April 1949; the founding of the West German Federal Republic in May; the Soviets' detonation of a nuclear weapon in September 1949; and the creation of the communist German Democratic Republic (GDR) on 7 October. As a result (and in the midst) of this intensifying conflict, American policy toward Germany shifted from one of occupation and denazification (as expressed in Joint Chiefs of Staff Directive 1067) to one of reconstruction and integration (JCS Directive 1779), occurring officially in July 1947. Accordingly, many observers began to feel that in this new context the prosecution of former Nazis had become counterproductive, if not entirely pointless. Further influencing the opinion of congressmen and ordinary Americans were reports of abuses by U.S. Army officials during the trial of German SS officers accused of executing American soldiers at Malmédy, Belgium, in 1944.

Protests against "victors' justice," emanating from German church leaders such as Bishop Theophil Wurm and pastor Martin Niemöller, resonated with several U.S. congressmen. Senator Robert Taft, the well-known conservative Republican from Ohio, became an outspoken critic of the tribunals, as did many other Republicans, who had regained control of Congress in 19476, some motivated by anticommunism, some by antisemitism, some by an overtly pro-German bias, some by genuine isolationism, and some by a mixture of all factors.[88] Even Supreme Court Justice Hugo Black denounced the subsequent proceedings and, along with Justice William O. Douglas, favored Oswald Pohl's request for habeas corpus during the review of his case.[89] As early as September 1946, a colleague of Benjamin Ferencz, the lead prosecutor in the *Einsatzgruppen* case, wrote that public apathy in America regarding the trials was shameful: "Anyone could have predicted that this would have been so, especially in view of the new plaguing international problems. The way things look now, I even predict that within a few months we will be very palsey-walsey with the Germans."[90]

According to Frank Buscher, while the cold war and the Malmédy fiasco were important factors molding public opinion, concerns about the integrity and constitutionality of the program most strongly affected the actions of U.S. authorities in Germany, especially before 1951; thereafter, political motives prevailed over legal considerations.[91] I would argue that political considerations played at least some role from the very beginning; whether this involved situating the trials within the overall strategy of denazification or containing communism. Buscher actually suggests this when he says that U.S. war crimes policy reflected changes in the priorities of the occupation as a whole, gradually discarding the punitive aspects of JCS directive 1067 in favor of JCS directive

1779. This is not to imply that the decisions of the tribunals were politically motivated or biased; to prove this, one must enter the minds of the judges, discard
their rulings, and hope to find hidden motives in their private writings. Unfortunately, with the exception of a few (such as Judge Wennerstrum), most of the
justices did not publicly comment about the tribunals afterward or leave personal papers to that effect, and when they did, their private opinions reflected
their professional rulings in each case. Even so, one could hardly have failed to
notice the political significance of the decisions, especially in the industrialist
cases, where a strict application of the law dovetailed conveniently with the
need to employ German industry in the struggle against communism.

Political concerns more obviously affected the clemency of war criminals
by 1951. Responding to pressure from German (and American) political and
religious leaders, both the High Commissioner and the Judge Advocate General established committees to address the issue of clemency—the former in
November 1949, the latter in March 1950.[92] McCloy's clemency review board,
led by David Peck, presiding judge of the New York State Supreme Court Appellate Division, refused to hear all the evidence from the trials but nonetheless
recommended the reduction of sentences or immediate clemency in 77 of 90
cases, including 7 of the 15 death sentences.[93] On 31 January 1951 McCloy and the
JAG boards under General Thomas Handy announced that of the 101 convicted
war criminals held in Landsberg prison, 33 were to be released immediately, an
additional 35 were to have their sentences reduced, and 16 death sentences were
to be commuted.[94] Among those granted clemency were Ernst Biberstein and
Franz Eirenschmalz, whose death sentences in the *Einsatzgruppen* and WVHA
cases, respectively, were commuted to life imprisonment; Erhard Milch, whose
life sentence was reduced to fifteen years; Wilhelm Speidel, whose life sentence
in the Hostages case was commuted to time served; and Alfried Krupp, whose
sentence of twelve years and forfeiture of property was rescinded.[95]

German journalists and politicians essentially welcomed the verdicts, although some criticized them for not being lenient enough.[96] According to
Edward Murphy, acting chief of the War Crimes Division of JAG, the "general
criticism in Germany has been to the effect that the war crimes trials were unjust, [that they] should be subject to review, and that convicted war criminals
should be released."[97] Joining German officials in support were several conser-

vative U.S. congressmen, including Senator Joseph McCarthy, who had led the Senate investigation into the charges of alleged U.S. Army brutality against the Malmédy defendants.[98]

Understandably, the response from Jewish groups and members of the American prosecution team was one of outrage. The World Jewish Congress expressed "profound dismay" over the sentences, believing that the decisions represented "a tragic error and a serious set-back to the democratic re-education of the German people."[99] Chief Counsel Telford Taylor condemned the clemencies as the "embodiment of political expediency."[100] Lead prosecutor Benjamin Ferencz concurred, here referring to the Krupp fiasco: "The Krupp pardons were not prompted by a recognition of the innocence of the officials concerned but by an attempt to achieve uniformity. It was pointed out that other convicted industrialists, such as Flick and the Directors of the I.G. Farben cartel, were already at large."[101]

Ferencz also pointed out that the panel handling the Krupp case regarded the evidence to convict as insufficient, despite never once reviewing it and having been instructed accordingly.[102] In an interview published two days after the clemency announcement, McCloy insisted that he had "made every effort to decide each individual case objectively, dispassionately, and on its own merits. . . . All of my decisions have been rooted in the firm belief in the basic principle of the rule of law which all must respect and to which all are answerable."[103]

Kai Bird, McCloy's biographer, justifiably disputes this contention. He insists that by January 1951, in the midst of the Korean War, American concerns about the spread of communism were at their height, prompting both a desire for German steel for armaments manufacture and speculation that the two-year-old West German republic might itself be rearmed. Neither could have been achieved, so it was thought, without the support of West German chancellor Konrad Adenauer: "Rearmament of Germany was HICOG's number-one priority in that bleakest of Decembers (1950), when it seemed for a moment that General MacArthur's forces might be pushed completely off the Korean peninsula. Adenauer was the only German leader willing to support German rearmament on American terms, and there was no better way to assist him politically than to do what was most popular on the clemency issue."[104]

Bird adds that McCloy reacted amiably to repeated entreaties for commutations from Adenauer. On December 5, when Adenauer wrote a letter specifically urging clemency for Krupp, the High Commissioner replied, "of the Krupp case I will give, I assure you, proper weight and attention to the comments and recommendations you make in your letter."[105] That McCloy had lifted the eleven-million-ton limitation on German steel production two months earlier suggests he was already moving in a direction favorable to Krupp.[106] In the end, Benjamin Ferencz maintains that "at the time, there was a sense of panic about the Soviets, a feeling that there was an urgent need for an understanding with the Germans. McCloy couldn't detach himself from that atmosphere."[107]

Whatever McCloy's motives may have been, the clemencies in many respects did more political damage than good. German nationalists seized upon the decisions to demonstrate that U.S. officials had lost faith in their war crimes program and to bolster their claim that the sentences had been based on "victor's justice." More important, perhaps, the commutations provided Soviet propaganda with an additional weapon to attack Western leniency toward Nazi criminals.[108]

Conclusion

The twelve subsequent trials at Nuremberg left a relatively dubious legacy. On the one hand, the legal issues that arose were broader and more complex in scope than those generated by either the IMT or the JAG processes. A wider spectrum of German society was recognized as implicated in various atrocities, and many of those charged at Nuremberg did not even belong to the Nazi Party. For these reasons, the subsequent trials gave the prosecution of war crimes a depth in legal theory and practice that heretofore did not exist. On the other hand, the tribunals were unpopular among large sections of the German populace, and they were quantitatively insignificant in terms of denazification: the 185 indictments constituted a minute fraction of the hundreds of thousands of suspected Nazi criminals who remained at large. Yet this inauspicious legacy resulted less from impartial litigation or biased adjudication than from inconsistencies in the Truman administration's overall program for Germany—specifically the shift, midway through the holding of the trials, from a policy of occupation and denazification to one of integration and reconstruction, designed to meet the new challenges of the cold war.

Notes

1. "Declaration on German Atrocities (Moscow Declaration)," signed by Franklin D. Roosevelt, Winston Churchill, and Josef Stalin, 1 November 1943.

2. "London Agreement of 8 August 1945," signed by Robert Jackson, Robert Falco, C. Jowitt, and I. Nikitchenko. The Moscow Declaration, the London Agreement, and other founding documents form the first section in each of the volumes of *Trials of War Criminals before the Nuernberg Military Tribunals under Control Council Law No. 10* (Washington DC: U.S. Government Printing Office, 1949; hereafter, *TWC*), the "green series" of Nuremberg-related official U.S. publications.

3. See "U.S. Army War Crimes Trials in Germany, 1945–1947" by Lisa Yavnai and "Early Postwar Justice in the American Zone: The 'Hadamar Murder Factory' Trial" by Patricia Heberer, both in this anthology.

4. Control Council Law No. 10 was reinforced by U.S. Executive Order 9679 of 16 January 946, U.S. Military General Ordinance nos. 7 and 11, of 18 October 1946 and 17 February 1947, respectively, and U.S. Forces European Theater General Order 301 of 24 October 1946.

5. Control Council Law No. 10, art. III, par. 1d.

6. Criminal liability for Crimes against Peace was normally extended only to individuals holding high political civil or military positions in the financial, industrial, or economic life of Nazi Germany. Control Council Law No. 10, art. II, par. 1a, 2f, and 3a–f; and Matthew Lippman, "The Other Nuremberg: American Prosecutions of Nazi War Criminals in Occupied Germany," *Indiana International and Comparative Law Review* 3:1 (1992): 10.

7. M. Dubost, the French delegate, wanted Röchling included, while Elwyn Jones, a delegate from Great Britain, proposed Schroeder. Taylor suggested pursuing the two Farben executives, and all three representatives agreed on the inclusion of Alfried Krupp. General N. D. Zorya of the Soviet Union had no comment throughout the meeting. One month before, Jones had recommended to Jackson that the Allies pursue the five defendants named above, along with Paul Pleiger of the Goering combine, Ernest Poensgen and Albert Voelger of Vereinigte Stahlwerke, and Wilhelm Zangen of Mannesmann. Minute Meetings, Counsel from the United States, Great Britain, France, and the Soviet Union, 15 May 1946, pp. 1, 3, 4, RG 260, OMGUS Functional Offices, Office of Chief of Counsel for War Crimes (hereafter, OCCWC), Box 1, Folder 1, National Archives, College Park MD (hereafter, NARA), and memo to Taylor from Captain D. A. Sprecher (signed Jackson), 12 April 1946, RG 260 OMGUS Functional Offices, OCCWC, Box 2, Subsequent Proceedings Division folder, NARA.

8. See Donald Bloxham, "'The Trial That Never Was': Why There Was No Second International Trial of Major War Criminals at Nuremberg," *History* 87:285 (January 2002): 41. Also, see Bloxham, *Genocide on Trial*; Frank M. Buscher, *The U.S. War Crimes Trial Program in Germany, 1946–1955* (Westport CT: Greenwood Press, 1989), p. 31; and Telford Taylor, *Final Report to the Secretary of the Army on the Nuernberg War Crimes Trials under Control Council Law No. 10* (Washington DC: U.S. Government Printing Office, 1949), p. 26.

9. Taylor, *Final Report*, p. 13.

10. The journalist Joseph Persico has speculated that Taylor's promotion sparked indignation among West Pointers who resented the fact that a uniformed civilian had won the

rank regular soldiers spent a lifetime pursuing. Joseph Persico, *Nuremberg: Infamy on Trial* (New York: Viking, 1994), p. 310.

11. As of May 1946, only 25 attorneys were on Taylor's staff, but by 4 July, that number had risen to 113. By October, when Taylor was officially named as the head of the Office of Chief of Counsel for War Crimes (OCCWC) of OMBUS, his team exceeded 400 American and Allied employees. Taylor memorandum to Howard Petersen, Assistant Secretary of War, 30 September 1946, p. 3, Abraham Pomerantz file, RG 153 Judge Advocate General E 132, War Crimes Branch, Box 10, NARA; Taylor to Jackson, 30 January 1946, pp. 1, 3, RG 260, OMGUS Functional Offices, OCCWC, Box 2, Subsequent Proceedings folder, NARA; and Taylor, *Final Report*, p. 13.

12. Taylor to Peterson, 30 September 1946, p. 3, Pomerantz file, RG 153, E 132, Box 10, NARA.

13. Communiqué to Taylor, cited in Washington to Nuremberg Teleconference, 22 August 1947, TT8455, p. 1 in Pomerantz File, RG 153, E 132, Box 10, NARA.

14. Robert Conot, *Justice at Nuremberg* (New York: Harper & Row, 1983), p. 283.

15. A background in international law was not always helpful. During the IMT, the French judge, Donnadieu De Vabres, who had such a background, was viewed as a distraction.

16. Taylor, *Final Report*, p. 16.

17. According to Ferencz, the reason that only 22 individuals were tried was because there were only 24 seats in the entire dock. Benjamin Ferencz, Oral History, RG-50.030*269 and RG-50.030*297, United States Holocaust Memorial Museum, Washington DC (hereafter, USHMM.)

18. Taylor, "The Program of War Crimes Trials to Be Brought by the Office of Chief of Counsel for War Crimes before Military Tribunals," memorandum to the Chief of Staff, OMGUS, 20 May 1947, p. 2, and Appendix, RG 260 OMGUS Functional Offices, OCCWC, Box 2, NARA.

19. Taylor, "Program of War Crimes Trials," p. 2.

20. Taylor, *Final Report*, p. 16.

21. See especially, August von Knieriem, *Nürnberg: Rechtliche und menschliche Probleme* (Stuttgart: Klett, 1953), and Wilbourn Benton, ed., *Nuremberg: German Views of the War Trials* (Dallas: Southern Methodist University Press, 1955).

22. Knieriem argued that German law would have been the more legitimate system to apply during the tribunals because, in his view, convictions arrived at on this basis would have stamped all convicted individuals as true criminals in the eyes of the German people. According to reviewer F. Honig, this assumption was dubious at best. Knieriem, *Nürnberg*, p. 104, and Honig, Review of Knieriem, in *International Affairs* 30 (1954): 207–8.

23. Dr. Hans Pribilla, one of the German lawyers in the Doctors' Case, was especially grateful that the defense was allowed to cross-examine any witness. Letter from Pribilla to Judge Walter Beals, 27 November 1947, in Walter Beals File, p. 2, RG 153 JAG WCB, E 132, Box 10, NARA, and Benjamin Ferencz, "Nuremberg Trial Procedure and the Rights of the Accused," *Journal of Criminal Law and Criminology of Northwestern University* 39:2 (August 1948): 145–51.

24. TWC, vol. 6, p. 1188.

25. Taylor, *Final Report*, p. 36.

26. Taylor, "An Outline of the Research and Publication Possibilities of the War Crimes Trials," November 1948 Brief, p. 3, RG 153, JAG Law Library E 135, Box 110, NARA.

27. John Mendelsohn, "Trial by Document: The Problem of Due Process for War Criminals at Nuremberg," *Prologue* 8 (1975): 228–34.

28. OMGUS Information Bulletin, 29 June 1948, p. 9, RG 153, JAG Law Library, E 135, Box 104, NARA.

29. The political affiliation of the judges appears to have been irrelevant. Wennerstrum and Toms were Republicans while Phillips, Musmanno, Speight, and Shake were Democrats. "Appointment of Judges at Nuremberg," *American Bar Association Journal* 33 (September 1947): 896–97, and Mendelsohn, "Trial by Document", pp. 223–34.

30. Tom Bower, *Blind Eye to Murder: Britain, America, and the Purging of Nazi Germany—A Pledge Betrayed* (London: Granada, 1981), pp. 396, 397, and RG 260, OMGUS HQ, Decimal File, 1945–1946, 000.5, 27 July 1946.

31. Charles Wyzanski, "Nuremberg in Retrospect," *Atlantic Monthly*, December 1946, p. 57.

32. TWC, vol. 3, p. 977.

33. TWC, vol. 10, pp. 532, 533; vol. 11, pp. 1234–39.

34. James Brown Scott, *The Hague Peace Conferences of 1899 and 1907* (Baltimore: Johns Hopkins Press, 1909), pp. 161, 529, 431.

35. Article 22 of Section II, chapter 1, likewise provided that the right of belligerents to adopt means of injuring the enemy is not unlimited. Annex to Hague Convention, no. 4; TWC, vol. 11, pp. 1239, 1240, and M. Cherif Bassiouni, *Crimes against Humanity in International Law* (The Hague: Cluwer Law International, 1992), pp. 160, 167, 168.

36. Many international lawyers argued that codes and standards of warfare were not new to the nineteenth and twentieth centuries, having precedents in ancient Greece, in decrees against piracy on the high seas in the seventeenth century, and in the writings of jurists and philosophers such as Hugo Grotius, a founder of international law from the late sixteenth and early seventeenth centuries. Even the concept of humanitarianism in armed conflict, as reflected in the notion of offenses against nations (*delicti just gentium*), predated the London Declaration. The first practical demonstration of humanitarian concerns in war came in the middle of the nineteenth century after the battle of Solferino in June 1859, at which the French army defeated the forces of Austria-Hungary. There, a Swiss businessman, moved by the horror of the battle scene, urged the creation of relief agencies to deal with the wounded and lobbied for an international agreement on the humane treatment of the sick and injured. In the United States, the Andersonville trial held after the Civil War was a first of its kind in the prosecution of war crimes. Finally, the phrase "crimes against humanity" as an outgrowth of the concept of "war crimes" emerged in 1915, when the governments of Britain, France, and the Soviet Union joined in a declaration against Turkey for the crime that was later to be articulated as genocide against its Armenian population. Bassiouni, *Crimes against Humanity*, pp. 147, 154, 155, 160, 168.

37. TWC, vol. 4, p. 453.

38. TWC, vol. 4, p. 460.

39. George Annas and Michael A. Grodin, eds., *The Nazi Doctors and the Nuremberg Code: Human Rights in Human Experimentation* (Oxford: Oxford University Press, 1992), p. 134. Michael Marrus takes a more critical view of the trial in his essay "The Nuremberg Doctors' Trial in Historical Context," *Bulletin of the History of Medicine* 73:1 (Spring 1999): 106–23.

40. TWC, vol. 3, p. 960.

41. TWC, vol. 3, pp. 1180–81.

42. TWC, vol. 11, pp. 1241–42, Oppenheim's International Law (5th ed., 1935), 452 ff., and *Ex Parte Quirin*, 317 United States 1 (1942).

43. Control Council Law No. 10, art. II, pt. C, and London Charter, art. 6, pt. C.

44. Taylor, *Final Report*, p. 16.

45. *TWC*, vol. 2, and vol. 8, pp. 1084, 1085.

46. Lippman, "Other Nuremberg," p. 85.

47. *TWC*, vol. 8, p. 1110.

48. *TWC*, vol. 14, p. 426.

49. *TWC*, vol. 9, p. 411.

50. *TWC*, vol. 2, p. 179. See "Early Postwar Justice in the American Zone: The 'Hadamar Murder Factory'" by Patricia Heberer in this volume.

51. For instance, the law did not require that crimes against humanity be "in execution of or in connection with any crime within the jurisdiction of the (International Military) Tribunal." Lippman, "Other Nuremberg," pp. 90, 91; and *TWC*, vol. 3, pp. 972–74.

52. *TWC*, vol. 2, p. 790.

53. *TWC*, vol. 8, p. 117.

54. *TWC*, vol. 6, p. 1215.

55. London Charter and Control Council Law No. 10, see note 43 above for passages.

56. Lippman, "Other Nuremberg," p. 87; and *TWC*, vol. 14, p. 339.

57. *TWC*, vol. 3, pp. 1137, 1138.

58. *TWC*, vol. 5, pp. 1051, 1052.

59. *TWC*, vol. 6, pp. 23, 1219–21.

60. *TWC*, vol. 2, p. 814.

61. *TWC*, vol. 8, pp. 1169–72; and Lippman, "Other Nuremberg," p. 88.

62. In contrast, the tribunals held that staff officers lacked command authority over their subordinates and did not incur criminal responsibility for transmitting illegal orders. However, they were culpable if they drafted an illegal military order or made a special effort to ensure that the order was distributed to those units who carried it out. Hermann Foertsch served as chief of staff to various generals during the Nazi invasion of Yugoslavia and Greece. In this position, Foertsch passed on various orders instructing subordinate units to take hostages and to exact reprisals. Nevertheless, citing a lack of evidence of the commission of an unlawful act and maintaining that a criminal is one who orders, abets, or takes a consenting part in a crime, the tribunal in the Hostage case acquitted Foertsch of war crimes. Lippman, "Other Nuremberg," p. 89.

63. *TWC*, vol. 14, pp. 576–78.

64. The tribunal in the *Einsatzgruppen* case also repudiated the defense claim that others would have obeyed illegal orders had the defendants refused to carry them out. *TWC*, vol. 11, p. 1238, and vol. 4, p. 485.

65. *TWC*, vol. 4, p. 486.

66. For more on this, see, Joseph Borkin, *The Crime and Punishment of IG Farben: The Unholy Alliance between Hitler and the Great Chemical Combine* (New York: Free Press, 1978), p. 148.

67. Borkin, *Crime and Punishment*, p. 464.

68. *TWC*, vol. 6, p. 1201.

69. Judge Paul Hebert disagreed with the decision of the court on the slave labor charge and penned a vigorous dissent to that effect. Bower, *Blind Eye to Murder*, pp. 406, 407; and *TWC*, vol. 8, pp. 1172–77, 1204, 1205.

70. *TWC*, vol. 9, pp. 1442, 1445; and Telford Taylor, "The Nuremberg War Crimes Trials: An Appraisal" (An Address before the Academy of Political Science, Columbia University, 1949), p. 27, RG 153, JAG Law Library, E 135, Box 110, NARA.

71. Taylor, *Final Report*, p. 91.
72. Taylor, *Final Report*, p. 92.
73. *TWC*, vol. 8, pp. 1336–37, vol. 5, p. 1254.
74. *TWC*, vol. 9, p. 1486.
75. Believing that the tribunal should have sustained more of the defense motions, Judge Leon Powers withheld his signature from several of the decisions confirming the original sentences. *TWC*, vol. 14, pp. 950, 960, 965, 1001, 1002.
76. *TWC*, vol. 14, p. 1004.
77. Taylor, *Final Report*, p. 92; and Robert Kempner, *Ankläger einer Epoche: Lebenserinnerungen* (Frankfurt: Ullstein, 1983), p. 321. Interestingly, in the Farben case, Judge James Morris drew criticism because his wife had been seen socializing with the wives of the I.G. Farben defendants. The intimation in the press regarding the influence this may have had on Morris's decision was none too clear. Morris Papers, North Dakota Historical Society, Bismarck ND.
78. Reporters from *Time* were less critical, asserting that the "victors had done their best to mete out justice." Howard W. Ambruster, "They Cheated the Gallows," *Nation*, 14 August 1948, p. 176; and "Finis," *Time*, 25 April 1949, p. 29.
79. *TWC*, vol. 5, pp. 168, 169.
80. *TWC*, vol. 9, pp. 1453–60.
81. "Presiding Judge at Nuremberg Disillusioned," *Chicago Tribune*, 23 February 1948, p. 5. See also Wennerstrum's personal papers held at Drake University in Des Moines IA.
82. "U.S. Prosecutor Blasts Attack on Nazi Trial," *Chicago Tribune*, 23 February 1948, p. 5, all in Wennerstrum File, RG 153, JAG WCB, E 132, Box 11, NARA. Taylor himself became embroiled in charges that the U.S. Army was monitoring newspaper copy, but it turned out that the Wennerstrum interview had been given to a low-ranking employee at Press Wireless in Frankfurt who then turned it over to Taylor. ICM from HQ EUCOM Frankfurt to CSUSA, 26 February 1948, Wennerstrum File, RG 153, JAG WCB, E 132, Box 11, NARA.
83. Edward Carter, Wennerstrum's colleague on the Hostages Tribunal, also disagreed with the justice's accusations. Carter, "The Nürnberg Trials: A Turning Point in the Enforcement of International Law," *Nebraska Law Review* 28:3 (1949): 370-86. See also Beals to Cecil Hubbert, Deputy Chief, War Crimes Branch (WCB), JAG, 17 March 1948, p. 1, Walter Beals File, RG 153, JAG WCB, E 132, Box 10, NARA; and Brand, Remarks on Wennerstrum Controversy, 18 October 1938, p. 4, James Brand File, RG 153, JAG WCB, E 132, Box 11, NARA.
84. Bower, *Blind Eye to Murder*, p. 314.
85. OMGUS, Information Bulletin, no. 138, June 1948, p. 12, RG 153, JAG Law Library, E 135, Box 104, NARA. For a different interpretation of the Justice case, see Carl Haensel, "Das Urteil im Nürnberger Juristenprozess," *Deutsche Rechts-Zeitschrift* 3:2 (1948): 40–43.
86. John Thompson, chief of *Newsweek*'s Berlin Bureau, reported: "Today, Germans are almost completely disinterested in the Nuremberg trials. Those who do think about them find it hard to understand why Nazis should still be tried and punished at Nuremberg for the kind of crimes Russians are committing every day in the Eastern zone of Germany." "War Crimes: The Last Judgments," *Newsweek*, 25 April 1949, p. 38.
87. See John Mendelsohn, according to Buscher, *War Crimes Trial Program*, p. 28.
88. For instance, William Langer of North Dakota claimed that the subsequent trials were dominated by Communists. *Congressional Record*, 81st Cong., 2nd sess., 96: 16708, and William Bosch, *Judgment on Nuremberg: American Attitudes toward the Major German War-Crime Trials* (Chapel Hill: University of North Carolina Press, 1970), p. 81.

89. John P. Frank, *Mr. Justice Black: The Man and His Opinions* (New York: Alfred A. Knopf, 1949), p. 131.

90. Sheldon Glueck to Ben Ferencz, 18 September 1946, Benjamin B. Ferencz Collection, RG 12, Drawer 13, Box 1, USHMM.

91. Buscher, *War Crimes Trial Program*, p. 50.

92. In mid-November, Chancellor Adenauer wrote to McCloy and asked for a "commutation of all death sentences" and the "widest possible clemency for persons sentenced to confinement." McCloy referred to this in a memo to the State Department, dated 3 January 1951, State Department.

93. Kai Bird, *The Chairman: John J. McCloy and the Making of the American Establishment* (New York: Simon & Schuster, 1992), pp. 360, 361.

94. Benjamin Ferencz to Editor, *New York Times Magazine*, 25 February 1951, p. 6, in Ferencz Collection, Drawer 24, Box 2, RG 12, USHMM. The JAG board reprieved 11 war criminals, including 6 defendants sentenced to death in the Malmédy trial.

95. *TWC*, vol. 15, p. 1146–1217.

96. Among the papers having favorable opinions of the clemency were the *Badische Zeitung* and the *Süddeutsche Zeitung*. "German Papers Call Rulings in War Crimes Cases 'Just,'" *Stars and Stripes*, 2 February 1951, p. 1, 16, and "Germans Applaud Action on War Criminals," *Stars and Stripes*, 2 February 1951, p. 16.

97. Murphy to Lt. Col. W. H. Johnson Jr., Chief, Administrative Division, JAG, 19 February 1951, in Executive Reading File, February 1951, RG 153, JAG, E 131, Box 7, NARA.

98. "Commutations 'Wise,' McCarthy Says," *Stars and Stripes*, 2 February 1951, p. 1.

99. "World Jewish Congress Raps Nazis' Release," *International Herald Tribune*, 3 February 1951.

100. Telford Taylor, "The Nazis Go Free," *Nation*, 24 February 1951, p. 171.

101. Joseph Kaufman also blasted the Krupp decisions: "Krupp: What Price Expediency?" *New Republic* 124 (1951): 15–16. See also Ferencz to *New York Times Magazine*, p. 7, and Ferencz Interview with John J. McCloy, (n.d.), p. 20, Ferencz Collection, RG-12, Drawer 24, Box 2, USHMM; and Bird, *Chairman,* p. 360.

102. Bird, *Chairman*, p. 360.

103. "High Commissioner Details Decisions on Sentences," *Stars and Stripes*, 2 February 1951, p. 10. In McCloy's defense, none of the death sentences for Oswald Pohl, Paul Blobel, Otto Ohlendorf, Werner Braune, and Erich Naumann were commuted, and all were executed on 7 June 1951.

104. Bird, *Chairman*, p. 363.

105. Adenauer to McCloy, 5 December 1950, and McCloy to Adenauer, 19 December 1950. Papers of the High Commissioner for Germany, NARA, as cited by Bird, *Chairman*, p. 711.

106. Bird, *Chairman*, p. 360.

107. Ferencz, as cited in Bird, *Chairman*, p. 368.

108. Taylor echoes this sentiment in "Nazis Go Free," p. 172.

The Nuremberg Doctors' Trial and the Limitations of Context

MICHAEL R. MARRUS

This essay follows a course I often warn my students against: it criticizes the proceedings of the Doctors' Trial more for what did *not* happen than for what did.
I want to argue that the Doctors' Trial—the first of the "subsequent Nuremberg
proceedings," the twelve trials held under United States auspices in the wake of
the International Military Tribunal (IMT)—missed an important opportunity
to define the principal crimes of German physicians during the Third Reich,
to identify the major perpetrators, to put them in a wider intellectual and institutional context, and to sketch an explanation of their crimes. A suggestion,
drawn from this observation, is that the focus of the trial contributed to the
evasion of medical responsibility that so many commentators have justifiably
commented on in recent years. My justification for this approach, fraught as it
is with the temptations of anachronism, is that those responsible for the trial
themselves defined the standards by which the trial can be assessed.

These standards, it should be said, were extraordinarily high and solemnly
declared. One thinks first, perhaps, of the opening address of the American
chief prosecutor, Justice Robert Jackson, at the Trial of the Major German War
Criminals, insisting on the gravity of Nazi wrongdoing: "The wrongs which
we seek to condemn and punish have been so calculated, so malignant, and so
devastating, that civilization cannot tolerate their being ignored because it cannot survive their being repeated."[1] "The groundwork of our case," Jackson told
President Harry Truman, "must be factually authentic and constitute a well-
documented history of what we are convinced was a grand, concerted pattern
to incite and commit the aggressions and barbarities which have shocked the
world." "Unless we write the record of this movement with clarity and preci-
sion," he continued, "we cannot blame the future if in days of peace it finds
incredible the accusatory generalities uttered during the war."[2] Jackson, of
course, was not alone in his reference to the historical record. The British chief

prosecutor, Sir Hartley Shawcross, made a related point in his own opening statement to the Nuremberg court: "This Tribunal will provide a contemporary touchstone and an authoritative and impartial record to which future historians may turn for truth and future politicians for warning."[3]

Famous for its graphic presentation of at least some of the most heinous medical atrocities of the Third Reich, the Doctors' Trial revealed the depths to which some doctors sank and the wide-ranging nature of their criminality—"the whole complex of stomach-churning 'medical' and 'scientific' experiments," as historian Michael Burleigh notes appreciatively.[4] In that sense, and that may perhaps be the most important achievement of the prosecution, the trial succeeded. My quarrel is rather with the proceedings' inattentiveness to historical context, something that Brigadier General Telford Taylor, the American chief counsel, declared as his objective at the beginning of the Doctors' Trial. "It is our deep obligation to all peoples of the world," Taylor said, "to show why and how these things happened. It is incumbent upon us to set forth with conspicuous clarity the ideas and motives which moved these defendants to treat their fellow men as less than beasts."[5] The Doctors' Trial was supposed to set the record straight—"to promote the interest of historical truth," as Taylor summed it up in his report to the secretary of the U.S. Army in 1949.[6] Like the other dignitaries associated with the trial, Taylor set his sights high—in terms of motivation, ideology, and historical explanation. With respect, and also with appreciation for what actually was accomplished, I want to suggest some ways in which the Doctors' Trial fell short.

The Courtroom and "Historical Truth"

Assembled in December 1946, in the courtroom recently vacated by the International Military Tribunal, United States Military Tribunal I began to hear evidence against twenty-three somewhat bedraggled defendants, all but three of them physicians, and some of them distinguished researchers, "charged with murders, tortures, and other atrocities committed in the name of medical science," as Telford Taylor said. According to the prosecution, the victims of these crimes numbered in the hundreds of thousands.[7] The three-judge court, presided over by Walter Beals, chief justice of the Supreme Court of the State of Washington, heard evidence until July 1947. Listening to testimony in English and German, the court sat for 139 days and received nearly 1,500 documents submitted by the prosecution and defense. The English-language transcript of the proceedings runs to over eleven thousand pages. The tribunal issued its judgment in August, finding sixteen of the defendants guilty and sentencing seven of them to death by hanging.

Those who go to the judgment expecting a ringing statement of explanation and responsibility—a call for "historical truth"—will certainly be disappointed. Quite unlike the style and scope of the judgment of the International Military Tribunal, Judge Beals and his colleagues issued a rather terse, technical document, mainly reviewing the evidence relating to particular defendants. The only memorable section was the so-called Nuremberg Code, a list of ten "basic principles" that the court contended were universally agreed to by "the protagonists of the practice of human experimentation." In the cases presented to the court, the judges found, "these ten principles were much more frequently honored in their breach than in their observance." The defendants were held to have acted "in complete disregard of international conventions, the laws and customs of war, the general principles of criminal law as derived from the criminal laws of all civilized nations."[8] Tucked into the passages dealing with individual defendants were occasional references to the organization of health services in the Third Reich, obligations in the face of superior orders, and the fraudulent methodology of the criminal experiments. But for a grand historic assessment of medicine in the Third Reich, for a human dimension of the catastrophe, or even for clues as to what went so very wrong in Nazi Germany, Judge Beals and his colleagues were practically silent. In what follows, I discuss some reasons why this was so.

An important clue lies in the indictment against the twenty-three accused. Drafted for the first of the subsequent proceedings, this was an important policy-making document, "in many respects the prototype of [other indictments] that were to follow," Telford Taylor later reported.[9] Understandably, it was designed to pursue American war crimes policy—to punish important Nazi criminals, stigmatize the criminality of the Nazi regime, and contribute thereby to the democratization of Germany. Framed by the war crimes concepts of the London Charter, the 1945 document negotiated by the Americans, British, French, and Russians to deal with the major German war criminals, and Control Council

Law No. 10, a four-power agreement on post-IMT war crimes proceedings, the indictment mentioned four counts—war crimes, crimes against humanity, the participation in a "common design or conspiracy" to commit these crimes, and membership in the SS, an organization declared criminal in the judgment of the International Military Tribunal.

The cast of this indictment, setting medical crimes within a formal legal framework painstakingly negotiated to fit the very general priorities of the four major victorious powers, is a reminder of how the trial served other masters than the historical record alluded to by Jackson and Taylor—or for that matter a specific reckoning with the crimes of Nazi medicine that so horrified Allied investigators at the end of the war. Notably, the counts against the accused focused exclusively on the wartime period, thereby skirting the delicate legal question, carefully considered in preparation for the IMT, of whether the victorious powers had jurisdiction over prewar Nazi crimes. Further, reflecting the prosecution strategy adopted before the IMT, the indictment portrayed the accused as members of a criminal conspiracy, something like a group of gangsters who planned and carried out a bank robbery, rather than as individuals who shared a common ideology or institutional culture.[10] Finally, while it did mention crimes against German civilians—who, in fact, constituted the overwhelming majority of victims of Nazi medical crimes—the indictment rather emphasized the non-German victims in countries at war with Nazi Germany. In all of these respects, as we shall see, strategically defined legal and political priorities shaped the course of the trial and the presentation of evidence, ultimately narrowing and distorting the history of medical crimes in the Third Reich.

Preparing the Doctors' Trial

In addition to these high-level priorities, more mundane circumstances weakened the impact of the Doctors' Trial. Launched amidst the ruins of postwar Germany, and the mountains of rubble in the city of Nuremberg, there was a haphazard, improvised character to the subsequent proceedings in general and the Doctors' Trial, as the first of these, in particular. Under the overall direction of Telford Taylor, the Office of Chief Counsel for War Crimes (OCCWC), responsible for all twelve trials, began with a staff of only twenty-five attorneys, hastily assembled in Nuremberg in mid-May 1946.[11] (The indictment of those accused in the Doctors' case was completed in October, and the trial began in December.) Preparation of the Doctors' Trial fell to one of six branches of the OCCWC, known as the SS Division, which had no special medical expertise and was rather preoccupied with the most highly Nazified of accused—Oswald Pohl and the managers of the Economic-Administrative Main Office (WVHA) of the SS, the SS Race and Resettlement Main Office (RuSHA), and the mass killers of the *Einsatzgruppen*. As Christian Pross and others have noted, the Doctors' Trial seems to have been poorly prepared in various respects. Overworked and understaffed, the prosecution team included only one full-time medical consultant, Leo Alexander, a Viennese-born neurologist with the rank of major in the U.S. Army. Only later, toward the end of the trial, did they call upon the much better-known Andrew Ivy, a recognized expert in the field of experimental physiology and vice-president of the University of Illinois at Chicago, a man with no specialized knowledge of Germany or its medical culture.[12]

Choosing whom to prosecute posed particular difficulties. The choice of defendants was supposed to depend upon a decision about at what level of responsibility a "bottom line" should be drawn; in practice it probably had as much to do with the size of the Nuremberg courtrooms, only two of which could hold up to twenty-four defendants. As Taylor later admitted, he and his colleagues were swamped with evidence and had real difficulty digesting what had been gathered for them. One result was that important perpetrators slipped through the Americans' net (the most notorious of whom was Josef Mengele, the "Angel of Death" of Auschwitz), while others were charged on the basis of insufficient evidence. Evidence of overhasty prosecution abounds in the cases of the seven accused who were acquitted—the average number of acquittals in the subsequent proceedings being three.[13] The uncertain hand is certainly evident in the case of Hitler's attending physician Karl Brandt, a major architect of the "euthanasia" program, who was almost released before his indictment. Prominent practitioners of racial policy who went about their business undisturbed or were overlooked included such luminaries as Ernst Rüdin and Fritz Lenz, or Josef Mengele's Berlin supervisor, Otmar Freiherr von Verschuer. Werner Heyde, one of the most notorious medical perpetrators, was also not indicted, possibly because of the difficulties investigators had in sorting out the authority of medical decision makers.[14]

Misinterpreting Nazi Medical Crimes

In keeping with the American understanding of German war crimes, the prosecutors portrayed the medical defendants as having been caught up in Nazism, a criminal, power-mad enterprise with a ruthlessly utilitarian philosophy. Alexander summed up his approach in the *New England Journal of Medicine* in 1949. "Science under dictatorship," the article contended, "becomes subordinated to the guiding philosophy of the dictatorship."[15] At Nuremberg, the commitment to this explanation was heavily conditioned by the Allied understanding of what went wrong after the First World War. In 1918, it was recalled, masses of Germans attributed their nation's catastrophe to the undermining of the German war effort by Jews and Communists at home, rather than to policies of their own government. Nuremberg—both the IMT and the subsequent proceedings—was intended to prevent a new *Dolchstosslegende*—the notion that Germany had been stabbed in the back by enemies at home, rather than defeated by its enemies abroad.

"This case, and others which will be tried in this building," Telford Taylor told the court at the opening of the Doctors' Trial, "offer a signal opportunity to lay before the German people the true cause of their present misery." That cause, he continued, was the "insane and malignant doctrines" of the Third Reich. To the American prosecutors the essential task of the Doctors' Trial was to link the defendants' atrocious medical crimes to the wider Nazi enterprise. Taylor underscored this point in addressing the court. The defendants' crimes "were the inevitable result of the sinister doctrines which they espoused, and these same doctrines sealed the fate of Germany, shattered Europe, and left the world in ferment. Wherever those doctrines may emerge and prevail, the same terrible consequences will follow. That is why a bold and lucid consummation of these proceedings is of vital importance to all nations. That is why the United States has constituted this Tribunal."[16]

A noble ambition, this strategy nevertheless shifted attention from *medical* origins of the medical crimes. The prosecutors took pains, for example, to outline the organization of medical services of the Third Reich, placing before the court a complicated chart topped by Adolf Hitler himself, following the pattern used before the IMT in attempting to prove the criminality of Nazi organizations. The purpose here was threefold: to link the defendants to the core of the Nazi enterprise headed by the Führer; to show how ten of them were integrated into the SS, an organization deemed criminal by the IMT; and finally to illustrate how these practitioners fit into a wider pattern of conspiracy, defined in the first count against the accused. The doctors' crimes, the prosecution claimed, "constituted a well-integrated criminal program in which the defendants planned and collaborated among themselves and with others." What moved them to do so? "The motivating force for this conspiracy came from two sources," Taylor explained:

> Himmler, as head of the SS, a most terrible machine of oppression with vast resources, could provide numberless victims for the experiments. By doing so, he enhanced the prestige of his organization and was able to give free rein to the Nazi racial theories of which he was a leading protagonist and to develop new techniques for the mass exterminations which were dear to his heart. The German military leaders, as the other main driving force, caught up the opportunity which Himmler presented them with and ruthlessly capitalized on Himmler's hideous overtures in an endeavor to strengthen their military machine.[17]

So much for the place of medicine in the Third Reich.

As it turned out, the prosecutors' arguments for a specific charge of conspiracy failed badly in the contest with the defense. Arguing legalistically, attorneys for the accused in the Doctors' Trial and two other trials in the subsequent proceedings contended that the American tribunals had no jurisdiction over such an offense, which the IMT judgment ruled had to be linked with "crimes against peace." Seven months into the trial, to the embarrassment of the prosecution, the various judges of several of the subsequent proceedings meeting in joint session agreed with this viewpoint, pointing out that such an offense was not mentioned in the Nuremberg Charter or Control Council Law No. 10. Thereby, the conspiracy count was dismissed.[18]

Significantly narrowing the historical field of inquiry, the prosecution strategy deliberately avoided the medical and scientific background of the atrocities committed by Nazi doctors. In their eagerness to establish the link with Nazism, the prosecutors and the judges largely ignored the degree to which racist and eugenic thought had become well established if not dominant in medical thinking in Germany even before the Nazis' seizure of power.[19] True, there was no straight line leading directly from such ideologies to Nazi crimes. Historians now show us how variegated scientific thinking was in the 1920s and early 1930s, and how complicated were the interactions among various factions and personalities during the Weimar and even Nazi periods. But virtually no one looking at this issue today would discount so totally the medical and ideological background of the atrocities that were the subject of the Doctors' Trial. As Michael Burleigh notes with reference to the "euthanasia" campaign, "these policies did not materialize out of thin air in response to unforeseeable wartime circumstances; they were entertained long in advance, by people who were very conscious of past precedents and of what they were doing."[20]

Similarly, the Nuremberg approach took no account of the special affinity between medical practitioners and Nazism, seeing Nazi doctors rather as supreme opportunists, bound together in the SS with a so-called *Blutkitt* (blood-cement)—as Alexander put it, "an age-old method used by criminal gangs everywhere: that of making suspects of disloyalty clear themselves by participating in a crime that would definitely and irrevocably tie them to the organization."[21] Much more powerful and extensive in impact than the *Blutkitt*, however, was the attraction of many physicians to the Nazi enterprise, which lavished status and authority on the medical profession. Under Nazism, doctors were encouraged to think of themselves as custodians of the health of the German *Volk*—with health often understood in racial and eugenic terms. National Socialism was "applied biology," said Fritz Lenz, one of the leading authorities on racial hygiene; Hitler, he claimed, was the "doctor of the German people." "Our starting point is not the individual," Joseph Goebbels told a Nazi Party rally in 1938, "we must have a healthy people in order to prevail in the world."[22]

As Michael Kater has shown, doctors at the medical grass roots offered themselves with alacrity to the regime: "physicians became Nazified more thoroughly and much sooner than any other profession, and as Nazis they did more in the service of the nefarious regime than any of their extra-professional peers."[23] At the clinical and academic heights the story is much the same: high-ranking Nazi doctors did not come from the margins of German medicine, but often from the very pinnacle of the professional establishment. Henry Friedlander lists seventeen top medical experts involved in Nazi crimes, most of whom dealt directly or indirectly in forcible sterilization or the murderous "euthanasia" campaign. Including distinguished university chairs of various medical specialties, hospital chiefs, and other top medical administrators, their names are part of a *Who's Who* of German medicine of the time.[24] "Contrary to the notion that Nazism somehow corrupted and distorted the temples of learning," Michael Burleigh and Wolfgang Wippermann note, "one could argue that a corrupt and inherently distorted science lent Nazism a specifically 'academic' and 'scientific' character."[25]

Out of Focus

Prosecution strategy not only distorted the origins of medical crimes but also drew attention away from some of the most egregious wrongdoing by physicians during the Third Reich. Understandably, the Doctors' Trial focused on crimes against non-German victims of Nazi aggression and observed other legal constraints agreed to by representatives from the United States, Great Britain, France, and the Soviet Union in their preparation of the International Military Tribunal. For the Doctors' Trial, this meant an almost exclusive attention to the wartime period and a focus on the ghastly concentration camp experiments as the principal instance of medical crimes. But it also entailed a downplaying of forcible sterilization and "medicalized killing"—the victimization of several hundred thousand people, mainly Germans, in which doctors were so heavily involved.

Although the indictment of the accused included crimes against German civilians, it did so only in reference to Count Three, Crimes against Humanity. German civilians were alleged to have been victims of "medical experiments without the subjects' consent" and to have been murdered in unspecified ways, including "the so-called 'euthanasia' program of the German Reich."[26] Behind these references there was a good deal of politics and negotiation. In the general understanding of many American officials, war crimes trials were not being held to punish Germans for domestic atrocities. Military Governor General Lucius Clay, commander of the American military zone and responsible for the establishment of the subsequent proceedings, believed that "our mandate was to try those who had committed crimes against the United States, or our Allies, not against the German people."[27]

Clay was not entirely right on this point, however. During the negotiations leading to the IMT, Jewish refugees and other anti-Nazi émigrés in the United States and Britain, fearing precisely this limitation, had urged the Allies to include the wrongs they had suffered in postwar trials. Responding to their appeals, the charge of "Crimes against Humanity" was drafted for this very purpose.[28] Nervous about an overly broad scope of such crimes, however, one that might theoretically trench upon American sovereignty, Justice Jackson insisted that such crimes be limited to acts committed in connection with or in execution of the launching of aggressive war—to the Americans the heart of the case against Nazi Germany.[29] But since this qualifying language was omitted from the definition of Crimes against Humanity in Control Council Law No. 10, the matter was subject to interpretation and judicial decision.

This issue was thrashed out in several of the subsequent proceedings, and the judges decided differently in different cases.[30] In the Doctors' Trial, the prosecution seems to have decided to skirt the matter, probably feeling that there was more than enough evidence of crimes against non-Germans to obtain convictions. In practice, therefore, both the prosecutors and the judges preferred to direct attention away from crimes committed against German civilians. As a result the trial suffered grievously as a chronicle of the medical crimes of the Third Reich.

Nowhere was this more obvious than with reference to forcible sterilization—a medical program instituted in 1934 for eugenic purposes, and that victimized about 1 percent of the entire German population, some 400,000 people in the Greater German Reich, most of them prior to the outbreak of the war in 1939.[31] Openly conducted, involving an elaborate apparatus of laws and procedures, genetic health courts, and appeal tribunals, this was a huge undertaking for the German medical profession. During the first four years of application of the 1933 Sterilization Law more than 50,000 people a year were victimized in this process. The circle of complicity became very wide. "Doctors competed to fulfill sterilization quotas," observes Robert Proctor, "sterilization research and engineering rapidly became one of the largest medical industries. Medical supply companies [. . .] made a substantial amount of money designing sterilization equipment. Medical students wrote at least 183 doctoral theses exploring the criteria, methods and consequences of sterilization."[32] The Doctors'

Trial raised the issue of forcible sterilization, seeing it as one of "the scientific tools for the planning and practice of genocide," but only in relation to experiments committed against concentration camp inmates—non-Germans—in the wider context of wartime criminal experiments.[33] To be sure, Germany was hardly alone in the the move toward forced sterilization. Paul Weindling suggests that Allied prosecutors were acutely aware that their medical compatriots were themselves deeply complicit in the application of eugenics to their own populations.[34] As a result, the trial missed an opportunity to elucidate eugenic and racist policies and to link them with the medical profession. A crime of extraordinary proportions was practically overlooked.

This was not the case with the "euthanasia" campaign, which occupied considerable time at the Doctors' Trial and for which there was a great mass of documents submitted in evidence. Some 200,000 people were killed in this cruel and inhuman process, which began with the murder of little children, expanded to include adults gassed in six killing centers in Germany, and developed further in 1942 at a number of institutions throughout the Reich. In 1941 "euthanasia" killings were also extended to include inmates throughout the German concentration camp system. The victims were overwhelmingly German, although not exclusively so.[35]

In documenting the extent of this killing and the mechanism by which it was carried out, the trial served the historical record well. But unfortunately the context was less than satisfactory for an accurate view. The prosecution regularly drew attention to non-German victims, ignoring the powerful ideological thrust of the campaign and presenting Nazi "euthanasia" in simple utilitarian terms—removing "useless eaters" from a country fully mobilized for war (presented as "the principal rationale") and pursuing the struggle against Germany's enemies. "Euthanasia became merely a polite word for the systematic slaughter of Jews and many other categories of persons useless or unfriendly to the Nazi regime," was how Telford Taylor put it.[36]

In their judgment, the judges had little to add about the "euthanasia" campaign, simply accepting the prosecution's contentions and turning to the matter in detail only in passages relating to specific defendants. Here, too, an important chapter in the medical history of the Reich was overlooked. For reasons we have explained, the judges took pains to emphasize that non-German nationals were among those killed. Responding to the claims of defendant Karl Brandt that there was a legal and even humanitarian basis for these killings, the judges were forthright if chilling in their language. "Whether or not a state may validly enact legislation which imposes euthanasia upon certain classes of its citizens is a question which does not enter into the issues," the judges said. "Assuming that it may do so, the Family of Nations is not obligated to give recognition to such legislation when it manifestly gives legality to plain murder and torture of defenseless and powerless human beings of other nations."[37]

As to origins, there was practically no challenge to the prosecutors' view that the "euthanasia" killings were a simple product of Nazi aggression. And yet, as Hans-Walter Schmuhl reminds us, "euthanasia" "was not a genuine National Socialist phenomenon." Rather, Nazism had simply taken up in the 1920s the most radical expression of racial-hygiene thinking.[38] The Doctors' Trial spared nothing in presenting the callousness, horror, and great extent of the "euthanasia" killing, but it offered only the crudest of explanations for what had occurred, made no links with eugenic thought and the medical culture of Germany or, as discussed below, the wider developed world.

Criminal Human Medical Experimentation

The real emphasis in the Doctors' Trial was, of course, upon the ghastly medical experiments conducted in concentration camps—upon which the great bulk of the evidence against the accused was presented, and in response to which the judges issued the famous "Nuremberg Code." This is the principal reason the Doctors' Trial is remembered today. However valuable this attention, and I freely acknowledge its importance in the evolution of the doctrine of informed consent, it distorted understanding of the impact of medical crimes in several ways. One of these involves the numbers of victims. As we have seen, there were about 400,000 victims of forcible sterilization, and 200,000 were killed in the "euthanasia" campaign. No one knows how many were subjected to the Nazi medical experiments, but the victims almost certainly did not exceed several thousand—nowhere near the totals of those other crimes, and far fewer than the murdered tubercular Poles mentioned in the indictment, for example, about whom there was far less discussion at the trial. In its preoccupation with experiments, the Doctors' Trial obscured rather than clarified.

Although the focus on experiments was useful in demonstrating the depravity of some German doctors, it deflected attention from the involvement of the medical profession as a whole in the Nazi enterprise. Unlike the case with forcible sterilization or "euthanasia," only a relatively small number of physicians and others conducted the experiments or even knew about them. That is why Andrew Ivy understood that there were no more than two hundred medical criminals—although "several hundred more were aware of what was going on."[39] The prosecution's view was that this "sinister assembly" of perpetrators, as Telford Taylor referred to them, experimented in a manner that served no useful purpose and that was both inefficient and unscientific. This is undoubtedly true for some of the experiments, yet may not be so for others. But I would suggest that, in highlighting this aspect of the Doctors' crimes as if it characterized the whole, the prosecutors may have assisted the postwar tendency for the profession to wrap itself in scientific credentials and to evade its social and ethical responsibilities.

Most of these experiments—extreme cold, high altitude, mustard gas, sulfanilamide, bone, muscle and nerve regeneration and bone transplantation, seawater, incendiary bomb, and other—were understood as having been undertaken at the behest of the military. Why did the defendants conduct these experiments? The overly simple answer at the Doctors' Trial was that they did so to assist the military triumph of Germany. "These experiments," said the judges, "were the product of coordinated policy-making and planning at high governmental, military, and Nazi Party levels, conducted as an integral part of the total war effort."[40] In this way, centering on the experiments drew attention away from the nonmilitary ideological and occupational motivations that subsequent historians have found so important in explaining the involvement of hundreds of doctors in the Nazi project.

Flushed with victory, and with their domestic opinion running powerfully against the defeated German Reich, the Allies were hardly eager to see lawyers for accused Nazi war criminals make what were called *tu quoque* arguments—the defense response, in the face of accusations of grave breaches of the laws and customs of war, that "you did it, too." Although explicitly precluded by the Nuremberg Charter, several defense counsel attempted to slip such arguments past the IMT judges. But with the exception of one instance having to do with submarine warfare, such strategies were ruled out of order. In the Doctors'

Trial, however, the indictment permitted greater attention to the conduct of the Allies because the defendants were accused of violating "general principles of criminal law as derived from the criminal laws of all civilized nations." As a result, the judges permitted testimony as to the state of medical ethics in the United States and elsewhere, testimony that was eagerly offered by the prosecution, which sought to contrast conduct in the Third Reich with comportment in "civilized nations."

However strenuously the lawyers for the accused worked to undermine the claims about medical ethics elsewhere, their arguments tended to be overwhelmed by evidence of Nazi cruelty and brutality. Defense counsel therefore made no headway when they contended that some Nazi legislation had its counterpart in other countries—that in matters having to do with eugenics, forcible experimentation, sterilization, and even "euthanasia," Germany was not entirely alone.[41] As we now appreciate, eugenic thought was widespread, even mainstream, during the 1930s when the Nazis were consolidating their hold on Germany. Following the First World War eugenics was an international movement, in which American and German scientists were leaders in the field. German experts looked appreciatively to the United States on such matters as sterilization laws, as Stefan Kühl has shown in some detail.[42] Racial categories and racial hygiene were part of the contemporary discourse.

Jewish scientists, for example, most of them doctors, adopted race science "as an instrument of self-definition," since the end of the nineteenth century, and had ruminated freely on the (usually positive) qualities of the Jewish "race."[43] Surveying the Jewish scene in 1934, Arthur Ruppin, lecturer in sociology at the Hebrew University of Jerusalem, included a chapter on eugenics in his widely read book, *The Jews in the Modern World*. "Eugenics," the section began, "is gradually leading to the demand that persons of defective predisposition should either not marry, or should at least practise birth control."[44] And in the fourth volume of the *Universal Jewish Encyclopedia*, first published in 1941, an article on eugenics referred to a wealth of biblical and Talmudic laws and maxims intended to "improve the inborn qualities of the Jewish people, and to guard against any practice that might vitiate the purity of the race, or 'impair the racial qualities of future generations' either physically, mentally or morally."[45] Understandably, this perspective was not heard at the Doctors' Trial.

On experimentation, the defense claimed that the German doctors had acted in emergency wartime circumstances, that the subjects had been prisoners, hence acceptable for medical experimentation, and that in any event those chosen had already been condemned to death. As to the status of the "subjects"—mostly concentration camp inmates—the prosecution demolished these contentions, most of which were simply misstatements of fact. But the Americans were much less persuasive against the claim that there really existed no internationally agreed-upon ethical code. Andrew Ivy testified that there existed well-established principles of medical ethics dealing with human subjects, recognized internationally. "To your knowledge," he was asked in direct examination, "have any experiments been conducted in the United States wherein these requirements which you set forth were not met?" "Not to my knowledge," was Ivy's reply.[46]

As became evident at the trial, Ivy painted far too rosy a picture. While certainly no American doctors sank to the depths of experimenters in Dachau or Auschwitz, in Allied countries there was extensive violation of the rules that he defined for the Nuremberg court. While in the United States the "agreement of the subjects" was assumed to be part of human experiments in wartime, according to David Rothman, in practice this "was often superseded by a sense of urgency that overrode the issue of consent."[47] During World War II scientists drew upon mental hospitals and prisons for people on whom to experiment and relied heavily upon conscientious objectors as well. One of the prosecutions' own witnesses, the German psychiatrist Werner Leibbrandt, contended in cross-examination that by using prisoners as subjects American researchers may themselves have been guilty of violating the Hippocratic Oath. In cross-examination, Andrew Ivy admitted that he himself had conducted dangerous experiments on conscientious objectors and prisoners in wartime, but he insistently denied that American research fell short in ethical terms.[48] As has now been established, Ivy "flirted with perjury" in his rejection of any parallel between Nazi wartime experiments and those conducted in the United States.[49]

In general, we can now appreciate, the record in the United States on human experimentation was quite mixed. Sometimes researchers were highly attentive to ethical concerns, but sometimes they were not, as Rothman observes. "The research into dysentery, malaria, and influenza revealed a pervasive disregard of the rights of subjects—a willingness to experiment on the mentally retarded, the mentally ill, prisoners, ward patients, soldiers, and medical students without concern for obtaining consent. Yet, research into survival under hardship conditions and into gonorrhea was marked by formal and carefully considered protocols that informed potential subjects about the risks of participation."[50]

Practice varied considerably, and one important reason for this was that during the war there were no formal requirements of the American Medical Association (AMA) on the subject of consent to human experimentation. Such requirements were prepared only in at the end of 1946, probably in response to Andrew Ivy's report to the AMA on the Nuremberg prosecution's case. As part of the case that the German experiments had violated generally accepted ethical principles, Ivy testified about these requirements at Nuremberg, but it was only during vigorous cross-examination that he admitted that these rules had not existed during the war and had in fact been prepared only when the Nuremberg proceedings were under way.[51]

What did the defendants achieve in their efforts to broaden the context of understanding? Looking at the judgment, one should say virtually nothing. In its unmemorable discourse, Military Tribunal I offered no food for thought about context beyond articulating the ten principles of the Nuremberg Code, probably drafted by Andrew Ivy and Leo Alexander.[52] From the courtroom contest, probably nothing as well was gained. Overall, the medical crimes discussed during the trial were so shocking, so cruel, so egregious in their violation not only of professional standards but of the most elementary notions of decency, that it seemed futile, even churlish, to identify common ideologies or weaknesses in the ethical standards elsewhere and thereby promote the exculpation of the accused. The Doctors' Trial, therefore, offered little international perspective on its subject.

Conclusion

As I noted at the beginning of this chapter, the prosecution hoped that the trial would explain to the world why and how the Nazi medical crimes happened. To an important degree, the organizers succeeded in their goal of presenting evidence of almost unbelievable medical wrongdoing. In addition to promoting enlightened rules for human experimentation, this was a major achievement, and one that continues to inspire action.[53] The "why," however, proved much more elusive. As I have suggested, politics, practical difficulties, legal strategy, and judicial practice limited the capacity of the trial to go very far in this direction. Indeed, by ignoring a searching inquiry into this question and by limiting the focus to largely unrepresentative criminality, the trial may even have facilitated the evasion of responsibility that has characterized much of postwar German medicine. The crimes of the doctors are only now being explained. This has become the task of historians and others who contemplate what went so wrong more than a half century ago.

Notes

1. Robert H. Jackson, *The Nürnberg Case as Presented by Robert H. Jackson, Chief of Counsel for the United States, Together with Other Documents* (New York: Cooper Square, 1971), pp. 30–31. This chapter is a revised and updated version of a paper that appeared in the *Bulletin of the History of Medicine* 73 (1999): 106–23.
2. *Report of Robert H. Jackson, United States Representative to the International Conference on Military Trials, London 1945* (Washington DC: Department of State, 1949), p. 48.
3. International Military Tribunal, *Trial of the Major War Criminals before the International Military Tribunal*, vol. 3, p. 92.
4. Michael Burleigh, *Death and Deliverance: "Euthanasia" in Germany, c. 1900–1945* (Cambridge: Cambridge University Press, 1994), p. 273. For a full account of the Doctors' Trial, and especially the background and attendant issues, see Paul Julian Weindling, *Nazi Medicine and the Nuremberg Trials: From Medical War Crimes to Informed Consent* (Houndmills/Basingstoke UK: Palgrave Macmillan, 2004).
5. *Trials of War Criminals before the Nuremberg Military Tribunals under Control Council Law No. 10, Nuernberg, October 1946–April 1949*, 15 vols. (Washington DC: U.S. Government Printing Office, 1949), vol. 1, p. 28. (Hereafter cited as TWC.)
6. Telford Taylor, *Final Report to the Secretary of the Army on the Nuernberg War Crimes Trials under Control Council Law No. 10* (Washington DC: U.S. Government Printing Office, 1949), p. 101.
7. TWC, vol. 1, p. 27.
8. TWC, vol. 1, pp. 181–84.
9. Taylor, *Final Report*, p. 64.
10. "Between September 1939 and April 1945, all of the defendants herein, acting pursuant to a common design, unlawfully, willfully, and knowingly did conspire and agree together and with each other and with diverse other persons, to commit war crimes and crimes against humanity." TWC, vol. 1, p. 10. Concerning the planning of the Doctors' Trial and its relation to contemporaneous zonal trials, see Ulf Schmidt, "'The Scars of Ravensbrück': Medical Experiments and British War Crimes Policy, 1945–1950," in this volume.
11. Taylor, *Final Report*, p. 14.
12. Christian Pross, "Nazi Doctors: Criminals, Charlatans, or Pioneers? The Commentaries of the Allied Experts in the Nuremberg Doctors' Trial," in Charles Roland, Henry Fried-

lander, and Benno Müller-Hill, eds., *Arbeitspapiere-Atti-Proceedings* Nr. 11 (*Medical Science without Compassion, Past and Present*, Fall Meeting, Cologne, September 28–30, 1988), pp. 253–54; Tom Bower, *The Pledge Redeemed: America and Britain and the Denazification of Post-War Germany* (Garden City NY: Doubleday, 1982), p. 245.

13. Taylor, *Final Report*, p. 241. In only one of the twelve cases were there more acquittals: the I.G. Farben case, in which the prosecution failed to prove that some of the defendants knew that the Zyklon B gas supplied to the was used for murder.

14. Taylor, *Final Report*, pp. 75–77; Gerald L. Posner and John Ware, *Mengele: The Complete Story* (New York: McGraw-Hill, 1986), ch. 3; Bower, *Pledge Redeemed*, pp. 220, 332; Weindling, *Nazi Medicine and the Nuremberg Trial*, p. 154.

15. Leo Alexander, "Medical Science under Dictatorship," *New England Journal of Medicine*, 241 (1949): 39–47.

16. TWC, vol. 1, p. 29.

17. TWC, vol. 1, p. 69.

18. TWC, vol. 2, p. 122; Taylor, *Final Report*, pp. 70–71.

19. Robert N. Proctor, *Racial Hygiene: Medicine under the Nazis* (Cambridge MA: Harvard University Press, 1988), p. 38; Geoffrey Cocks, "The Old as New: The Nuremberg Doctors' Trial and Medicine in Modern Germany," in *Medicine and Modernity: Public Health and Medical Care in Nineteenth-and Twentieth-Century Germany*, ed. Manfred Berg and Geoffrey Cocks, pp. 173–91 (Cambridge: Cambridge University Press, 1997).

20. Burleigh, *Death and Deliverance*, p. 38.

21. Alexander, "Medical Science under Dictatorship," p. 44.

22. Proctor, *Racial Hygiene*, pp. 50, 62; Michael Burleigh and Wolfgang Wippermann, *The Racial State: Germany, 1933–1945* (Cambridge: Cambridge University Press, 1991), p. 69.

23. Michael H. Kater, *Doctors under Hitler* (Chapel Hill NC: University of North Carolina Press, 1989), pp. 4–5.

24. Henry Friedlander, *The Origins of Nazi Genocide: From Euthanasia to the Final Solution* (Chapel Hill NC: University of North Carolina Press, 1995), p. 128; Benno Müller-Hill, *Murderous Science: Elimination by Scientific Selection of Jews, Gypsies, and Others, Germany 1933–1945*, trans. George R. Fraser (Oxford: Oxford University Press, 1988). See also the contribution "Early Postwar Justice in the American Zone: The 'Hadamar Murder Factory Trial'" by Patricia Heberer in this volume.

25. Burleigh and Wippermann, *Racial State*, p. 56. In this vein, see William Seidelman, "Medical Selection: Auschwitz Antecedents and Effluent," *Holocaust and Genocide Studies* 4 (1989): 435–48; and Mario Biagioli, "Science, Modernity, and the 'Final Solution,'" in *Probing the Limits of Representation: Nazism and the Final Solution*, ed. Saul Friedlander, pp. 185–205 (Cambridge MA: Harvard University Press, 1992).

26. TWC, vol. 1, pp. 16–17.

27. Jean Edward Smith, *Lucius D. Clay: An American Life* (New York: Henry Holt, 1990), p. 301.

28. Bradley F. Smith, *The Road to Nuremberg* (New York: Basic Books, 1981).

29. *Report of Robert H. Jackson*, p. 333.

30. William Allen Zweck, "Nuremberg: Proceedings Subsequent to Goering, et al.," *North Carolina Law Review*, 26 (1948): 374–75; Matthew Lippman, "The Other Nuremberg: American Prosecutions of Nazi War Criminals in Occupied Germany," *Indiana International and Comparative Law Review* 3 (1992): 90–91.

31. Gisela Bock, *Zwangssterilisation im Nationalsozialismus: Studien zur Rassenpolitik und Frauenpolitik* (Opladen: Westdeutscher Verlag, 1986), pp. 237–38.

32. Proctor, *Racial Hygiene*, pp. 108–9.

33. TWC, vol. 1, pp. 48–50, 694–738.

34. Proctor, *Racial Hygiene*, p. 97; Weindling, *Nazi Medicine and the Nuremberg Trial*, p. 229.

35. Ernst Klee, *"Euthanasie" im NS-Staat: Die „Vernichtung lebensunwerten Lebens"* (Frankfurt: S. Fischer Verlag, 1983); Hans-Walter Schmuhl, *Rassenhygiene, Nationalsozialismus, Euthanasie: Von der Verhütung zur Vernichtung "lebensunwerten Lebens," 1890–1945* (Göttingen: Vandenhoeck und Ruprecht, 1987). For a recent summary, see Christopher R. Browning, with contributions by Jürgen Matthäus, *The Origins of the Final Solution: The Evolution of Nazi Jewish Policy, September 1939–March 1942* (Lincoln: University of Nebraska Press, 2004), pp. 93–184.

36. TWC, vol. 1, pp. 66, 809.

37. TWC, vol. 2, pp. 179–80, 196–98.

38. Schmuhl, *Rassenhygiene, Nationalsozialismus, Euthanasie*, p. 370.

39. Andrew Ivy, "Statement," in Alexander Mitscherlich and Fred Mielke, *Doctors of Infamy: The Story of the Nazi Medical Crimes*, trans. Heinz Norden (New York: Henry Schuman, 1949), p. x; Weindling, *Nazi Medicine and the Nuremberg Trial*, p. 283.

40. TWC, vol. 2, p. 181.

41. Weindling, *Nazi Medicine and the Nuremberg Trial*, p. 270.

42. Stefan Kühl, *The Nazi Connection: Eugenics, American Racism, and German National Socialism* (Oxford: Oxford University Press, 1994).

43. John M. Efron, *Defenders of the Race: Jewish Doctors and Race Science in Fin-de-Siècle Europe* (New Haven CT: Yale University Press, 1994), p. 9.

44. Arthur Ruppin, *The Jews in the Modern World* (London: St. Martin's Press, 1934), ch. 16.

45. Max Reichler, "Eugenics," *The Universal Jewish Encyclopedia* (10 vols., new ed., New York: KTAV Publishing House, 1969), vol. 4, p. 191.

46. TWC, vol. 2, pp. 83–84.

47. David J. Rothman, *Strangers at the Bedside: A History of How Law and Bioethics Transformed Medical Decision Making* (New York: Basic Books, 1991), p. 30.

48. TWC, vol. 2, pp. 111–18. Ivy's testimony, argues Dr. Evelyne Shuster, "reflects what has remained to this day the double standard of human experimentation, i.e., therapeutic goals and rules are used to justify otherwise unjustifiable experiments. [. . .] Ivy condemned Nazi medical experiments because they violated Hippocratic moral ideals, while at the same time abandoning Hippocratic ethics to justify his own experiments." Shuster, "Medical Ethics at Nuremberg: Leo Alexander, Andrew C. Ivy and Werner Leibbrandt," unpublished paper, 1996. I am grateful to Dr. Shuster for the opportunity to have seen this paper. See Evelyne Shuster, "Fifty Years Later: The Significance of the Nuremberg Code," *New England Journal of Medicine* 337 (1997): 1436–40.

49. John M. Harkness, "Nuremberg and the Issue of Wartime Experiments on U.S. Prisoners," *JAMA: The Journal of the American Medical Association* 276 (27 November 1996): 1674.

50. Rothman, *Strangers at the Bedside*, pp. 47–48.

51. Jay Katz, "The Nuremberg Code and the Nuremberg Trial," *JAMA: The Journal of the American Medical Association* 276 (27 November 1996): 1663–64.

52. Michael Grodin, "Historical Origins of the Nuremberg Code," in *The Nazi Doctors and the Nuremberg Code: Human Rights in Experimentation*, ed. George J. Annas and Mi-

chael A. Grodin, pp. 121–44 (Oxford: Oxford University Press, 1992), p. 134. For the most recent detailed discussion, see Weindling, *Nazi Medicine and the Nuremberg Trial*, ch. 15.

53. See Michael A. Grodin, George J. Annas, and Leonard H. Glantz, "Medicine and Human Rights: A Proposal for International Action," in *Medicine, Ethics, and the Third Reich: Historical and Contemporary Issues*, ed. John J. Michalczyk, pp. 199–209 (Kansas City MO: Sheed/Ward, 1994).

"The Scars of Ravensbrück"

Medical Experiments and British War Crimes Policy, 1945–1950

ULF SCHMIDT

Although the sixtieth anniversary of the Nuremberg Doctors' Trial (1946–1947) sparked significant debate about medical ethics and the origins of the Nuremberg Code, historians have so far paid little, if any, attention to Allied war crimes policy on the investigation of German medical atrocities, of which the Ravensbrück trials formed part.[1] British war crimes policy, in particular, was concerned with medical war crimes committed by German researchers at the Ravensbrück concentration camp. Much of the evidence against some key defendants at the Doctors' Trial, most notably Karl Gebhardt, Fritz Fischer, and Herta Oberheuser, was compiled by British war crimes experts and made available to the U.S. chief of counsel.[2] Following the Belsen Trial in the autumn of 1945, British investigators were among the first to document comprehensively the criminal medical experiments that German doctors had carried out on prisoners at Ravensbrück.[3] Most of the subjects were women. For the most part the doctors involved in these experiments were either associated with or employed by the Hohenlychen sanatorium, located in close proximity to the camp. These researchers thus became known as the "Hohenlychen group." Although the British investigated this group as part of the first of the Ravensbrück trials, some of the defendants were later extradited to the American zone of occupation and tried with the Nuremberg doctors.

To date, little has been written about the broader political and legal context of the first Ravensbrück Trial, its origins, and its overall place in the context of Allied denazification policy. This essay examines the genesis of the Ravensbrück Trial and the extensive investigations and international discussions that preceded its opening. It looks at how members of the German public perceived the Ravensbrück Trial, and contextualizes the British response to criticism leveled against it at the dawn of the cold war. The article aims, in part, to reconstruct the wider historical context of postwar British policy on medical war crimes. It suggests that British war crimes investigations conducted in preparation for the Ravensbrück trials formed one of the most substantial bodies of legal testimony and scientific expertise on human rights violations in experimental research *before* the establishment of the Nuremberg Doctors' Trial. The article also acknowledges Britain's contribution to the war crimes program and emphasizes that the memory of the first Ravensbrück trial has largely been overshadowed by the publicity surrounding the Nuremberg proceedings.[4]

British War Crimes Investigations into Ravensbrück

According to the Moscow Declaration of October 1943, war criminals were to be tried by the countries in which the crimes had been committed.[5] The Moscow agreement, however, excluded criminals whose crimes were not restricted to a defined geographical area. Those criminals were tried on the basis of the London Agreement on the Punishment of the Major War Criminals of the European Axis of August 1945, which established the legal basis for the International Military Tribunal (IMT).[6] Allied legislation was further defined by Control Council Law No. 10, of December 1945, which introduced a uniform legal basis in Germany for the prosecution of war criminals other than those covered by the IMT.[7] Thus, with a few exceptions, most post-war British military trials, including the Ravensbrück trials, were based on Control Council Law No. 10, which included crimes against peace, war crimes, crimes against humanity, and membership in an organization declared criminal by the IMT.[8] That law excluded crimes committed by Germans against other German nationals—such as the "euthanasia" program—and against other citizens from European Axis countries.[9] Such crimes were meant to be tried by German courts.[10] The guidelines for British military trials had been established in the Royal Warrant, Regulations for the Trials of War Criminals of 14 June 1945, Army Order 81/45.[11] The warrant followed the general procedures of British military law, whereby the court consisted of three to five military officers who served as judges. The Judge Advocate had to advise the judges on all legal and procedural questions, including the investigation, documentation, and evaluation of war crimes. He was appointed by the Judge Advocate General (JAG) in London, who was responsible for the administration of military jurisdiction. The number of British military trials after the Second World War was substantial. According to a Public Record Office directory, British military authorities held a total of 358 trials, including one in Austria, with approximately 1,100 defendants.[12] A total of 7 British trials focused on the Ravensbrück concentration camp.[13] In the first, Ravensbrück Trial No. 1, which opened on 3 December 1946 in Hamburg, the camp personnel, including some of the doctors and medical staff involved in criminal medical research, were indicted for war crimes and crimes against humanity.[14]

British investigations into Ravensbrück medical war crimes followed a long and twisted road. Officials in London had neither foreseen the extent of these investigations, nor had they anticipated the tensions that would arise from them. The period from the beginning of the investigation to the conclusion of Ravensbrück Trial No. 1 in March 1947 can be divided into four loosely connected phases. Conducted shortly after the end of hostilities, the first phase saw British intelligence securing witness testimonies and compiling registers of potential defendants.[15] The second began at the end of 1945, when further investigations were temporarily suspended in anticipation of a Foreign Office ruling over which country would be given jurisdiction to mount the upcoming Ravensbrück Trial No. 1. The third started in the spring of 1946, when the British Judge Advocate General (JAG) ordered substantial investigations in preparation for the first Ravensbrück Trial. The last phase began with Britain's transferal of both evidence and the Hohenlychen defendants to the U.S. chief of counsel in order to support the establishment of the Nuremberg Doctors' Trial.

British war crimes investigations into the Ravensbrück camp, where German doctors had committed criminal human experiments on prisoner populations without their consent, were carried out by the British War Crimes Group (North-West Europe). British intelligence was tracing war criminals under the two code names: "Operation Fleacomb" and "Operation Haystack."[16] By April 1945 the 21st British Army Group, later transformed into the British Army of the Rhine (BAOR), set up a number of small War Crimes Investigation Teams, which were later amalgamated into various Investigation Units. Those units were supported by the British War Crimes Liaison Groups, established to coordinate general policy decisions with the other three major Allied powers.[17] As a result of these sometimes hastily established new command structures, administrative tensions were commonplace in the immediate postwar period.

While some of these frictions were residual in nature, others had their origin in the war crimes investigations.

In the case of Ravensbrück, Polish and French witnesses played a crucial role in the early investigations, for most of the victims of medical experimentation and abuse were from those two countries. Whereas most of the Polish victims had been rescued by the Danish and the Swedish Red Cross in the Aktion Bernadotte and were transported either to Sweden or Poland, most of the French victims were concentrated in Paris, where many belonged to the Fedération Nationale de Déportés et Internés Patriotes.[18] This organization was of great importance for war crimes experts, for it helped them trace victims and perpetrators alike. It held periodic meetings at which British intelligence identified some of the former camp staff by means of photographs. Though little was known about the identity of individual members of the medical personnel, some of the victims remembered the faces of those who had beaten and sometimes seriously abused them. As one victim, Mademoiselle Lascroux, pointed out: "Their faces are burned on my memory, but their actual names are very rarely known."[19]

By October 1945 British investigations had come to a halt. Caught amidst negotiations between London and the Polish government-in-exile on the jurisdiction of cases involving Polish citizens, the BAOR was instructed to "suspend all preparations for trials of war criminals where victims [were] solely persons of Polish nationality."[20] The Foreign Office stressed that almost all of the victims of medical experiments at Ravensbrück were of Polish nationality, and that consequently Poland should be in charge of mounting the trial. The JAG, who investigated the cases and was considering establishing a trial against those accused already in British custody, opposed this position. The ruling of the War Office maintained that all evidence should be transferred to the military attaché of the Polish Embassy, with the request that his government consider taking over the cases. The debate highlighted the fact that, until the autumn of 1945, British policy focused mainly on cases involving British subjects, with the idea of passing all other cases to those countries requesting them. This policy became much broader after Control Council Law No. 10 was issued in December 1945, as this strengthened considerably the position of the JAG.[21] In the same month the JAG informed the War Office that plans had been made to try all cases that had initially been offered to the Polish government, despite Poland's prior acceptance of the cases.[22] The JAG's differing view on the matter was based upon the fact that evidence against some of the leading Ravensbrück defendants had steadily increased during the foregoing months. By December the United Nations War Crimes Commission (UNWCC) had listed their crimes, and potential witnesses and sources had presented him with the latest intelligence, as well as a detailed register of eighty-six camp officials. This sensitive file remained closed until 1997.[23] Among others, it named Karl Gebhardt, Fritz Fischer, and Herta Oberheuser as key perpetrators of medical experiments at Ravensbrück. All three were later included in the Nuremberg Doctors' Trial, as distinct from the Ravensbrück Trial.[24]

Although incriminating evidence had mounted, British officials showed great uncertainty about the extent to which the German medical profession had been involved in criminal human experiments. Commitment to large-scale investigations was therefore limited. Intelligence reports also varied to such an extent that experts had difficulties in shaping a uniform British war crimes policy. A top-secret report from December 1945, for example, stated that up to 90 percent of members of the German medical profession at the highest levels were involved, in one way or another, in unethical medical experiments.[25] This dramatic figure resulted from random investigations at half a dozen universities and hospitals. Nevertheless, the report had a strong impact in London, where experts realized the extent of work necessary in order to draw more precise conclusions. Faced with the prospect of time-consuming investigations by large numbers of personnel, some legal experts contemplated terminating medical war crimes investigations altogether. Others argued that the investigations might show that the German medical profession, as a whole, was so deeply involved in medical crimes that the investigations could jeopardize the employment of doctors by the Allied governments and thus interfere with the reconstruction of the German health care system.[26] At the same time, British legal experts were anxious to prosecute medical war crimes to ensure that unethical medical research practices would stop in Germany and not spread to other countries, including the United Kingdom.

The whole debate lost much of its speculative flavor after the total figures of doctors in detention for war crimes became available. By March 1946, Group

Captain Antony G. Somerhough who belonged to JAG's War Crimes Branch and was in charge of the British investigations into the Ravensbrück camp, explained that the Americans and the British had about thirty doctors under arrest for medical war crimes. As a result, he remarked, "the absence of these medical men will not disturb the smooth running of the medical profession in Germany."[27] According to Somerhough, the available evidence showed that only the "dregs of the profession" had participated in criminal experiments, and this made it unlikely that the investigations would interfere with the German medical profession. "On the contrary," he remarked, "it would probably cleanse it of some of its filthiest elements."[28] Thus, for legal and ethical reasons, he believed that the government was well advised to expedite further research into German medical war crimes.

The Ravensbrück case made British legal authorities realize the potential for a major war crimes trial against the German medical profession. As early as May 1946, British war crimes experts were preparing a case against Gebhardt and the doctors from the Hohenlychen sanatorium.[29] A conflict of interest arose, however, between those experts wanting to investigate medical war crimes and those interested in the exploitation of German experimental results. Thus, on 15 May 1946, American, French, and British war crimes experts held their first informal meeting in Frankfurt am Main to discuss the ethics of German experiments on human subjects and to explore their scientific utility.[30] There was no Soviet representative present at the meeting, as tensions between the Western Allies and the Soviet Union had been increasing since the opening of the IMT.[31]

The participants agreed that each of the countries present should prepare a specific medical war crimes case. Individual zonal trials were given preference over another international trial such as the IMT. The meeting showed that concerted efforts were being undertaken to co-ordinate Allied war crimes investigations, and that each of the three Allied nations planned to prepare its own trial against the German medical profession. The Americans were preparing a case for the Dachau high-altitude and freezing experiments. The French were building up a case on typhus, and the British were pursuing a case against the Ravensbrück experiments on gas gangrene.[32] British experts suggested a four-pronged approach, including the confiscation of the perpetrators' facilities, the reconstruction of the experimental procedure, the compilation of witness testimonies, and the full interrogation of the accused in order to establish the motives for the crimes. They were of the opinion that the Ravensbrück investigations would also uncover evidence on other human experiments, including bone transplantation experiments, sterilization experiments, artificial insemination, and various gynecological experiments performed by the notorious Auschwitz doctor Carl Clauberg.[33]

The first in a series of informal conferences revealed that British war crimes experts and the JAG in London had gathered significant evidence on medical war crimes in general and on the Ravensbrück experiments in particular. Apart from the Dachau freezing and high-altitude experiments, which had been investigated in the summer of 1945 by scientifically qualified members of the Combined Intelligence Operative Subcommittee (CIOS), the Americans presented the other Allies with little, if any, evidence on medical war crimes. The U.S. investigator, Dr. Leo Alexander, had already compiled seven CIOS intelligence reports on the German medical and scientific community, but these had been classified and were known only to a small number of specialists.[34] Informally, British investigators noted that although the Americans were willing to cooperate, they were not particularly enthusiastic for several reasons, one being that the cases were not "big enough" and required too much work in preparation. The Americans wanted to try the "major" war criminals, preferably after the evidence had been gathered and prepared by some of the other Allies. By June, one British official stated that the "knowledge and energy" of the Americans was "not very impressive" and concluded: "Information at present available at US War Crimes is not considerable."[35] Thus, in the summer of 1946, British and French investigators were left to undertake the groundwork.[36]

Based in Bad Oeynhausen, British war crimes investigators worked under the leadership of Group Captain Somerhough. He had been appointed in late 1945 and had quickly realized that his group received little support with regard to manpower and equipment. Finding himself lacking the necessary logistics, he engaged in constant struggles with the War Office for better transport facilities, equipment, and qualified personnel. The original focus of his brief was narrow. The task of a small group of intelligence officials was to investigate those crimes that German camp personnel had committed on British prisoners of war. Their efforts concentrated on the women of the Special Operations Executive (SOE) who had been interned and, in some cases, executed at Ravensbrück.[37] During the investigations, however, British experts broadened the scope of their inquiry to include crimes such as torture, executions, and criminal medical experimentation on humans. Somerhough's group of investigators consisted of six officers and the Special Medical Section, headed by the pathologist Major Keith Mant of the Royal Army Medical Corps (table 1).[38] One of the investigators was Lieutenant W. Wierzbowski, who had been assigned to the War Crimes Investigation Unit by Polish forces. The French later supported the investigations by dispatching the French Navy specialist Françoise Bayle.[39] In search of reliable witnesses to the sulfonamide drug experiments and bone transplantations, this group traveled to many European countries, including Denmark, Norway, Sweden, the Netherlands, Luxembourg, Belgium, France, Switzerland, Austria, and Czechoslovakia. In Britain they searched for witnesses who would testify in front of a British military court. In total, they secured over one hundred affidavits from witnesses. Contacts between British investigators and German scientists were also crucial in understanding the complexities of German medical science. Mant, for example, had close contacts with the Göttingen physiologist Hermann Rein, who provided British and American intelligence experts with information about various research programs.[40] An interim report from the autumn of 1946 outlined the conduct of the investigation and the selection of potential defendants:

> "In order to establish a definite case and determine both which of the accused were to be included in the major case and the direction in which investigations could most profitably be pursued, all witnesses were interrogated prior to the examination of any suspect persons. Those eventually chosen were the persons most frequently mentioned in the depositions or those who held such a high position of authority that regardless of direct evidence against them they can be held responsible for conditions prevailing in the camp.[41]

Progress reports on medical war crimes investigations were periodically transmitted to the JAG in London. By the spring of 1946 Somerhough reported that British forces had arrested eight key personnel in connection with medical war crimes carried out at Ravensbrück. They included Karl Gebhardt, Fritz Fischer, Karl Brunner, Herta Oberheuser, Percy Treite, Rolf Rosenthal, Augusta

Table 1. British War Crimes Investigators Examining the Ravensbrück Concentation Camp

Name	Department and Function
Group Capt. A. G. Somerhough	Chief, Legal Staff, JAG War Crimes Branch, Main HQ, BAOR; Head of Investigation Unit
Lt.-Col. R. A. Nightingale	Int. Corps, War Crimes Investigation Unit, Main HQ, BAOR
Maj. A. K. Mant	Special Medical Section, Royal Army Medical Corps
Maj. B. Silley	War Crimes Investigation Unit
Maj. E. H. Vernon	War Crimes Investigation Unit
Capt. D. G. Worcester	War Crimes Investigation Unit
Capt. G. E. Kaiser	War Crimes Investigation Unit
Capt. J. W. Da Cuhna	War Crimes Investigation Unit
Lt. W. Wierzbowski	War Crimes Investigation Unit (Polish Forces)
Miss S. Jansen	Secretary of Investigation Unit

Hingst (senior operating nurse in Hohenlychen), and Karl Brandt. These medical personnel became known as the "Hohenlychen group" since they had either been associated with or employed by the Hohenlychen sanatorium. It was there that the medical experiments were organized, and from there that the doctors traveled to the camp to perform their experiments on humans. Somerhough proposed a separate trial for the Hohenlychen group, for as he explained, "the case against them is essentially different from that against the medical staff of the camp."[42] Yet, he did not make clear under what terms and conditions such a case would eventually be established. One may assume that he regarded their crimes to be of such a nature that only a mixed inter-Allied military court, if not an international military tribunal, would suffice to rule on these defendants. As a result of his proposal, however, the investigations first developed along two different lines: one stressing the ill-treatment of Allied nationals by the camp staff, including the medical personnel, and the other focusing on criminal medical experiments carried out by the Hohenlychen group. By April 1946 investigators were ordered to confine their search to activity within the camp and to use evidence gathered from members of the Hohenlychen group against members of the Ravensbrück camp:

> It [the Ravensbrück investigation] should not be part of the investiga-
> tions to produce evidence against doctors of the Hohenlychen [sana-
> torium] as it is intended that their case will form the subject of a
> separate investigation on another brief. It is possible therefore to use
> any of the latter doctors as evidence against members of the camp.
> This investigation should result in a legally substantial case not only
> against the particular doctors and nurses concerned but also against
> the remaining members of the camp to be accused for allowing or
> actively procuring the existence of such a state of affairs. It is impor-
> tant for this purpose to establish that the experiments were of such a
> nature that they constituted a maltreatment or killing of the victims
> and that they were undertaken for no purpose concerned with medi-
> cal assistance of the victims.[43]

The investigations, as it later turned out, were difficult to separate from each
other, and the division between the two was conceptual in nature rather than
substantive. But the consequences of these two lines of investigation were significant. With respect to the experiments conducted at Ravensbrück, British
authorities now distinguished between "major" war criminals (i.e., the Hohenlychen group) and "minor" defendants. When, in the fall of 1946, preparations
for the Doctors' Trial reached their final stage, U.S. officials wanted to indict all
"major" medical war criminals and asked to include the Hohenlychen group in
the Nazi Doctors' Trial. Some members of the Hohenlychen group were eventually tried by the American authorities, not the British, and received milder
sentences as a result. For Fischer and Oberheuser, in particular, being tried
alongside the Nuremberg doctors was instrumental in saving their lives, for
their overall responsibility for ordering the experiments appeared less significant when compared with that of high-ranking medical officers. As the verdicts
in the Ravensbrück trials show, if tried by a British military court, both would
have probably been sentenced to death (table 2).

Human Experiments at Ravensbrück

The origins and motives of the Ravensbrück medical experiments have been
thoroughly researched.[44] The scars that they left on their victims are well documented.[45] One of them was Jadwiga Dzido. Born in 1918 in Suchowola, she

Table 2. Nuremberg Medical Trial Defendants Originally Assigned to the
British Medical War Crime Trial as Part of the Hohenlychen Group

Defendant	Date of Birth	Sentence	Commutation
Karl Brandt	(8 January 1904)	Death	
Karl Gebhardt	(23 November 1897)	Death	
Fritz Fischer	(5 December 1912)	Life	15 years
Herta Oberheuser	(15 May 1911)	20 years	10 years

studied chemistry and pharmacy at the University of Warsaw before becoming a member of the Polish resistance movement "Conspiracy" in November 1940.[46] Following her arrest by the Gestapo in March 1941, Dzido was taken to Ravensbrück, where she first worked on a farm and later sewed boots for the German army. On 22 November 1942 she was taken to the sick quarters with nine other Polish girls. Her legs were shaved, and two days later she was operated on. For five weeks she was gravely ill, could not eat, had a high fever, and was delirious. After the war Dzido remembered only the enormous pain she had endured, having been sleepless and restless for most of the time. On 20 December 1946 Dzido and three other women, Maria Broel-Plater, Władysława Karolewska, and Maria Kuśmierczuk, gave testimony at the Doctors' Trial.[47] Their stories resembled those of seventy-four other women who had been subjected to involuntary sulfonamide drug and bone transplantation experiments at the Ravensbrück camp.

In all cases the prisoners, most of whom were Polish, were used for medical experiments without having given their clear and voluntary consent. No case has been reported in which the women were at liberty to withdraw from the experiment. Often the experiments were performed by unqualified medical personnel and undertaken at random for no scientific reason and under appalling hygiene conditions. All of the Ravensbrück experiments caused unnecessary suffering, and generally no safeguards were taken to protect the women from severe and multiple injuries, mutilation, disability, or death. All of the women experienced extreme pain, and almost all of those who are alive today suffer from physical injuries and trauma, either as a direct result of the experiments or from a total lack of post-operative care.

Owing to heavy German casualties from gas gangrene on the Eastern Front in the winter of 1941–1942 and the deleterious effect on German morale that had been wrought by Allied propaganda about the value of sulfonamide drugs, leading SS authorities demanded an evaluation of these drugs. Experiments with sulfonamide drugs were ordered by the Nazi leadership after the head of the Reich Security Main Office (RSHA), SS-Obergruppenführer Reinhard Heydrich, died in Prague from a gas gangrene infection caused by an assassination attempt in May 1942. Gebhardt, who had been sent to Prague to look after Heydrich, was informally accused of negligence by Dr. Theodor Morell, Hitler's private physician, who alleged that sulfonamide drugs might have saved Heydrich's life. Morell had invented, tested, and marketed the sulfonamide drug Ultraseptyl, and thus had good (if not financial) reasons for being critical of Gebhardt's lack of confidence in sulfonamide drugs.[48]

Gebhardt, nevertheless, had more experience than Morell with war wounds. He had extensive knowledge of American and British literature on sulfonamide drugs, and through his personal experience on the front lines, he knew the limitations of these drugs in the treatment of severe battle wounds. Gebhardt was of the opinion that sulfonamide drugs were no substitute for good front-line surgery. Himmler and the SS, however, saw sulfonamide drugs as a "miracle cure" (*Wundermittel*) that could prevent all infections if correctly administered. The rationale for the experiments was to find a definite answer to the question as to whether battle wounds should be treated with surgical methods performed by doctors and nurses in front-line hospitals, or with sulfonamide drugs by medical officers in the field. In the latter case they would then be fit to travel down the lines of communication to a base hospital for further medical treatment.[49] Gebhardt's motive for conducting the experiments was to clear himself of the responsibility for Heydrich's death and to convince Himmler and leading SS officials that his judgment on sulfonamide drugs was correct. Thus, the experiments were no more than a "mere medico-political gesture," as one of the investigators pointed out after the war.[50] The fact that Gebhardt knew the outcome of the experiments in advance was an aggravating factor in the decision to charge him with war crimes, and in the end it secured his death sentence at the Doctors' Trial.

The initial order for experiments on humans probably came from Himmler and Ernst Robert Grawitz, Reichsarzt-SS and acting president of the German Red Cross. Gebhardt, however, was left in charge of the general direction.[51] His objective was to test the efficiency of various commercial sulfonamide drugs, both Swiss and German, especially Morell's drug Ultraseptyl. The companies producing the drug included the pharmaceutical conglomerates I.G. Farben, Schering-Kahlbaum, Ciba-Gesellschaft, and Nordmarkwerke Hamburg, and the company Haupt und Sohn.[52] Sulphonamide drug experiments started at the end of July 1942, with those on the seventy-four Polish women beginning in August 1942. The first twenty operations were performed on twenty male prisoners from Sachsenhausen. Thirty additional operations were performed on Polish women, who suffered much more serious infections owing to the introduction of foreign bodies such as fragments of wood or powdered glass. In one case, a curved surgical needle and twenty centimeters of silk were left in a wound.[53] After the completion of the first series of experiments, Grawitz visited the camps and examined the young women. As no deaths had occurred among the experimental subjects, Grawitz gave orders to fire actual bullets through the legs of the women in order to produce battle-like gas gangrene infections. Fischer and Gebhardt decided not to carry out these instructions, but to produce severe tissue damage by tying off the blood supply to an area of muscle and implanting bacterial cultures in the avascular area. This technique was used in two groups of ten Polish women.[54] Though most of the Polish women believed that Gebhardt had performed the operations, he in fact carried out only the first one on the men's group, doing so in order to demonstrate the "technique" to his assistant, Fischer.[55] Five of the women died from the effects of the operations, and six were later executed. Gebhardt's experiments convinced his nonscientist superiors that sulfonamide drugs were of little use for certain types of wounds, that they were no substitute for surgery, and that their application had been much overrated.

Experiments on human beings at Ravensbrück were anything but secret among the Nazi medical profession and were in fact openly discussed at a conference in May 1943, where Fischer presented the preliminary findings of the experiments to over two hundred army physicians. His talk revealed that the experiments had been carried out on concentration camp inmates without their consent, and that in three cases the outcome had been fatal. To date, there is no record that any of the attending physicians protested against these experiments. However, they must have known that the experiments violated every conceivable moral standard of clinical research on humans, including the German "Regulations Concerning New Therapy and Human Experimentation" that had been issued in 1931.[56] Some of the scientists involved in the Ravensbrück experiments did not even hesitate to publish their "results" in established academic journals such as the *Deutsche Zeitschrift für Chirurgie*. In 1944, for example, the camp physician Ludwig Stumpfegger published a detailed account of bone transplantations that he had conducted on Ravensbrück inmates. The experiments described in his article showed a striking correspondence with testimony given two years later by some of the mutilated witnesses.[57]

Members of the camp staff were also perfectly aware of the immoral nature of the experiments. Camp commandant Fritz Suhren, who attempted to boycott some of the experiments by refusing to provide Gebhardt with further Polish inmates for experimental purposes, exemplified this. Although Suhren apparently objected to the experiments, complaining to the RSHA in Berlin, he was overruled and had to apologize to Gebhardt. The victims were also conscious of the criminal character of the experiments. All of the women selected from a transport arriving at Ravensbrück from Lublin were alleged members of the Polish resistance movement. According to the Geneva Convention, they were therefore political prisoners. The women received no trial, and their alleged membership in the Polish underground movement carried an automatic death sentence.[58] In March 1943 a group of Polish women, who called themselves "guinea-pigs," protested in front of the camp commandant that the experiments had been carried out without their consent and therefore violated international law. As political prisoners, they demanded to be shot and not to be experimented upon against their will. One of the women, Zofia Sokulska, was a student from Berlin. She protested that the Hohenlychen doctors had operated on her twice, and that she refused to be operated upon a third time.[59] For some women in this group of Polish prisoners, the experiments were discontinued, though investigators later found out that other victims were shot after the operations had been completed. Sokulska survived the camp and was taken to Sweden by the Red Cross. Having been interrogated by British investigators in Lund, she served as a key witness in the Ravensbrück Trial. She was also among

Table 3. Victims of Medical Experiments Carried Out in the Ravensbrück Concentration Camp

Name	Age	First Operation	Transport/Date	Experiment[1]
A. Waclawa	20	22 September 1942	Lublin, 23 September 1941	Inf.
B. Bogumila	27	17 November 1942	Lublin, 23 September 1941	Inf.
B. Irena	19	4 November 1942	Lublin, 23 September 1941	Bone
B. Zofia	27	4 November 1942	Lublin, 23 September 1941	Bone
B. Jadwiga	20	22 November 1942	Lublin, 23 September 1941	Inf.
B. Leokadia	24	14 November 1942	Lublin, 23 September 1941	Bone
B.-P. Maria	28	22 November 1942	Lublin, 23 September 1941	Inf.
B. Wojciecha	22	22 November 1942	Lublin, 23 September 1941	Inf.
C. Maria	36	19 November 1942	Lublin, 31 May 1942	Bone + Inf.
C. Krystyna	19	23 November 1942	Lublin, 23 September 1941	Inf.
C. Stanislawa	18	23 November 1942	Lublin, 23 November 1942	Muscle
D. Krystyna	24	28 August 1942	Lublin, 23 September 1941	Bone
D. Jadwiga	24	22 November 1942	Lublin, 23 September 1941	Inf.
G. Jadwiga	39	22 November 1942	Lublin, 23 September 1941	Inf.
G. Maria	22	1 August 1942	Lublin, 23 September 1941	Inf.[2]
G. Maria	35	20 November 1942	Lublin, 23 September 1941	Bone + Inf.
G. Rozalia	20	1 August 1942	Lublin, 23 September 1941	Inf.[3]
H. Helena	25	23 November 1942	Lublin, 23 September 1941	Muscle
H. Zofia	28	30 September 1942	Lublin, 23 September 1941	Inf.
I. Janina	20	14 August 1942	Lublin, 23 September 1941	Inf.
I. Krystina	22	14 August 1942	Lublin, 23 September 1941	Inf.
J. Stanislawa	37	8 October 1942	Lublin, 31 May 1942	Inf.
J. Alicja	20	14 August 1942	Lublin, 23 September 1941	Inf.
K. Jadwiga	27	14 August 1942	Lublin, 23 September 1941	Inf.
K. Maria	35	8 October 1942	Lublin, 31 May 1942	Inf.
K. Maria	25	14 August 1942	Lublin, 23 September 1941	Inf.
K. Wladyslawa	33	14 August 1942	Lublin, 23 September 1941	Inf.
K. Urzula	33	14 August 1942	Lublin, 23 September 1941	Inf.
K. Zofia	21	14 August 1942	Lublin, 23 September 1941	Inf.
K. Zofia	35	8 October 1942	Lublin, 23 September 1941	Inf.
K. Genowefa	21	8 October 1942	Lublin, 31 May 1942	Inf.
K. Zofia	30	14 August 1942	Lublin, 23 September 1941	Inf.
K. Czeslawa	33	8 October 1942	Lublin, 23 September 1941	Inf.
K. Weronika	30	30 September 1942	Lublin, 23 September 1941	Inf.
K. Irena	42	8 October 1942	Lublin, 31 May 1942	Inf.
K. Wanda	20	1 August 1942	Warsaw, 23 September 1941	Inf.
K. Kazimiera	29	8 October 1942	Lublin, 23 September 1941	Inf.
K. Maria	22	8 October 1942	Lublin, 23 September 1941	Inf.
K. Leokadia	32	8 October 1942	Lublin, 23 September 1941	Inf.
L. Aniela	34	8 October 1942	Lublin, 23 September 1941	Inf.
L. Stefania	29	30 September 1942	Lublin, 23 September 1941	Inf.
L. Jadwiga	24	8 October 1942	Warsaw, 31 May 1942	Inf.

Table 3. continued

Name	Age	First Operation	Transport/Date	Experiment[1]
M. Pelagia	43	8 October 1942	Lublin, 23 September 1941	Inf.
M. Eugenia	21	22 November 1942	Lublin, 23 September 1941	Inf.
M. Janina	18	28 December 1942	Lublin, 23 September 1941	Bone
M. Janina	23	13 December 1942	Lublin, 23 September 1941	Bone
M. Wladyslawa	32	3 January 1943	Lublin, 23 September 1941	Bone
M. Pelagia	20	2 December 1942	Lublin, 23 September 1941	Bone
M. Stanislawa	35	5 January 1943	Lublin, 23 September 1941	Bone
M. Eugenia	30	22 November 1942	Lublin, 23 September 1941	Inf.
M. Janina	22	28 August 1942	Lublin, 23 September 1941	Bone
M. Stanislawa	32	30 September 1942	Lublin, 23 September 1941	Inf.
M. Zofia	23	23 January 1943	Lublin, 23 September 1941	Muscle
N. Maria	21	30 September 1942	Warsaw, 23 September 1941	Inf.
O. Aniela	23	1 August 1942	Lublin, 23 September 1941	Inf.
P. Janina	22	30 September 1942	Warsaw, 23 September 1941	Inf.
P. Helena	24	16 August 1943	Lublin, 23 September 1941	Bone
P. Maria	30	30 September 1942	Lublin, 23 September 1941	Inf.
P. Barbara	16	3 November 1942	Warsaw, 23 September 1941	Bone
P. Halina	29	16 January 1943	Lublin, 23 September 1941	Inf.
P. Alfreda	22	30 September 1942	Lublin, 23 September 1941	Inf.
P. Barbara	26	3 November 1942	Lublin, 23 September 1941	Muscle
R. Apolonia	45	30 September 1942	Warsaw, 23 September 1941	Inf.[4]
R. Izabella	20	3 November 1942	Lublin, 23 September 1941	Bone
S. Stefania	35	16 August 1943	Lublin, 23 September 1941	Bone
S. Anna	21	22 November 1942	Lublin, 31 May 1942	Inf.
S. Stanislawa	18	3 November 1942	Lublin, 23 September 1941	Muscle
S. Aniela	24	22 August 1942	Lublin, 23 September 1941	Bone[5]
S. Zofia	26	21 September 1942	Lublin, 23 September 1941	Muscle
S. Zofia	21	13 September 1942	Lublin, 23 September 1941	Inf.
S. Weronika	16	30 September 1942	Warsaw, 23 September 1941	Inf.
S. Joanna	35	16 August 1943	Lublin, 23 September 1941	Bone
W. Wanda	21	1 August 1942	Lublin, 23 September 1941	Inf.
Z. Maria	22	1 August 1942	Lublin, 23 September 1941	Inf.[6]

Source: Public Record Office, WO235, 531; WO309, 420; also Dunja Martin, "Die Funktion des Krankenreviers in NS-Konzentrationslagern am Beispiel des Frauenkonzentrationslager Ravensbrück" (master's thesis, Hannover, 1994), appendix.

Notes: 1. Inf. = Infection Experiment; Bone = Bone Transplantation Experiment; Muscle = Muscle Transplantation Experiment.
2. Maria G. was shot after the operations on 12 February 1943 at Ravensbrück.
3. Rozalia G. was shot after the operations 28 September 1943 at Ravensbrück.
4. Apolonia R. was shot after the operations in the fall of 1943 at Ravensbrück.
5. Aniela S. was shot after the operations in the fall of 1943 at Ravensbrück.
6. Maria Z. was shot after the operations in the fall of 1943 at Ravensbrück.

those who provided the names of all seventy-four Polish victims and offered information on the kinds of medical experiments that had been performed (table 3). Sokulska's testimony was crucial, for it showed that the perpetrators knew full well that their acts violated both international law and the established code of medical practice.[60]

The Genesis of the Ravensbrück Trial

Since after May 1945 the Ravensbrück concentration camp was located in the Soviet zone, the Soviets were formally responsible for establishing the appropriate war crimes trial. Although London had anticipated that the Soviets would follow up the case, Moscow showed no particular interest in indicting specific camp personnel.[61] Initial Soviet intelligence reports had documented some of the horrific conditions and war crimes at Ravensbrück, but this material was not passed on to the other Allied powers, nor did the Soviets conduct further investigations.[62] Soviet interest in war crimes trials seems to have been linked with the number of potential defendants that the Soviets had in custody—for example, in the case of the Sachsenhausen concentration camp.[63] With most of the Ravensbrück war criminals having escaped to the West, primarily to northern Germany, and having been arrested by the British army, applications for extraditing the defendants from Britain became a necessary precondition for any prospective Soviet trial. Thus, commitment for investigating and prosecuting German atrocities at Ravensbrück received little attention in postwar Soviet politics and was silently left to Britain. The Soviets may have also been disinclined to pursue the case because they knew that Poland wanted some of the accused for trial. With most of the victims being of Polish or French nationality, any Soviet involvement must have looked increasingly futile. The Ravensbrück case was probably seen as a matter of secondary importance and thus not necessarily in the national interest.

By the end of 1945, British officials were asking for advice on how to handle the "Russian cases" that the Soviets declined to take over for trial. By March 1946 the War Office sent a secret cable to the JAG in London to expedite a general Foreign Office ruling.[64] However, it became more and more difficult to carry out investigations in the Soviet zone, not only because of various communication problems, but also because the zone became increasingly unsafe for British agents and was seen as a "sanctuary" for German war criminals. Hence, the British JAG was anxious to obtain Soviet clearance to continue both the investigations and preparations for the trial. Further problems arose after Poland claimed formal responsibility for mounting a trial against the doctors of the Hohenlychen sanatorium.

On 31 May 1946 Dr. Mieczyslaw Szerer, the Polish representative of the UNWCC, officially requested the extradition of members of the Hohenlychen group for trial in Poland.[65] This came in response to information that the British JAG had launched extensive investigations into the Ravensbrück case. The Polish application caused high-level debates among various British departments. Realizing the importance of the Hohenlychen group, the military deputy to the JAG pointed out that the "whole question of handing over Dr. Gebhardt and others to the Poles is bound up with the case against the German doctors in carrying out improper medical experiments on persons interned in German concentration camps."[66] Although acknowledging that most of the experiments were performed on Polish nationals, the JAG wanted to exploit Gebhardt as a vital source in the forthcoming British investigations into Ravensbrück and thus opposed his extradition.[67]

By 3 June 1946 British and American investigators met in Wiesbaden to discuss unethical medical experiments and the problem posed by Poland's request to try the Hohenlychen group. Both parties were of the opinion that a case involving gross breaches of medical ethics would have to be widely publicized and that only the Western zones were capable of doing this. Though the Hohenlychen sanatorium was located in the Soviet zone, British intelligence had sufficient evidence that the Soviets were not going to proceed with the case and concluded: "It goes to us by default."[68] British officials saw the Hohenlychen case as part of the larger Ravensbrück case and claimed jurisdiction over both:

> The Poles should not be allowed to try this case. We are trying Ravensbrück and so we should also try the doctors of Hohenlychen who carried out their experiments at Ravensbrück. It is an integral part of the Ravensbrück case and only schematic and not substantive reasons compel one to try it as a separate case at all. If the Poles take over this, then they should take over every other case of maltreatment, etc. of Polish subject [sic] in Ravensbrück and then finis Ravensbrück.[69]

Political pressure on British officials was mounting since the Polish government-in-exile was awaiting a final ruling. To secure American support, U.S. investigators were told that Britain would abandon all its concentration camp cases if Poland were to try the Hohenlychen doctors. As a result, American authorities would have been faced with a much larger share of war crimes trials than previously anticipated. Furthermore, this potentially defeated U.S. plans to persuade Britain to shoulder a large number of war crimes trials for minor war criminals. Outlining the British strategy, one official noted:

> If it is suggested that the Poles try the case because the women operated on were Poles then on the same reasoning we ought to abandon all our Concentration Camp cases to our Allies whether Eastern or Western. The fact that the women were Poles is quite fortuitous, they might as easily have been French or any other nationality, and the experiments were not as such directed against any nationality as some other concentration camp actions. The principle to be established in this case when it is tried is that such exp. were morally and legally wrong as carried out on human beings and the fact that the human beings were Polish subjects is no more relevant to the decision as to who tries the alleged criminals than the fact they were black-haired or fat.[70]

By mid-1946, it had become clear that Poland had a genuine interest in bringing the Hohenlychen doctors to trial. Not only had hundreds of witnesses given testimony about the Ravensbrück experiments, but the Polish authorities also conducted their own investigations into medical atrocities. By the summer of 1946 the Medical Academy of Danzig examined most of the victims of sulfonamide drug and bone transplantation experiments and published an incriminating report in the second edition of the journal *Biuletyn Glownej Komisji Badania Zbrodni Hitlerowskich w Polsce*.[71] On 12 June 1946 Brigadier Henry Shapcott of the JAG office informed his American counterpart, Colonel Clio E. Straight, about the progress in the Ravensbrück investigations and the likelihood that Poland would have a justified claim for the extradition of the Hohenlychen doctors: "With regard to Ravensbrück and particularly the *Aussenkommando* at Hohenlychen, the Poles are showing a very keen interest in the experiments conducted there by Dr. Gebhardt. According to my information all the persons on whom experiments were made at the hospital were Poles, and I think they will put up a very strong case to be allowed to try Gebhardt and his assistants."[72] Shapcott's approach was meant to secure American support in the event that Britain would pursue the doctors' case alone in the future and, more important, against Poland's claim.

Discussions to extradite doctors detained in the British zone revolved around Brandt, Gebhardt, Fischer, Oberheuser, and Treite. Apart from Poland, requests from Eastern countries were generally turned down by Britain. In August 1946 the Czechoslovakian government requested the extradition of Brandt, Hitler's attending physician (*Begleitarzt*), for war crimes.[73] The response by the JAG was firm: "Brandt is wanted by us and cannot be handed to the Czechs."[74] In the same month the Polish government requested the extradition of Herta Oberheuser to stand trial in front of a Polish court.[75] Britain's response was the same as in Brandt's case. U.S. authorities had previously turned down a similar request issued by Poland by referring to Oberheuser's status as a British prisoner. Britain, in turn, referred to her status as a "major accused" in the Ravensbrück Trial, and the JAG stated that "under no circumstances must she be handed to the Poles or anybody else."[76] Thus, eventually, and in accordance with previous policy, the British government turned down the request to extradite the Hohenlychen group to Poland.

Having rejected Poland's claim, British authorities were faced with further problems when it surfaced that French officials were seemingly preparing a trial against some of the Ravensbrück personnel in French custody. France proposed to bring the "whole case" before the Tribunal General of Rastatt. Arguing along Poland's lines, France claimed to have a unique interest in this trial since numerous French inmates had died in that camp. The idea was to convene an "International Court" that would be constituted by a British officer.[77] This put British legal officials on the defensive, for it endangered the successful establishment and outcome of the Ravensbrück Trial. Furthermore, the French had previously promised to hand over certain persons to the British Army of the Rhine to stand trial in the British zone. The Chief of Staff of the BAOR therefore suggested that in view of the new situation each nation "should try in its own courts the persons it already holds for war crimes committed at Ravensbrück."[78] One month later, it turned out that the entire French proposal had been issued without the authority of the senior French prosecutor during his absence, and that all previous agreements between the British and the French were still valid.[79]

British preparations for the Ravensbrück Trial finally were running at high speed. By 9 September 1946 Somerhough forwarded the Interim Report on the Ravensbrück investigations to the JAG in London and proposed a conference among some key British investigators in the case.[80] Only a month later, British experts discussed their findings on Ravensbrück at the International Scientific Commission for the Investigation of Medical War Crimes in Paris.[81] Only Somerhough and Mant attended the meeting on behalf of Britain. Having agreed to supply Britain with witnesses and defendants, France wished to be represented on the bench and in the prosecution team. Madame Aline Chalufour was selected as the French member of the prosecution since she had compiled extensive information about the conditions in the Ravensbrück camp. And Françoise Bayle was asked to support the investigations and monitor the progress of the trial.[82] British prosecutors were well aware that the case would produce a great deal of publicity and that the reliability of the witnesses was crucial. Shortly before the final arrangements for the trial were laid out and agreed upon, one military official described the Ravensbrück case as the "swan-song" of British concentration camp trials and encouraged his colleagues to do their best, as "we all want it to end triumphantly."[83]

In preparing the case for trial, British legal experts suggested that those countries whose nationals were the main victims should be represented on the court.[84] France and Britain also agreed to invite the Fedération Nationale de Déportés et Internés Patriotes to send a number of witnesses to the trial. By the beginning of October 1946, plans to invite the governments of France, Poland, and Luxembourg were already underway. Brigadier General Shapcott was hesitant to invite other governments, as the trial procedure laid out under the Royal Warrant required that at least half of the military court be British. Locations under discussion were Hamburg and Bad Oeynhausen, with the latter being preferred by military officials. It was at Hamburg, however, that Britain staged Ravensbrück Trial No. 1, probably for pragmatic reasons with regard to courtroom facilities, hotels, and press attention.[85] Yet symbolism also played a significant role. Referring to Hamburg's active role in supporting Hitler's racial

Table 4. Members of the Court in Ravensbrück Trial No. 1

Name

President: Major-General V. J. E. Westropp, CBE

Members of the Court: Lt.-Colonel J. A. Glendinning, Royal Artillery, Permanent WCC President; Major D. S. Bowling-Smith, MC, Royal Tank Regiment; Captain E. H. Buckland, The Duke of Wellington's Regiment; Captain W. H. Scott, Royal Army Service Corps; Major Kasimierz Olszewski, Polish Military Authority; Colonel Henri de Bonnechose, Judge du Tribunal de la Seine.

Judge Advocate: Mr. C. C. Stirling, Deputy Judge Advocate General.

Prosecuting Officers: Major S. M. Stewart, JAG's Branch HQ BAOR; Captain J. W. da Cunha, 23rd Hussars (RAC); Mme. Aline Chalufour, Docteur en Droit.

Defence Counsel: Dr. Adolf Meyer-Labastille (for Ramdohr and Mewes); Dr. Alfred Beyer (for Binz and Bösel); Dr. Günther Bruch (for Binder and Schwarzhuber); Dr. Alfred Rücker von Klitzing (for Winkelmann); Dr. Richard Gädke (for Peters and Hellinger); Dr. Otto Zippel (for Mory); Dr. H. Meyer; Dr. Rudolf Martin; Dr. Lappenberg; Dr. H. H. Todsen; Dr. W. von Metzlar.

Interpreters: CSM v. Neftel, REME; Sgt. K. Ellington, RA; Sgt. H. Aitchison, Rur Corps.

Witnesses for the Prosecution: Violette Le Coq (French); Jacqueline Hereil (French); Helena Piasecka (French); Renee Lascroux (French); Yanina Ivanska (Polish); Dr. Louise le Porz (French); Sylvia Salvesan (Norwegian); Helena Dziedziecka (Polish); Stanislaw Szewzykova (Polish); Zofia Sokulska (Polish); Anna Weng Seidemann (Danish); Mary O'Shaughnessy (British); Lt. Sanson, GC, MBE (British); Yvonne Basedem (British); Sqn. Officer. V. M. Atkins (British); Hermine Salvini (Austrian); Irma Trksakova (Czechoslovakian); Anna Hand (Austrian); Countess Lancroronska (Polish); Erika Buchmann (German); Neeltje Epker (Dutch); Annette Eekmann (Belgian); Claire van der Boom (Belgian); Mudr. Zdenka (Czechoslovakian).

policies, one British official noted that they had given the city "the doubtful honour of staging this Trial."[86]

Shortly before the opening of the first Ravensbrück trial, former camp commandant Suhren managed to escape from prison, causing much embarrassment among British military authorities. He was later captured and tried in one of the subsequent Ravensbrück trials.[87] The trial opened on 3 December 1946, six days before the United States opened the Nazi Doctors' Trial in Nuremberg. It was expected that the Ravensbrück Trial would last about six weeks. The president of the court was Major-General V. J. E. Westropp, who presided over six members of the court, two of whom did not belong to the British forces. Major Kasimierz Olszewski represented Poland, and Colonel Henri de Bonnechose represented the French government.[88] The prosecution consisted of Major S. M. Stewart from the JAG's branch, himself a witness in the Belsen Trial,

Table 5. Outcome of Ravensbrück Trial No. 1

Defendant	Judgment	Sentence Purged	Released
Johann Schwarzhuber	Death	3 May 1947	
Ludwig Ramdohr	Death	3 May 1947	
Gustav Binder	Death	3 May 1947	
Heinrich Peters	15 years		20 May 1954
Dorothea Binz	Death	2 May 1947	
Margerete Mewes	10 years		26 February 1952
Greta Boesel	Death	2 May 1947	
Eugenia von Skene	10 years		21 December 1951
Carmen Mory	Death	Committed suicide	
Vera Salvaquart	Death	2 May 1947	
Elisabeth Marschall	Death	2 May 1947	
Gerhard Schiedlauski	Death	3 May 1947	
Percy Treite	Death	Committed suicide	
Rolf Rosenthal	Death	3 May 1947	
Adolf Winkelmann	No finding announced by Court. Defendant as accused died on 1 February 1947		
Martin Hellinger	15 years		14 May 1955

Source: Public Record Office, wo235, 305.

Captain J. W. da Cunha, one of the Ravensbrück investigators, and Madame Aline Chalufour (table 4).

In his opening address Major Stewart drew attention to the fact that almost all the victims were women, and most of them had been Allied nationals. His address emphasized the ill-treatment of the Ravensbrück inmates, rather than the ethics of the medical experiments carried out there.[89] Stressing the camp's "efficient and enduring intimidation" of the population of German-occupied territory, Stewart applied the definition of "war crimes" established by Oxford law professor James Leslie Brierly; he argued that the atrocities committed during the war by camp personnel showed that they regarded their fellow men as less than beasts. As Stewart argued: "this is a question a court will have to answer. Can this killing which would normally be murder, can this injury which would normally be unlawful wounding—be defined as an act of war? If not, it will be a war crime."[90] Five women and six men were sentenced to death in the first of the Ravensbrück trials (table 5).[91] Two of them, Carmen Mory and Percy Treite, committed suicide shortly after the pronouncement of sentences. On 2 May 1947 the remaining female prisoners were hanged in Hameln prison; one day later the male prisoners were hanged.[92]

Responses to the Ravensbrück Trial

Press coverage of the Ravensbrück Trial was substantial since citizens repre-senting many nations from all over Europe were involved. News of the experi-ments had already been made known during the war and was broadcast by the BBC in early 1945.[93] With a stolen camera, some of the victims had also taken photographs of their infected wounds and mutilated legs. For security reasons, the exposed film was given to one of the French prisoners, Germaine Tillion, who managed to smuggle it out when the camp was eventually evacuated.[94] Representatives of all European countries attended the trial to report on both the proceedings and the sentences.[95] Newspaper correspondents and govern-ment officials stated that "nearly every European United Nation is deeply con-cerned."[96] During the first three weeks, a total of twenty-one witnesses from nine countries testified about the living conditions that prevailed in the camp. In early January 1947, newspaper reports began showing the extent to which German doctors had committed medical war crimes in the concentration camps.[97]

Sources providing an accurate account of the German population's percep-tion of the Ravensbrück Trial are rare, and accounts were often written from a certain political perspective. However, aside from newspaper accounts, pub-lic statements, and radio interviews, some sources contain almost unfiltered insights into the trial's perception by segments of the German public. These include classified notes taken by the British Censorship Office, which regularly taped telephone conversations and opened letters of Germans to monitor how the general public perceived British denazification policy.[98] Bearing the repre-sentative limitations of such material in mind, these sources give partial insight into the various views some members of the German public expressed with respect to the trial.

Unlike other British trials, the Ravensbrück Trial received substantial press attention. British newspapers such as the *Daily Mail*, the *Sunday Despatch*, and the *Daily Express* sent correspondents to Hamburg to report on the ill-treat-ment of Allied nationals. National and local newspapers reported almost daily on the latest developments and revelations at the trial.[99] An extra 120 seats had been allocated for German citizens who wanted to hear about the nature of the crimes their countrymen had committed during the war. This form of re-education was widely accepted by most citizens, especially those from Hamburg who regularly attended the trial. For others it may have been a sense of sensationalism that attracted them to the courthouse. One commentator noted that the "gallery allocated to the Germans is full to overflowing."[100] Opinions about the trial varied considerably, ranging from positive voices in favor of Allied denazification policy to hostile resentment against "victors' justice" (*Siegerjustiz*).

From a taped telephone conversation from December 1946, British censors gained insight into how some Germans perceived the Ravensbrück Trial and expressed their general contempt for Allied policy:

> *Voice 1: Have you read the evidence in the Ravensbrück Trial?*
>
> *Voice 2: Yes but you know I do not give much for this French or Belgian evidence. These so-called witnesses have been influenced and prepared. They only want to exterminate the Germans, and they do not care at all whether they tell a few lies or even perjure themselves.*[101]

Others expressed satisfaction that the Ravensbrück camp staff had been indicted, and that the Allies were uncompromising with regard to war criminals. One woman, who had knowledge about the camp, expressed a kind of *Schadenfreude* that some of the Ravensbrück staff had been sentenced to death, but she was doubtful about the quality of the witnesses. Following the announcement of sentences in March 1947, she wrote to her friend:

> *I have followed the Ravensbrück Trial and I am satisfied that the witch, Binz [defendant], is kaput. Now her angel's head will begin to rot. I am not happy with the other verdicts. I had the feeling that the witnesses were not clear enough. . . . Well, tell me Käte, where are all the others? . . . They are still missing; are they not detained?*[102]

Some contemporaries also criticized the slow British trial procedure. A telephone conversation taped by the British censors revealed the extent to which the local population was still caught up in wartime sentiment, particularly when Allied imposition of punishment was swift.

> *1: Listen—I have talked with Otto, he has been to the court-room and has been looking at the whole performance.*

2: The one from Ravensbrück?

1: Yes, the British make a terrible fuss about it.

2: How do you mean?

1: Instead of hanging up the criminals, they make long stories about it, typically English.

2: Yes, you know what they are like.[103]

This conversation also seems to indicate that segments of the German population may have been less indifferent to the war crime trials than is sometimes suggested. Indeed, the trials were widely discussed, both in public and in private. The citizens of Hamburg took a special interest in the trial. By January 1947, with publicity at its peak, some citizens of Hamburg regularly visited the courthouse and discussed their impressions at dinner parties and other social gatherings. Apart from its judicial and re-educational aspects, the very act of visiting the courthouse and hearing victims' accounts developed into a social convention. To some extent the trial had become a social event, and the general population was anxious that justice would be done at last. At the beginning of January 1947, British censors taped the following conversation:

1: I have been to the Ravensbrück Trials. They start every day at 2 o'clock. You ought to go there, it is extremely interesting.

2: How do the accused behave?

1: Well, they are smiling and shaking their heads and . . .

2: Do they deny anything?

1: No, but their faces show clearly enough that they are completely indifferent to the trial. These beasts who pulled the gold teeth from innocent people and beat and destroyed them, they do not realize that they stand justly accused by the German nation and not by the British. Most of them are quite young, and they look somewhat altered, but one sees at once that they have finished with life. The former camp-commander looks like an old gypsy.

2: I must go there.

1: You ought to, you will get a much better picture of the realities than from the high-flown reports in the papers.[104]

Apart from these positive accounts, there were many critics of the Ravensbrück trial, among them Madame Geneviève Anthonioz, née de Gaulle, the niece of General Charles de Gaulle, who herself had been deported to Ravensbrück during the war. At the end of January 1947, and after the sentencing of the defendants, she organized a concerted press campaign that attacked the British trial procedures and the quality of the verdicts. Under the heading "French Criticise the British Way of Justice," the *Manchester Guardian* reported on the French press conference that protested against the actions of the Ravensbrück trial. Together with two fellow inmates from Ravensbrück, Madame Anthonioz criticized the rules of procedure that prohibited a general indictment and inquiry into the system of the camp. She complained that the court, and especially the judges, failed to appreciate the character of the camp and the atmosphere of torture and fear that the prisoners had endured. Furthermore, the judges had apparently repeatedly asked witnesses and victims to remember precise dates concerning when they were beaten or when specific operations were being performed. As a result observers had gained the impression that in some cases the context of the camp environment had not been adequately taken into account.

Criticism leveled against British judges and the Ravensbrück trial was given serious consideration in London, for it was important how British justice was perceived abroad. British legal authorities vividly remembered the blow to British jurisprudence that occurred when the verdicts in the Belsen Trial were announced without ever being explained to the general public. Moreover, the French public was well aware of the small number of British citizens imprisoned at Ravensbrück, especially when compared with the thousands of their own and of other continental nationalities. Observers also noted that the nations from which most of the victims came were not those in charge of the trial. Although the British authorities had added one French and one Polish judge to the bench, this gesture was generally regarded as insufficient. Responding to the *Manchester Guardian*, British legal authorities stiffly explained the rules of British military trial procedures and attempted to ward off any criticism by suggesting that Madame Anthonioz was a follower of communist ideas and that her orchestrated press campaign was little more than "a plank in the Communist platform."[105] Opposition to British war crimes trials became at this point enmeshed with the political currents of anticommunism at the dawn of the cold war and was seen as criticism of denazification and of the European policy of the Western Allies in general.

Conclusion

British war crimes experts were among the first to launch substantial investigations into the criminal medical experiments that German doctors carried out at Ravensbrück during the war. Having compiled detailed registers of potential defendants and much documentation on German medical atrocities, British legal authorities were initially unwilling to leave the Ravensbrück Trial to other European nations. Thus, they refused to comply with requests issued to the London government for the extradition of some of the defendants. In the end, British pragmatism aimed at coordinating Allied denazification policy and liaising with U.S. policies. With the cold war becoming chillier, Britain provided substantial support in the Nuremberg war crimes trials. Members of the Nuremberg staff, who claimed credit for the successful establishment of the subsequent Nuremberg tribunals, have suggested that the Americans mounted the Doctors' Trial with great speed and with much improvisation.[106] Such accounts of postwar U.S. policy glossed over the fact that much of the incriminating evidence against some of the defendants at the Doctors' Trial had been compiled beforehand by British war crimes experts and made available for the U.S. chief of counsel by the fall of 1946. Though it is true that the Americans expedited the subsequent Nuremberg proceedings by shipping enormous legal and administrative machinery to Europe, the painstakingly researched evidence from British and French investigators was crucial for the success of the trials and deserves historical consideration. British authorities also agreed to plans allowing the trials of minor war criminals to be conducted by the British military government or left to the German judicial authorities. Following the foundation of the Federal Republic in 1949, however, political support and public interest in war crimes trials faded both in Europe and America. It was the beginning of a long and twisted process of German *Vergangenheitspolitik*—the politics of dealing with a country's past—which, in its first decade, aimed to annul Allied war crimes policy by invalidating trial sentences and by granting amnesty to alleged and real war criminals.[107] The legacy of this policy reaches far into the current political culture of a unified Germany, where the third generation is presently trying to come to terms with its past. As recent debates about the Holocaust memorial and the compensation of forced and slave laborers show, German society is anything but united on how the Holocaust should be remembered.

Notes

For some of the debates on this issue, see Ulf Schmidt, *Karl Brandt, The Nazi Doctor: Medicine and Power in the Third Reich* (London: continuum, 2007). I wish to thank three anonymous referees for their helpful and constructive suggestions and my colleagues at the University of Kent and elsewhere for their ongoing support. The article has previously been published in *German History* 23:1 (2005): 20–49. It is published with the kind permission of the editors of *German History*, the journal of the German History Society, United Kingdom.

1. For some of the debates on this issue, see Ulf Schmidt, *Justice at Nuremberg: Leo Alexander and the Nazi Doctors' Trial* (Basingstoke UK: Palgrave, 2004); also Ulf Schmidt, "German Medical War Crimes, Medical Ethics, and Post-War Justice: A Symposium Held at the University of Oxford to Mark the 50th Anniversary of the Nuremberg Medical Trial, 14 March 1997," *German History* 15:3 (1997): 385–91; Ulf Schmidt, "Die Angeklagten Fritz Fischer, Hans W. Romberg und Karl Brandt aus der Sicht des medizinischen Sachverständigen Leo Alexander," in *Vernichten und Heilen: Der Nürnberger Ärzteprozeß und seine Folgen*, ed. Klaus Dörner und Angelika Ebbinghaus, pp. 374–404 (Berlin: Aufbau, 2001); Ulf Schmidt, "Der Ärzteprozeß als moralische Instanz? Der Nürnberger Kodex und das Problem 'zeitloser Medizinethik,' 1946–47," in *Medizingeschichte und Medizinethik: Kontroversen und Begründungsansätze, 1900–1950*, ed. Andreas Frewer and Josef N. Neumann, pp. 334–73 (Frankfurt am Main: Campus, 2001); see also George J. Annas and Michael A. Grodin, eds., *The Nazi Doctors and the Nuremberg Code: Human Rights in Human Experimentation* (New York: Oxford University Press, 1992); Jürgen Peter, *Der Nürnberger Ärzteprozeß im Spiegel seiner Aufarbeitung anhand der drei Dokumentensammlungen von Alexander Mitscherlich und Fred Mielke* (Münster: Literatur Verlag, 1994); Claudia Wiesemann and Andreas Frewer, eds., *Medizin und Ethik im Zeichen von Auschwitz* (Erlangen: Palm und Enke, 1996); Evelyne Shuster, "Fifty Years Later: The Significance of the Nuremberg Code," *New England Journal of Medicine* 337:20 (1997): 1436–40; Paul J. Weindling, "From International to Zonal Trials: The Origins of the Nuremberg Medical Trial," *Holocaust and Genocide Studies* 14:3 (2000): 367–89; Paul J. Weindling, "The Origins of Informed Consent: The International Scientific Commission on Medical War Crimes, and the Nuremberg Code," *Bulletin of the History of Medicine* 75:1 (2001): 37–71; Dörner and Ebbinghaus, *Vernichten und Heilen*; for primary sources, see also www.nuremberg.law.harvard.edu.

2. See Schmidt, "Die Angeklagten."

3. The Belsen Trial lasted from 17 September to 17 November 1945. The court was one of the first British military courts convened under the Royal Warrant of 14 June 1945; see *Law Reports of Trials of War Criminals: Selected and Prepared by the United Nations War Crimes Commission*, vol. 2, *The Belsen Trial* (London: HM Stationery Office, 1947), pp. 1–156.

4. For primary sources, see Public Record Office (hereafter PRO), Judge Advocate General's Office, War Crimes Papers. These papers include the trials nos. 1–357 and one trial that was conducted in Austria. For Bergen-Belsen, see PRO, WO235, JAG 108, 124, 132,

137, 140, 142, 146, 166, 316; for Groß-Rosen, JAG 347; for Mauthausen-Loiblpaß, JAG 355; for Natzweiler JAG 147, 241; for Ravensbrück JAG 225, 289, 330, 333, 334, 335; also Trials of War Criminals before the Nuremberg Military Tribunals under Control Council Law No. 10, vols. 1–15, October 1946–April 1949. For British war crimes policy, see Anthony Glees, "The Making of British Policy on War Crimes: History as Politics in the UK," *Contemporary European History* 1 (1992): 171–97; for postwar trials in Hamburg, see Helge Grabitz, "Die Verfolgung von NS-Gewaltverbrechen in Hamburg in der Zeit von 1946 bis heute," in *Die Normalität des Verbrechens: Bilanz und Perspektiven der Forschung zu den nationalsozialistischen Gewaltverbrechen*, ed. Helge Grabitz et al., pp. 300–24 (Berlin: Hentrich, 1994); also Hermann Kaienburg, "Die britischen Militärgerichtsprozesse zu den Verbrechen im Konzentrationslager Neuengamme," in *Die frühen Nachkriegsprozesse*, ed. KZ-Gedenkstätte Neuengamme, pp. 56–64 (Bremen: Temmen, 1997); Katrin Stoll, "Walter Sonntag—Ein SS-Arzt vor Gericht," *Zeitschrift für Geschichtswissenschaft* 10 (2002): 918–39; Anette Kretzer, "'His or Her Special Job': Die Repräsentation von NS-Verbrecherinnen im ersten Hamburger Ravensbrück-Prozess und im westdeutschen Täterschafts-Diskurs," in *Entgrenzte Gewalt: Täterinnen und Täter im Nationalsozialismus*, ed. KZ-Gedenkstätte Neuengamme, pp. 134–50 (Bremen: Temmen, 2002); also Schmidt, "German Medical War Crimes"; Schmidt, *Justice at Nuremberg*. Nina Stähle of Oxford University is currently writing her doctoral thesis: "British Trials of Nazi Medical War Crimes: Medical Ethics in a Political Context."

5. *Law Reports of Trials of War Criminals*, vol. 1, p. viii.

6. *Law Reports of Trials of War Criminals*, vol. 1, pp. ix–xvi.

7. *Law Reports of Trials of War Criminals*, vol. 1, pp. xvi–xx; see also Annas and Grodin, *Nazi Doctors*, pp. 317–21.

8. Kaienburg, "Die britischen Militärgerichtsprozesse," p. 56.

9. See *Trials of War Criminals*, vol. 1I, pp. 909–25; also Paul J. Weindling, "Gerechtigkeit aus der Perspektive der Medizingeschichte: 'Euthanasie' im Nürnberger Ärzteprozeß," in *Medizingeschichte und Medizinethik, 1900–1950*, ed. Andreas Frewer and Josef N. Neumann, pp. 311–33 (Frankfurt am Main: Campus, 2001).

10. See also Fritz Bauer, Christian F. Rüter, and Adelheit L. Rüter-Ehlermann, eds., *Justiz und NS-Verbrechen: Sammlung deutscher Strafurteile wegen nationalsozialistischer Tötungsverbrechen 1945–1966*, vol. 1 (Amsterdam: University Press Amsterdam, 1968).

11. For British legislation concerning trials of war criminals by military courts, see *Law Reports of Trials of War Criminals*, vol. 1 (London: HM Stationery Office, 1947), pp. 105–10.

12. Kaienburg, "Die britischen Militärgerichtsprozesse," pp. 56ff.

13. For the other British Ravensbrück Trials, see PRO, WO235, 433–34 (Case no. 2); 520 (SS Personnel Case no. 2); 516A and 516B (Case no. 3), 530–36 (Case no. 4), 526–27 (SS Personnel Case no. 5a); 528, 529A and 529B (Case no. 6); for files and clippings about the Ravensbrück Trial no. 1, see "Collection Warsaw" at the Gedenkstätte Ravensbrück (hereafter RA), RA 4, nos. 12–19. I am indebted to Ms. Herzog for drawing my attention to this collection; see also Hanna Elling and Ursula Krause-Schmitt, "Die Ravensbrück-Prozesse vor den britischen Militärgerichten in Hamburg," *Informationen: Studienkreis Deutscher Widerstand* 35 (1992): 13–29; Hanna Elling and Ursula Krause-Schmitt, "Die Ravensbrück-Prozesse vor französischen Militärgerichten in Rastatt und Reutlingen," *Informationen: Studienkreis Deutscher Widerstand* 37/38 (1993): 22–36.

14. The Ravensbrück Trial was neither the first British military trial nor, as it appears, one

that people remembered much thereafter. The Belsen Trial or the Neuengamme Trials, for example, are still much more present in the public conscience. One of the reasons for the latter being remembered might have been that both trials were held in close proximity to where the actual crimes had been committed. For Ravensbrück this was essentially different, because the Ravensbrück camp was some three hundred kilometers away from Hamburg and at the time in the Soviet zone of occupation.

15. PRO, WO309, 420.

16. PRO, "Operation Fleacomb," WO309, 476–77, 1458, 1460, WO311, 650; "Operation Haystack," WO309, 1606.

17. PRO, WO309, 372 (formation and organization of investigation units); for "Liaison Groups," see WO309, 459 (Soviet zone), 460 (French zone), 461 (American zone).

18. PRO, WO309, 417; see also Simone Erpel, "Rettungsaktion in letzter Minute: Die Befreiung von Häftlingen aus dem Frauen-Konzentrationslager Ravensbrück durch das Internationale Komitee des Roten Kreuzes, das Dänische und Schwedische Rote Kreuz," in *"Ich grüsse Euch als freier Mensch": Quellenedition zur Befreiung des Frauen-Konzentrationslagers Ravensbrück im April 1945*, ed. Sigrid Jacobeit and Simone Erpel, pp. 22–79 (Berlin: Stiftung Brandenburgische Gedenkstätten, 1995).

19. PRO, WO309, 15.

20. PRO, WO309, 15.

21. PRO, WO309, 15.

22. PRO, WO309, 15.

23. PRO, WO311, 658.

24. The index cards were made accessible in 1997; for Gebhardt, Fischer, and Oberheuser, see PRO354, 13, 12, 33.

25. PRO, WO309, 468.

26. PRO, WO309, 468.

27. PRO, WO309, 468.

28. PRO, WO309, 468.

29. PRO, WO309, 468.

30. PRO, WO309, 471.

31. See also Schmidt, *Justice at Nuremberg*.

32. PRO, WO309, 1652.

33. PRO, WO309, 1652.

34. Schmidt, *Justice at Nuremberg*.

35. PRO, WO309, 468.

36. PRO, WO309, 1652.

37. British intelligence was especially interested in the case of the three British parachutists, Violette Szabo, Lillian Rolff, and Danielle Williams, who were executed in March 1945 by direct order of Himmler. PRO, WO235, 316, Interim Report of the War Crimes Investigation Unit, British Army on the Rhine on Ravensbrück Concentration Camp, p. 7 (in the following "Interim Report").

38. The six officers in charge of the investigations were Lt.-Col. R. A. Nightingale, Maj. E. H. Vernon, Capt. D. G. Worcester, Capt. G. E. Kaiser, Capt. J. W. Da Cunha, Lt. W. Wierzbowski; PRO, WO235, 316, Interim Report; also Keith Mant, "The Medical Services in the Concentration Camp of Ravensbrück," *Medico Legal Journal* 17 (1949): 99–118.

39. PRO, WO309, 1652.

40. PRO, WO309, 468; PRO, WO309, 473.

41. PRO, WO235, 316, Interim Report.

42. PRO, WO309, 468.

43. PRO, WO309, 417.

44. For some of the sources and literature on the Ravensbrück medical experiments, see Alexander Mitscherlich and Fred Mielke, *Doctors of Infamy: The Story of Nazi Medical Crimes* (New York: Henry Schuman, 1949); Alexander Mitscherlich and Fred Mielke, *Medizin ohne Menschlichkeit* (Frankfurt am Main: Fischer, 1960); National Archives and Records Administration, Records of the United States Nuremberg War Crimes Trials. *United States of America v. Karl Brandt et al.* (Case 1), 21 November 1946–20 August 1947 (Washington DC: National Archives and Records Service, 1974); Angelika Ebbinghaus, ed., *Opfer und Täterinnen* (Nordlingen: Greno, 1987); Freya Klier, *Die Kaninchen von Ravensbrück* (Munich: Droemer Knaur, 1994); Dunja Martin, "Menschenversuche im Krankenrevier des KZ Ravensbrück," in *Frauen in Konzentrationslagern: Bergen-Belsen, Ravensbrück,* ed. Claus Füllberg-Stolberg et al., pp. 99–112 (Bremen: Temmen, 1994); Dunja Martin, "Versuchskaninchen—Opfer medizinischer Experimente," in Füllberg-Stolberg, *Frauen in Konzentrationslagern,* pp. 113–122; Angelika Ebbinghaus and Karl Heinz Roth, "Kriegswunden: Die kriegschirurgischen Experimente in den Konzentrationslagern und ihre Hintergründe," in Dörner and Ebbinghaus, *Vernichten und Heilen,* pp. 177–218; Angelika Ebbinghaus, "Zwei Welten: Die Opfer und die Täter der kriegschirurgischen Experimente," in Dörner and Ebbinghaus, *Vernichten und Heilen,* pp. 219–40; Schmidt, "Die Angeklagten," pp. 374–404.

45. See especially Kornel Michejda, "Operacje Doświadczalne w obozie koncentracyjnym Ravensbrück," *Biuletyn Glownej Komisji Badania Zbrodni Hitlerowskich w Polsce* 2 (1947): 123–75; also RA 4, no. 16 ("Collection Warsaw"), Protokoll der Hauptkommission zur Untersuchung von hitlerschen Verbrechen (27.4.1957–25.5.1957); Mitcherlich, *Medizin ohne Menschlichkeit,* pp. 131–59; Loretta Walz, "Gespräche mit Stanisława Marczewska und Maria Plater über die medizinischen Versuche in Ravensbrück," in Dörner and Ebbinghaus, *Vernichten und Heilen,* pp. 241–72.

46. NARA, RG 238, Case History of Polish Witnesses—Broel-Plater, Karolewska, Dzido, and Kusmierczuk by Dr. Leo Alexander, Office of Chief of Council for War Crimes, 17 December 1946.

47. Alexander papers, Alexander diary, 20 December 1946.

48. PRO, WO309, 469; Morell was described by contemporaries and those who interrogated him after his internment by American forces as a "greedy quack" and a "charlatan," who was inarticulate and supposedly had the "hygienic habits of a pig."

49. PRO, WO309, 469.

50. PRO, WO309, 469.

51. PRO, WO309, 469.

52. PRO, WO309, 469; for the role of the chemical industry in using the concentration camps as "research laboratories," see, for example, Ebbinghaus and Roth, "Kriegswunden," pp. 177–218. Christine Wolters from the University of Berlin is currently writing her dissertation, "Tuberkulose im Konzentrationslager Sachsenhausen." Her work examines the role of the chemical and pharmaceutical industry in some of the concentration camps.

53. Deposition by Zofia Baj on 12 August 1946 in Brussels in the presence of Major A. K. Mant; Ebbinghaus, *Opfer und Täterinnen,* pp. 256–59.

54. PRO, WO309, 469.

55. PRO, WO309, 469.

56. See Schmidt, *Justice at Nuremberg*; also Hans-Martin Sass, "Reichsrundschreiben 1931: Pre-Nuremberg German Regulations Concerning New Therapy and Human Experimentation," *Journal of Medicine and Philosophy* 8 (1983): 99–111.

57. PRO, WO309, 1791; see also Ludwig Stumpfegger, "Die freie autoplastische Knochentransplantation," *Deutsche Zeitschrift für Chirurgie* 259 (1944): 495; also Ebbinghaus and Roth, "Kriegswunden," pp. 192, 208.

58. PRO, WO309, 469.

59. PRO, WO235, 318, deposition on oath by Zofi Sokulska on 11 July 1946 at Lund, Sweden; also PRO, WO235, 531; first deposition by Maczka on 16 April 1946; second on 2 July 1946 in Stockholm by Major Mant; also Duke University Medical Center, Durham NC, Box 1, File 3, Summary of 3rd Interrogation of Dr. Zofia Maczka, 7 January 1947.

60. Schmidt, *Justice at Nuremberg*.

61. Jacobeit and Erpel, *"Ich grüsse Euch als freier Mensch."*

62. On 9 May 1945 Soviet investigators completed the "Evidence File Ravensbrück" for the "Extraordinary Commission" that summarized the conditions at Ravensbrück. This is probably one of the earliest documents that provides detailed information, however incomplete, about the ill-treatment of prisoner populations and about criminal medical experiments; Bärbel Schindler-Saefkow, "Die Befreiung des Konzentrationslagers Ravensbrück durch die Rote Armee und die erste Beweisaufnahme von Verbrechen," in Jacobeit and Erpel, *"Ich grüsse Euch als freier Mensch,"* pp. 137–208.

63. See also RA, 4, no. 18 ("Collection Warsaw"), extract from letter of Legal staff, BAOR, 9 May 1946.

64. PRO, WO309, 459.

65. PRO, FO371, 57645; see also Szerer's letter of 23 May 1946 to Colonel Richard C. Halse, Judge Advocate Department, informing the British government that Poland "would be most anxious to hold the trial against the chief culprit Prof. Gebhardt and his assistants in Poland. This implies of course their extradition to Poland"; RA 4, no. 18 ("Collection Warsaw").

66. PRO, FO371, 57645.

67. PRO, FO371, 57645.

68. PRO, WO309, 468.

69. PRO, WO309, 468.

70. PRO, WO309, 468.

71. Michejda, "Operacje Doświadczalne," pp. 123–75.

72. PRO, WO309, 468.

73. See Schmidt, *Karl Brandt*.

74. PRO, WO309, 418.

75. PRO, WO354, 33.

76. PRO, WO309, 418.

77. PRO, WO309, 683.

78. PRO, WO309, 418.

79. PRO, WO309, 762; after the opening of the British Ravensbrück Trial No. 1, the French authorities, nevertheless, conducted several military trials of the Ravensbrück camp staff. The first French trial opened on 28 December 1946 in Reutlingen. The others were held at Rastatt; see Elling and Krause-Schmitt, "Die Ravensbrück-Prozesse vor französischen Militärgerichten."

80. PRO, WO309, 418.

81. PRO, WO309, 470 and 471; also Paul Weindling, "Ärzte als Richter: Internationale Reaktionen auf die medizinischen Verbrechen während des Nürnberger Ärzteprozess im Jahre 1946–47," in Wiesemann, *Medizin und Ethik im Zeichen von Auschwitz*, pp. 31–44.

82. PRO, WO309, 471.

83. PRO, WO309, 418; final arrangements were discussed at the beginning of November 1946 when leading British administrators and military and legal officials met for a conference to decide on the responsibilities at the Ravensbrück Trial; see PRO, FO1014, 536.

84. PRO, WO309, 419; for mixed inter-Allied military courts under the Royal Warrant, see *Law Reports of Trials of War Criminals*, vol. I (London: HM Stationery Office, 1947), p. 106.

85. PRO, WO309, 419.

86. PRO, WO309, 1655.

87. PRO, WO309, 1791.

88. PRO, FO1014, 536.

89. It was left to the U.S. prosecution in Nuremberg, under the leadership of the young and charismatic Brigadier General Telford Taylor, to focus on German medical atrocities and the violation of ethical standards in human experimentation; see Annas and Grodin, *Nazi Doctors*; Schmidt, *Justice at Nuremberg*.

90. PRO, WO235, 305.

91. For a summary of the deeds of the defendants at the Ravensbrück Trial No. 1, see PRO, WO235, 316; also Lord Russel of Liverpool, *The Scourge of the Swastika* (London: Kassel, 1955), pp. 191–225.

92. PRO, WO309, 689; also records of the British executioner Albert Pierrepoint, RA-No. II13–Y11.

93. PRO, WO235, 305.

94. Martin, "Versuchskaninchen," p. 120; Michejda, "Operacje Doświadczalne w," pp. 136–61; also Germaine Tillion, *Ravensbrück*, trans. Gerald Satterwhite (Garden City NY: Anchor Press, 1975).

95. PRO, WO309, 686.

96. PRO, WO309, 684.

97. "Bewußte Gasbrandinfizierungen: Erschütternde Aussagen in Ravensbrückprozeß," *Hamburger Echo* 2 (January 1947); "Ravensbrück-Prozeß: Unmenschliche Operationen: Die Verteidiger haben das Wort," *Hamburger Echo* 3 (January 1947); also Lord Russel of Liverpool, *Scourge of the Swastika*, pp. 191–225.

98. PRO, WO309, 417; surveillance of German postal correspondence was also meant to find new leads in the investigations. At the end of 1945, for example, one of the former nurses from the Hohenlychen sanatorium, Roswitha Goritzka, informed her long-time friend in Bitterfeld, near Halle: "Our Chief [Gebhardt] has been arrested, he is in prison in Nürnberg as a war criminal. Many of our doctors, including an operation sister [Oberheuser] are also in Nürnberg."

99. RA 4, no. 12 ("Collection Warsaw") for newspaper clippings by *Die Welt* and *Hamburger Echo*.

100. PRO, FO1014, 536.

101. PRO, WO309, 419.

102. PRO, WO309, 420.

103. PRO, WO309, 1655.

104. PRO, WO309, 1655.
105. PRO, WO309, 1791; and WO309, 420.
106. For an account of the Doctors' Trial, held under American auspices at Nuremberg, see Michael R. Marrus, "The Nuremberg Doctors' Trial and the Limitations of Context," in this volume; see also Schmidt, *Justice at Nuremberg,* and Schmidt, *Karl Brandt.*
107. Norbert Frei, *Vergangenheitspolitik: Die Anfänge der Bundesrepublik und die NS-Vergangenheit* (Munich: Beck, 1996), pp. 133–306.

The Sachsenhausen Trials
War Crimes Prosecution in the
Soviet Occupation Zone
and in West and East Germany

JONATHAN FRIEDMAN

On 18 June 1936, less than two months before the staging of the summer Olympics in Berlin, Gestapo officials informed the Prussian Forestry Office that a new concentration camp was to be built in the outskirts of the city of Oranienburg—in the suburb of Sachsenhausen, some thirty miles from Berlin.[1] On 12 July, fifty prisoners from the Esterwegen concentration camp (located in the moor lands of northwest Germany) began construction on the 160,000-square-meter triangular site. Prisoners were to be interned in sixty-seven barracks built to hold between 100 and 120 individuals (but that ultimately held over 600 each). A main cell block (*Zellenbau*), with seventy cubicles, became the central torture chamber, while two open areas served as the official execution grounds. A 2.7-meter-high brick wall enclosed the camp, and it was guarded by between 1,500 and 3,000 SS-men from eighteen different companies of the SS Death's Head Divisions.

Sachsenhausen opened in September 1936 with a total of 2,000 inmates, all of them male and most of them political prisoners, such as Communists and Socialists. Members of other groups eventually found themselves incarcerated as well, including Jews, "Gypsies" (Roma and Sinti), homosexuals, Jehovah's Witnesses, resistance leaders, and Soviet prisoners of war. Some of the more notable prisoners included pastor Martin Niemöller, former Austrian premier Kurt von Schuschnigg, Nobel laureate Carl von Ossietzky, and onetime Nazi diplomat Dr. Martin Luther. By March 1945, one month before its liberation by a unit of the Soviet 47th Army, the number of inmates in the camp had swollen to over 95,000. It is estimated that over 200,000 individuals passed through the camp between 1936 and 1945. Half of them perished, through disease and starvation, by shooting and hanging, through deadly medical experimentation, and some by gassing, which was instituted at Sachsenhausen in March 1943.

One of the goals of this essay is to investigate these atrocities from the perspective of postwar tribunals in order to deepen our understanding of the con-centration camp system. Its main purpose, however, is to present new research on the prosecution of Sachsenhausen's many guards by Soviet and German authorities, offering insight into the complex union of law and politics by com-paring their varied approaches to postwar justice.

The Soviet Military Tribunal

On 23 October 1947 Soviet occupation forces brought former personnel of the Sachsenhausen camp before a military tribunal. The trial was unique in many respects: it was the only public hearing in the Soviet zone; it was quickly set-tled (in contrast to trials in the American and British zones); its defendants all pleaded guilty; and none were sentenced to death.[2] On 1 November, the sixteen defendants under indictment were sentenced to various terms of imprison-ment. Although only a minute fraction of the tens of thousands of individuals tried by Soviet military tribunals, the Sachsenhausen defendants were among the most notorious figures directly involved in the murder of innocent civilians and prisoners of war.

Despite the demise of communism, we do not have an accurate count of the number of legal proceedings instituted by Soviet occupation courts against German nationals between 1945 and 1949. According to legal historian Adalbert Rückerl, we can safely assume "that the number of those convicted was many times more than the aggregate number of persons sentenced by all the tribu-nals of the Western occupying powers together."[3] A report issued by the West German minister of justice in 1965 is more specific, estimating from a variety of Soviet sources that over ten thousand individuals sentenced by Soviet mili-tary tribunals were surrendered to East German officials in January 1950, three months after the founding of the German Democratic Republic.[4] Fortunately, for the purposes of this essay, documents from the KGB archives on the Sach-senhausen trial have recently been declassified, affording new opportunities to research war crimes prosecutions by Soviet officials and to build upon the few existing studies of the Soviet occupation.

The Soviet Military Administration of Germany (SMAD) was established on 6 June 1945 to oversee Germany's compliance with the unconditional surrender, to facilitate the implementation of the most important Allied decisions, to supervise denazification efforts,[5] and to bring suspected war criminals to justice.[6] For this task, the Soviets set up military tribunals in accordance with Control Council Law No. 10, passed by the Allies in December 1945 to streamline their code of prosecution. The tactics of these tribunals, however, were often severe:

> *The occupation of Eastern and Central Germany ushered in a virtually indiscriminate spate of arrest and imprisonment of all Germans considered by the Soviets to be dangerous. Tens of thousands were sent to penitentiaries, prisons, and concentration camps including, for example, Buchenwald, Sachsenhausen, Neubrandenburg, Mühlberg, and Bautzen. Starvation and in some cases torture were used there to extract "confessions" as the basis for trials by Soviet military tribunals, i.e., if the prisoners had not already died as a result of their privations, illnesses, and maltreatment. . . . Even ordinary German soldiers who had been taken prisoner appeared in their thousands before military tribunals, which usually sentenced them to uniform terms of 25 years imprisonment or in many cases to death after summary proceedings often built up on extorted confessions or simply the accused's membership in a certain military unit.[7]*

Sachsenhausen itself became an internment camp for captured Germans on 10 August 1945; the Soviets renamed it Special Camp Nr. 7 Under the MVD (the Soviet secret police). In 1946 the camp was divided into two zones, one for "political internees" (i.e., opponents of the Soviet regime, including Christian Democrats, Liberals, and Social Democrats), and the other for POWs and individuals later sentenced by Soviet tribunals. From the time of its inception to its closure at the beginning of 1950, the camp held over 50,000 Germans, 40 percent of whom died under deplorable conditions.[8] This was despite the fact that by 1948, in the midst of the escalating cold war, Soviet officials were recruiting individuals into service for the nascent East German state without regard to their antifascist credentials.[9]

Mistrust of the West also promoted a disengaged quality to Soviet war crimes prosecution. Soviet officials refused to join the United Nations War Crimes Commission and to cooperate with CROWCASS (the Central Registry of War Criminals and SS).[10] Moreover, they displayed little interest in handing over former Nazis to the other occupying powers. On the one occasion in which a transfer of prisoners did take place (an exchange of Sachsenhausen guards with the British in June 1946), Colonel-General I. A. Serov, the commander of the Soviet garrison in Berlin, refused all requests for British teams to investigate crimes in Soviet-occupied territory.[11] Alan Nightingale, a delegate of the British War Crimes Group, remembered that Serov "kept on chuckling . . . and calling me an intelligence agent, which of course I denied."[12]

Trial Preparations

For all their mistrust of the West, Soviet authorities did not dispute the legitimacy of either Control Council Law No. 10 or the Charter of the International Military Tribunal, agreed upon in the summer of 1945. In fact, they turned to both in their prosecution of Nazi crimes. Each defendant in the Sachsenhausen case stood accused of committing war crimes, crimes against peace, and crimes against humanity—all provisions of Law No. 10 and the Charter. Each defendant had the additional (and ironic) benefit of being sentenced under the Soviet penal code, which at the time had eliminated the death penalty as a component.

Arrests of individuals with direct ties to Sachsenhausen began as early as the German surrender in May 1945. Some of the defendants were already in Soviet prisoner of war camps, while others were arrested after having eluded authorities. Camp doctor Heinrich Baumkötter, for instance, was taken into custody after being recognized on a highway outside Helmstedt. SS Second Lieutenant and prison camp director August Höhn fell into Soviet hands as a result of the June 1946 transfer. In December 1946 the Soviets issued official arrest orders, jail orders, and search orders for sixteen individuals[13]:

1. Anton Kaindl—SS Colonel and Camp Commandant

2. August Höhn—SS Second Lieutenant and Prison Camp Director

3. Michael Körner—SS First Lieutenant and Camp Leader

4. Ludwig Rehn—SS Second Lieutenant and Work Detail Leader

5. Heinrich Baumkötter—SS First Lieutenant and Camp Doctor

6. Heinrich Freesemann—SS First Lieutenant and Director of the Subsidiary Camp's Brick Work Factory (*Klinkerwerke*)

7. Kurt Eccarius—SS Sergeant-Major and Cell Block Chief

8. Gustav Sorge—SS Sergeant-Major, Work Coordinator, and Director of the Subsidiary Camp Berlin-Lichterfelde

9. Wilhelm Schubert—SS Sergeant and Block Leader

10. Martin Knittler—SS Sergeant and Block Leader

11. Fritz Ficker—SS Sergeant and Block Leader

12. Menne Saathoff—SS Sergeant and Block Leader

13. Horst Hempel—SS Sergeant Second Class and Reporter

14. Dr. Ernst Brennscheidt—Reich Economics Ministry Official in charge of shoe testing at Sachsenhausen

15. Karl Zander—prisoner and Block Elder

16. Paul Sakowski—prisoner who became an executioner

Interrogations of the accused, some conducted with more than one defendant as a way of inducing confessions, began shortly thereafter.[14] On 27 December the Soviet Ministry for State Security created a commission to investigate the activities of the defendants. Headed by Dr. W. I. Prosorovski, with the assistance of five Soviet and three German forensic specialists, the commission was charged with researching and reporting on the living conditions of the camp, the mortality rate of the prisoners, the capacity of the crematorium and gas chamber, and the origins of ashes, hair, and dental crowns found by Soviet soldiers during liberation. Prosorovski's group had the additional task of estimating the total number of fatalities in the camp from 1936 to 1945.

On 10 January 1947 the commission issued its report. In the first part it described the structure of the camp—with particular regard to the shooting grounds and "Station Z," which held the gas chamber, the crematorium, and a facility where inmates were shot. The report then turned to living conditions in the camp and medical experiments, specifically the use of gas vans, testing of explosive bullets, and poisoning of inmates. Based on daily statistical reports, the commission concluded that approximately 100,000 inmates died in the camp between 1936 and 1945.[15] Despite the speed with which Prosorovski's group collated and published its findings, it took more than ten months before the Soviet Military Tribunal (SMT) issued indictments. This delay coincided with a period of legal confusion following the removal of the death penalty from the Soviet penal code in May 1947.[16]

The Case Presented

Five days after the SMT handed down indictments on 18 October 1947, the Sachsenhausen trial began. Justices N. J. Majorov, S. D. Klimovich, and W. A. Svonarev presided over the hearings. Twenty-seven eyewitnesses were called to testify, and Chief Prosecutor F. A. Beliaev presented extensive evidence of atrocities committed by the defendants. Seven days later, the prosecution rested and pleaded for life imprisonment for the accused, using the newly revised Soviet Penal Code instead of Control Council Law No. 10, as a gesture of Soviet "humanitarianism."

The basis for the life sentence plea was the extraordinary nature of the defendants' crimes. Prisoners in the camp endured unspeakable living conditions— the prevalence of disease, eleven-hour workdays, and starvation-level rations. According to camp physician Heinrich Baumkötter, "Sachsenhausen was incredibly overfilled. In the barracks, there were three-level bunk-beds, each for two prisoners. There were no mattresses. The prisoners' underwear was old and torn. Many of them had no over garments. Wearing leather shoes was forbidden, and so they were given wooden shoes."[17]

Medical exams following liberation showed that 417 out of 498 inmates were suffering from malnutrition, and of these, 122 had reached an incurable state. It was estimated that between 1936 and 1945, some 20,000 inmates had died of starvation alone.[18] Fatalities that could not be traced to starvation and disease were the result of a systematic program of execution involving mass shootings, hangings, gassings, and lethal experiments. August Kaindl gave a detailed description of this shooting process during his interrogation:

> The place for the execution of prisoners in our camp was a special room in the Industriehof (the so-called Station Z). It had two doors, one of which led to an exit, the other to the "death chamber," which was used for stacking up corpses. On the outside, this room looked like a sanitation room. In the room there was a normal device for

measuring the height of a person and an alphabet to check eyesight.
Over the scale of the measuring device was an opening of about two
centimeters wide which led into the next room, the shooting room
[also the room with the corpses].

The victim stood on the scale, allegedly to have his measurements
taken, and in a second, when the command "ready" was given, the
prisoner was shot in the neck through the gap in the wall.

The blood from the shooting was then hosed away. The corpse was
taken into the next room, the so-called morgue, and a new prisoner
was led into the shooting room. The procedure then began again.[19]

The execution of 18,000 Soviet prisoners in the fall of 1941, in which defendants
Höhn, Eccarius, Sorge, Schubert, and Ficker participated, also took place in the
infamous Station Z.[20]

Many POWs were killed in experimental gas vans as well. According to Gustav
Sorge: "The two gas vans . . . looked like mobile refrigerators. The vans had two
trailers. In the first there was an oven, to burn the corpses. The second, which
was open, was the conduit for the stock of fuel for the mobile crematorium.
Both the gas van and the trailers bore the label 'Reich Post Office.'"[21]

In 1943 a permanent gas chamber went into use in Station Z.[22] Made to appear like a shower, the chamber had an opening in the wall through which
preparations of hydrocyanic acid (Zyklon-A liquid capsules and Zyklon-B crys-
tals) were pumped. Because of a lack of specific evidence, it is impossible to
estimate the exact number of prisoners gassed at Sachsenhausen, but we do
know that the chamber was used infrequently. In September 1944 camp officials
began sending prisoners to other camps for gassing. By 1945, nearly 26,000 prisoners declared "unfit for labor" by Labor Director Ludwig Rehn had been sent
to their deaths in other concentration camps in Germany.[23]

Hangings in the camp were carried out on the shooting grounds (in front of
the cell block or *Zellenbau*). Three to four persons could be hanged at one time
on the stationary gallows. Paul Sakowski, the youngest of the defendants and
a prisoner who had been promoted to hangman, remembered that after each
execution he would put a nail into the base of the gallows as a sort of "death
count."[24] Sakowski further admitted that he and other executioners purpose-

fully dragged out the hangings to make them more painful.[25] Sakowski presents us with a truly disturbing case; not a fanatical Nazi, he had gone to Spain to fight against Franco. He was later arrested by German authorities and, upon his release from prison, was transferred to the Sachsenhausen *Klinkerwerke.* Sakowski ended up in an isolation cell for hitting a guard who was strangling a Jewish prisoner. After weeks in isolation, SS guards came to him and offered him the "job" of hangman, in return for better living conditions. Sakowski readily accepted. On Pentecost Monday in 1942 he carried out his first execution.[26]

Torture was also a grisly feature of daily life inside the camp. Kurt Eccarius, leader of the cell block, recalled that prisoners were often beaten, hosed with ice-cold water, and forced to run around the building barefoot in the dead of winter.[27] Ernst Brennscheidt, a non-SS government official, engaged in similar brutality as the head of the "Shoe Testing Branch," a division within the camp under the direction of the Reich Economics Ministry. Prisoners dragooned into the "Shoe Test" were forced to march back and forth on a designated stretch for a total of forty kilometers; they did so regardless of the weather and despite being weighed down with one hundred kilograms of ballast.[28] Finally, in the so-called Punishment Company, male prisoners were made to load heavy clay blocks onto carts for hours and were often required to stand in water up to their knees for a similarly long duration. Twelve to fifteen men from this "company" committed suicide daily.[29]

Medical experimentation was an additional method of execution. Supervised by Heinrich Baumkötter, these experiments included the testing of explosives, diseases, and harmful chemicals on inmates. Camp physicians often performed unnecessary surgery on healthy prisoners in order to give them blood poisoning and to experiment with anti-sepsis drugs.[30] In the summer of 1943, twenty-five such operations took place; eighteen resulted in fatalities. In 1944 Baumkötter initiated tests of a salve designed to heal skin burned by phosphorous. During these experiments, prisoners were strapped down onto a table and covered from head to toe with molten phosphorous. That same year, following orders from Himmler, Baumkötter tested lethal injections on four Soviet and Polish inmates. Poisonous capsules were injected into the lower abdomen of each, and within minutes all four were dead.[31]

Accounts of brutality cut across racial, political, cultural, and national lines:

in 1942, 250 Jews in the camp were shot following Heydrich's assassination.[32] That same year, 2 Jehovah's Witnesses were executed for not saluting Himmler.[33] In 1944, 27 political prisoners were shot and 200 were sent to Mauthausen concentration camp after guards discovered an illegal radio in the prisoners' barracks.[34] In 1945 camp officials began executing POWs from Britain, Luxembourg, the Netherlands, Poland, and the United States; in one case, an American flyer was shot by the defendant Freesemann for smoking a cigarette during his interrogation.[35]

The final atrocities for which the defendants stood accused were crimes committed during the camp's evacuation. On 1 February 1945, Gestapo chief Heinrich Müller ordered Kaindl to destroy the camp and liquidate its remaining prisoners. Finding the order impractical, Kaindl told his subordinates simply to kill all unfit and sick inmates.[36] In the span of two months, 5,000 prisoners were executed and an additional 16,000 were shipped to other concentration camps.[37] On 18 April the Inspector of Concentration Camps decreed that the remaining 45,000 prisoners in Sachsenhausen were to be marched to Lübeck, where they would be taken out to sea and drowned. Kaindl gave the additional order to shoot prisoners who, over the course of the death march, were no longer able to walk.[38]

The Tribunal's Verdict

After the prosecution rested on 30 October, the five attorneys assigned to the defense from Moscow began their short cross-examination, seeking to obtain milder sentences for their clients, who had already pleaded guilty. To that end, the defense lawyers frequently invoked pleas of duress (*Notstand*). S. K. Kasnatscheyev argued that his defendants, Kaindl and Höhn, had been forced to carry out criminal orders.[39] K. D. Tshishov (the defense attorney for Brennscheidt, Sakowski, and Zander) and N. T. Sidorenko (the defense counsel for Eccarius, Freesemann, Ficker, and Hempel) did the same.[40] Tshishov also reminded the court that defendants Zander and Sakowski had been prisoners in the camp.[41] In the pretrial interrogations, however, it was revealed that many of these defendants had committed deeds without receiving specific orders. Höhn had confessed to executing prisoners under these circumstances, and Kaindl had admitted to instituting the gas chamber partially on his own initiative.[42] Finally, N. P. Belov, who represented Körner, Baumkötter, Sorge, and Schubert, made an issue of the age of his defendants: at the time of Hitler's appointment as chancellor in 1933, Schubert was sixteen; Körner, eighteen; Baumkötter, twenty; and Sorge, twenty-one. Belov contended that, as youths, they had been particularly susceptible to Nazi propaganda.[43]

In the end, the arguments of the defense proved unpersuasive. Fourteen of the sixteen were given the most severe punishment allowed under Soviet law—life imprisonment. Brennscheidt and Zander received fifteen-year sentences, but the justices gave no explanation for these decisions in their final judgment. It is possible that Brennscheidt's non-SS status and Zander's commission of comparatively fewer atrocities played a role in mitigation.[44] Why Sakowski was not given a similar sentence but received life instead is unclear as well.

Viewed broadly, the Soviet tribunal was a curious mixture of rational jurisprudence and old-fashioned show trial. There were, for instance, discrepancies in some of the indictments and convictions. As an example, Höhn was convicted of shooting a group of Polish prisoners sometime in 1945, this despite a lack of evidence linking him to that crime on a specific date.[45] More problematic were the confessions, which, after one views Soviet newsreels of the proceedings, appear to have been extracted forcibly.[46] Although there is no evidence of this in the pretrial transcripts and although the defendants never made an accusation to that effect, even after they were handed over to German authorities in 1955, the unanimity of the guilty pleas is at best suspicious, at worst suggestive of torture. Still, had they wished to do so, the Soviets could have ignored their own criminal statutes and approached the case with an "off-with-their-heads" mentality, which they clearly did not do.

After the tribunal rendered its sentences, the sixteen defendants were remanded into Soviet custody and taken to prisons within the USSR. Five of the defendants, including camp commandant Kaindl, died shortly thereafter.[47] As hinted above, between 1955 and 1956, ten of the eleven remaining convicts were transferred to West Germany, where they were to serve out the rest of their sentences. Paul Sakowski was sent to East Germany. Those in the West German Federal Republic (FRG) had the benefit of being turned over to authorities who never recognized the legitimacy of the Soviet tribunal. The uproar sparked by the reprieves prompted state courts to investigate charges that many of the defendants' crimes had yet to be punished and might well be prosecuted now as murder, manslaughter, and so forth, under the existing German Penal Code. This decision to regard Nazi offenses as violations of German law instead of international law (e.g., the IMT Charter or Control Law No. 10) became a central feature of war crimes prosecution in West Germany.[48]

The Sachsenhausen Trials in West Germany, 1949–1970

The re-establishment of courts in Germany's western zones of occupation occurred within months of the Allied victory in Europe.[49] Although U.S. and British occupiers intended to inject elements of Anglo-American political culture into the "new" Germany, they permitted the German legal system to preserve its codified tradition. The prosecution of crimes was to revert back to the rules of the German Code of Criminal Procedures (*Strafprozessordnung* or StPO) of 1877 and the Penal Code (*Strafgesetzbuch*) of 1871. Nullifying specific laws enacted under Hitler and purging the judiciary of known or suspected Nazis, the Western Allies re-opened all ordinary courts (i.e., magistrate courts or *Amtsgerichte*, district courts or *Landgerichte*, and circuit courts, *Oberlandgerichte*) and the offices of the state attorney (*Staatsanwaltschaft*).[50] During the early stages of the occupation, the Allies permitted German courts to deal only with everyday crimes. While special courts (*Spruchkammer*) were set up to deal with the issue of denazification, Nazi war crimes remained primarily—although not exclusively—the preserve of Allied tribunals.[51]

Following the issuance of Control Council Law No. 10, German courts were permitted to try "crimes against humanity" committed by German nationals against other persons of German citizenship or nationality or against stateless persons. In cases involving crimes that already violated customary German law, such as murder, German courts could apply both the Penal Code and Law No. 10. The use of the latter, however, made the conviction of Nazi criminals easier by including deeds not previously prohibited by German law, removing distinctions between perpetrator and accomplice, rejecting the defense of superior orders, and providing for penalties higher than did the Penal Code. In 1955, six years after the establishment of the FRG, Law No. 10 was discontinued; thereafter, war crimes were prosecuted solely as violations of the 1871 Code. The *Landgerichte* became the venues for these trials, and most of them were presided over by a mixed court of both lay and professional judges.[52]

In the immediate postwar years, German courts in the Western zones tried Nazi crimes that primarily involved random acts of assault against Jews. Of the 5,228 individuals prosecuted by these tribunals between 1945 and 1949, roughly 100 warranted convictions for murder and manslaughter.[53] The lone Sachsenhausen trial that took place during the occupation years, the case against Franz Kernke, was one of the exceptions. Brought to trial by the *Landgericht* Berlin, Kernke was charged with committing crimes against humanity as defined by Control Council Law No. 10.[54] Kernke was a bookbinder who was interned in Sachsenhausen in 1942 after beating up an SS officer. In 1944, still in the camp, he became the leader of Block 38, a barracks of political and criminal prisoners. There he subjected inmates to frequent and severe whippings; on one occasion, he brought about the death of a Polish prisoner by hitting him seventy-two times on the back and head. Although Kernke admitted his offense, the Berlin court gave him a short, four-year prison term, mainly because it took into consideration the fact that he had been a prisoner and an alcoholic.[55]

As the cold war between the western Allies and the Soviet Union intensified and pressure to denazify diminished, the number of convictions against former Nazis in West Germany dropped—from over 1,500 in 1949 to 21 in 1955.[56] That same year a statute of limitations on crimes that could receive a maximum sentence of ten years went into effect.[57] Yet the trials of Nazi crimes that *did* take place in the early years of the West German republic, between 1950 and 1955, generally investigated more serious infractions, that is, capital offenses. Cases involving wrongful death fell under the sections of the Penal Code dealing with murder (Article 211), manslaughter (Article 212, paragraph 1), homicide in aggravated circumstances (Article 212, paragraph 2), depraved indifference with fatal consequences (Article 222), bodily harm with fatal consequences (Article 226), and unlawful detention with fatal consequences (Article 239, paragraph 3). Cases of physical assault that did not result in fatality included aggravated bodily injury (Article 223) and bodily harm with malice prepense (Article 225).

Distinguishing murder from manslaughter in cases of war crimes was a point of controversy in numerous hearings. Article 211 restricted the definition of murder to the killing of another person for a "thirst for blood, satisfaction of sexual desires, avarice, or other base motives (*niedrige Beweggründe*) in a malicious or brutal manner" or with concealment of the criminal act. The mandatory sentence for murder was life imprisonment (a provision that had an all-too-clear impact on the decisions of the courts).[58] Manslaughter, by way of contrast, was interpreted as wrongful killing that did not satisfy the "thirst for blood" or "base motives" conditions of Article 211. Sentences for manslaughter could not exceed fifteen years.[59] Whether to treat defendants as principals or accessories to crimes proved equally vexing for West German tribunals. Article 49 of the Penal Code classified anyone who aided the main perpetrator of a crime as an accomplice (or *Gehilfe*).[60] But after 1950 nearly all the judgments in cases of Nazi crimes indicated that those principally responsible were Hitler, Himmler, Heydrich, and other persons holding senior command posts. The courts regarded most everyone else, even those who had carried out executions, as accessories.[61]

Three of the four Sachsenhausen cases brought to trial in West Germany in the early 1950s involved charges of homicide.[62] In 1952 a regional court in Osnabrück indicted Bernhard Rakers, an SA official and one of the camp's cooks, on charges of murder, attempted murder, accessory to murder in five cases, and aggravated assault. Eyewitnesses testified that prisoners who worked in the kitchen were beaten (occasionally to death) by the defendant. Although the court dropped the assault charge, because of the statute of limitations, it imposed a life sentence plus fifteen years for his other crimes.[63]

The courts trying former prisoner K. and former camp official August Kolb were more lenient, although the defendants committed quantitatively more crimes. In each case the judges distinguished murder from manslaughter and classified the defendants as accomplices. Kolb was found guilty of both accessory to murder in one case and manslaughter in ten cases and sentenced to a light, four-year prison term; the court credited his two-year internment to his sentence. In the murder portion of the trial, Kolb stood accused of unlawfully hanging a young Ukrainian prisoner named Wassilenko, who had ripped up a dozen shoe soles earmarked for saddlebags. Witnesses testified that Kolb presided over Wassilenko's execution, making particular reference to its brutality. Before being led to the gallows, the young inmate was brought to a state of semi-consciousness after enduring fifty blows at the stockade. Concluding that Kolb had acted with malice prepense and "base motives," and the court categorized the Wassilenko episode as murder. At the same time, it held that ten similar instances of hangings under Kolb's auspices constituted manslaughter because they involved "true" saboteurs who threatened "camp discipline" and because they were not carried out in an excessively cruel manner.[64] Similarly, the court hearing the case of K., a career criminal whose informant network in Sachsenhausen led to the unlawful killing of seventeen political prisoners, charged the defendant with manslaughter—contending that he was deceived by the Gestapo, acted out of fear, and never personally demonstrated "base motives." K.'s sentence, eight years, was nonetheless higher than Kolb's.[65]

The prosecution of former Sachsenhausen guards in West Germany regained momentum after Soviet authorities released thousands of German prisoners of war in 1955–1956. Among those released were the defendants in the 1947 Soviet trial. Although initially freed, the former camp officials soon found themselves back in court. Gustav Sorge and Wilhelm Schubert stood trial in 1959 on additional charges of murder; August Höhn was re-tried in 1960, Heinrich Baumkötter and Kurt Eccarius in 1962.[66] In each case the courts ignored the rulings of the Soviet tribunal and justified bringing new charges by arguing that the defendants had violated aspects of the German Penal Code. Sorge, Schubert, and Höhn also stood trial as co-principals (*Mittäter*), unlike the general trend.[67]

On 6 February 1959 the regional court in Bonn gave Gustav Sorge and Wilhelm Schubert life sentences plus fifteen years for mass murder. Sorge was found guilty of murder (in sixty-seven cases), attempted murder (twenty cases), accessory to murder, and manslaughter. Schubert was convicted on forty-six counts of murder and eight counts of attempted murder. Despite sentencing Schubert to life, the court regarded him as less culpable, and he was released in 1987 for good behavior. Sorge, meanwhile, died in prison.[68]

In October 1960 the regional court in Düsseldorf found August Höhn guilty of murder in eight instances, accessory to murder in five instances, and accessory to manslaughter in two instances. The court regarded the killing of two prisoners who broke out of the camp as manslaughter, but not because it viewed their attempted escape as grounds for execution; rather, it took into consideration the fact that the fugitive prisoners had broken into a printing press and commissioned a Czech partisan to procure false identity papers, acts that, in the opinion of the court, constituted grounds for "severe punishment."

For his crimes, Höhn received a life sentence. The court sentenced Otto Böhm to life as well for murder in forty-one cases and accessory to murder in five others. It gave Horst Hempel, another original defendant in the Soviet trial, five years for accessory to murder but credited him with time served in prisons in the USSR.[69]

A few lesser-known officials from Sachsenhausen went on trial at the same time as the major criminals mentioned above. But while their crimes were no less heinous than those of Sorge, Höhn, and others, their sentences were comparatively lighter. In 1961 Albert Widmann, a chemist, was convicted as an accessory to murder for his involvement in a poison-gas pellet experiment in which five prisoners were murdered. In mitigation, the court ruled that Widmann was young and had no choice but to conduct the test. It sentenced him to five years imprisonment, a ruling that was set aside by the Supreme Court in 1962 and lowered to three years, six months that same year.[70] Widmann was later tried and convicted in 1967 for aiding in the development of gas vans, a crime for which he received a six-year, six-month sentence.[71]

Another "lesser" trial, the hearing against Otto Wessel, confronted the controversial issue surrounding the German statute of limitations (*Verjährung*) and sent an unclear message in the process. Pursuant to Article 67 of the Penal Code, crimes punishable by life were to be immune from prosecution after the passage of twenty years; crimes liable to a term of more than ten years, such as manslaughter, were to become immune after fifteen years. Because the limitations period for all Nazi offenses was set to begin on 8 May 1945, crimes such as manslaughter were to become statute-barred in May 1960. Wessel, in his trial, was convicted of accessory to murder in sixteen cases and sentenced to a seven-year, six-month prison term. He was found guilty of manslaughter in the unlawful shooting of a prisoner named Kunczevitz, but the court dismissed the charge because the statute of limitations had expired.[72]

Although the West German government had done little to prevent the statute of limitations from taking effect on manslaughter, it felt compelled to act as the date for limitations on the more serious offense of murder approached. At the end of March 1965, less than two months before the limitations deadline, the Bundestag voted to reset the starting date for felony murder at 31 December 1949. That meant that the statute of limitations was not to begin until the last day of December 1969. As that date approached, the Bundestag voted to extend the statutory period for murder to thirty years. In 1979, the German government finally decreed that there would be no statute of limitations for Nazi crimes involving murder.[73]

The last of the Sachsenhausen trials in West Germany took place between 1965 and 1970, and the rulings in four of these five cases were noticeably mild. Hans Zimmermann, convicted in 1969 by the regional court in Cologne for complicity in the deaths of Soviet POWs, received a one-year prison term because he had repented and had good character witnesses.[74] In 1970 Kurt Eccarius was retried and given a sentence of eight and a half years, the time he had served, despite his involvement in the unlawful shooting of Heinrich Petz, a prisoner whom Eccarius had forced into a restricted area of the camp in order to justify executing him.[75] In 1965 a Fulda court sentenced Erich Schemel to five years for "abetting" the killing of fourteen prisoners during the infamous "death march" from the camp, contending that he never killed anyone on his own initiative.[76] The German Supreme Court struck down the ruling a year later, and in his 1967 retrial Schemel was found guilty on only five of the fourteen counts. He was sentenced to a prison term of four and a half years, three of which the court credited as time served.[77] In another 1965 trial, eight of nine defendants convicted on multiple counts of accessory to murder received minor terms ranging from twelve to twenty-two months. The court believed that the defendants had acted under duress and demonstrated sufficient repentance for their crimes.[78] The only defendant to "warrant" a lengthy sentence was Otto Heinrich Kaiser, who was given fifteen years for attempted murder in six cases involving the deaths of Soviet prisoners.[79] Retried in 1969 on new charges, Kaiser and four others received harsher, life terms for mass murder, but these sentences were exceptional.[80]

West Germany's record of prosecuting former Sachsenhausen officials was mixed. Although regional courts brought numerous camp guards to trial, including those sentenced by the Soviet Military Tribunal in 1947, the accusations and punishments in many of those hearings did not fit the severity of the crimes. As we shall see, communist East Germany (the former German Democratic Republic, or GDR) prosecuted Nazi crimes differently from its Western counterpart—despite maintaining a similar court structure and adhering to roughly similar versions of the 1871 Penal Code.

Trials in East Germany

Research into war crimes trials in East Germany, an endeavor made possible only after German unification in 1990, is hampered by the same obstacle plaguing researchers into Soviet and West German tribunals, namely access to documentation. Adding to this difficulty is a dearth of legal commentary. One of the few repositories of information on East German trials is the Institute of Criminal Law at the University of Amsterdam, whose director, C. Frederik Rüter, oversaw the publication of the multivolume series on war crimes trials in West Germany, *Justiz und NS-Verbrechen*. Rüter is also one of the few individuals who have offered a general overview of war crimes prosecution in the GDR. This section uses trial indictments and judgments from the institute's files on Sachsenhausen to add nuance to his synopsis.[81]

Not surprisingly, some of the differences between prosecution in West and East Germany were political. The GDR was, after all, an outgrowth of the Soviet occupation zone and an essential component of the Communist bloc. In terms of law, socialist ideology was infused into the East German constitution.[82] East German jurists, under pressure from the ruling Socialist Unity Party (SED), made more of an effort to investigate the subjugation of Communists and Socialists.[83] In one egregious example, the so-called Waldheim Trials, they meted out justice in "kangaroo" courts: 3,224 former Nazi officials were convicted over the course of two and a half months in 1949 in trials that averaged only twenty minutes.[84]

However, much of the difference between prosecuting war crimes in East and West Germany was a matter of law, both in theory and practice.[85] The GDR may have followed the 1871 Penal Code like its Western counterpart and established a court structure parallel to that of the Federal Republic, but the similarities ended there. Up to the collapse of the GDR in 1990, East German officials prosecuted the vast majority of defendants accused of Nazi crimes as principals (not accessories) who had committed crimes against humanity (not murder or manslaughter). After Control Council Law No. 10 was repealed in 1955, East German jurists turned to the London Charter of the International Military Tribunal for legal justification. In 1968 they incorporated crimes against humanity and war crimes into their revised version of the 1871 Penal Code, something that the West Germans never did.[86] Moreover, despite prosecuting roughly the same number of individuals by the mid-1960s (approximately fourteen thousand), the GDR tried a higher proportion because its population was one-fourth that of the Federal Republic. The acquittal rate in East Germany was also much lower than in the West; indeed, after 1952 not a single defendant was acquitted in the GDR.[87] Where West Germany made more of an effort was in the prosecution of senior officials involved in the killing of Jews and non-Jews in occupied Eastern Europe. West German officials tried 110 members of the *Einsatzgruppen* and held 93 members of the concentration camp personnel of Auschwitz, Treblinka, Sobibor, and Majdanek. In East Germany, only 7 people were tried—6 from Auschwitz and 1 from Treblinka.[88]

In addition, until 1952, 53 percent of the trials in East Germany dealt with individuals who had denounced opponents of the Nazi regime. According to C. F. Rüter, this was five times higher than in West Germany.[89] One of the earliest Sachsenhausen trials in the GDR involved a woman who had denounced her cousin for making anti-Nazi remarks, a Ukrainian woman, and, in a bizarre twist, her husband. (She apparently mistook a note, which she discovered in one of his pairs of pants, for a love letter, whereupon she went to a guard at Sachsenhausen and told him that her husband, who worked in the camp laundry, was stealing. Her husband was subsequently incarcerated.) In 1948 the three professional judges and three lay judges (*Schöffen*) of the Eberswalde court determined that because the defendant evinced psychopathic tendencies and had herself been a prisoner in the Fehrbellin concentration camp, she warranted a light prison term of one and a half years.[90]

In the early Sachsenhausen trials, East German jurists indicted only former prisoners of the camp who became prison functionaries, for reasons that are unclear. The sentences in these cases were also disproportionately harsh—including the first death penalty we have so far encountered. In January 1949 the regional court in Chemnitz sentenced to death M. R., an alcoholic, ex-SA official incarcerated in Sachsenhausen who became a block elder, for fatally beating prisoners with a police truncheon.[91] Two years earlier a court in Plauen tried E. B., a morphine addict who was sterilized and then sent to Sachsenhausen, for crimes committed while also serving as a block elder. The court convicted him of crimes against humanity, sentencing him to life for beating and shooting inmates in Block 9 and for overseeing the transport of prisoners to Bergen-Belsen.[92] Sentences became more lenient over the course of 1949. In June a Potsdam court gave A. J., a career criminal interned in Sachsenhausen between 1938 and 1944, only six years for assault and battery during his tenure as an elder in Block 25.[93] And in a trial with clear ideological implications, a court in Schwerin sentenced W. H., a block elder with a communist past, to fifteen years for beating Jewish prisoners to death and gouging out their eyes.[94]

With the onset of the cold war and the establishment of the GDR in October 1949, the number of cases involving Nazi crimes dropped from approximately two hundred per year to an average of seven per year.[95] From available documentation at the University of Amsterdam Institute of Criminal Law, it appears that no one from Sachsenhausen was brought to trial again until the early 1960s. The defendants in these cases were, for the most part, lower-ranking SS officials, and their sentences were more severe than those handed down at the same time in West Germany—even harsher than those from the early days of the GDR. And they could have been worse.

In 1963 R. P., a deserter from the Czech army who joined the SS and was stationed in Sachsenhausen in 1938, was found guilty of crimes against humanity and sentenced to death for single-handedly executing 30 to 40 Soviet prisoners of war.[96] Five years later and by way of contrast, a regional court in Rostock gave its defendant a life sentence, even though it had convicted him of the murder of 3,000 Soviet POWs and 400 old and sick inmates.[97] In 1966 the same court imposed another life sentence on a defendant regarded as a fanatical and unrepentant Nazi. A. Z., an SS *Lagerschreiber* (camp clerk), was sentenced in the unlawful shootings of Soviet prisoners and British pilots.[98]

One of the higher-ranking officials from Sachsenhausen who stood trial in East Germany was Dr. O. H., a physician accused and convicted in 1965 of committing crimes against humanity for his involvement in the "euthanasia" program. H. was commissioned by Himmler in 1941, in accordance with the so-called "14f13" effort, to extend "euthanasia" killings to ill and exhausted camp inmates at Sachsenhausen; this technically placed him outside the authority of the camp's medical staff. His duties included selecting thirty prisoners at a time from work details for "mercy killing." In its final decision, the court sentenced H. to life, considering his repentance in mitigation.[99]

Conclusion

Central to the story of postwar war crimes prosecution has been the influence of the cold war and the politics of individual nations. The example of the Sachsenhausen trials confirms this complex relationship between law and politics. Soviet and East German officials combined the IMT Charter and Control Council Law No. 10 with their own penal codes (in many respects, as in the case of the Soviet tribunal, for political reasons), while the West Germans simply employed their own criminal statutes. At the same time, the severity of the punishments did not correspond to an immutable political pattern. The sentences handed down by West German courts were comparatively lighter than those from the totalitarian systems of East Germany and the Soviet Union, but not uniformly so. Conversely, verdicts from the latter nations were milder than one might have expected. Those seeking deeper insight into the interplay between law and politics in the prosecution of war crimes committed at Sachsenhausen might, for future research, focus on those individuals who were not brought to trial and the reasons they were able to escape indictment.

Notes

1. Gestapo to Prussian Forestry Office Sachsenhausen, 18 June 1936, Gedenkstätte Museum Sachsenhausen, Oranienburg. See also *Sachsenhausen: Dokumente, Aussagen, Forschungsergebnisse, und Erlebnisberichte über das ehemalige KZ Sachsenhausen* (Berlin: VEB Deutscher Verlag der Wissenschaften, 1986), and *Damals in Sachsenhausen: Solidarität und Widerstand im KZ Sachsenhausen* (Berlin: Kongress Verlag, 1961). It should be noted that one of the first "wild camps" of the Nazi regime was located in Oranienburg. Viewed as the predecessor to Sachsenhausen, it was shut down in 1935.
2. The Subsequent Nuremberg Trial No. 9, *U.S. v. Otto Ohlendorf et al.*, for instance, lasted nearly seven months, from September 1947 to April 1948.
3. Adalbert Rückerl, *The Investigation of Nazi Crimes, 1945–1978: A Documentation* (Hamden CT: Archon Books, 1980), p. 30.
4. Report of the Federal Minister of Justice to the Bundestag President, 26 February 1965, Bundestag Documents, Doc. 1V 3124, p. 10f, and Rückerl, *Investigation of Nazi Crimes*, p. 30.
5. Moreover, although the Soviets allowed German courts to deal with nominal and low-ranking Nazi officials (as Western officials did), they often lost patience with the pace of proceedings, took them over, and punished the defendants by themselves.
6. The extent to which SMAD accomplished these goals efficiently is another matter. The Soviet occupation was above all chaotic and uncoordinated—cluttered with a multitude of administrative units that shared authority without a clear sense of hierarchy. Norman M. Naimark, *The Russians in Germany: A History of the Soviet Zone of Occupation, 1945–1949* (Cambridge MA: Harvard University Press, 1995), pp. 11–21. See also Peter

Strunk, "Die sowjetische Militäradministration in Deutschland und ihr politischer Kon-trollapparat," *Historische und Landeskundliche Ostmitteleuropa-Studien 7* (1991): 143–76; Alexander Fischer, ed., *Studien zur Geschichte der SBZ/DDR* (Berlin, 1993); David Pike, *The Politics of Culture in Soviet-Occupied Germany* (Stanford CA: Stanford University Press, 1992); and Gregory Sandford, *From Hitler to Ulbricht: The Communist Reconstruction in East Germany, 1945–1946* (Princeton: Princeton University Press, 1983).

7. Bundestag Document 4 3124, quoted from Rückerl, *Investigation of Nazi Crimes*, p. 30.

8. *Alltag im KZ: Das Lager Sachsenhausen bei Berlin*, pp. 142, 143; Günter Agde, *Sachsen-hausen bei Berlin: Speziallager Nr. 7, 1945–1950* (Berlin: Henschel, 1987); Gerhard Finn, *Sachsenhausen 1936–1950* (Bad Münstereifel: Westkreuz Verlag, 1988); Bodo Ritscher, "Die NKVD/MVD 'Speziallager' in Deutschland—Anmerkungen zu einem Forschungs-gegenstand," and Eva Ochs, "Mit dem Abstand von vier Jahrzehnten: Zur lebensge-schichtlichen Verarbeitung des Aufenthalts in sowjetischen 'Speziallagern,'" both in *In-ternierungspraxis in Ost-und Westdeutschland nach 1945*, ed. Renate Knigge-Tesche et al. (Erfurt: Eichborn, 1993).

9. Soviet Command 201, issued in August 1947, was intended to speed up the entire denazi-fication process by 1948. Ruth Kristin Rössler, *Die Entnazifizierungspolitik der KPD/SED 1945–1949* (Goldbach: Keip, 1994), and Norman M. Naimark, "To Know Everything and to Report Everything Worth Knowing: Building the East German Police State, 1945–1949," Woodrow Wilson Center, Cold War International History Project Working Paper, August 1994, p. 3.

10. Tom Bower, *The Pledge Betrayed: America and Britain and the Denazification of Postwar Germany* (New York: Doubleday, 1982), p. 202.

11. The Soviets also never gave the British the men they promised in exchange for the Sach-senhausen guards. Bower, *Pledge Betrayed*, p. 203.

12. Ironically, the Soviets were among the most vocal opponents of a U.S.-imposed mora-torium on extraditions from the American zone, which took effect on 1 November 1947. According to Tom Bower, apart from Poland, international criticism of the mora-torium was the loudest from the two nations that had done the least to track down suspected war criminals, namely France and the Soviet Union. On 1 November, the day after the Sachsenhausen verdicts, U.S. Military Governor Lucius Clay received a letter from Soviet General Vassily Sokolovsky demanding the extradition of 31 Germans "guilty of the mass killing of peaceful citizens." This request actually reflected more the disorganization of the Soviets than their suspicion of the West: 3 of the 31 were being held by the British, while the other 28 were being tried by the Americans in their subse-quent tribunals. Bower suspects that a member of Sokolovsky's staff, lacking a central war crimes bureau, simply listed the names easiest at hand. In the end, the Soviets ex-tradited only 45 suspects, compared to nearly 4,000 by the Americans. Bower, *Pledge Betrayed*, pp. 203, 217.

13. Facsimiles of these orders, plus biographical sketches (*aketa arrestovannogo*), are in each of the defendants' files in the KGB Archives Collection. KGB Archive Collection, Folders 1460–1546, N19092 Tom 1, RG 06.025, United States Holocaust Memorial Museum, Washington DC (hereafter USHMM).

14. See, for instance, interrogation of Anton Kaindl and August Höhn, 21 December 1946, Folder 1601, interrogation of Kaindl and Heinrich Baumkötter, 22 December 1946, Folder 1602, and interrogation of Höhn and Michael Körner, 21 December 1946, in KGB Collection, Folders 1601–22, N19092, Tom 6 (in German), RG 06.025, USHMM.

15. Agde, *Sachsenhausen*, pp. 237, 238.

16. The death penalty was reinstated in 1951.

17. Testimony of Heinz Baumkötter in the Soviet Military Tribunal Indictment, 19 October 1947, in KGB Collection, p. 20, N19092, Tom 61, RG 06.025, USHMM.

18. SMT Indictment, p. 23.

19. According to defendants Ficker and Hempel, during these executions, music was played in the morgue to drown out the sound of the pistol fire. SMT Indictment, pp. 4, 5, 10, and Kaindl interrogation, 20 December 1946, in KGB Collection, pp. 1–44, Folder 1548, N19092, Tom 2, RG 06.025, USHMM.

20. SMT Indictment, pp. 9–13, and Höhn interrogation, 19 December 1946, in KGB Collection, pp. 1–33, Folder 1549, N19092, Tom 2, RG 06.025, USHMM.

21. Sorge maintained that gas vans were already being used in Sachsenhausen in 1938, but there is nothing to corroborate his testimony. SMT Indictment, p. 7; Ernst Klee, *Dokumente zur Euthanasie* (Frankfurt am Main: Fischer Verlag, 1992), p. 69; and Adalbert Rückerl, *NS-Vernichtungslager im Spiegel deutscher Strafprozesse* (Munich: Deutscher Taschenbuch Verlag, 1977), p. 268, n. 55.

22. Kaindl interrogations, KGB Collection, and Kaindl interrogation in *Todeslager Sachsenhausen: Ein Dokumentarbericht vom Sachsenhausen-Prozess* (Berlin: SWA-Verlag, 1948), p. 66.

23. Ludwig Rehn interrogation, in *Todeslager Sachsenhausen*, p. 90.

24. SMT Indictment p. 5.

25. SMT Indictment p. 5.

26. *Alltag im KZ*, pp. 136, 137; and eyewitness Harry Naujoks, *Mein Leben im KZ-Sachsenhausen 1936–1942* (Cologne: Röderberg, 1987), pp. 308ff.

27. Kurt Eccarius interrogation, in *Todeslager Sachsenhausen*, p. 78.

28. Ernst Brennscheidt interrogation, in *Todeslager Sachsenhausen*, pp. 92, 93.

29. In the "Standing Commandos," prisoners were also forced to stand for nine to ten hours at a stretch. The defendant Zander recalled that Gustav Sorge once forced all 28,000 inmates to stand at attention for twelve hours because a prisoner was absent during roll call. Ficker testimony in SMT Indictment, p. 22, and Zander testimony, p. 21.

30. Interrogation of Baumkötter, 21 December 1946, in KGB Collection, pp. 1–22, Folder 1552, N19092, Tom 2, RG 06.025, USHMM; and SMT Indictment, p. 8.

31. SMT Indictment, pp. 8–9.

32. Sakowski testimony, SMT Indictment, p. 18.

33. Eccarius testimony, SMT Indictment, p. 18.

34. Höhn testimony, SMT Indictment, p. 17.

35. Höhn testimony and Freesemann interrogation, SMT Indictment, p. 14.

36. Kaindl interrogation, in *Todeslager Sachsenhausen*, pp. 67, 68.

37. SMT Indictment, p. 27.

38. In February 1945 SS-*Obergruppenführer* Heissmeyer ordered Kaindl to dispose of the ashes of corpses and to begin falsifying records to say that executed prisoners had actually died of natural causes. Kaindl testimony, SMT Indictment, pp. 26, 27.

39. Kasnatscheyev closing statement, in *Todeslager Sachsenhausen*, pp. 145, 151.

40. Tshishov closing statement, in *Todeslager Sachsenhausen*, p. 171, and Sidorenko closing statement, in *Todeslager Sachsenhausen*, pp. 191–93.

41. Tshishov statement, in *Todeslager Sachsenhausen*, pp. 173, 176.

42. During his interrogation, Kaindl admitted to holding a conference in March 1943 in

which he and head doctor Baumkötter chose to construct a gas chamber because the methods of execution in the camp no longer sufficed. This followed general instructions to that effect by Richard Glücks, the Inspector of Concentration Camps. *Todeslager Sachsenhausen*, pp. 66, 71; Kaindl testimony, in SMT Indictment, p. 6; and Eugen Kogon et al., eds., *Nazi Mass Murder: A Documentary History of the Use of Poison Gas* (New Haven CT: Yale University Press, 1993), p. 184.

43. W. N. Gavrilov, who represented Rehn, Knittler, and Saathoff, also made references to the power of Nazi propaganda. Belov closing statement, in *Todeslager Sachsenhausen*, pp. 155, 156; and Gavrilov closing statement, in *Todeslager Sachsenhausen*, pp. 181, 182.

44. Judgment of the SMT, 1 November 1947, in *Todeslager Sachsenhausen*, p. 214; and KGB Collection, pp. 18, 19, Folder 2246, N19092, Tom 48, RG 06.025, USHMM.

45. *Todeslager Sachsenhausen*, p. 204; and Agde, *Sachsenhausen*, p. 245.

46. "Berlinskij Prozess," Documentary Film of the Sachsenhausen Trial, Gedenkstätte und Museum Sachsenhausen.

47. The date of Kaindl's death is known only by Russian authorities. Körner died in February 1948, Freesemann and Saathoff in the spring, Ficker in June. Agde, *Sachsenhausen*, pp. 245, 246.

48. See Rebecca Wittmann, "Tainted Law: The West German Judiciary and the Prosecution of Nazi War Criminals," in this volume.

49. Allied Control Council Law No. 4, "Reorganization of the German Judiciary System," was issued on 30 October 1945. It took effect one month later. Rückerl, *Investigation of Nazi Crimes*, p. 32.

50. The Soviets excluded all Nazi judges and put in people who were not qualified but politically reliable. The British implemented a 50/50 rule, whereby every unimplicated, that is non-Nazi, jurist could bring in one Nazi jurist. Courts in the American and French zones, meanwhile, were slow to commence functioning because they had difficulties finding qualified jurists who had not been Nazi Party members. Henry Friedlander, "The Judiciary and Nazi Crimes in Postwar Germany," *Simon Wiesenthal Center Annual* 1 (1984): 28.

51. Dick de Mildt, *In the Name of the People: Perpetrators of Genocide in the Reflection of Their Post-War Prosecution in West Germany: The "Euthanasia" and "Aktion Reinhard" Trial Cases* (The Hague: Martinus Nijhoff, 1996), pp. 22, 23; Henry Friedlander, "The Deportation of the German Jews: Postwar German Trials of Nazi Criminals," *Leo Baeck Institute Yearbook* 29 (1984): 202; Karl Loewenstein, "Reconstruction of the Administration of Justice in American-Occupied Germany," *Harvard Law Review* 61 (1948): 419–67; and Eli Nobleman, "The Administration of Justice in the United States Zone of Germany," *Federal Bar Journal* 8 (1946): 70–97.

52. Before German reunification in 1990, there were ninety-three *Landgerichte* in West Germany. The Criminal Division of the *Landgericht* was organized into two chambers, one small and one large. The small chamber, made up of one professional and two lay judges, heard appeals from the *Amtsgerichte*, while the large chamber, made up of three professional and two lay judges, heard indictable offenses at first instance. Cases of unlawful killings were usually presented before a jury, but most of the capital war crimes trials had mixed courts. Nigel Foster and Satish Sule, *German Law and Legal System* (Oxford: Oxford University Press, 1993), pp. 39, 85, 86.

53. Rückerl, *Investigation of Nazi Crimes*, p. 39, and Jadwiga Gorzkowska et al., *Nazi Criminals before West German Courts* (Warsaw: Zachodnia Agencja Prasowa, 1965), p. 19.

54. This case, held in Berlin, was technically under Four Power jurisdiction.

55. *Strafsache gegen Franz Kernke*, LG Berlin, 1 November 1948, Lfd. Nr. 93, in *Justiz und NS-Verbrechen* (Amsterdam: University Press Amsterdam, 1969), vol. 3, pp. 339–41 (hereafter *JuNSV*).

56. Rückerl, *Investigation of Nazi Crimes*, pp. 43, 44.

57. Rückerl, *Investigation of Nazi Crimes*, p. 46.

58. Art. 211, par. 1 and 2, *German Penal Code of 1871*, trans. Gerhard O. W. Mueller and Thomas Buergenthal (South Hackensack NJ: F.B. Rothman, 1961), p. 113.

59. Art. 212, par. 1 and 2, *German Penal Code*, p. 113.

60. Art. 49, par. 1 and 2, *German Penal Code*, p. 39.

61. See Rückerl, *Investigation of Nazi Crimes*, pp. 42–43; Friedlander, "Judiciary and Nazi Crimes"; and Wittmann, "Tainted Law"; and Jürgen Matthäus, "'No Ordinary Criminal': Georg Heuser, Other Mass Murderers, and West German Justice," in this volume.

62. The case against defendant R. was dismissed due to lack of evidence. LG Hamburg, 24 September 1952, Lfd. Nr. 327, in *JuNSV*, vol. 10, pp. 127, 130.

63. *Strafsache gegen Bernhard Rakers*, LG Osnabrück, 10 February 1953, Lfd. Nr. 340, in *JuNSV*, vol. 10, pp. 349, 353, 389–91.

64. *Strafsache gegen August Heinrich Kolb*, LG Nürnberg-Fürth, 13 October 1954, Lfd. Nr. 405, in *JuNSV*, vol. 12, pp. 648–53.

65. Similar to the Kolb case, however, two years of internment were deducted from K.'s sentence. The German Supreme Court refused to overturn the judgments in either case. In 1961 Kolb was tried and convicted on an additional charge of assault with fatal consequences. He received a six-year prison sentence. *Strafsache gegen K.*, LG Deggendorf, 1 March 1954, Lfd. Nr. 394, in *JuNSV*, vol. 12, pp. 269, 270, 292, 294, 297, 299–304 and Kolb, in *JuNSV*, vol. 12, p. 637, LG Nürnberg-Fürth, 16 March 1961, Lfd. Nr. 504, in *JuNSV*, vol. 17.

66. In 1962 Baumkötter was convicted of accessory to murder in two cases and depraved indifference in fourteen cases. The regional court in Münster sentenced him to eight years but credited him with time served in the Soviet Union. That same year the *Landgericht* Coburg gave Kurt Eccarius four years for manslaughter and attempted manslaughter. Martin Knittler, meanwhile, escaped prosecution by committing suicide in his prison cell in Bonn on 13 July 1958. *Strafsache gegen Heinrich Baumkötter et al.*, LG Münster, 19 February 1962, Lfd. Nr. 529, in *JuNSV*, vol. 17, pp. 219–332, and Agde, *Sachsenhausen*, p. 246.

67. Richard Bugdalle, a Block Leader at Sachsenhausen was also tried as a co-principal in his 1960 murder hearing. He was found guilty of beating a prisoner to death and sentenced to life. *Strafsache gegen Richard Bugdalle*, LG München, 20 January 1960, Lfd. Nr. 488, in *JuNSV*, vol. 16, pp. 277–89.

68. *Strafsache gegen Gustav Sorge and Wilhelm Schubert*, LG Bonn, 6 February 1959, Lfd. Nr. 473, in *JuNSV*, vol. 15, pp. 415, 416, 653–58.

69. *Strafsache gegen August Höhn, Otto Böhm, and Horst Hempel*, LG Düsseldorf, 15 October 1960, Lfd. Nr. 497, in *JuNSV*, vol. 16, pp. 611, 612, 639–40, 718–20.

70. *Strafsache gegen Albert Widman*, LG Düsseldorf, 16 May 1961, LG Düsseldorf, 10 October 1962, and Bundesgerichthof, 21 February 1962, Lfd. Nr. 542, in *JuNSV*, vol. 18, pp. 690, 691, 703.

71. LG Stuttgart, 15 September 1967, Ks 19/62, not published.

72. *Strafsache gegen Otto Wessel*, LG Verden, 6 June 1961, Lfd. Nr. 537, in *JuNSV*, vol. 18, pp. 497, 559–63.

73. On the importance of statutes of limitations see Wittmann, "Tainted Law."

74. *Strafsache gegen Hans Zimmermann,* Schwurgericht Köln, 20 January 1969, Case 719, pp. 2, 10. Unpublished cases, University of Amsterdam, Institute of Criminal Law.

75. *Strafsache gegen Kaspar Drexl, Franz Ettlinger, and Kurt Eccarius,* LG München, 21 September 1970, Case 721, pp. 1, 15, 89, 90. Unpublished cases, University of Amsterdam, Institute of Criminal Law. Ettlinger was acquitted, and Drexl was sentenced to four years time served.

76. *Strafsache gegen Erich Schemel,* LG Fulda, 15 October 1965, Lfd. Nr. 598, in *JuNSV,* vol. 22, p. 289.

77. *JuNSV,* vol. 22, pp. 272–82.

78. *Strafsache gegen Otto Kaiser et al.,* 28 May 1965, LG Köln, Lfd. Nr. 591, in *JuNSV,* vol. 21, pp. 67, 68, 138, 139, 149, 151. Former SS-*Hauptscharführer* Friedrich Meyerhoff was convicted of accessory to murder in four cases and given one and a half years. Paul Strunk, also a former SS-*Hauptscharführer,* was given one year for accessory to murder in one instance. Kurt Hickl was sentenced to one year and eight months for accessory to murder in three cases. SS-*Oberscharführer* Johann Sosnowski received one year for accessory to murder in one instance. SS-*Hauptscharführer* Alfred Klein was given one year and ten months for accessory to murder in one instance. Werner Krämer received one year and eight months for accessory in five cases. Willi Wöhe was given one year and three months for accessory in three cases, while Heinrich Meier received one year and six months for accessory to murder in four instances.

79. *Strafsache gegen Otto Kaiser et al.,* 28 May 1965, LG Köln, Lfd. Nr. 591, in *JuNSV,* vol. 21, pp. 67–68.

80. *Strafsache gegen Otto Kaiser et al.,* LG Köln, 20 January 1969, Case 729, Judgment. BGH, 2 August 1962, pp. 2, 3. Unpublished cases, University of Amsterdam, Institute of Criminal Law. The other life sentences went to Richard Hoffmann, Erwin Seifert, Willy Busse, and Josef Nägele. Kurt Simke received a ten-year sentence for attempted murder. Heinz Willi Beerbaum and Artur Braun were acquitted. In August 1972 the Supreme Court temporarily suspended Busse's sentence on two counts because it determined that the lower court had not sufficiently proved Busse's guilt.

81. The USHMM has recently acquired from German archives (*Bundesarchiv; Bundesbeauftragte für die Unterlagen des Staatssicherheitsdienstes der ehemaligen DDR*) copies of documentation compiled by East German courts and prosecutors' offices on the adjudication of Nazi crimes. This material was not available to me at the time of the writing of this essay.

82. Even the study of constitutional law in East Germany was susceptible to political repression. The discipline was banned from 1958 to 1972. See Wolfgang Bernet, "Entwicklung und Zustand der Verwaltungsrechtswissenschaft der DDR," *Staat* 29 (1990): 389–405.

83. The SED or *Sozialistische Einheitspartei,* was a fusion of the Communist and Social Democratic Parties.

84. C. F. Rüter, "The Trials of Nazi Criminals in East Germany," unpublished paper, p. 5; and Kurt Pätzold, "NS-Prozesse in der DDR," in *Vereint vergessen? Justiz-und NS-Verbrechen in Deutschland* (Düsseldorf: Landeszentrale für politische Bildung, 1993), p. 41.

85. This is contrary to the arguments of Otto Kirchheimer, who believes that the GDR was a state where politics unduly influenced the application of law. Kirchheimer, *Politische Justiz* (Princeton: Princeton University Press, 1961). For a left-wing critique of this thesis, see Uwe Jens Hewer and Michael Schumann, "Politik und Justiz in der Auseinan-

dersetzung um die DDR Geschichte," and Ingo Wagner, "War die DDR-ein Unrechts-staat?" both in *Unrechtsstaat: Politische Justiz und die Aufarbeitung der DDR-Vergangenheit*, ed. Lothar Bisky et al. (Hamburg: VSA-Verlag, 1994). See also Inge Markovits, *Imperfect Justice: An East/West German Diary* (Oxford: Oxford University Press, 1995); John Daniel Meador, *Impressions of Law in East Germany: Legal Education and Legal Systems in the GDR* (Charlottesville: University of Virginia, 1986); and Erika Lieser-Triebnigg, *Recht in der DDR: Einführung und Dokumentation* (Cologne: Landeszentrale für Politische Bildung, 1985).

86. See paragraphs 91 and 93 of the Revised Penal Code of 1968.

87. Rüter, "Trials of Nazi Criminals in East Germany," pp. 1–12.

88. Rüter, "Trials of Nazi Criminals in East Germany," pp. 10, 11.

89. Rüter, "Trials of Nazi Criminals in East Germany," p. 10.

90. *Strafsache gegen M. H.*, LG Eberswalde, 23 March 1948, Dossier 3232–1230, Indictment, p. 12, and Judgment, pp. 1, 5, 6. Unpublished cases, University of Amsterdam, Institute of Criminal Law.

91. *Strafsache gegen M. R.*, LG Chemnitz, 24 January 1949, Dossier 3232–1431. Unpublished cases, University of Amsterdam, Institute of Criminal Law.

92. *Strafsache gegen E. B.*, LG Plauen, 30 May 1947, Dossier 3232–1096, Judgment, p. 12. Unpublished cases, University of Amsterdam, Institute of Criminal Law.

93. His sentence was upheld on appeal in 1950 by an appeals court in Potsdam. *Strafsache gegen A. J.*, LG Potsdam, 14 September 1949, and Appeal, 13 February 1950, Dossier 3232–1598. Unpublished cases, University of Amsterdam, Institute of Criminal Law.

94. *Strafsache gegen W. H.*, LG Schwerin, 9 June 1949, Dossier 3232–1527, Judgment, pp. 1, 2, 4. Unpublished cases, University of Amsterdam, Institute of Criminal Law.

95. Rüter, "Trials of Nazi Criminals in East Germany," p. 11.

96. The East German Supreme Court (*Oberstes Gericht*—in West Germany, *Bundesgerichtshof*) overturned the lower court's ruling that the defendant had committed crimes against the peace, arguing that he was in no position to commit such a crime. *Strafsache gegen R. P.*, LG Neubrandenburg, 16 December 1963, Dossier 3232–2031, Judgment, pp. 1, 15, 19, 20, Revision from the East German Supreme Court, 17 January 1964, p. 15. Unpublished cases, University of Amsterdam, Institute of Criminal Law.

97. *Strafsache gegen P. B.*, LG Rostock, 28 June 1968, Dossier 3232–2045, Judgment, p. 1, 45. Unpublished cases, University of Amsterdam, Institute of Criminal Law.

98. *Strafsache gegen A. Z.*, LG Rostock, 3 June 1966, Dossier 3232–2039, Judgment, pp. 1, 31, 32, 49, 50, East German Supreme Court, 2 September 1966, Judgment upheld, p. 1. Unpublished cases, University of Amsterdam, Institute of Criminal Law.

99. *Strafsache gegen Dr. O. H.*, LG Cottbus, 12 July 1965, Dossier 3232–2036, Indictment, p. 11, Judgment, pp. 1, 29, 30. Unpublished cases, University of Amsterdam, Institute of Criminal Law. See also Walter Grode, *Die "Sonderbehandlung 14f13" in den Konzentrationslagern des Dritten Reiches* (Frankfurt/Main: Lang, 1987), pp. 86, 87; and Patricia Heberer, "Early Postwar Justice in the American Zone: The 'Hadamar Murder Factory' Trial," in this volume.

III

Postwar Society and the Nazi Past

"No Ordinary Criminal"
Georg Heuser, Other Mass Murderers, and West German Justice

JÜRGEN MATTHÄUS

During West Germany's formative period, dealing with the criminal record of the Nazi past played a key role in the process of nation-building. Rampant, if tacit, compliance and widespread complicity on the part of large sectors of German society during the war had accompanied, as well as facilitated, systematic mass murder of unprecedented proportions. After 1945 West German elites—most notably politicians, jurists, and law enforcement officers—viewed Allied attempts at adjudicating Nazi crimes with great skepticism. It took a decade after the founding of the Federal Republic of Germany in 1949 for the state to establish mechanisms that facilitated thorough investigations of the crimes and their perpetrators. By that time many of the agents of genocide had found a safe haven in the very profession that had helped execute these crimes and that was now called upon to bring about a measure of justice.

The case of Georg Heuser exemplifies this phenomenon. Heuser, born in 1913, was a Gestapo officer during the war and was involved in the deportation and killing of thousands of civilians, primarily Jews, in the occupied Soviet Union and in Slovakia. After the end of the "Third Reich," he obscured his Gestapo career and in the early 1950s rejoined the police in the state of Rhineland-Palatinate (Rheinland-Pfalz), where he finally became the head of the criminal police. In mid-1959 Heuser was arrested, and in late 1962, together with some of his former fellow officers, he was put on trial in the city of Koblenz. The investigations, the trial, and its aftermath highlight some of the problems inherent in West Germany's dealing with wartime mass murder and its agents.[1]

Heuser's Career before and after 1945

At the beginning of the war, Georg Heuser was twenty-six years old, a lawyer by training and a policeman by profession. Since Hitler's coming to power, the German police functioned as the executor of Nazi policies, a development intensified by the appointment of *Reichsführer-SS* Heinrich Himmler in 1936 as chief of the German police. As a result of Germany's victorious military campaigns in 1939 and 1940, policemen of all trades—members of the Gestapo, criminal and order police (*Ordnungspolizei*) officers—were in high demand in the occupied countries of Eastern and Western Europe. Here, in addition to the Wehrmacht, the police played a decisive role in maintaining German law and order.[2] Following his exam at the "*Führerschule*" of the Security Police in Berlin-Charlottenburg, Heuser joined the SS and was transferred to the capital crimes section of the Berlin criminal police (*Kriminalpolizei*).

After his promotion to the rank of SS second lieutenant (*SS-Untersturm-führer*) in early 1941 and to superintendent of the criminal police in fall 1941, Heuser was attached to a subunit of *Einsatzgruppe* A. With the beginning of "Operation Barbarossa" on 22 June 1941, this special task force of the Security Police and the SD followed, as did the other three *Einsatzgruppen*, the advancing German army into the Soviet Union, where it helped execute the emerging "Final Solution."[3] With bloody effectiveness, the fewer than 1,000 men of *Einsatzgruppe* A, led by SS Brigadier General Dr. Walter Stahlecker, and their local auxiliaries swept through the Baltic States and parts of Belorussia. In mid-October *Einsatzgruppe* A reported that they had already killed 128,432 Jews. By February 1942, the death toll recorded by Stahlecker's unit had reached 229,052 Jews.[4]

When Heuser joined *Sonderkommando* 1b in Riga, this detachment of *Einsatzgruppe* A was about to be relocated to Minsk in Belorussia and integrated into the newly established civil administration under Alfred Rosenberg, the Reich minister for the occupied eastern territories. The western part of Belorussia came to be called Generalkommissariat Weißruthenien (GKW) and formed, together with the Baltic States, under Hinrich Lohse the *Reichskommissariat Ostland*—an artificial administrative entity created (like the adjacent *Reichskommissariat Ukraine*) to systematically subjugate, exploit, and "pacify" this vast area. Step by step, the mobile units of the *Einsatzgruppen* were transformed into stationary posts of the Security Police and the SD within the area under civil administration. The Wehrmacht, the German railways, and a variety of other agencies established offices in Minsk, the capital of the GKW. Heuser and his colleagues set up the office of the Commander of the Security Police and SD (*Kommandeur der Sicherheitspolizei und des SD*, or KdS) headed first by the chief of *Sonderkommando* 1b, SS-Lieutenant Colonel Erich Ehrlinger and, after early 1942 until mid-1943, by Eduard Strauch.[5]

Georg Heuser, by then SS first lieutenant (SS-*Obersturmführer*), remained in charge of KdS Division IV—Gestapo—until fall 1943 when he took over a special assignment investigating the thriving partisan movement. In a number of cities, the KdS established outposts that reported to Heuser's office. Given the imbalance between manpower and space, relatively few Germans could be deployed in these towns, fewer still in rural areas. It was only by causing massive terror and through the help of non-German collaborators that control could be exerted temporarily.[6] In 1944 the advancing Red Army drove the Germans out of the Ostland; along with the retreating Wehrmacht, Heuser escaped from Minsk on 1 July 1944.

From early 1942 until the German retreat, those responsible for the implementation of the "Final Solution" as well as for the "pacification" of the region worked in close cooperation with other branches of the occupation apparatus. They applied various means of mass murder—primarily executions, but also gassings by so-called gas vans developed by police technicians in Berlin. Although Minsk differed in many respects from the extermination camps in Poland, the killing process unfolded with the same effectiveness. Of the approximately 100,000 inmates of the Minsk ghetto, 3,000 to 4,000 survived, and an unknown number managed to escape to the woods. Of the nearly 22,000 Jews deported to Minsk, about 30 lived to see the German retreat. The other ghettos in the GKW were systematically destroyed in 1942–1943. According to a recent in-depth study, of the 9 million people in Belorussia at the time of the German occupation, up to 1.7 million—including 700,000 Soviet POWs and between 500,000 and 550,000 Jews—were murdered.[7]

After escaping the Red Army in Minsk, Heuser taught briefly at a police school in Eastern Prussia before, in August 1944, he became chief of *Einsatzkommando* (EK) 14 of *Einsatzgruppe* H with which he and several other former members of the KdS Minsk took part in crushing the Slovak uprising. After a wave of deportations in 1942, the remaining Jews in Slovakia (approximately 20,000) experienced a period of relative quiet until the German invasion of Slovakia in August 1944. From the very beginning of his deployment, Heuser and his men used their experience gained in the occupied Soviet Union to bring about a "radical solution of the Jewish question by deporting them to a concentration camp outside of Slovakia" in view of the intended "rapid pacification of the area."[8] In close cooperation with other German agencies EK 14 started organizing the deportation to the transit camp of Sered in early September. In late September the "resettlement" of the Jews of Bratislava began; by the end of November 9,000 of them had been sent to Auschwitz via the Sered transit camp.[9]

At the end of the war Georg Heuser exchanged his SS uniform as a captain (*SS-Hauptsturmführer*) for civilian clothes in order to avoid being taken prisoner by the Allies. He blended in easily with those of his compatriots who had been uprooted by the war and were trying to adapt to life after Germany's defeat. Unlike many Germans at the time, Heuser seems to have suffered no material deprivation: already in Minsk he had boasted that once the war was over, the gold taken from the Jews would make him a rich man.[10] Whenever asked officially about what he had done before 1945, he kept his SS membership and his deployment in Minsk secret, claiming to have been a captain in the German Air Force. Heuser worked in a number of jobs, such as a lawyer and as liaison for British or American agencies, while cultivating his contacts with former colleagues, some of whom had already succeeded in circumventing Allied courts and in reentering the West German public service as bureaucrats, administrators, or policemen.[11]

As a result of the unprecedented havoc spread by the Third Reich, its utter defeat in May 1945, and the negative experiences made after the First World War, the Allies did not intend to leave the adjudication of war crimes to the vanquished. However, German complaints about "victors' justice" ignored the fact that between May 1945 and January 1950 (with Allied regulations restricting the jurisdiction of German courts to crimes committed by Germans against their fellow countrymen or against stateless persons) nearly one-quarter of all sentences passed by German courts for murder related to the killing of non-Germans.[12] Heuser, like the great majority of perpetrators, initially succeeded in posing as an insignificant cog in the Third Reich's giant machine. In August 1949 the board of enquiry in the West German city of Ludwigshafen, where Heuser had established residence, provided him with a certificate exempting him from denazification procedures.[13]

Following the creation of the Federal Republic of Germany and the transfer of authority from Allied into German hands in 1949–1950, the German penal code (*Strafgesetzbuch*) became the basis for adjudicating Nazi crimes. By that time the initial postwar impulse among the German population to punish the guilty had given way to a mentality that called for drawing a "final line" (*Schlußstrich*) to the past or, as Chancellor Konrad Adenauer put it, for tabula rasa. In this perspective, Nazi crimes in general and the Holocaust in particular sank into oblivion behind the suffering of the German population from the consequences of the war, be it Allied strategic bombing, the breaking up of the Reich, or the expulsion of Germans from its Eastern provinces.[14]

In the prevailing climate of cold war anxiety and reconstruction euphoria, vociferous pressure groups in West Germany demanded a full-scale amnesty for war-related crimes and the release of prisoners in Allied custody. When in early 1950 the newly appointed minister of justice in Adenauer's cabinet pleaded before parliament that "one should come to an end with these things," he could be sure that he had a significant number of his countrymen behind him.[15] By the mid-1950s, due to a wave of amnesties, fewer than 200 German war criminals remained in the custody of the Western Allies.[16] The disinclination to punish those responsible for Nazi crimes was paralleled by an increasing willingness to admit civil servants (*Beamte*) of the Third Reich into West Germany's rapidly expanding bureaucratic apparatus.

Based on article 131 of the West German constitution (*Grundgesetz*), a law was enacted in 1951 stipulating that "displaced public servants" (*verdrängte Beamte*) who had not been convicted of a crime had the right to be re-employed and, until this could be done, to receive financial compensation.[17] While the number of newly opened Nazi-related investigations had reached a record low, the percentage of former SS and police officers integrated into West Germany's public service had increased—the dimensions and implications of this development became clear only when, years later, prosecutors started their investigations.[18] Georg Heuser's career can serve as a typical example: after having worked in a number of white-collar jobs, he was, as of 1 May 1954, employed (on the basis of article 131) as senior superintendent (*Kriminaloberkommissar*) in the criminal police of the state of Rheinland-Pfalz. By then, a network of mutual assistance was in place to ease the way of former Nazi functionaries toward tenured respectability. Heuser solicited letters of reference from former colleagues: a fellow officer already employed in Rheinland-Pfalz testified to the state minister that he had served under Heuser in Slovakia, that Heuser had been deployed in the East where he received several decorations "for bravery," and that he was "one of the few personalities who are equally gifted in theory and practice."[19] Heuser rapidly climbed the career ladder. By May 1956 he had been promoted to acting chief of a police district until finally, in January 1958, he became director of the criminal investigative office (*Landeskriminalamt*) in Rheinland-Pfalz.

Despite his professional success, Heuser started to feel uneasy about the growing inquisitiveness of West German prosecutors; as the most senior criminal policeman in the state, he could witness the process from a unique vantage point. The upsurge in Nazi-related investigations (*NSG-Verfahren*) in the Federal Republic reflected a heightened awareness of the dimensions of the crimes. Individual cases opened on the basis of allegations against one or two suspects developed a tendency to soon encompass entire administrative, regional, or functional units. In the wake of the so-called *Ulm Einsatzkommando* Trial dealing with crimes committed by members of the SS and police in Lithuania, judicial officials from the West German states decided in October 1958 to create a central office for the purpose of coordinating their investigative efforts: the *Zentrale Stelle der Landesjustizverwaltungen zur Aufklärung nationalsozialistischer Verbrechen* (zsl) in the city of Ludwigsburg.[20] This office commenced its work on 1 December 1958. The zsl generated a massive wave of investigations: 400 in the first year of its existence, nearly 104,000 up to 1992.[21]

In the late 1950s the urgency of legal action increased as more and more crimes committed during the Third Reich would, according to the German penal code, reach the statute of limitations: manslaughter and other, less serious crimes on 8 May 1960, and murder five years later. This could be prevented by a parliamentary extension of the statute of limitations (as happened in 1965 and 1969 for murder), or, for individual crimes, by any action of a judge, such as an interrogation or a court order. The latter helps to explain why so many cases were opened in the late 1950s and the mid-1960s. Arrest warrants for some of Heuser's co-defendants were issued on 7 May 1960. Nevertheless, there remained a huge imbalance between investigations, indictments, and convictions: of a total of 103,823 criminal investigations started between the end of the war and January 1992 by West German judicial authorities, only 6,487 (about 6 percent) led to a conviction, which in 5,513 cases (85 percent) related to lesser Nazi crimes or crimes committed prior to the outbreak of war. Of the 974 convictions related to crimes of World War II, only 472 cases (about 7 percent of all convictions) involved the murder of Jews.[22]

German legal parameters such as statutes of limitations and the wording of the penal code were clearly of crucial importance for the success or failure of NSG-Verfahren; however, their application and interpretation have to be considered within a wider context. The ZSL and individual prosecutors eager to pursue cases such as Heuser's were operating in a vacuum. Having to rely in their investigations on a "renazified" police force in whose ranks a considerable number of perpetrators had found refuge, these prosecutors were outsiders in a legal profession that had, even in regard to judges who had passed death sentences during the Third Reich, never really been denazified, and they faced disinterest or outright hostility from within West German society at large.[23] Fritz Bauer, chief prosecutor in Frankfurt who initiated the momentous Auschwitz trial, remarked in the 1960s that whenever he left his office he felt as if he were entering enemy territory.[24]

Although the ZSL lacked the authority to prosecute, it enabled the bringing of charges and the preparation of trials. In summer 1959, in the course of an ZSL-investigation against Erich Ehrlinger, former commander of Sonderkommando 1b and later KdS in Minsk and Kiev, evidence surfaced that Georg Heuser had significantly participated in mass murder in Minsk.[25] The ensuing investigation focused on events in Belorussia while at this time Heuser's activities in 1944-1945 in Slovakia remained outside the scope of judicial interest. In due course, the ZSL passed on the task of compiling further evidence to Staatsanwalt Bornscheuer in Koblenz, the city where Heuser was living. Over the next three years, in close cooperation with the ZSL and with a specially created police investigation unit, Bornscheuer reconstructed the historical setting and the sequence of murderous events in and around Minsk.

More than any other active policeman in West Germany, Heuser was uniquely positioned to arrange for defense strategies with former fellow officers.[26] At one of his meetings with his old comrades in spring 1959, Heuser expressed concern: "Everything is going wrong now," he said, "but don't panic."[27] Heuser's past was indeed catching up with him: an arrest warrant was issued on 15 July 1959; senior justice officials convened in Rheinland-Pfalz to discuss the case on 22 July. One day later, Heuser was arrested on the charge that in Belorussia he had given "orders to carry out executions [and gassing] of Jews and 'potential enemies' [of the Nazi regime], among them women and children, for predominantly racial reasons" and that he had participated in these murders.[28] Newspapers reported on the allegations against the high-ranking police officer.[29] In his first interrogation after arrest, Heuser denied all accusations.[30]

Evidence and Evasion

The investigation that led to Heuser's arrest and, some months later, to the arrest of other suspects was not the first judicial attempt at coming to terms with wartime events in Minsk.[31] Already in January 1946, Soviet authorities in the city of Minsk had charged and sentenced 18 German officials from the Wehrmacht, SS, and other agencies for war crimes.[32] Subsequently, the murders committed by members of the KdS office in Belorussia surfaced again and again in a number of trials, most notably in the 1947–1948 American Military Tribunal case against members of the *Einsatzgruppen* and in the West German case of Adolf Rübe, an officer who later testified against his former colleagues.[33] The massive amount of material collected by the Koblenz prosecutor's office proved that within the universe of destruction in and around Minsk, the deeds of Heuser and his fellow officers at the KdS stood out.[34]

According to the indictment, between early 1942 and the German retreat in late June and early July 1944 the defendants were involved in nine large-scale "*Aktionen*," killing at least 31,970 Jews by mass executions and, subsequent to June 1942, by gas vans. In addition, the KdS members participated, collectively or individually, in a number of killings of non-Jews: Sinti and Roma ("Gypsies"), partisans, mental patients, members of the clergy, and other civilians. The victims came from the Minsk ghetto, the prisons, their places of work, or the deportation trains arriving from the West, or they were killed on the spot. Maly Trostinets, a farm twelve kilometers southeast of Minsk, emerged as the main killing site where, according to estimates, 60,000 persons were murdered.[35]

It became evident that as head of the Gestapo in Minsk, Heuser had played a key role in the apparatus of annihilation. Heuser was subordinate only to

Strauch and his successors as KdS, so his position gave him considerable freedom of action. He participated directly in the killings—by shooting Jews and suspected Soviet agents, in one case even by burning two persons alive at Maly Trostinets; he arranged, in cooperation with German railway officials, for ways to overcome problems regarding the scheduling of deportation trains and the "reception" of persons about to be murdered; and he compiled information for his superiors on the progress of the "Final Solution" in the area. According to a postwar statement, Heuser proudly told one of his KdS colleagues in summer 1943: "Well, now in our reports we have reached the figure of 70,000 executed Jews."[36]

Heuser and his fellow officers at the KdS represented a mixture of the two archetypical types of perpetrators as described by the long-time head of the ZSL, Adalbert Rückerl: desk murderers (*Schreibtischtäter*) at the centers of decision making, and direct killers (*Direkttäter*) at the actual killing sites.[37] The success of the prosecution's efforts depended to a large extent on the ability of investigative officers to trace evidence and interrogate witnesses. Policemen with a clean service record were selected to form a special task force (*Sonderkommission*) in order to establish the facts properly. The few *Sonderkommission* policemen in Rheinland-Pfalz who investigated the Heuser case saw themselves confronted with a task that required exceptional professional skill and at least some historical knowledge. Following leads provided by a number of other agencies and archives, the *Sonderkommission* went on extensive interview trips covering a great number of witnesses all over West Germany.[38]

Very few victims had survived to tell their story; most of them could not recollect having met any of the accused in Minsk.[39] As in many other *NSG-Verfahren*, the prosecution had to rely to a significant extent on evidence from the close surroundings of the accused. Commenting on the historical accuracy of postwar depositions by perpetrators, Christopher Browning recognizes elements of truth hidden behind layers of denial, distortion, and outright lies—a constellation that makes it impossible to ignore the context of these testimonies. In order to use these kinds of sources appropriately, the historian has to apply the methods of *Quellenkritik* with special care.[40] One of the most fascinating aspects of the Heuser investigation is that it provides an additional filter mechanism to separate facts from fiction: file notes by the members of the

Sonderkommission about the value of individual witness statements. Written directly after the interrogation, these comments reflect the impression left on the investigator—information that usually is absent from the records and that allows at least some insight into the mindset of both the interrogated and the interrogators.[41]

In their postwar testimonies Heuser's fellow officers displayed little inclination to dissociate themselves from their former colleague. Most referred to Heuser with a mixture of awe and respect: Erich Ehrlinger, the first KdS commander, described him as a harsh personality (*"sehr hart veranlagt"*) and as a perfectionist (*"ausgesprochener Routinier"*).[42] Some were more outspoken: codefendant Kaul recollected Heuser's comment after he had shot a Jew from Austria: "Bang it went, then it was over," and noted, "You should have seen Heuser at the execution site."[43] Others found it incomprehensible that he "had participated in *Judenaktionen* or even [sic] in unusual brutality" and that he "could mentally deal with the execution of so many people and at the same time remain, in dealing with us, always a sensitive person."[44] Few expressed their contempt for his increasingly brutal, "cold and numbed" behavior or for his "somewhat sinister" character.[45]

In addition to Heuser's circle of colleagues, the spectrum of perpetrators and bystanders who testified included various groups: female staff of the KdS, officers from SS and police units, as well as representatives of other agencies deployed in and around Minsk. Acutely aware of the dangers of saying too much, the majority of former KdS members displayed no feelings about a past that seemed to have left little impression on them. Some appeared to the interrogators as remorseless, full-fledged Nazis and proud former SS members.[46] Some started to cry when told that they were lying or when they were confronted with the murderous facts.[47] As in other Nazi institutions, behind the facade of selfless devotion to the cause of the Fatherland, corruption as well as alcoholic and sexual excesses dominated the scene to such an extent that even former members called the KdS a "pigsty" (*Sauhaufen*).[48] Maly Trostinets was not perceived as a killing center but, compared with downtown Minsk, as a place of tranquility where one could go for horseback riding or to pick up a fur coat taken from Jewish victims. While some witnesses said that every German in Minsk talked about "what happened to the Jews," others denied having heard anything.[49]

Among the group of witnesses with wartime experiences in Minsk, those who—like Heuser—had after the war regained entry into the police force stood out. Their background provided them with expert knowledge on the most effective means of self-defense. Some rejected being interrogated by their colleagues from the *Sonderkommission* or complained about "Gestapo methods" of the interrogators; others lied, pretended not to remember anything, or insisted that it would be better to put to rest this aspect of the past.[50] As in other cases, policemen in adjacent precincts or cities exchanged information in order not to contradict each other when giving evidence.[51] A frequently used last line of defense was the suspects' claim to have acted under duress (as defined in paragraph 52, article 1 of the West German penal code).[52] Despite years of intensive search by defense lawyers after the war, no single incident could be found in which a person declining to implement an order to kill innocent civilians was threatened by an "immediate or otherwise not avertable danger," such as by being sentenced to death.[53] Consequently, the accused tried to stress that at the time they had *believed* they would be severely punished for disobedience, thus experiencing "putative duress" (*Putativnotstand*).

Lawyers assisted the accused in transforming postwar apologia into legal procedure; Heuser even picked a former KdS colleague as his first counsel.[54] The evidence, however, spoke a different language. Asked to give his expert advice on the question of superior orders, historian Hans-Günther Seraphim concluded that "the decisive factor in Minsk was not an order, but the proper attitude from which everything else resulted."[55] Unlike in other cases, the Koblenz court ruled out the defendants' claim of *Putativnotstand* as they had shown "no serious attempts to avoid being involved into the numerous murders."[56]

Help for the Koblenz prosecutors in building their case came from an unlikely source. While the attempt at interrogating witnesses in the USSR failed, during the trial the Soviet foreign ministry handed over a 318-page collection of photocopied contemporaneous German documents that included a wealth of material taken from Belorussian archives inaccessible to Western researchers.[57] In addition to some documents compiled for the Nuremberg proceedings in 1945, this material was of special importance to prove beyond doubt the involvement of Heuser and his fellow officers in the deportation and killing process. Copies of these documents were given to the ZSL, where they formed the first part of a growing source collection from the USSR ("*Sammlung UdSSR*") heavily used in subsequent years by prosecutors and historians until, with the end of the cold war and the opening of Soviet archives in the late 1980s, the original documents finally became available to Western users.[58]

In May 1961 the Regional Court (*Landgericht*) Koblenz opened the pre-investigation (*gerichtliche Voruntersuchung*) against Heuser and nine co-defendants.[59] Some months later, prosecutors had caught up with two more suspects: Erich Gn., a former gas van driver, and Artur Wilke, who had been living under the name of his dead brother and who admitted to participating in mass executions.[60] The success in identifying Wilke was overshadowed by a severe drawback in the case of Gn., who, after admitting that gas vans in Minsk always operated well ("*Es hat bei uns immer gut geklappt*"), hanged himself in his jail cell.[61] While the Koblenz prosecutors had the opportunity to use material from older investigations, they in turn generated additional evidence on perpetrators outside the circle of KdS officers. In late November 1961 the pre-investigation was closed.[62] Six weeks later, *Staatsanwalt* Bornscheuer presented the indictment against Heuser and others and applied for the opening of the court case (*Hauptverfahren*). In more than three hundred pages, the indictment summed up what had emerged during the investigation.[63] In June 1962 the *Landgericht* Koblenz decided to open the *Hauptverfahren*; the first day of trial was set for 15 October 1962.[64]

Trial, Punishment, and Re-integration

The Koblenz Court of Assizes (*Schwurgericht*), consisting of six lay and three professional judges, sat for 63 days until, on 21 May 1963, the verdict was handed down. The trial proceeded quickly and quietly, receiving only occasional press coverage. A long line of former members of German agencies in Minsk, from SS men to judges and railway officials, testified on matters directly or indirectly related to the charges. Even in a society used to having the past interpreted by former Nazi officials, the degree of amnesia displayed by some witnesses seemed staggering, especially when—as in the case of the former chief of the finance department in the *Reichskommissariat Ostland*—wartime records proved their personal involvement in the job-sharing enterprise of mass murder.[65] The accused followed the court proceedings passively and showed few signs of concern. Harder, one of the defendants who had already been released on bail, once even appeared at court under the obvious influence of alcohol, for which he received two days' arrest for contempt of court.[66]

Heuser's trial attorney, *Rechtsanwalt* Egon J. Ge., tried his best to get his client off the hook. Two days after the start of the trial, he filed an unsuccessful bias complaint (*Befangenheitsantrag*) against the presiding judge, partly because the judge had described the conditions in the Minsk prison as "bad."[67] In relation to the most shocking of the charges—the burning alive of two victims in fall 1943—Ge. submitted an application to investigate the finding of "medical experts" that "the death struggle of a person incinerated by a burning liquid is short; already within seconds the person will fall unconscious."[68] He was also eager to prove that Heuser was held in high esteem by other German officers in Minsk and that he was "not regarded as one involved in a leading capacity in the killing measures."[69]

Despite the huge imbalance between the scope of the crimes and the level of punishment that characterized German *NSG-Verfahren* in general, the sentences passed in this specific case were comparatively high. For Heuser, the prosecutor had requested life imprisonment, plus another seven years and abrogation of his civil rights (*Aberkennung der bürgerlichen Ehrenrechte*).[70] The court, however, ruled that the former Gestapo chief in Minsk, found guilty of nine crimes as an accessory to murder (*gemeinschaftliche Beihilfe zum Mord*) and one count of accessory to manslaughter, had to serve fifteen years imprisonment and a five-year-suspension of his civil rights. None of Heuser's former fellow officers were acquitted: Harder received imprisonment of three and a half years; Dahlheimer and Oswald, four; Feder, von Toll, and Kaul, four and a half; Merbach, seven, Schlegel, eight; Wilke, ten; and Stark, life in prison plus eight years. For the duration of their term-sentence the time spent in jail since arrest was to be taken into account.[71]

Their direct participation in murder turned none of the defendants, in the mind of the court, into a main perpetrator (*Haupttäter*)—a term German courts reserved for those few who, such as Hitler, Himmler, and Heydrich, planned and ordered the "Final Solution." In deciding whether a crime constituted murder, it was the "inner attitude toward the deed" (*innere Einstellung zur Tat*) that counted, not the nature of the deed itself.[72] Heuser was acquitted on three counts (the execution of 300 civilians, and the killing of a Catholic priest and a Soviet agent). On the count of burning two persons alive, Heuser was sentenced as an accessory to murder as the court assumed (without documentary proof) that the order for this crime had come directly from the Reich Security Main Office in Berlin.

The ten counts on which Heuser was found guilty involved the killing of more than 11,100 men, women, and children, Jews and non-Jews. In setting a cumulative prison term of fifteen years, the court thus applied a sentence of less than half a day per person murdered. For this stunning judgment, the court presented the standard reasoning that Heuser, though he had "partly rather actively participated" in implementing the Final Solution, was merely an assistant to the main perpetrators. The judges also applied in their ruling a specific understanding of the character of the accused and society's obligation toward him:

> The punishment has necessarily the character of retaliation [Vergel-tungscharakter]; it only peripherally serves the purpose of preventing the accused to commit similar crimes in the future. For the court is not dealing with the ordinary type of criminals. None of the accused committed the crimes out of their own desire [aus eigenem Antrieb]; they rather followed the orders of a government that no longer exists. None of them was sentenced before and, aside from the events dealt with in this trial, none had conflicts with the law. After the war, without exception, they regained reputable jobs and led a proper life in honorable circumstances. For this reason, they as well as their families are especially hard hit by the late punishment. . . . Given the exceptional circumstances which made them criminals, their guilt does not seem so grave as to call for lifelong imprisonment as a means of expiation.[73]

Most of his co-defendants appealed the judgment; Heuser, however, accepted the verdict and tried to reduce the inconvenience of life in prison. Less than a month after the verdict, his lawyer approached the Koblenz Regional Court asking for a four-week hospital treatment due to Heuser's "extraordinarily bad" health after four years of imprisonment and the stress of a seven months' trial.[74]

During the next years Heuser frequently changed prisons until, in mid-1969, he applied for early release. Having had time to reflect on his past, Heuser became convinced "that in my case the imprisonment served suffices as recompense," especially as all his former fellow officers convicted to term imprisonment by the Koblenz court had already been released.[75] The director of the Freiendiez prison supported the application by reiterating that Heuser was "no ordinary criminal," that he saved money for the time after his release, and that expiation has been achieved.[76] His attorney followed up by claiming that, "especially the fact that the deeds Herr Heuser was convicted for were accessory acts (*Beihilfshandlungen*) to the deeds of the Nazi-leadership supports the assumption that, given the personality of the defendant who after the war had been—professionally as well as socially—fully rehabilitated, he will also in the future lead an orderly life according to current laws."[77]

The Koblenz judgment and its aftermath reflect conservative thinking in West Germany in the late 1960s. Perceiving Nazi murderers as no "ordinary criminals" legitimized the demand that, in a society oriented toward the future, a "final line" (*Schlußstrich*) should be drawn under this ugly chapter of the past by integrating, not segregating, the guilty. This interpretation had severe practical ramifications at a time when the parliament of the Federal Republic was called upon to decide the statutes of limitations for those crimes that had not yet expired. The debate turned out to be more controversial than in former years since supporters of the *Schlußstrich* faced opposition. In 1969 the Bundestag decided to extend the expiration date for crimes of murder to 1979. At the same time, instead of an outright parliamentary decision to terminate the prosecution of noncapital Nazi-related crimes, a clause altering paragraph 50 of the German penal code achieved the same objective. This change, buried in a law enacted in connection with the reform of the penal code, had a profound—and, for the work of many state prosecutors, disastrous—effect.[78]

With social and generational change in full swing, defenders of Nazi perpetrators deliberately applied the rhetoric of liberalism. Demanding Heuser's release, his attorney sharply criticized that the non-application of Paragraph 26 of the West German penal code (regulating the early release of sentenced prisoners) to Nazi perpetrators constituted a perversion of the democratic concept of law.[79] A few months later, Heuser repeated his plea that "the public interest in continued imprisonment should be superseded by the interest of re-integrating me into society," this time by taking advantage of parliamentary plans to reform the penal code in general and Paragraph 26 in particular.[80] Enacted in December 1969, the modified Paragraph 26 worked perfectly for convicted Nazi criminals such as Heuser. In deciding for the early release of prisoners, the parliamentary commission argued that "the idea of expiation (*Schuldausgleich*) and general prevention is not to hinder a conditional release, given a favorable prognosis, even in relation to grave deeds like e.g., Nazi-related crimes if two-thirds of the sentence has been served."[81]

In a letter to the *Landgericht* Koblenz, the prosecutor's office agreed that Heuser was right and that it was up to the court to decide this matter.[82] On 12 December 1969, the Regional Court ruled that Heuser was to be immediately released despite the fact that the "new law" was taking effect only in April 1970. The very same day at 4 p.m., Georg Heuser left the Freiendiez prison a free man and moved to his house in Koblenz.[83] Heuser's release led to the termination of judicial efforts regarding the KdS Minsk complex. In early 1971 the Koblenz *Landgericht* granted a motion of *nolle prosequi* in the case of thirty-sight persons whose involvement in murder had been proven during the Heuser investigation.[84]

Not surprisingly, the court's prediction that Heuser would have little problems in integrating himself into West German society turned out to be correct. Within one year of his release, he had found a job at a company in Wiesbaden.[85] If Heuser ever suffered from psychological problems when confronted with his Nazi past, he overcame them quickly as a result of his restored social status. In September 1971, when approached by the prosecutor's office in a form letter, he burst out in indignation:

> Now they talk about reform and rehabilitation, and then one reads in every letter "vs. you re murder." . . . Every time I receive such a letter I am completely distressed because I expect a similar letter to be sent to my employer. You can be sure that I would lose my job at once because only two company executives know about my past. And even when the letter reads "criminal matter vs. you re murder," I am finished with the entire business. . . . After all, I too have a right to be left alone, especially as the burdens of the trial and its aftermath are hardly bearable for me.[86]

After his release from prison, Georg Heuser was indeed left alone, but not for long. Compared with the investigation into the Minsk complex, the judicial efforts of 1977 to link Heuser to crimes committed by *Einsatzgruppe* H and its six subunits in 1944 in Slovakia were much more haphazard. Although the case files are voluminous, about two-thirds of the material was not generated by German prosecutors.[87] In June 1977 a special commission appointed by the government of Czechoslovakia presented a memorandum to German authorities together with a thirty-two-volume compendium of documents, witness statements, and photographs of German crimes committed in Slovakia in the wake of the 1944 uprising. Via the zsl, the material reached Koblenz prosecutors in October 1977.[88] While a previous investigation had yielded no result, the Czechoslovak material warranted a new effort at retracing the steps of Heuser and his *Einsatzkommando* 14.[89]

Irrespective of the massive documentation about the historical setting available to Koblenz prosecutors, the direct involvement of Heuser in crimes committed in Slovakia remained nebulous. Most of the former members of EK 14 or of other units deployed in the area could not be traced; if they gave evidence, they avoided any mention of executions or organized mass murder. Only one former German official—the very same man who in 1954 had recommended Heuser's readmission into the West German police force on the basis of his wartime "bravery"—admitted that there had been a "general order to 'liquidate' all Jews."[90] The material provided by the Czechoslovak commission did little to clarify questions of responsibility beyond a reasonable doubt. Whenever surviving witnesses described specific crime scenes, they frequently referred to the perpetrators in general terms such as "the Germans" or "the Gestapo," neither of which helped in establishing individual guilt. Georg Heuser, aware of the frailty of the actual charges against him, challenged the prosecution even on historical facts by claiming that he "cannot imagine that there were still Jews in the area" at the time of the uprising. Confronted with contemporary German documents, some of them signed by himself, Heuser warned that reports were often puffed up and that for Slovakia "in no way an order existed to exterminate the Jews as, e.g., in the East."[91]

It can hardly be overlooked that, compared with the Minsk case, in the investigation of the crimes of EK 14 in Slovakia, the roles of prosecutor and accused as well as the ways of gathering evidence had changed. Although open resistance in German society against *NSG-Verfahren* had quieted down when compared with the years around the founding of the zsl, tracing witnesses and using their testimonies for trial purposes had become increasingly difficult. In a judicial system based on direct evidence, the totality of the crimes provided the best defense for the perpetrators—there was no one left to testify. Archival documentation rarely contained the kind of proof necessary to gain a conviction in court. At the same time, the accused felt they could more easily get away with denial and distortion.

In Heuser's case his years of imprisonment and his belief that, having received pardon, he had a right to lead an ordinary life added to his self-confidence in confronting the Koblenz prosecutors. In fact, Heuser made it a habit to drop in at the *Staatsanwaltschaft* and tell his version of the story.[92] In February 1980, after more than two years of investigations, his case was closed.[93] Georg Heuser lived out his life as an ordinary citizen who had no further clash with the law. For him, it was all over when he died in January 1989; for German society, dealing with the legacy of its judicial investigations into the crimes of the Third Reich remains an issue that defies closure.

Notes

1. For details on Heuser's biography, see *Justiz und NS-Verbrechen: Sammlung deutscher Strafurteile wegen nationalsozialistischer Tötungsverbrechen* (hereafter *JuNSV*), vol. 19, lfd. Nr. 552 (Verdict by Landgericht Koblenz of 21 May 1963), pp. 167–68; also Heiner Lichtenstein, *Himmlers grüne Helfer: Die Schutz-und Ordnungspolizei im "Dritten Reich"* (Cologne: Bund-Verlag, 1990), pp. 97–118; Jürgen Matthäus, "Georg Heuser—Routinier des sicherheitspolizeilichen Osteinsatzes," in *Karrieren der Gewalt: Nationalsozialistische Täterbiographien*, ed. Klaus-Michael Mallmann and Gerhard Paul, pp. 115–25 (Darmstadt: WBG, 2004).
2. On the role of the German police in occupied Eastern Europe, see Christopher Browning, *Ordinary Men: Reserve Police Battalion 101 and the Final Solution in Poland* (New York: HarperCollins, 1992); Edward Westermann, *Hitler's Police Battalions: Enforcing Racial War in the East* (Lawrence: University Press of Kansas, 2005).
3. *JuNSV*, vol. 19, lfd. Nr. 552, pp. 167–69; indictment, 15 January 1962, 9 Ks 2/62, pp. 10082–87. For "Operation Barbarossa" and the *Einsatzgruppen* in the Soviet Union, see Christopher R. Browning (with contributions by Jürgen Matthäus), *The Origins of the Final Solution: The Evolution of Nazi Jewish Policy, September 1939–March 1942* (Lincoln: University of Nebraska Press, 2004), pp. 213ff.; Helmut Krausnick and Hans-Heinrich Wilhelm, *Die Truppe des Weltanschauungskrieges: Die Einsatzgruppen der Sicherheitspolizei und des SD* (Stuttgart: DVA, 1981).

4. Browning, *Origins*, pp. 244–45.

5. See Christian Gerlach, *Kalkulierte Morde: Die deutsche Wirtschafts-und Vernichtungs-politik in Weißrußland 1941 bis 1944* (Hamburg: Hamburger Edition, 1999); Christian Gerlach, "Deutsche Wirtschaftsinteressen, Besatzungspolitik und der Mord an den Juden in Weißrußland, 1941–1943," in *Nationalsozialistische Vernichtungspolitik 1939–1945: Neue Forschungen und Kontroversen,* ed. Ulrich Herbert, pp. 263–91 (Frankfurt: Fischer Taschenbuch Verlag, 1998); Paul Kohl, *"Ich wundere mich, daß ich noch lebe": Sowjetische Augenzeugen berichten* (Gütersloh: Verlagshaus G. Mohn, 1990), pp. 92–93; Bernhard Chiari, *Alltag hinter der Front: Besatzung, Kollaboration und Widerstand in Weißrußland 1941–1944,* (Düsseldorf: Droste Verlag, 1998).

6. See Timothy P. Mulligan, *The Politics of Illusion and Empire: German Occupation Policy in the Soviet Union, 1942–1943* (New York: Praeger, 1988).

7. Gerlach, *Morde,* p. 1158; Kohl, *Augenzeugen,* pp. 74–75, 107.

8. EK 14, situation report, 6 September 1944, Bundesarchiv Lichterfelde (hereafter BA) R 70 Slowakei, vol. 189, pp. 42–47; situation report, 8 September 1944, BA R 70 Slowakei, vol. 189, pp. 50–52. On the German occupation of Slovakia, see Tatjana Tönsmeyer, *Das Dritte Reich und die Slowakei 1939-1945: Politischer Alltag zwischen Kooperation und Eigensinn* (Paderborn: Schöningh, 2003). With special focus on EK 14, Konrad Kwiet, "Der Mord an Juden, Zigeunern und Partisanen: Zum Einsatz des EK 14 der Sicherheitspolizei und des SD in der Slowakei 1944/45," in *Jahrbuch für Antisemitismusforschung,* ed. Wolfgang Benz, vol. 7, pp. 71–81 (Frankfurt: Campus, 1998).

9. Einsatzgruppe H to RSHA, 8 September 1944, BA R 70 Slowakei, vol. 194, pp. 75–76; Einsatzgruppe H, situation report no. 16, 22 September 1944, BA R 70 Slowakei, vol. 194, pp. 179-82; Einsatzgruppe H, report 29 September 1944, BA R 70 Slowakei, vol. 197, p. 8; Einsatzgruppe H, Tagungsprotokoll Abt.III, 22 November 1944, BA R 70 Slowakei, vol. 302, pp. 101–9.

10. Statement by Alfred Re., 13/14 September 1961, Staatsanwaltschaft Koblenz (subsequently StK), 9 Ks 2/62, vol. 61, p. 9082. Names of witnesses involved in the case (other than those convicted) have been rendered anonymous throughout this text.

11. Statements by Bernhard Do., 5 August 1959, StK, 9 Ks 2/62, vol. 1; Herbert Di., 20 August 1959, StK, 9 Ks 2/62, vol. 1; vol. 44, pp. 6651–6652; vol. 45, p. 6694.

12. See Annette Weinke, *Die Verfolgung von NS-Tätern im geteilten Deutschland: Vergangenheitsbewältigungen 1949-1969 oder: Eine deutsch-deutsche Beziehungsgeschichte im Kalten Krieg* (Paderborn: Schöningh, 2002); Marc von Miquel, *Ahnden oder amnestieren? Westdeutsche Justiz und Vergangenheitspolitik in den sechziger Jahren* (Göttingen: Wallstein Verlag, 2004; pp. 182–83 with reference to the Heuser case); Henry Friedlander, "The Judiciary and Nazi Crimes in Postwar Germany," in *The Nazi Holocaust: Historical Articles on the Destruction of European Jews,* ed. Michael Marrus, vol. 9, pp. 668–70 (Westport CT: Meckler, 1989); Ulrich Herbert, *Best: Biographische Studien über Radikalismus, Weltanschauung und Vernunft, 1903–1989* (Bonn: Dietz, 1996), pp. 435–36; Mildt, *In the Name of the People,* p. 22.

13. *JuNSV,* vol. 19, lfd. Nr. 552, p. 168.

14. See Norbert Frei, *Vergangenheitspolitik: Die Anfänge der Bundesrepublik und die NS-Vergangenheit* (Munich: C.H. Beck, 1996), with extensive bibliography on the Federal Republic's early history. Adenauer's remark: *"Wir haben so verwirrte Zeitverhältnisse hinter uns, daß es sich empfiehlt, generell tabula rasa zu machen"* (Cabinet meeting, 26 September 1949), Frei, *Vergangenheitspolitik,* p. 31.

15. Protocol of a meeting of the Federal Parliament, 11 January 1950, p. 783, quoted from Herbert, *Best*, p. 440.

16. Quoted from Frei, *Vergangenheitspolitik*, p. 280, n. 58. See also pp. 29–53, 266–95.

17. Frei, *Vergangenheitspolitik*, pp. 69–99; Herbert, *Best*, pp. 483–87.

18. See Frei, *Vergangenheitspolitik*, pp. 79–82; Willi Dreßen, "The Role of the Wehrmacht and the Police in the Annihilation of the Jews: The Prosecution and Postwar Careers of Perpetrators in the Police Force of the Federal Republic of Germany," *Yad Vashem Studies* 23 (1993): 296–319.

19. Statement by Heuser, 29 June 1959, StK 9 Ks 2/62, vol. 3, p. 392; copy of a letter by Kriminalrat Johannes Ho. to the Ministry of the Interior Rheinland-Pfalz, 21 March 1954, StK 9 Ks 2/62, vol. 3.

20. The Central Clearing House of the State Justice Administrations for the Investigation of National Socialist Crimes.

21. See Adalbert Rückerl, *Die Strafverfolgung von NS-Verbrechen, 1945–1978* (Heidelberg/Karlsruhe: C.F. Müller, 1979), pp. 49–52; Adalbert Rückerl, "Nazi Crime Trials," in Marrus, *Nazi Holocaust*, vol. 9, pp. 621–34; Kerstin Freudiger, *Die juristische Aufarbeitung von NS-Verbrechen: Versuch einer Bilanz* (Tübingen: Mohr Siebeck, 2002).

22. Miquel, *Ahnden*; see also Mildt, *In the Name of the People*, pp. 20–21; Rückerl, *Strafverfolgung*, pp. 53–56.

23. See Friedlander, "Judiciary," pp. 675–76.

24. *Der Spiegel* 31/1995, p. 42, "Feindliches Ausland," Miquel, *Ahnden*, contains a twelve-page appendix of West German judges with a Nazi past. On the Frankfurt Auschwitz trial, see Rebecca Wittmann, "Tainted Law: The West German Judiciary and the Prosecution of Nazi War Criminals," in this volume.

25. See *JuNSV*, vol. 18, lfd. Nr. 526 (with special emphasis on Ehrlinger's career in Kiev).

26. Statement by Franz Ge., 4 January 1961, StK 9 Ks 2/62, vol. 42, pp. 6333–34. For collective attempts at warding off allegations by former SS and policemen, see Michael Okroy, "'Man will unserem Btl. was tun . . .': Der Wuppertaler Bialystok-Prozess 1967/68 und die Ermittlungen gegen Angehörige des Polizeibataillons 309," in *Im Auftrag: Polizei, Verwaltung und Verantwortung*, ed. Alfons Kenkmann and Christoph Spieker, pp. 301–17 (Essen: Klartext, 2001).

27. Statement by Paul Ru., 28 December 1960, StK 9 Ks 2/62, vol. 42, pp. 6235–67.

28. Arrest warrant by Amtsgericht Karlsruhe against Georg Heuser, 15 July 1959, StK 9 Ks 2/62, vol. 3, p. 365 (the additions in square brackets include passages from the renewed arrest warrant issued by the Amtsgericht Koblenz in December 1959, StK 9 Ks 2/62, vol. 7, pp. 1020–23).

29. See, e.g., "Nach dem Baden verhaftet: Schwerer Verdacht gegen Kriminalchef von Rheinland," *Hamburger Abendblatt*, 25/26 July 1959.

30. Interrogation of Georg Heuser, 24 July 1959, StK 9 Ks 2/62, vol. 3, pp. 369–71.

31. Arrest warrants for Merbach, Kaul, We., Dalheimer, and von Toll were issued by the Amtsgericht Koblenz on 7 May 1960 (StK 9 Ks 2/62, vol. 20, pp. 2933–38); for Feder by the Amtsgericht Köln on 26 July 1960, StK 9 Ks 2/62, vol. 28, p. 4187.

32. Extracts from the trial proceedings have been edited by Hannes Heer, *Der Minsker Prozeß* (Hamburg: Hamburger Edition, 1996).

33. *Trials of War Criminals before the Nürnberg Military Tribunals under Control Council Law No. 10*, vol. 4, Nürnberg 1949, Case no. 9 (vs. Otto Ohlendorf et al.); *JuNSV*, vol. 9, lfd. Nr. 298. For other West German court-cases regarding Minsk, see *JuNSV*, vol. 17, lfd.

Nr. 512, 519; vol. 19, lfd. Nr. 555; vol. 22, lfd. Nr. 601. For a look at Austrian proceedings growing out of the investigation of this complex of crimes, see Patricia Heberer, "Justice in Austrian Courts? The Case of Josef W. and Austria's Difficult Relationship with Its Past," in this volume.

34. The investigation and trial material collected by the Staatsanwaltschaft Koblenz vs. Heuser et al. (9 Ks 2/62) comprises more than 14,000 pages in 89 volumes plus additional files (Handakten, Vollstreckungs-, Gnadenheft, collection of contemporary German documents handed over by the Soviet Union).

35. See Gerlach, *Morde*, pp. 503–773; Kohl, *Augenzeugen*, pp. 91–96.

36. Statement by Artur Wilke, 10 August 1961, StK 9 Ks 2/62, vol. 58, p. 8646.

37. See Rückerl, *Strafverfolgung*, pp. 85–88.

38. The Heuser case files contain acquittals on travel expenses for trips totaling more than 100,000 kilometers (StK 9 Ks 2/62, vol. 11, p. 1561; vol. 18, p. 2624; vol. 29, p. 4290; vol. 44, p. 6563; vol. 48, p. 7167).

39. See file note by Sonderkommission "P" re statement by Walter Ma., 8 December 1959, StK 9 Ks 2/62, vol. 10, p. 1416.

40. See Browning, *Ordinary Men*, pp. xviii–xvix.

41. I thank Bettina Birn for her advice on the uniqueness of the Heuser case.

42. Statement by Erich Ehrlinger, 8 May 1959, StK 9 Ks 2/62, vol. 1.

43. Statement by Kaul, 13 June 1960, StK 9 Ks 2/62, vol. 23, pp. 3474–75.

44. Statements by Dietrich Sch., 22 September 1959, StK 9 Ks 2/62, vol. 6, pp. 912–15; Karl Dalheimer, 24 August 1959, StK 9 Ks 2/62, vol. 3.

45. Statements by Theodor Fe., 4 December 1959, StK 9 Ks 2/62, vol. 10, pp. 1357–76; Ernst We., 8 June 1960, StK 9 Ks 2/62, vol. 23, pp. 3417–35; Irma Sch., 29 March 1961, StK 9 Ks 2/62, vol. 48, pp. 7126–35; Fritz Mi., 2 June 1961, StK 9 Ks 2/62, vol. 52, pp. 7799–7811.

46. Note by Sonderkommission "P," 23 May 1960, re statements by Theodor On., StK 9 Ks 2/62, vol. 21, pp. 3196; note by Sonderkommission "P," 1 July 1960, re statement by Jakob Oswald, StK 9 Ks 2/62, vol. 26, pp. 3973a-b; idem, 20 November 1961, re statement by Adam Ba., StK 9 Ks 2/62, vol. 64, pp. 9536–38.

47. Note by Sonderkommission "P," 3 February 1960, re statement by Heinrich Ga., StK 9 Ks 2/62, vol. 13, p. 1852; Note by Sonderkommission "P," 29 June 1960, re statement by Otto Ed., StK 9 Ks 2/62, vol. 26, pp. 3934a-b; statement by Max Re., 23 March 1961, StK 9 Ks 2/62, vol. 48, pp. 7168–92.

48. Statement by Edith Sch., 10 January 1961, StK 9 Ks 2/62, vol. 42, p. 6380. Regarding sexual excesses, see statement of Ulrich Fr., 8/9 August 1960, StK 9 Ks 2/62, vol. 29, p. 4340; Ryszard Sch., 25 March 1961, StK 9 Ks 2/62, vol. 48, pp. 7193–7202; Ruth Ze., 16 March 1961, StK 9 Ks 2/62, vol. 47, fol. 7058–67. One KdS officer administered 20,000–30,000 bottles of vodka for use by the executioners during mass shootings (statement by Karl Graf von der Go., 10 April 1961, StK 9 Ks 2/62, vol. 49, pp. 7350–55).

49. Statement by Irma Sch., 29 March 1961, StK 9 Ks 2/62, vol. 48, pp. 7126–35. A gas van driver brought his fourteen-year-old son from Germany to Minsk where he became an office boy but, according to his father, never saw any atrocities being committed (statement by Karl Ge., 2 April 1962, StK 9 Ks 2/62, vol. 71, pp. 10590–99; letter Ge. to Staatsanwaltschaft Koblenz, April 1962, StK 9 Ks 2/62., vol. 73, pp. 10845–46).

50. Statement by Wilhelm Sch., 19 November 1959, StK 9 Ks 2/62, vol. 8, p. 1184; file note by Sonderkommission "P," 23 July 1960, re statement by Georg Bu., StK 9 Ks 2/62, vol. 28, p. 4166; file note by Sonderkommission "P," 5 August 1960, re statement by Willy Sch., StK 9 Ks 2/62, vol. 28, p. 4244a.

51. Note by Sonderkommission "P," 5 August 1960, re statement by Willy Sch., StK 9 Ks 2/62, vol. 28, p. 4244a; note by Sonderkommission "P," 11 November 1960, re statement by Johannes Sch., StK 9 Ks 2/62, vol. 38, pp. 5667–68. A disproportionately high number of police witnesses for the case lived and worked in the Ruhr area from which, during the war, they had been transferred to Minsk (letter of Staatsanwaltschaft Koblenz to Polizeipräsident Essen, 21 March 1961, StK 9 Ks 2/62, vol. 47, p. 7086).

52. "No act constitutes an offense if its perpetrator was compelled so to act by irresistible force or by a threat entailing an immediate or otherwise not avertable danger to his own or one of his family members' body or life." *The German Penal Code of 1871*, trans. Gerhard O. W. Müller and Thomas Bürgenthal (South Hackensack NJ: Rothman, 1961), p. 41.

53. Rückerl, *Strafverfolgung*, p. 81; Dreßen, "Annihilation," pp. 306–7. See also statement by Irmin Ho. (former judge at SS-und Polizeigericht Minsk), 18 October 1961, StK 9 Ks 2/62, vol. 62, pp. 9337–40.

54. On Dr. Eberhard St., see "Haftbeschwerde," 27 July 1959, StK 9 Ks 2/62, vol. 3; investigation by Koblenz prosecutor, 27 January 1960, StK 9 Ks 2/62, vol. 12, pp. 1786–90; StK 9 Ks 2/62, vol. 14, pp. 2097–98; interrogation of St., 23 March 1960, StK 9 Ks 2/62, vol. 16, pp. 2421–28; interrogation of St., 28 February 1961, StK 9 Ks 2/62, vol. 46, p. 6835.

55. Expert opinion by Dr. Hans-Günther Seraphim, n.d. (1962), StK 9 Ks 2/62, vol. 72, pp. 10733.

56. Ruling by Amtsgericht Koblenz, 20 May 1960, StK 9 Ks 2/62, vol. 21, p. 3122.

57. Trial protocol, 15 February 1963 (41st day of the trial); StK 9 Ks 2/62, vol. 82, p. 12651. The document collection was referred to during the trial as the "brown book" and is contained as a separate volume in StK 9 Ks 2/62.

58. See Rückerl, *Strafverfolgung*, pp. 100-101; ZSL Sammlung UdSSR, Heft 1: "Verzeichnis der anläßlich des Heuser-Prozesses in Koblenz von einer sowjetrussischen Delegation vorgelegten Dokumente."

59. Landgericht Koblenz, 3 May 1961, StK 9 Ks 2/62, vol. 50, p. 7508.

60. Statement by Artur Wilke, 8/10 August 1961, StK 9 Ks 2/62, vol. 58, pp. 8629–51; statement by Artur Wilke, 15/24, August 1961, StK 9 Ks 2/62, vol. 59, pp. 8807–42; Landgericht Koblenz, 30 August 1961, re-opening of "Voruntersuchung" vs. Wilke, StK 9 Ks 2/62, vol. 59, pp. 8861–70.

61. Statement by Erich Gn., 19 July 1961, StK 9 Ks 2/62, vol. 57, pp. 8477-85. Staatsanwaltschaft Koblenz, file note, 1 August 1961, StK 9 Ks 2/62, vol. 57, p. 8495.

62. Landgericht Koblenz, 30 November 1961, StK 9 Ks 2/62, vol. 64, p. 9602.

63. Oberstaatsanwalt Koblenz, Anklageschrift, 15 January 1962, StK 9 Ks 2/62, vol. 67, pp. 9922–10081, vol. 68, pp. 10082–239.

64. Landgericht Koblenz, Erste Große Strafkammer, 18 June 1962, StK 9 Ks 2/62, vol. 74, pp. 10963–80.

65. See *Der Spiegel* 17 (1963), p. 37, "Ein Haushaltsmann aus Riga;" StK 9 Ks 2/62, vol. 74, 21/1963, pp. 26–28.

66. 12 December 1962 (26th day of the trial), StK 9 Ks 2/62, vol. 80, p. 12164.

67. 17 October 1962 (third day of the trial), StK 9 Ks 2/62, vol. 77, pp. 11488–89.

68. 12 December 1962 (26th day of the trial), StK 9 Ks 2/62, vol. 80, p. 12154.

69. 7 January 1963 (31st day of the trial), StK 9 Ks 2/62, vol. 80, p. 12287a.

70. 29 April 1963 (57th day of the trial), StK 9 Ks 2/62, vol. 84, p. 13009.

71. Verdict read 21 May 1963 (63rd day of the trial), StK 9 Ks 2/62, vol. 84, pp. 13053–56. For the written verdict, see StK 9 Ks 2/62, vol. 86, pp. 13200–579; JuNSV vol.19, lfd. Nr. 552.

72. See Friedlander, "Judiciary," pp. 673–75.
73. *JuNSV*, vol.19, lfd. Nr. 552, pp. 308, 310.
74. Letter Ge. to Landgericht Koblenz, 12 June 1963, StK 9 Ks 2/62, Vollstreckungsheft, pp. 7–8.
75. Letter by Heuser, 27 June 1969, StK 9 Ks 2/62, pp. 44–45.
76. Director of Strafanstalt Freiendiez to Staatsanwaltschaft Koblenz, 1 July 1969, StK 9 Ks 2/62, pp. 52–53.
77. Letter by Rechtsanwalt Ge., 28 June 1969, StK 9 Ks 2/62, pp. 47–50.
78. See Miquel, *Ahnden*, pp. 224ff; Herbert, *Best*, pp. 507–10; Friedlander, "Judiciary", pp. 675–76; Mildt, *In the Name of the People*, pp. 30–35. The statute of limitations for murder was abolished by the Bundestag on 3 July 1979.
79. Rechtsanwalt Ge., 28 June 1969, StK 9 Ks 2/62, Vollstreckungsheft, pp. 47–50.
80. Heuser to Landgericht Koblenz, 13 November 1969, StK 9 Ks 2/62, pp. 68–69.
81. Bundestags-Drucksache V/4094, pp. 13–14 (also quoted in ruling by Landgericht Koblenz, 12 December 1969, StK 9 Ks 2/62, Vollstreckungsheft, pp. 72–74). I am indebted to Bernd Volckart and Helmut Kramer for their advice on the revision of paragraph 26 and for providing me with a copy of this document.
82. Oberstaatsanwalt Koblenz to Landgericht, 26 November 1969, StK 9 Ks 2/62, Vollstreckungsheft, p. 71.
83. Ruling by Landgericht Koblenz, 12 December 1969, StK 9 Ks 2/62, Vollstreckungsheft, pp. 72–74; note by Strafanstalt Freiendiez, 12 December 1969, StK 9 Ks 2/62, Vollstreckungsheft, p. 75.
84. Staatsanwaltschaft Koblenz to Landgericht, 21 December 1970, and ruling by Erste Strafkammer, 6 January 1971, StK 9 Ks 2/62, vol. 89, pp. 13995–14065.
85. File note, 16 December 1970, StK 9 Ks 2/62, Vollstreckungsheft, p. 85.
86. Heuser to Staatsanwaltschaft Koblenz, 14 September 1971, StK 9 Ks 2/62, Vollstreckungsheft, p. 89.
87. StK 101 Js 2244/77, ca. 8,000 pages in 47 case and supplementary files (Beiakten).
88. StK 101 Js 2244/77, vol. 36, pp. 6461–6548.
89. Closing statement re 9 Js 48/73, August 1974, StK 101 Js 2244/77, vol. 44, pp. 7584–86.
90. Statement by Johannes Ho., 7 December 1971, StK 101 Js 2244/77, vol. 35, pp. 6394–99.
91. Statements by Heuser, 13 July 1979 and 24 January 1980, StK 101 Js 2244/77, vol. 44, pp. 7508–13, 7578–79.
92. See StK 101 Js 2244/77, vol. 44, pp. 7499-501, 7508–83.
93. Concluding statement, 29 February 1980, StK 101 Js 2244/77, vol. 46.

Tainted Law
The West German Judiciary and
the Prosecution of Nazi War Criminals

REBECCA WITTMANN

When we think of trials of Nazi criminals, two major proceedings come immediately to mind: the Nuremberg Trial of the Major War Criminals in 1945 and the Eichmann Trial in 1961. Both trials were public affairs, and both affected how the international community deals with war crimes and crimes against humanity now. It is surprising to many to discover that in West Germany an enormous number of Nazi-and regime-supporting defendants were brought to trial—over 6,000, in fact. Many more—about 100,000—were investigated but never tried. The defendants sat in court accused not of crimes against humanity but of regular murder, as defined by the German penal code in 1871. In this essay I would like to shed light on these trials, and particularly on the extraordinary difficulty prosecutors had in bringing former Nazis to trial, in getting them convicted, and, finally, in ensuring that they served their sentences in full.

Focusing on the period between 1960 and 1980, I argue that there was a massive divide between the young and eager prosecutors and the older, more conservative, largely former Nazi judiciary. There is no clear-cut picture of complicit jurists; in nearly every state in West Germany there was a young, committed, and probing prosecution. But they had to work within a system that was defined by the generation of jurists who had come before them and who still wielded extraordinary influence over the West German judicial system; in some states, 100 percent of Nazi judges had maintained or returned to their former posts. These judges sent a message to the public—through their interpretation of the laws—that the Nazi past was being dealt with properly. They developed the notion of the middleman as neutral, and therefore innocent; this representation of Nazi crime, reinforced time and again by trial verdicts, created a society in which there was little public will to punish Nazism fully. This is what Joachim Perels has called a normalization of the NS (Nazi) system from the elites.[1] Through an examination of the legal reforms in the 1960s, and by giving examples from three major investigations—the Auschwitz Trial, the RSHA (*Reichssicherheitshauptamt*) investigation, and the Majdanek Trial—I show that changes to the law made it increasingly easy for those who had the most power in the Nazi regime—the desk murderers (*Schreibtischtäter*)—to go free or escape trial, and in the end only the exceptionally sadistic Nazi criminals, usually camp guards, were tried and convicted of murder. On the one hand, there are thousands of trials. On the other, the continuities in the judicial personnel rendered interpretation of the laws and sentencing extremely favorable to the defendants.

New Beginnings and Old Elites

During the past decade there has been an explosion of historical research on the West German confrontation with the past. In their work, most historians point to an undeniable presence of former Nazis in all parts of public life: in the civil service, the government branches, academia, the press, and, most especially, in the judiciary. According to Ingo Müller, despite the best intentions of the Allies to purge the judicial system of its Nazi members, this endeavor proved to be virtually impossible as it would have left the justice system with few, if any, functionaries. Therefore, during the reconstruction period of 1945-1949, the Allies made more and more exceptions to their initial rule that anyone who had even nominally participated in the Hitler regime should lose his or her job. First, most of those who had retired or been fired in 1933 were called back; next, anyone who joined the party after 1937 was given a clean slate; then, for every judge with a clean record, a tainted judge could be hired; and finally, all judges who had gone through the flimsy denazification process could be brought back. This meant that by 1949, for example, 93 percent of court officers in the state of Westphalia had been affiliated with the Nazi Party; in the city of Schweinfurt, 100 percent; and in the enormous state of Bavaria, 81 percent of judges were former Nazis.[2]

Astonishingly, as Joachim Perels has pointed out, historians have not been willing to make the connection between the jurists and the interpretations that they generated, arguing that the new laws of the Federal Republic were basically purged of any anti-democratic tendencies from the Nazi period. This attitude is a reflection of the response of the general public during the postwar restructuring of the judicial system. The vast majority of German citizens willingly put their faith into this "new" justice system, accepting the notion that the new democratic state no longer possessed anti-democratic legal norms. The mass repression of the truth—that most representatives of the legal system in postwar Germany were former Nazis—may have been a necessity in order to embrace the new "democracy" and put trust in the justice system; however, this willful blindness led to an acceptance of criminal norms shaped entirely by a judiciary trying to shield itself from legal scrutiny.

The personalities of the former Nazi judges showed themselves in the conservative interpretations of the law, and these generally led to lesser convictions. Perels calls this an "interpretational monopoly" held by a postwar judiciary consisting largely of former functionaries of the Nazi state.[3] Legal theorists actively introduced roadblocks to the conviction of former Nazis. This was an intentional act so that jurists could avoid prosecution as lawmakers and law enforcers during the Nazi period. The best proof of the lasting heritage of Nazi law on West German postwar jurisprudence is the fact that there were only two judgments of lawyers or judges who instituted and carried out the Nazi program, and both were before 1949 (by the West German courts).[4] In those few trials—usually of judges from the *Volksgerichtshof* (People's Court) accused of having sentenced resistance fighters to death—the explanation used to give them milder sentences was that the National Socialist *Rechtsdenken* (the attitude toward law and legality) was responsible for the death sentence, not the judge himself. But who, if not the jurists, was responsible for the *Rechtsdenken*?

There is an important comparison here with the Weimar period. General consensus among historians of the Weimar period sees the failure of the democracy in large part as a result of the continuity of the elites in the civil service (government, education, and justice). This lack of purging of the old imperial system contributed to the rise of the right and the downfall of Weimar. Perels argues that these old Weimar elites remained in place during the Nazi era and in the postwar period as well, doing serious damage to the idea of a *Rechtsstaat*. Jurists accommodated themselves quickly to what was required of them. This strategy of accommodation was not unique to the judiciary: in government, in academia, in the press, and in the civil service, the most influential members of society readily complied with the demands of the regime, pursued professional programs that would please the Nazi state, and allowed the foundations of the new West German state to be built—at least partially—on the remnants of the Nazi political and social structure.[5]

The perception of Nazi crime was very different in the early postwar period; according to Norbert Frei, during the Adenauer years, "a widespread desire to see the purging project's circle of 'victims' narrowed to the smallest possible group of 'main offenders' corresponded to an increasingly prevalent theory limiting the blame for Nazi crimes to the narrow band of top Nazi leaders."[6] This perception of Nazi crime—that only the top leaders were guilty—was slowly eroded after the Nuremberg trials, whereby the prosecution of desk-top murderers lost its urgency in West German courts, and in turn in public consciousness as well. Tired of "victors' justice," swayed by the perception that all the major Nazis had already been tried by the Allies, and wanting to move forward instead of continuing to look back in shame, West Germans were ready and willing to accept the changes enforced by the judiciary. These changes led to a very different kind of Nazi convict and, I would argue, a distorted perception of Nazi crime. In effect, jurists made concerted efforts to shift legal focus away from the administrators, bureaucrats, professionals, doctors, and judges on the stand at Nuremberg and to focus instead on cruel, sadistic, hands-on murderers—people whom the Nazis themselves investigated for excessive brutality and for corruption.[7]

Penal Code and Politics

How and why was the legal representation of Nazi crime transformed after Nuremberg? During the period of reconstruction of the German judicial system, negotiations between West German officials and the Allies included discussion about how the new justice ministry would prosecute Nazi crimes. Specifically, there was debate as to whether West Germany would adopt the international criminal charges used at Nuremberg or whether the new state would reject these in favor of their own criminal system.[8] Whereas countries such as France and Israel incorporated charges such as war crimes and crimes against humanity into their penal code, West German jurists decided against a similar policy, for numerous reasons. Specifically, their own penal code had existed since 1871 and was in place throughout the Nazi period.

The existence of these laws made murder illegal throughout the Third Reich and circumvented the harshly criticized use of retroactive or ex post facto laws. In addition, it allowed the new democratic West German state to demonstrate its ability to deal with its own past through its own laws. And finally, it removed the political element present at Nuremberg and made the activities of former Nazis a purely criminal matter. These were the arguments made at the time of this debate. In retrospect it becomes clear, however, that West German jurists—often former Nazi jurists—were loath to institute laws that could hold them accountable as lawmakers during the Nazi period. The American Subsequent Nuremberg Trial No. 3, or the Judges' Case, was a humiliation that many post-war judges had narrowly escaped; they were not inclined to make themselves vulnerable under their own legal system.

West German state prosecution offices began investigating Nazi cases in the early 1950s. Only in the late 1950s did these trials really address the "Final Solution" and receive widespread public attention. There were serious problems with using the West German penal code to prosecute crimes of mass murder. Prosecutors had to adhere to rigid interpretations of the murder statute and subjective definitions of perpetrators and accomplices that, in the end, condemned only those who had gone above and beyond ordered acts of murder. In effect, those who carried out the state-ordered genocide were convicted only—if they were convicted at all—as accomplices to murder; and after 1968, not even accomplices could be tried.

The German penal code was inadequate for dealing with Nazi crimes because of the legal interpretations that were used. First, the murder charge stipulated that the prosecution prove the subjective inner motivation of the defendant. Elements of intent in murder included lust for murder, sexual drive for killing, treachery, malicious intent, cruelty, and, finally, base motives (which the postwar German courts defined as race hatred for the Nazi trials).[9] Second, the distinction between perpetrator and accomplice in the penal code specified that the primary perpetrator must show individual initiative and knowledge of the illegality of the act.[10] This meant that the state had to prove beyond doubt that each defendant had acted individually and with personal initiative

in order to be convicted of murder. In the case of bureaucratic or political entities of the Third Reich, where physical acts of murder did not take place, the
only unquestioned perpetrators of murder—those with base motives—were
the people who dreamed up the "Final Solution": Hitler, Himmler, and Heydrich. All other state functionaries, no matter their rank, could (and usually
did) claim that they were simply doing their jobs. Third, the statute of limitations prevented the courts from using the manslaughter charge, as any crimes
with possible sentences of fifteen years or less were statute barred fifteen years
after the crimes had been committed; in the case of Nazi crimes, this meant that
manslaughter could not be charged after 1960. This made the state's task much
more difficult, as it was limited to proving murder or the far lesser charge of
aiding and abetting.[11]

Within judicial circles there were important discussions that led to the constant redefining of the murder charge, the manslaughter charge, and the definition of perpetrator and accomplice. Specifically, in the 1950s and 1960s legal
theoreticians fell into different camps regarding the definition of perpetration
as an objective or subjective act. The objective definition saw the perpetrator as
the one who pulled the trigger and was generally considered too narrow a definition. Ultimately more conservative scholars, and in turn the German High
Court of Appeals, adopted an entirely subjective definition, which determined
perpetration entirely by the presence of will, regardless of whether the defendant physically committed the act—thus allowing for the possibility that the
person who committed the act not be guilty of murder. This was the standard
adopted by most judges in pre-1968 trials of Nazis.

In addition to this, German criminal law requires, uniquely, that the prosecution prove that the defendant possesses "knowledge of the illegality of the
act"; this means that, unlike Anglo-American law where it is assumed that citizens know the law, defendants in the German case *can* use the excuse that they
did not know they were committing a crime. This leads, in Nazi trials, to a
perverse result: the more a defendant claimed that he believed in and identified
with the Nazi worldview, the less likely he was to be convicted. In turn, the more
doubt a defendant showed about the morality and legality of Nazi laws—that
is, the more remorse he showed—the more likely he was to be convicted.[12] We
see this standard applied in its most egregious form in the West German trials

of Nazi doctors. Repeatedly, doctors who participated in "euthanasia" and experimentation were exculpated in the judgments because of what was defined as the general perversion of medicine at the time; this created in effect a "legal blindness" that the doctors could use to their advantage. According to Perels, "this means that the convinced Nazi perpetrator—and this applied especially for Nazi judges—was privileged, and in this way the system of legal distortion was immunized from delegitimization."[13]

Cases: The Frankfurt Auschwitz Trial, the RSHA Investigation, and the Düsseldorf Majdanek Trial

Prosecutors had difficulty convicting anyone who did not show individual initiative. This becomes most obvious in the Frankfurt Auschwitz Trial. This enormous public trial—probably the first and last major Nazi trial that either the newspapers or the public really cared about—had on its defendants' stand twenty Auschwitz perpetrators, from a *kapo* (prisoner barrack guard) to two adjutants to the commander, representing a cross-section of all the possible criminals at Auschwitz. The trial began in 1963, lasted two years, produced tens of thousands of pages of files, made use of over four hundred witnesses, and made history in that it brought to light for the first time the horrific, specific details about the inner workings of the Auschwitz concentration camp, to a German public that was willfully uninformed.

Fritz Bauer, attorney general of the state of Hesse, led a team of determined and dedicated state attorneys. They were—contrary to dominant scholarship on the reluctance of West German prosecutors to try Nazi crimes—devoted to putting the whole of the "Auschwitz complex" on trial.[14] Because of the incredibly narrow interpretation of the laws and a very conservative (and former Nazi) judge, however, only the most sadistic defendants, who had murdered people drunkenly, wantonly, and without official orders, were convicted of murder and sentenced to life in prison. The rest, the vast majority, got mild sentences that usually were reduced to time served at the end of the trial. They remained ordinary citizens who were basically seen as decent and reluctant Nazis, while the others, the sadists and "excess perpetrators," were monsters who in no way bore resemblance to the majority of society. The murder of millions in the gas chambers, or the creation and execution of laws that allowed for the murder of

Jews, the disabled, and political prisoners, became a lesser crime, with a lighter sentence, than the murder of one person without orders from superiors. The German public learned to chastise and denounce the sadistic "excess perpetrators" of Auschwitz and to forgive the order-followers whose crimes of complicity were never the true focus of the trial or of the extensive press coverage from which people obtained their information about the trial and about Auschwitz itself.

Consider in this regard the case of defendant Robert Mulka. Mulka was an SS first lieutenant and captain, and became adjutant to Auschwitz camp commandant Rudolf Höß from February 1942 to March 1943. Mulka was charged with having taken part

> in the realization of the National Socialist extermination program (establishment, activity, securing of the gassing facilities, provision of the Zyklon B necessary for gassing, organization, processing, and securing of the selection of incoming transports of civilians through the watch guards, participation in the sorting process on the platform, transport of selected people for gassing to the gas chambers on trucks, supervision of selections in the camp for the commander), as adjutant/commander, who, according to camp procedure was responsible for the quickest and most precise execution of his orders, in the knowledge of the illegality of these orders, in the measures created for killing these people.[15]

This charge was leveled against only the highest officials at the camp; it included the important stipulation that the defendant possessed the requisite "knowledge of the illegality of these orders," presumably in order to secure a conviction of perpetrating murder under the motivation of "base motives." Mulka could and did insist, however, that he possessed no understanding of the illegality of his orders, nor did he possess any base motives of racial hatred or antisemitism. Without solid evidence that Mulka knew his actions to be illegal, or that he had uttered antisemitic tirades in the presence of witnesses who could corroborate this on the stand, the prosecution stood very little chance of getting the conviction they wanted. Prosecutors and civil plaintiffs attempted in their closing statements to reinforce the criminality of Mulka's actions as a high official at the camp. Civil plaintiff Christian Raabe declared Mulka to be a "vital cog" in the machinery of mass murder at Auschwitz, and in fact called for over thirty thousand life sentences for Mulka.[16] Defense lawyers, however, used the narrow legal definitions to their advantage and insisted that the court must not be swayed by the magnitude of the crime complex and instead must soberly judge the defendant according to the standards predetermined by the reigning legal interpretation of the day: that a murderer must show individual initiative or base motives. Although it was decided that Mulka did have some understanding that the order to murder the Jews of Europe was illegal, he could not be convicted as a perpetrator because he did not issue any orders or show personal initiative. In the end he was convicted of aiding and abetting murder, and sentenced to fourteen years in prison. He served less than three years, however, and was released from prison in 1968 due to illness.

In stark contrast to Mulka's case was the verdict against another defendant on the stand at the Auschwitz Trial, Oswald Kaduk. Kaduk had none of the responsibility and influence that Mulka had; he was a low-ranking SS corporal who worked as a block and reporting officer at Auschwitz between 1942 and 1945. Kaduk had much closer contact with prisoners as his work entailed guarding some of the barracks. He was accused of thousands of counts of murder, but most important, of acting with individual initiative. The indictment against him charges, among other crimes, that "in early 1942, in Block 8, more than once, and often in a drunken state, he beat prisoners and then strangled them. He would lay a walking cane over their necks and stand on it. In this manner he killed, amongst others, the diamond handler Moritz Polakewitz, the former Secretary of the Antwerp Jewish council, Teidelbaum, and another unidentified prisoner from Block 8."[17]

Significant here is the description of Kaduk's drunken state and the use of a walking stick to torture and murder prisoners; it was determined quite easily that Kaduk was never ordered to use such a device to murder prisoners, and his individual sadistic crimes became the main focus of the law and the press coverage. Certainly Kaduk deserved at least the life sentence he received for six individual convictions of perpetrating murder.[18] More problematic, however, was the legitimization of the Nazi state through a judgment that made acting *above and beyond* the call of duty—by killing prisoners already selected for death—a crime worse than implementing and participating in the mass murder of the Jews. Narrow legal definitions—created by legal theorists and jurists the majority of whom had Nazi pasts and knew very well that they could be held accountable for their actions should the law function as it had at Nuremberg, for example, or had they defined murder more objectively—shifted the focus of legal reckoning from the crimes of complicit architects and implementers of genocide to the actions of a few wanton, exceptional, excessive perpetrators.[19]

The prosecution of desk murderers and Nazi lawmakers became even more difficult with the introduction of a controversial amendment to the criminal code in 1968. Arguably introduced in order to reduce the sentences of defendants convicted of traffic offenses, jurists began already in 1955 to discuss ways to amend the law and introduce more "humane" and "democratic" sentences for less serious offenses. According to the old version of Article 50 in the penal code, anyone who was convicted as an accomplice to a crime was subject to the same penalty as the perpetrator. This meant, ostensibly, that a Nazi defendant who was convicted as an accomplice to murder could be sentenced to life in prison. In 1968 the amendment to Article 50 was finally introduced: now, in order to sentence a convicted accomplice to life in prison, the prosecution had to show that the defendant possessed "base motives." Otherwise, the defendant had to be given a shorter sentence, which would be fifteen years or less.

You will recall that base motives, in the case of Nazi trials, meant racial hatred or antisemitism. In the case of desktop murderers—civil servants, bureaucrats, and jurists—base motives were virtually impossible to prove, as defendants could always claim that they had no antisemitic impetus. So prosecutors were faced with the daunting task of somehow showing that a pen-pusher or a lawmaker had hatred as an inner motivation. If the prosecution could not do this, then a guilty defendant had to be given a milder sentence. The problem here lies with the abovementioned statute of limitations: all crimes carrying sentences of fifteen years or less were no longer prosecutable after 1960 because they became statute-barred fifteen years after the crime was committed. Effectively, this amendment meant that no one could even be tried as an accomplice after 1968 unless their base motives could be proven.[20]

Historians and legal scholars disagree about the rationale behind the introduction of this amendment: Adalbert Rückerl, Joachim Perels, and Michael

Wildt each argue that the change was brought in without regard for what it would mean for trials of Nazis, and its disastrous effect on the prosecution of Nazis was the result of an oversight; Ingo Müller, a much more ferocious critic of the German legal system, contends that it was introduced precisely to make it impossible to try Nazi desktop killers. Müller may be imputing too much importance to the Nazi past for jurists in the 1960s, who had long repressed their own complicity and were much more preoccupied with immediate crimes against the state (not the least of which were the increasingly violent student protests of the New Left). However, it is also striking that the main jurist heading the commission for criminal law reform during the 1960s was Eduard Dreher. Dreher was the former prosecutor at the *Sondergericht*—special Nazi courts set up that regularly sentenced people to death for the smallest of infractions—in Innsbruck during the Nazi period and is presumed to have been responsible for the execution of hundreds of innocent people.[21] He represents perhaps the most powerful of many former Nazi jurists in the postwar period, as he wrote the most widely used commentary on the criminal law during the 1960s. Surely Dreher's past, and that of so many jurists making reforms to the legal system, played a role their worldview.[22]

Whatever the case, this amendment had devastating effects for a massive investigation that was going on in Berlin at this time. The Berlin Court of Appeal, in conjunction with East Berlin prosecutors, had opened an investigation of the high command of the RSHA (*Reichssicherheitshauptamt*), or Reich Security Main Office. Located in Berlin, the RSHA was responsible—on the bureaucratic level—for all aspects of state security, including the Gestapo, the *Einsatzgruppen*, and the transfer of prisoners into concentration camps. About 3,000 people worked for the RSHA (which was headed first by Reinhard Heydrich, later by Ernst Kaltenbrunner), and so the prosecution had their work cut out for them.[23] Before this investigation was opened, the Americans tried ten RSHA officials at Nuremberg, and the West Germans had adjudicated only four such officials by 1964.[24]

Prosecutors had high hopes for the investigation and divided the proposed proceedings into three groups: those who had been involved in implementing the "Final Solution"; those involved in the administration of the *Einsatzgruppen* and development of the mobile gas vans; and those in charge of POWs, slave laborers, and political prisoners and their eventual murder.[25] Unlike the Auschwitz Trial, where prosecutors tried to prove the individual crimes of particularly sadistic people, in Berlin state attorneys had to explain the whole world of the RSHA, its structure and hierarchy, as well as the acts of individuals. The RSHA was a political entity and was therefore even more difficult to investigate than the world of hands-on murder that was Auschwitz. The main perpetrators in the RSHA were not physically involved in the act of killing; their motives would be very difficult to prove. And yet, before 1968, prosecutors were not concerned with this problem and felt optimistic about the prospects for this colossal trial.

When the 1968 amendment was introduced, the RSHA investigation fell apart. Defense lawyers for former Nazis who had already been indicted were the first to recognize this new loophole as advantageous for their clients. For example, in 1969, Otto Bovensiepen, former head of Gestapo in Berlin, found himself on the defendant's dock. His lawyer wrote to Werner Best, former head of Office I of the RSHA, later Reich's representative in Denmark, who after the war was one of the most active jurists in the largely successful movement to amnesty former Nazi civil servants. Bovensiepen's lawyer judiciously observed to Best that "if our interpretation is correct, nobody accused of aiding and abetting can be punished anymore, if base motives cannot be established."[26] This proved to be correct, and Bovensiepen's trial was suspended.

What is ironic about this loophole for Nazi defendants is that, in practice, no defendant who was convicted of aiding and abetting was ever actually subjected to a life sentence: only perpetrators were. Judges were already lenient with accomplices, as is evidenced in the Auschwitz Trial, where only six defendants got life in prison (all for perpetrating murder), three were acquitted, and the eleven remaining all received less than fifteen years as accomplices. So even though judges could mete out harsher punishment, in the case of Nazi defendants they rarely did. After 1968, however, they no longer had to face this dilemma because no prosecutor would be given the green light to indict anyone as an accomplice if his base motives were not provable.

The Berlin prosecution office scrambled to stop their investigation from falling apart; they argued, cleverly, that the base motives of racial hatred or antisemitism should, logically, apply to the crime itself, and not to the person who committed the crime. After all, the mass extermination of the Jews was clearly a crime with base motives and therefore all Nazi crimes should be exempt from the amendment that was otherwise being used to deal with individual crimes like traffic offenses. The Federal Court of Appeals, however, denied this motion and insisted that base motives had to be shown in the defendant, not just in the crime.[27]

The devastating result of this ruling was that the plan to try the whole administrative complex responsible for the mass murder of the Jews fell apart on a technicality. The prosecution's effort to have the amendment overturned in the case of Nazi trials was a wasted one. According to Adalbert Rückerl, one of the harshest critics of the conservative legal community during the 1960s, "it is too late. . . . The small men, who shot, will continue to be caught through their treachery or cruelty. But the big men, who didn't commit the murder with their own hands, can be prosecuted only for aiding and abetting murder with base motives. Since today it's virtually impossible to prove that they possessed these motives, they benefit the most."[28]

My preliminary research into later trials in West Germany confirms Rückerl's dismal projection. After 1968, only four RSHA members were ever tried, and only for crimes related to base motives and hands-on murder. The largest trial of the 1970s, the Majdanek Trial in Düsseldorf, was a trial of camp guards who were mainly charged with crimes of excess and gruesome cruelty.[29] The trial lasted from 1975 to 1981 and was plagued by legal limitations; endless debates about eradicating the statute of limitations on murder; aging and dying defendants; survivors whose memories were fading and who were more and more reluctant to appear at yet another trial for fear of being branded "professional witnesses"; a disinterested press; and a public who felt that these senior citizens who had lived productive lives for the previous thirty years were harmless in comparison to the "state enemies" on trial in Stuttgart at the same time, namely the terrorists from the radical left-wing Red Army Faction (RAF).

Contexts and Continuities

It is illuminating to note the different legal response to crimes committed by members of left-wing movements in contrast with those committed by former Nazis. Perversely, the standards used at Nazi trials did not apply at all to political criminals on trial during the same period. When it came to trials of communists, courts often set aside the very rule that all be tried equally. This is because of the inner-disposition clause: because communists were disposed to detest the state, their motivation could be brought into court and made them more likely to be charged for participating in May Day activities than noncommunists.[30] The subjective interpretation of the law—that individual initiative is required to prove perpetration of murder—was used to benefit Nazis, who were deemed less responsible for their beliefs because they were performing state-ordered actions, and to the detriment of communists, whose inner motivation was to destroy the democratic state. This becomes devastatingly clear during the 1970s, at the sensational Stammheim Trial of the leaders of the RAF or "Baader-Meinhof gang." The four defendants—Andreas Baader, Gudrun Ensslin, Ulrike Meinhof, and Jan-Carl Raspe—complained that they were deprived of many basic rights and subjected to conditions (limiting their access to defense lawyers, solitary confinement, charges from crimes that had not previously been defined by law) that Nazi defendants never experienced. They were judged more harshly than Nazi defendants on the stand at the time because of their *Unrechtsbewußtsein* (knowledge of the illegality of the act) and their goal to commit crimes against the state.[31] After all, the Nazi defendants had been acting in the name of the state, had not shown individual initiative except in the most extreme and rare of cases, and had, for the preceding thirty years, been represented in legal language as mainly functionaries of a perverted state.

Demonstrative of the priorities of the conservative judiciary and the frightened public during the height of the cold war was the fact that while over 100,000 Nazis were investigated and 6,000 tried in the postwar period, over 125,000 Communists were investigated and 6,500 tried.[32] By 1975, when the Stammheim Trial was fully underway, the state and the public were no longer very interested in the distant crimes of a few old men and women, despite the fact that their atrocities far outweighed the crimes of the RAF in magnitude. In the end, at the Majdanek Trial, the press showed up only at the very beginning and at the very end. While the Auschwitz Trial had over 20,000 visitors and generated 900 press articles, the Düsseldorf courtroom was mainly empty except for a new kind of spectator, the right-wing extremist. Of the fifteen indicted defendants, nine were men and six were women; the focus was entirely on the sadistic actions especially of the female guards, whose excessive cruelty was especially shocking and sensational because of their gender.

Otherwise, the trial dragged on interminably; four defendants were acquitted at an early phase because of lack of evidence. Only one defendant, known as "*Die Stute* (the mare), was sentenced to life in prison, and of the rest no one was sentenced to more than twelve years in prison. In contrast, the Stammheim Trial, which lasted two years, was the greatest public and media sensation of the era. It was marred by swirling controversy: the restriction of defense lawyers' rights and access to information; the arrest of defense lawyers; the holding of suspects without charge; the suicide of Ulrike Meinhof in 1976; the introduction of new emergency laws, which were applied to proceedings already running; and the use of a *Staatsschutzgericht*—State Security Court—a court designed to deal with the actions of the terrorists, despite the fact that the 1949 constitution specifically prohibited the creation of new *Ausnahmegerichte* (exceptional courts) because of the Nazis' flagrant violations of law in the *Volksgerichtshof* and *Sondergerichte*. The defendants were sentenced to multiple life sentences, and defense lawyers criticized the court heavily for not abiding by the rule of law. The three remaining convicts committed suicide in the famous "German Autumn" of 1977, some six months after their conviction for murder.

Scholars have recently turned to the question of continuity between Nazi and postwar Germany. A handful of new books have demonstrated that there was a general willful failure among early postwar German journalists, scholars, politicians, and jurists, to earnestly face up to their roles in perpetuating the racist, persecutory policies of the Third Reich.[33] Challenging the protestations of almost all professionals that they remained outside of Nazism as silent resistors, scholars of postwar Germany now agree that the most influential members of society readily complied with the demands of the regime, pursued professional programs that would please the Nazi state, and by their denial allowed the foundations of the new West German state to be built—at least partially—on the remnants of the Nazi political and social structure. However, just as these continuities are being recognized, there is still not enough examination of the continuities in the law, the legal personnel, and what this meant not only for Nazi trials but for the public perception of Nazi criminality.

We know, of course, that the most heinous of Nazi laws were repealed: the

Nuremberg laws, arbitrary death sentences, persecution on racial and religious grounds, or based on sexuality or mental capacity; all were removed from the penal code during the reconstruction period. However, many changes made in the Nazi period remained. For example, Paragraph 175 of the penal code, introduced in 1871, forbade homosexual intercourse; it was amended by the Nazis in 1935 in order to close any loopholes and make punishments much harsher, up to ten years imprisonment; this amendment was not repealed in West Germany until 1973, and the law itself was not repealed until 1994. Similarly, legal precedents set during the Nazi period, often by the same judges who would later work on trials of Nazis, were judged wholly appropriate in the postwar setting. A good example of this continuity in legal interpretation was the bathtub case of 1940. It went a long way toward defining perpetrator motivation: in a case where a woman drowned her sister's baby, it was determined that the mother of the child had willed the act and that therefore the actual killer of the child, the sister, was not guilty of perpetrating but aiding and abetting murder due to her lack of will. Precisely this interpretation was used again and again in postwar Nazi trials, in which hands-on killers without individual initiative were convicted only as accomplices.[34]

Finally, it is astounding to note that the *Volksgerichtshof*—the Nazi People's Court, formed in 1934 to prosecute treason—was not recognized as a state-operated instrument of terror until 1985, and the summary dismissal of all criminal judgments issued during the Nazi period occurred finally in 1998.[35] Such delays in historical justice are not surprising, considering the constituency of the postwar judiciary. The desire of former Nazi judges to protect themselves from possible prosecution led to a deeply conservative postwar legal system, whereby most Nazi perpetrators, although valiantly pursued by state attorneys, escaped punishment, and the public absorbed a largely distorted image of the Nazi criminal. Why was there so little protest against these legal diversions? The problem is this: to address the extent to which Nazi jurists infiltrated and shaped the West German justice system meant questioning the legitimacy of the entire legal system of West Germany. The will to do this did not exist. In fact, the minority who did question the fundamental basis of the postwar legal system—the students of the left-wing movements—were openly demonized and harshly silenced by the very laws and lawmakers they were criticizing.

The student movement's frustration with the conservatism and what they perceived as lingering Nazism in all aspects of West German society, and especially the legal system, was met with emergency laws, tear gas, and a clampdown on the basic legal right to protest.[36] The vast majority of Germans saw this protest of the younger generation as a threat to their fragile new democracy and to their carefully constructed representation of the past. No one, and especially none of the jurists at the center of this deliberate amnesia and distorted definition of Nazi crime, wanted to face the possibility of being held accountable for his actions. And because the newly minted legal system was largely in the hands of former Nazis, jurists were relatively successful at achieving their goal of obscuring their own crimes, appearing to be heralds of the new democracy, and eliminating public will for change. The postwar judiciary created an image whereby the governmental system, the justice ministry, was conveniently separate from the people, the individuals who made up this structure. Where individuals may have had Nazi pasts, the law apparently did not.

The law was not the setting in which Germans would come to recognize the wholesale complicity of an entire generation: this would occur through different channels. The student movement's frustration with the results of proceedings such as the Auschwitz Trial, dropped investigations such as the RSHA inquiry, and the silence of their parents led to a sober reconsideration of the complicity of an entire generation during the Nazi period. This new attitude was best reflected in Willi Brandt's momentous acknowledgment of German responsibility for the Holocaust during his 1970 genuflection before the Warsaw ghetto memorial. Mainstream television broadcasts, such as the American mini-series *Holocaust* in 1979, aired on West German television and provoked fresh discussion about the Nazi past. And, finally, the 1980s brought earnest historical inquiry and a dramatic expansion of archival research, sound scholarship, debate, and information to a young, curious German public. These were the forces that helped—and are still helping—to erode prevailing myths about Nazi crime.

Notes

An earlier, shorter version of this essay appears in *Judging Nuremberg*, ed. Herbert Reginbogin and Christoph Safferling (Frankfurt am Main: Sauer Verlag, 2006).

1. Joachim Perels, *Das juristische Erbe des "Dritten Reiches": Beschädigungen der demokratischen Rechtsordnung* (Frankfurt am Main: Campus, 1999), p. 198.

2. Ingo Müller, *Hitler's Justice: The Courts of the Third Reich* (Cambridge MA: Harvard University Press, 1992), pp. 202–3.

3. Perels, *Juristische Erbe*, p. 25.

4. Perels, *Juristische Erbe*, p. 23.

5. For more on the conformity of professionals during the Nazi period, see Norbert Frei, *Adenauer's Germany and the Nazi Past: The Politics of Amnesty and Integration* (New York: Columbia University Press, 2002); Lutz Hachmeister and Friedemann Siering, eds., *Die Herren Journalisten: Die Elite der deutschen Presse nach 1945* (Munich: C. H. Beck, 2002); and Bernd Weisbrod, ed., *Akademische Vergangenheitspolitik: Beiträge zur Wissenschaftskultur der Nachkriegszeit* (Göttingen: Wallstein, 2002).

6. Frei, *Adenauer's Germany and the Nazi Past*, p. 304.

7. In 1943, for example, the SS created a special commission based in Krakow, in which SS judges were sent to Auschwitz to investigate and to prosecute guards and officers suspected of corruption or brutality not ordered by Nazi officials. These investigations led to the dismissal of Maximilian Grabner, head of the Political Department at Auschwitz, and the transfer of Wilhelm Boger, an officer in the Political Department accused of creating a torture device called the "Boger Swing," which had not been authorized by the camp administration. This very evidence provided by the documentation from the Krakow SS commission was introduced against Boger in the Frankfurt Auschwitz Trial; the head of that commission, Konrad Morgen, was a practicing lawyer in the 1960s who testified to Boger's acts on the stand on Frankfurt. For more on this, see Rebecca Wittmann, *Beyond Justice: The Auschwitz Trial* (Cambridge MA: Harvard University Press, 2005), pp. 160–74.

8. See Henry Friedlander, "The Judiciary and Nazi Crimes in Postwar Germany," *The Simon Wiesenthal Center Annual* (New York: Rossel Books, 1984), pp. 27–44.

9. *Strafgesetzbuch mit 77 Nebengesetzen* [StGB], 34th ed. (Munich: C.H. Beck'sche Verlagsbuchhandlung, 1963), p. 88.

10. *Strafgesetzbuch mit 77 Nebengesetzen*, p. 22.

11. For more on the debate on the statute of limitations, see Wittmann, *Beyond Justice*, pp. 48–53.

12. Perels, *Juristische Erbe*, p. 27.

13. Perels, *Juristische Erbe*, p. 27.

14. See Hannah Arendt, *Eichmann in Jerusalem: A Report on the Banality of Evil* (New York: The Viking Press, 1964), pp. 14–15.

15. 4 Ks 2/63, *Strafsache gegen Mulka und andere*, First Frankfurt Auschwitz Trial, 20 December 1963–8 August 1965, jury trial at the District Court, Frankfurt-am-Main *Anklageschrift*, 78: p. 14620.

16. Christian Raabe in Bernd Naumann, *Auschwitz: Bericht über die Strafsache gegen Mulka u.a. vor dem Schwurgericht Frankfurt* (Frankfurt am Main: Fischer Bücherei, 1968).

17. 4 Ks 2/63, *Anklageschrift*, 52: p. 9486.

18. 4 Ks 2/63, *Urteil*, pp. 390–99.

19. See also Wittmann, *Beyond Justice*, ch. 5.

20. Michael Wildt, *Generation des Unbedingten: Das Führungskorps des Reichssicherheitshauptamtes* (Hamburg: Hamburger Edition, 2003), p. 831.

21. See Norbert Podewin, ed., *Braunbuch: Kriegs-und Naziverbrecher in der Bundesrepublik und in Berlin (West)* (1968; reprint, Berlin: Edition Ost, n.d.), p. 128.

22. See Eduard Dreher and Hermann Maasen, *Strafgesetzbuch mit Erläuterungen und den*

wichtigsten Nebengesetzen, 2nd ed. (Munich: C.H. Beck'sche Verlagsbuchhandlung, 1956).

23. Wildt, *Generation*, p. 23.
24. Wildt, *Generation*, p. 817.
25. Wildt, *Generation*, p. 825.
26. Quoted in Wildt, *Generation*, p. 833.
27. Wildt, *Generation*, p. 834.
28. Adalbert Rückerl in *Der Spiegel*, 1 January 1969, in Wildt, *Generation*, p. 835.
29. See Volker Zimmermann, *NS-Täter vor Gericht: Düsseldorf und die Strafprozesse wegen nationalsozialistischer Gewaltverbrechen*, vol. 10 (Düsseldorf: Justizministerium des Landes Nordrhein-Westphalen, 2001).
30. Zimmermann, *NS-Täter vor Gericht*, p. 28.
31. For more on the double standards used at the Stammheim Trial, see Pieter Bakker Schut, *Stammheim: Der Prozeß gegen die Rote Armee Fraktion* (Kiel: Neuer Malik Verlag, 1989), pp. 37–51.
32. Müller, *Hitler's Justice*, p. 223.
33. See Ulrich Herbert and Olaf Groehler, *Zweierlei Bewältigung: Vier Beiträge über den Umgang mit der NS-Vergangenheit in den beiden deutschen Staaten* (Hamburg: Ergebnisse Verlag, 1992); Hans Mommsen, *Auf der Suche nach historischer Normalität: Beiträge zum Geschichtsbildstreit in der Bundesrepublik* (Berlin: Argon, 1987); Peter Reichel, *Vergangenheitsbewältigung in Deutschland: Die Auseinandersetzung mit der NS-Diktatur von 1945 bis heute* (Munich: C.H. Beck, 2001); and Annette Weinke, *Die Verfolgung von NS-Tätern im geteilten Deutschland: Vergangenheitsbewältigung 1949–1969, oder: Eine Deutsch-Deutsche Beziehungsgeschichte im Kalten Krieg* (Paderborn: Ferdinand Schöningh, 2002).
34. Wittmann, *Beyond Justice*, p. 39.
35. Perels, *Juristische Erbe*, p. 37.
36. See Jeremy Varon, *Bringing the War Home: The Weather Underground, the Red Army Faction, and Revolutionary Violence in the Sixties and Seventies* (Berkeley: University of California Press, 2004), pp. 254–90.

Justice in Austrian Courts?

The Case of Josef W. and Austria's Difficult Relationship with Its Past

PATRICIA HEBERER

On 14 September 1942 a transport of Jews from the city of Vienna arrived in German-occupied Minsk.[1] Here, beginning in April 1942, the forces of the *Kommandeur der Sicherheitspolizei und des SD* (Commander of the Security Police and SD, or KdS) in Minsk were engaged in murdering trainloads of Jews, deported from the Reich, by shooting and by asphyxiation in gas vans at the nearby agricultural estate of Maly Trostinets, some thirteen kilometers from the Belorussian capital.[2] That September afternoon, the Austrian Jews arriving at the freight yard in Minsk were met by five large vans, waiting to collect them. Unloaded car by car, the crowd of men, women, and children were instructed to leave their baggage on the pavement and to form an orderly line. From her place in the queue, a women focused her attention on one of the van drivers, speaking in German to his colleagues. Heartened by the familiar dialect—for she could recognize the accent of Vienna's Erdberg neighborhood—the woman approached and engaged in brief conversation with him. Returning to her acquaintances in the line, she was heard to remark: "*Wenn ein Wiener da ist, kann uns nicht viel passieren*" (If a Viennese is here, nothing much can happen to us).[3]

The Viennese man in the freight yard that day was gas van driver Josef W., on loan to the KdS Minsk from *Einsatzkommando* 8 (EK 8), a mobile killing unit of the *Einsatzgruppen*, stationed two hundred kilometers away in Mogilev. This self-admitted perpetrator of Nazi crimes, and the story of the Austrian justice apparatus that failed to convict him, are the focus of this essay.

Josef W. was born to a working-class Viennese family on 3 September 1910. Apprenticed in his teens to a hairdresser, he spent most of the initial years of the Depression era unemployed. Perhaps it was this early experience of joblessness in a newly truncated Austria that drove him to join the Austrian Nazi Party in 1931 and the SS two years later. His political stance and his status as an "Illegal" following a national ban on Nazi activity in Austria in 1934 ensured that he lost a succession of job opportunities, including a brief stint with the Austrian *Bundesheer*.[4] After 1933 he supported himself through chance employment, often as a driver or chauffeur.[5] In 1938 W. was in temporary service as a waiter in the southern province of Styria. Upon hearing of the *Anschluss*, he immediately returned to Vienna and made his way to the Hotel Regina, an early, temporary headquarters of the Viennese Gestapo, looking for work.[6] In the years following Austria's annexation to the Reich, W. worked as a driver in the Gestapo motor pool, but in early 1942, the thirty-two-year-old was instructed to report to the Reich Security Main Office (*Reichssicherheitshauptamt*, or RSHA) headquarters in Berlin. Here he received orders to take possession of a five-ton Saurer cargo van and to link up with the special operations unit *Einsatzkommando* 8 in Mogilev in the occupied East.[7]

The Saurer was no ordinary van. In August 1941 *Reichsführer-SS* Heinrich Himmler had traveled east to Minsk, where he observed the shooting actions of the mobile killing units attached to *Einsatzgruppe* B. Visibly shaken by his visit to the shooting pits, Himmler tasked Arthur Nebe, chief of RSHA Office V and head of Germany's Criminal Police, to devise a more "convenient" method of killing, particularly one that would spare the shooting commandos an element of their grisly assignment.[8] Murder with carbon monoxide gas—already utilized on German soil for the systematic murder of Germany's institutionalized disabled population—was contemplated, but transporting the chemically produced gas in bottled form, as it was currently used for this "euthanasia" program, seemed too cumbersome a method for mobile killing units operating in the East. Nebe turned to his own Technical and Forensic Institute of the Criminal Police (*Kriminaltechnisches Institut*, or KTI) and to chemist Albert Widmann, so instrumental in developing the gassing technology for the "euthanasia" campaign, to find the most expedient solution.[9] Widmann's ultimate answer to Nebe's dilemma was the gas van: a large cargo truck with a modified chassis that allowed a length of tubing attached to the engine's exhaust to pipe deadly carbon monoxide gas into a sealed chamber in the rear of the vehicle.[10] This "special purpose vehicle" (*Sonderwagen*) was the perfect solution for the German-occupied Soviet Union: it was mobile, drivable, and could be used for transport and portage; it could convey and gas the "enemies of the Reich," and its routine appearance had an element of camouflage that could allay the fears of its victims and conceal their fates from the preying eyes of onlookers. Gas vans are believed to have made their first appearance on the Eastern Front near Poltava in November 1941 and were famously used at Chelmno, the first extermination camp of the "Final Solution."[11]

Josef W. arrived with his gas van in Mogilev in mid-March 1942.[12] By most accounts the forces of the *Einsatzgruppe* B had two other vans operating in Belorussia by this time, including one assigned to the *Befehlshaber der Sicherheitspolizei und des* SD (commanding officer of the Security Police and SD, or BdS) Minsk, so that the van attached to EK 8 was the third operating in this territory. EK 8, then under the command of Dr. Otto Bradfisch, comprised a force of sixty to one hundred men, including police officials, SD functionaries, *Waffen-SS* reserves, and a dozen SS drivers.[13] The commando was engaged at least partially in combating partisans, who were particularly active in the region; but anti-partisan warfare mingled seamlessly with antisemitic persecution, and a major preoccupation of the unit lay in anti-Jewish actions both in the town of Mogilev and in the outlying districts. With the van in disrepair upon its delivery to Belorussia, W., by his own admission, participated as a driver of transport vehicles in at least one shooting action, near Smolensk, shortly after his arrival in May 1942.[14] His initial participation in direct killing operations with his gas van was the clearing of a local prison in Mogilev, which routinely housed 100 to 120 Jewish prisoners, including women and children. This prison "evacuation" was W.'s chief occupation in Mogilev, for according to fellow gas van driver Heinz Sch., who joined EK 8 in August 1942, prisoners were removed from the jail once or twice weekly and driven in a series of convoys to the edge of the city. There they were gassed in the van's interior and buried in a pit by a small commando of Jews from the ghetto, who themselves were shot shortly thereafter. Sch. would later testify that by the early autumn of 1942 some 6,000 Jews had been murdered by gassing in the context of prison clearing.[15] We have also seen that W. participated in at least one instance in the killing of Jews from the Reich when, on loan to the KdS Minsk in September 1942, he gassed transports of Viennese Jews at Maly Trostinets. In the late autumn of that year he was granted leave and traveled home to Vienna to marry his now pregnant fiancée.[16] On his return to the East, he suffered an attack of kidney stones and was not fit for active duty until late January 1943. From this time until his departure from Belorussia nine months later, the state's attorney's office of the city of Vienna asserted—conservatively—that W. had driven his gas van on at least three separate occasions in the Minsk-Mogilev area, claiming the lives of at least 340 Jewish men, women, and children.[17] Unconfirmed by Austrian justice authorities were well-based allegations that in the course of his assignment with EK 8, he had also gassed inmates from the local mental institution by inserting the metal tubing from his gas van into the window of a hermetically sealed outbuilding of the asylum where the patients had been confined and forcing the lethal exhaust into the makeshift gas chamber.[18]

In September 1943 Josef W. returned to Vienna on leave to take a training course for a future career with the Viennese police. It was there that he learned that he had been dismissed from his service in Mogilev and spent the last year of the war as a chauffeur and driver for an RSHA unit in Budapest. At war's end W.'s SS membership landed him in American captivity, finally in the internment camp Glasenbach, near Salzburg.[19] Now, Austrian—and American—justice authorities had it in their power to try Josef W. for his participation in Nazi crimes. Yet in 1945 the actions of the *Einsatzgruppen* were still imperfectly understood, and evidence of W.'s involvement with EK 8 apparently went undiscovered. In early 1946 an Austrian court tried and convicted W. of high treason in light of his SS and Nazi Party membership. He received a fifteen-month sentence, which was commuted to time served in the internment camp. No mention was made of his gas van service in Mogilev.[20]

It was the early 1960s by the time Josef W.'s criminal past began to catch up with him. By 1960 West Germany's first full-scale effort to adjudicate crimes of the *Einsatzgruppen*, in the Ulm *Einsatzkommando* trial of 1958, had spurred federal German justice officials to create a centralized national clearinghouse for capital crimes committed during the Nazi era.[21] The concrete result of this effort was the Central Office of the State Justice Administrations for the Investigation of Nazi Crimes (*Zentrale Stelle der Landesjustizverwaltungen zur Aufklärung nationalsozialistischer Verbrechen*), headquartered in Ludwigsburg. The foundation of the *Zentrale Stelle* and a waning statute of limitations for murder committed under the auspices of the Third Reich—then set to expire in May 1965—inspired a rash of indictments of suspected Nazi perpetrators in

German courts.[22] Not so, however, in Austria, where postwar national identity was fashioned from its self-styled status as "first victim" of German aggression. Under the gaze of its postwar occupiers, Austrian courts tried 28,148 cases in the ten years following the war and convicted 13,607 individuals.[23] Yet in the 1960s, even as Germany began to emerge from a decade of suppression of its Nazi past, Austria continued to exist in what the Viennese historian Hans Safrian has called an era of "amnesia through amnesty," pointedly ignoring the extensive involvement of native Austrians in the crimes of the Holocaust.[24] Since 1955, the year in which Austria gained independence from Allied occupation, Austrian justice officials launched only 35 trials of accused Nazi perpetrators, with 28 of those proceedings between the years 1955 and 1978.[25]

Josef W. was interrogated about his activities in Mogilev for the first time in 1963, as West German prosecutors investigated the Minsk BdS and KdS complexes and prepared cases against individuals such as Georg Heuser, the Gestapo chief of the latter unit.[26] In that year two *Austrian* criminal investigators were present to interview W.[27] The interrogation seemed light going, with the officials rarely challenging W.'s patently false claims that he had only been a cargo driver and ignoring his manipulation of facts and dates.[28] W. fared less well in a follow-up interview on 10 March 1964, when German investigators accompanied their Austrian colleagues to the interrogation room.[29] Under the more intense scrutiny of German detectives, W. quickly folded and gave a full account of his involvement with the EK 8, including a revealing description of his experience with the gas van and solid identifications of implicated men in his unit.[30] We know much about the activities of Josef W. and his colleagues because of this particularly frank interview. W. described his complicity in detail and did so in the cynical confidence that despite the presence of German police officials, Austrian justice authorities would not move to try him. We know this because after an initial complaint was launched against him a year later by the Vienna public prosecutor in February 1965, W. refused to cooperate with Austrian investigators. "[I] was supposed to testify as a witness in a German proceeding," he protested; "it was *not* explained to me at either interrogation that I could refuse to testify concerning certain events, by which I could place myself in danger of criminal prosecution."[31]

Although Austrian prosecutors were sufficiently encouraged by Josef W.'s admission to open an investigation against him in early 1965, it would be another five years before the public prosecutor's office in Vienna succeeded in pressing an indictment for murder.[32] Although German investigators had accumulated an enormous amount of evidence with regard to the KdS Minsk and the activities of *Einsatzkommando* 8 in the Minsk-Mogilev region from prior proceedings in Frankfurt and Kiel, Austrian authorities seem to have found corroborating details concerning W.'s actions hard to come by, and the witnesses whom they could locate proved generally uncooperative. Former comrades in the EK 8 remembered W.—or more commonly recalled the van driver with the heavy Austrian accent—but even those who had already been tried in Germany and were thus in little danger of further self-incrimination seemed loath to provide justice officials with the information they needed.[33] Once proceedings against him were pending, W. and his attorney attempted to stave off further interrogations by filing dilatory motions and by suggesting that the fifty-nine year-old W. was too ill to meet with investigators.[34] Finally, however, on 12 May 1970 the Vienna public prosecutor's office (StA Wien) issued an indictment charging W. with murder in the deaths of at least 340 Jewish men, women, and children in the Minsk-Mogilev area in the years 1942 and 1943.[35] W. was arrested in his home on the evening of 20 May and held in remand in the expectation of an autumn trial date.[36]

W.'s trial began on 6 October 1970. Fellow EK 8 member Otto D., who ran the unit's kennel, was to have shared the dock with W. as a co-accused, but he had successfully dodged prosecutors' attempts to interrogate him and in early May was officially dropped from the investigation for lack of evidence.[37] The proceeding, which lasted four days, was, significantly, a jury trial, with eight jurors sworn in before presiding judge Dr. Werner Ortis and two further jurists.[38] Already in the trial's first day, W.'s testimony, along with the voluminous witness accounts gleaned from earlier German judgments, succeeded in revealing in disturbing detail the murderous actions of the *Einsatzkommando* 8. So gruesome were some of W.'s revelations that one of the jurors, war veteran Leopold T., asked to be excused from the jury pool. He had "gone through a lot of things during the war," T. explained to the presiding judge, so that listening to the defendant's statements made his "whole body shake"; the bench replaced him with an alternate juror.[39] As the trial's first witness, W. made no attempt to hide his crimes and indeed recalled for the court the instance in which he had gassed the Viennese Jews in Maly Trostinets, including the woman with whom he had conversed in the freight yard in Minsk.

> *I heard also that Jews from the Reich were coming and would be gassed. . . . Resistance would have been useless, so I didn't offer any. I loaded these people in and drove to the pit. I had seen that the van was nearly full, that about fifty people were inside. . . . The van ran on idle while gassing. It really should have been run with the choke, so that the gas mixture would be richer, and the people inside could die more quickly. But the choke didn't work on my van. I then drove back . . . [and] received orders to bring all the luggage to Trostinets. On the day I was on assignment there, 600 people were gassed.*[40]

As is often the case in trials involving National Socialist criminality, W.'s complicity was clear from his own testimony and from earlier admissions that had been entered into evidence. Thus, the defense's sole hopes rested on the two fundamental modes of justification for perpetrators of Nazi war crimes: duress and superior orders. W., along with his defense counsel Rudolf Stonitsch, asserted that the defendant had initially refused responsibility for the gas van at RSHA headquarters in Berlin, and that his experience thereafter had taught him that resistance was both futile and dangerous. Subsequently, he had allegedly attempted a course of action to break free of his service and the EK 8 by covert means. He suggested, for example, that he had delivered the van to Belorussia in a state of disrepair, intimating that he had sabotaged the brakes in order to render the vehicle inoperable.[41] Further, he insisted, he had done all in his power to gain release from his assignment by using repeated attacks of kidney stones to withdraw from active duty, and by attempting, without success, to find an SS colleague who might replace him.[42] Yet W.'s most persistent claim was that any refusal to drive his gas van in Mogilev put him in danger of life and limb. He was discouraged from endeavoring a determined resistance, he maintained, because he feared transfer to a punishment battalion or to the infamous Dirlewanger units, manned by impressed criminals and often subjected to particularly dangerous assignments at the front. When the presiding judge, Dr. Ortis, inquired why the defendant could not have declared himself psychologically unable to perform his duty, as the excused juror Leopold T. had done, W. stated flatly that there was a fundamental difference between the duties of a juror in peacetime and an SS member in time of war.[43]

W.'s allusions to his fears in refusing to carry out his function at the EK 8 brought to the fore the crucial issue of duress as a legal defense. In Allied postwar proceedings, and often in German courts, pleas for clemency based on superior orders were categorically rejected as an exonerating defense and might only be accepted by jurists and jurors concerning Nazi criminality as a mitigating factor. Explaining the complex set of statutes surrounding duress to the proceeding's lay jurors proved a formidable task. At the close of the testimony the jury was instructed they might convict W. for murder according to §135 of the Austrian penal code if the defendant had committed his crimes through base motives, if the crime had been carried out through malice aforethought (*Heimtücke*), or if the killing qualified as "gruesome" (*grausam*), "as when the victim is tormented physically or emotionally." According to binding legal interpretation at the time, the unlawful killing of a person because of his or her identity as a member of an ethnic or social minority fell under the first category.[44] Concerning the question of duress, jurors were advised that the imposed force must be such that "the average man, without exceptional moral courage, [could] not be expected to effect resistance and not enter into the criminal act." Further, there had to be a clear and present danger (*gegenwärtige und dringende Gefahr*) "which threatens in the immediate present and not in an unforeseen future."[45] In W.'s case, certainly no such danger had existed or materialized; indeed, it is a growing consensus among historians that no one paid with his or her life for refusing to carry out crimes against humanity. What W. maintained was that he had *believed* the threat of danger implicit in refusal, legally defined as putative duress (*Putativnotstand*), which put him on thinner ice still. According to the statute, presiding judge Dr. Ortis counseled that putative duress could exist only where the perpetrator's inference of danger was a justifiable misunderstanding of the situation in which he found himself.[46]

On the morning of 9 October 1970, after three days of testimony, the eight lay jurors in the Criminal Matter of Josef W. retired to the jury room to deliberate. After consulting briefly, the panel of three men and five women found W. guilty of all three counts of murder listed on the indictment but, in supplementary questions (*Zusatzfragen*) attached to the verdict, confirmed the presence of putative duress in W.'s case. Apparently without understanding the full consequences of their actions, the jury had voted to allow putative duress as an exonerating circumstance in the proceedings. After their initial findings had been read to the court, the foreman immediately sent word to the bench, informing the judges that the group had not wished to acquit W. and petitioning to deliberate again.[47] In a highly unusual second polling, the jurors were told to debate whether W. stood "in fear of the harshest punishment that a refusal to obey orders would bring with it."[48] At 2:00 p.m. the jury returned once more with a unanimous consensus of guilt on the three counts of murder. The members split over the notion that W. had stood under true duress, but all still voted affirmatively on the existence of putative duress.[49]

In Austrian courts this decision was sufficient for an acquittal. The Vienna public prosecutor's office appealed the ruling in the immediate aftermath of the trial, contending that the jury had been insufficiently prepared to grapple with the difficult concept of duress and pointing out that the jurors themselves had been horrified to learn that their decision had allowed W. to go free.[50] After months of wrangling, the public prosecutor's efforts finally proved unsuccessful, and on 10 March 1971 the original verdict—an acquittal—was reaffirmed.[51] W. melted back into obscurity. He died at his home in Vienna's third district in 1996, aged 86.[52]

In the end, the most significant aspect of the case is not so much what occurred in regard to the W. proceedings, but rather what did not occur. The trial of Josef W. appears emblematic of Austria's inability and unwillingness to deal with its Nazi past in a significant way. It has been noted that since Austria reemerged as an independent state in 1955, its courts have adjudicated only 35 trials associated with National Socialist crimes, despite the fact that Austria was home to hundreds of Nazi perpetrators, including many in key positions in the planning and execution of the "Final Solution." Clearly the verdict in the W. case bears comparison with a complex of proceedings in the 1960s and 1970s focusing on the actions of Adolf Eichmann's associate, Franz Novak. It took Austrian prosecutors four separate trials finally to convict Novak, the "transport officer" responsible for the deportations of thousands of Jews, to just seven years in prison and to make the sentence stick.[53] In the case of both Josef W.

and Novak, the jurors, perhaps representative of the society at large, exhibited a reluctance to sentence "upstanding citizens" to prison sentences for crimes committed during the Nazi era, while justice authorities themselves did little to impede the defense's manipulation of the legal system to the advantage of the accused. Since Novak's last trial in 1972, there have been only seven trials involving accused Nazi perpetrators. The last, begun in 2000, involved the case of "euthanasia" physician Heinrich Gross. Gross, a psychiatrist interested in brain pathology, handpicked children for killing in the pediatric ward Am Spiegelgrund, attached to the Viennese psychiatric facility then known as Am Steinhof. Gross was tried in 1947 for manslaughter, but his conviction was overturned on a technicality. Throughout the 1960s, Gross and his students continued to use the brain materials "collected" at Am Spiegelgrund, and Gross himself became prominent, attaining a position as head of his own Boltzmann Institute.[54] The local Social Democratic Party, of which he was now a loyal member, protected him from the threat of prosecution, and in the 1980s he won an initial libel suit in Austrian courts against a historian who accused him of participating in the "euthanasia" (T4) program, because, as Gross pointed out, he had not been convicted of such an offense. The discovery of his brain preparations in a building of the University of Vienna medical faculty in the late 1990s at last spawned public debate about the issue of Austrians' participation in "German" crimes and led to an indictment in 1999 on nine counts of murder. In March 2000 an Austrian court in its first hearing of the case ruled that Gross was unfit to stand trial due to advanced senile dementia and postponed proceedings until such a time as Gross might prove *verhandlungsfähig*.[55] Dr. Gross, who appeared disoriented and confused during the session, adjourned with his attorney to a nearby coffeehouse following the trial, where he held a lucid and lively hour-long interview with ORF (*Österreichischer Rundfunk*) television journalists. The presiding judge, who himself viewed the ORF broadcast that evening, reinstated the proceedings, but in all subsequent hearings Gross continued to exhibit the appearance of senility, and the case, likely to be the last trial of Nazi perpetrators in Austria, was discontinued.[56] Gross died shortly before Christmas of 2005 a free man.[57]

Although the cases are dissimilar in many respects, the proceedings against Josef W., Frank Novak, and Heinrich Gross do lead us to one conclusion. The

Austrian Republic's national identity as "first victim" of Nazi aggression and its enduring refusal to accept responsibility for its citizens for the crimes of the Nazi era have allowed it over the decades to turn a blind eye to murder. And as we can see by more recent examples than the W. trial, Austria's *schwerer Umgang mit der Geschichte*—its difficult dealings with its history—continues till this day.

Notes

In accordance with Austrian and German privacy laws, the surnames of plaintiffs, suspects, and witnesses in juridical proceedings not convicted of wartime offenses have been abbreviated throughout the text.

1. Landesgericht für Strafsachen Wien (hereafter LgfStW), *Strafsache gegen Josef Michael W.*, 27 evr. 1100/65 (hereafter *Strafsache gegen Josef W.*), Band IV, ON 48, Amtsgerichtsrat Dr. Ulrich Richter, Schwurgericht Koblenz, betr. 9 Ks 2/62, Auswertung von Unterlagen des International Tracing Service Records, "Records of Jews Deported from the Reich." Of deportations from Vienna to Minsk, W.'s indictment sheet pinpoints the September 1942 date as the most likely for W.'s participation; see *Strafsache gegen Josef W.*, Band VIII, ON 93, Anklageschrift gegen Josef Michael W., Staatsanwaltschaft (StA) Wien, 12 May 1970.

2. See Christian Gerlach, *Kalkulierte Morde: Die deutsche Wirtschafts-und Vernichtungspolitik in Weissrußland, 1941-1944* (Hamburg: Hamburger Edition, 1999), pp. 764ff.

3. *Strafsache gegen Josef W.*, Band I, ON II, Vernehmung von Josef W., Bundesministerium für Inneres, 10 March 1964, p. 10.

4. That is, the Austrian army.

5. *Strafsache gegen Josef W.*, Band IX, ON 117, Trial transcript, Testimony of Josef W., p. 4.

6. Throughout most of the legitimate Nazi period in Austria, the Hotel Metropol in the I. District served as official Gestapo headquarters in Vienna. Yet, in March 1938 the Hotel Regina was an important base, housing in the immediate pre-*Anschluss* days such prominent "illegal" Nazis as Odilo Globocnik, an early *Gauleiter* of the city of Vienna and later a major executor of the "Final Solution."

7. *Strafsache gegen Josef W.*, Band IX, ON 117, Trial transcript, Testimony of Josef W., p. 5f.

8. *Amt V für Verbrechensbekämpfung* (Office for Combating Criminality).

9. See Matthias Beer, "Die Entwicklung der Gaswagen beim Mord an den Juden," in *Vierteljahrshefte für Zeitgeschichte* 35 (1987): 407-8.

10. Beer, "Die Entwicklung der Gaswagen," p. 409.

11. This would have been the *Einsatzgruppe* C, *Sonderkommando* 4a.

12. *Strafsache gegen Josef W.*, Anklageschrift, p. 8.

13. Soon after W.'s arrival, Bradfisch was replaced by Georg Richter.

14. *Strafsache gegen Josef W.*, Band IX, ON 117, Trial transcript, Testimony of Josef W., p. 11.

15. *Strafsache gegen Josef W.*, Band IX, ON 117, Trial transcript, Testimony of Josef W., p. 13; Eugen Kogon, Hermann Langbein, and Adalbert Rückerl, eds., *Nazi Mass Murder: A Documentary History of the Use of Poison Gas*, trans. Mary Scott and Caroline Lloyd-Morris (New Haven: Yale University Press, 1993), p. 58.

16. National Archives and Records Administration (hereafter NARA), RG 242 (Seized Foreign Records), RuSHA dossier of Josef Michael W.

17. *Strafsache gegen Josef W.*, Anklageschrift, p. 1.

18. *Strafsache gegen Josef W.*, Band V, ON 49, Verantwortliche Vernehmung von Hans Hasse, OStA b. LG Kiel, Lübeck, 19 December 1962; Vernehmung von Hans Sch., Kripo Frankfurt am Main, 23 January 1961.

19. *Strafsache gegen Josef W.*, Band IX, ON 117, Trial transcript, Testimony of Josef W., p. 20.

20. *Strafsache gegen Josef W.*, Band IX, ON 117, Trial transcript, Testimony of Josef W., pp. 19–25.

21. For a closer exploration of the adjudication of war crimes in the Federal Republic of Germany, see Rebecca Wittmann, "Tainted Law: The West German Judiciary and the Prosecution of Nazi War Criminals," in this volume.

22. Before 1962, the German penal code set the cap on the statute of limitations for homicide (§211) at twenty years; therefore the limitations for Nazi crimes prosecuted in West Germany were set to expire on 8 May 1965, the twentieth anniversary of the end of World War II in Europe. In August 1969, after a fierce national debate, the statute of limitations (*Verjährungsfrist*) was extended to thirty years; and in 1979 the *Bundestag*, influenced by a long-standing United Nations convention, abolished the statute of limitations for murder, crimes against humanity, and genocide; see Adalbert Rückerl, *The Investigation of Nazi Crimes: A Documentation*, trans. Derek Rutter (Hamden CT: Archon Books, 1980), pp. 53ff.

23. Winfried Garscha, *Österreichische Nachkriegsjustiz* (*www.nachkriegsjustiz.at*); "Seit 1955 gab es nur 35 Prozesse wegen NS-Verbrechen," *Der Standard*, 1 December 2005, 13:03.

24. Hans Safrian, "Amnesie durch Amnestie: Zur österreichischen Entsorgung der Vergangenheit," in *Denn sie töten den Geist nicht, ihr Brüder: Festschrift für Richard Berczeller*, ed. Joachim Riedl, pp. 171–98 (Vienna: Österreichischer Kunst-und Kulturverlag, 1992).

25. See Garscha, *Österreichische Nachkriegsjustiz*. Compare this with the 682 trials of German Federal courts in the same time period.

26. The prosecution of Heuser and his colleagues involved in the actions of the KdS Minsk are examined in detail in Jürgen Matthäus, "'No Ordinary Criminal': Georg Heuser, Other Mass Murderers, and West German Justice," in this volume.

27. *Strafsache gegen Josef W.*, Band I, ON 3, Vernehmung des Beschuldigten, LgfStW, 26 February 1965.

28. *Strafsache gegen Josef W.*, Band I, ON 3, Vernehmung von Josef Michael W., Bundesministerium für Inneres, Gruppe Staatspolizei, 28 October 1963.

29. *Strafsache gegen Josef W.*, Vernehmung des Beschuldigten, 26 February 1965.

30. *Strafsache gegen Josef W.*, Zeugenvernehmung Josef Michael W., 10 March 1964.

31. *Strafsache gegen Josef W.*, Band I, ON3, Vernehmung des Beschuldigten Josef W., LgfStW, in *Strafsache gegen Josef W. et al.*, 26 February 1965 (emphasis in original).

32. *Strafsache gegen Josef W.*, Anklageschrift, 21 May 1970.

33. See, e.g., *Strafsache gegen Josef W.*, Band II, ON 30, Zeugenvernehmung von Helmut H., Amtsgericht Altenkirchen, 24 April 1968.

34. *Strafsache gegen Josef W.*, Band I, ON 4, Dr. jura Rudolf Stonitsch an das LgfStW, Betr. Beschwerde, 2 March 1965; Band I, ON 3, Attest von Dr. med., Herbert Kotzinger, 7 January 1969. As we shall see, claiming physical illness in order to postpone preliminary and trial proceedings was a favorite defense strategy of suspected Nazi perpetrators, particularly where, as here, several years separated the trial from the actual events surrounding the crime.

35. *Strafsache gegen Josef W.*, Anklageschrift, 12 May 1970.
36. *Strafsache gegen Josef W.*, Band VII, ON 97, Bundespolizeidirektion Wien an die Untersuchungsanstalt beim LgfStW, Einlieferung v. Josef W., 21 May 1970.
37. *Strafsache gegen Josef W.*, Band VIII, ON 70, Bundespolizeidirektion Wien X (Favoriten), betr. Ladung des Verdächtigen Otto D., 23 February 1965; StA Wien an Untersuchungsrichter, LgfStW, 12 May 1970. Otto D. did serve as a witness on the second day of the proceedings.
38. *Strafsache gegen Josef W.*, Band IX, ON 117, Trial transcript, p. 1.
39. *Strafsache gegen Josef W.*, Band IX, ON 117, Trial transcript, p. 16.
40. *Strafsache gegen Josef W.*, Band IX, ON 117, Testimony of Josef W., p. 16.
41. *Strafsache gegen Josef W.*, Band IX, ON 117, Testimony of Josef W., p. 8. Because of the extra weight imposed on the modified chassis, brake problems consistently plagued the fleet of gas vans employed in the occupied East. Thus, it remains a matter of conjecture as to whether W.'s claims of sabotage were legitimate or not.
42. *Strafsache gegen Josef W.*, Band IX, ON 117, Testimony of Josef W., pp. 20–21.
43. *Strafsache gegen Josef W.*, Band IX, ON 117, Testimony of Josef W., p. 21.
44. *Strafsache gegen Josef W.*, Band IX, ON 120C, Rechtsbelehrung an die Geschworenen, pp. 2–3.
45. *Strafsache gegen Josef W.*, Band IX, ON 120C, Rechtsbelehrung an die Geschworenen, pp. 2–3.
46. *Strafsache gegen Josef W.*, Band IX, ON 120C, Rechtsbelehrung an die Geschworenen, p. 4.
47. *Strafsache gegen Josef W.*, Band IX, ON 120F, LgfStW, Beratungsprotokoll, 9 October 1970, p. 5.
48. *Strafsache gegen Josef W.*, Band IX, ON 120I, Niederschrift der Geschworenen, 9 October 1970.
49. *Strafsache gegen Josef W.*, Band IX, ON 121, Verdict, 9 October 1970.
50. *Strafsache gegen Josef W.*, Band IX, ON 126, Dr. Bratusch-Marrain, StA Wien, an das LgfStW, betr. Nichtigkeitsbeschwerde, 29 December 1970.
51. *Strafsache gegen Josef W.*, Band IX, ON 129, Dr. Oktavian Coca, StA Wien an Generalprokurator beim Obersten Gerichtshof, 10 March 1971.
52. I am grateful to the filmmaker Serge Bluds, who interviewed W. shortly before his death and provided information about his passing.
53. Winfried Garscha, "The Eichmann Trial and Austria's Nazi Past" (unpublished paper), p. 6.
54. See Marianne Enigl, "'Ich bin nicht verhandlungsfähig': Der NS-Arzt Heinrich Gross über sein Verfahren wegen Mordverdacht," *Profil* 46 (November 1998): 60–63; Marianne Enigl, "Fluch der bösen Tat: Kommt die Anklage wegen neunfachen Mordes gegen den früheren NS-'Euthanasie-Arzt Heinrich Gross zu spät?" *Profil* 16 (19 April 1999): 52–54. For a broader discussion of the Nazi "euthanasia" program, see pertinent sections of Patricia Heberer, "Early Postwar Justice in the American Zone: The 'Hadamar Murder Factory' Trial," in this volume.
55. The German legal term for physical or mental fitness to stand trial.
56. "Nazi Era Doctor Heinrich Gross," *Washington Post*, 23 December 2005, p. B4.
57. After Gross's death, the Viennese public prosecutor's office permanently set aside the proceedings, which had been ongoing since 2000.

IV

Current Aspects and Implications

Crimes-against-Humanity Trials in France and Their Historical and Legal Contexts
A Retrospective Look

RICHARD J. GOLSAN

In the autumn of 1994, at the height of the controversy generated by revelations concerning the nature and duration of President François Mitterrand's service to the Vichy regime, the distinguished American historian Robert Paxton wryly observed that the Vichy past appeared to interest the French more than money or sex.[1] While Paxton's tongue-in-cheek remark might well have been an exaggeration, there is no doubt that from the early 1970s through the 1990s and even up to the present, many in France have been preoccupied with, if not obsessed by, the period of the nation's recent past commonly referred to as *les années noires*, or the "Dark Years" of the German Occupation during World War II. As the debates, scandals, and controversies associated with what Henry Rousso has aptly labeled the "Vichy Syndrome" reveal, the memory of official (and unofficial) French collaboration with the Nazi Occupier remains troubling, controversial, and occasionally even explosive. That memory has frequently left its mark not only on politics, political leaders, and governments, but also on the nation's legal and judicial system, as well as its cultural practices. Such is the unsettling and haunting power of the memory of the Vichy period, and at least the perception of the uniqueness of the historical moment itself, that the historian Gérard Noiriel has noted that for many its impact on French history is comparable to the French Revolution itself.[2]

The "Vichy Syndrome"

As Rousso points out in his classic study *The Vichy Syndrome*, as well as in subsequent works, the troubled memory of the period has undergone a number of transformations during the long postwar period. Immediately following the Liberation and up through the early 1950s, the nation experienced what Rousso describes as a period of "unfinished mourning," during which time it attempted to come to terms with the immediate impact of the regime itself, the implications of collaboration with the Nazis, and the "Franco-French" civil war pitting the Resistance against Vichy and its supporters in the months preceding the Liberation. The early postwar period was marked by the purge of former collaborators, including the trials and executions of many of Vichy's political leaders, as well as pro-Nazi cultural figures, writers, and journalists most prominent among them. It was also marked by political struggles between the victorious Resistance groups, the far right's efforts to reassert its legitimacy, and the Gaullists' efforts to impose the so-called Gaullist Myth of Resistance: the claim that the vast majority of the French had resisted, that France owed its liberation from Nazi hegemony almost entirely to its own efforts, and that Vichy essentially comprised a small group of misfits and traitors. Of course, none of this was really accurate.

In the early 1950s the Fourth Republic passed a series of amnesty laws dealing with former collaborators. Both the net effect and intent of the laws was to put an end to postwar divisiveness. The result, according to Rousso, was a lengthy period of "repressions," during which time the political, social, and cultural divisions provoked by the Occupation, collaborationism, and Vichy's excesses were in effect largely swept under the rug in the name of national unity. That these conflicts and divisions were not in reality resolved but only put in abeyance and kept out of sight is suggested not only in Rousso's choice of terms to describe the period but also in the explosive return of the memory of Vichy at the outset of the 1970s. At that time, to use Rousso's colorful expression, the "mirror" was "broken," and the French could no longer delude themselves by admiring a flattering and false self-image of their own past.

To a significant degree, the student revolts of May 1968, with their challenge to Gaullist authority and the legitimacy of postwar French culture and society, as well as the students' deliberate and provocative comparisons of police actions with Nazi oppression, helped pave the way for the breaking of the "mirror." But it was the *succès de scandale* of films such as Marcel Ophuls's monumental documentary *The Sorrow and the Pity* (1971) and Louis Malle's *Lacombe Lucien* (1974) that focused national attention on the troubling realities of France during the Dark Years. These films emphasized the pervasiveness of *attentisme* and overt collaborationism among the French, and even the presence of a homegrown fascism. Along with the fiction associated with the so-called *mode rétro*—the fetishistic fascination with the seamy side of the period explored, for example, in the early novels of Patrick Modiano—they also downplayed and even undermined the "Gaullist Myth of Resistance" and its comforting and misleading reassurances. When President Georges Pompidou clumsily attempted in 1971 to, as he later put it, "draw a veil over the past" and put the conflicts associated with Vichy to rest once and for all by secretly pardoning the former Vichy militiaman and pro-Nazi fanatic Paul Touvier (who is discussed in detail later in this chapter), his effort backfired completely. The outrage provoked by Pompidou's pardon served only to trouble further the waters and make the memory and legacy of the period even more controversial in the eyes of the public. The result of all this has been, according to Rousso, an extended "obsessions" phase stretching roughly from the mid-1970s through the 1990s and even up to the present. As Rousso has stressed in his recent *Vichy: L'Événement, la mémoire, l'histoire*, this last phase can be further subdivided to demonstrate, from 1980 to 1990, the increasing presence of the Holocaust and French complicity as the central focus of the memory of Vichy and, from 1990 roughly to the present, efforts to deal with that past and its implications through reparations and especially judicial proceedings.[3]

French Proceedings and the Holocaust

In effect, the increasing "judeocentrism" of the memory of Vichy in the 1980s and 1990s had as its most visible and controversial stage the courtroom. Beginning as early as the mid-1970s, efforts were undertaken in a variety of circumstances and by a number of parties to prosecute several individuals on charges of crimes against humanity for their respective roles in the Nazi genocide of the Jews. The first successful outcome of these efforts was the 1987 trial and conviction of the Nazi Klaus Barbie, the "Butcher of Lyons," primarily for his role in the deportation and death of Jewish children hidden in the village of Izieu. More significant, perhaps, than the trial of Barbie, who was after all German, were efforts to prosecute four Frenchmen and former Vichy officials involved in crimes against Jews and, in most cases, directly linked to the implementation of the "Final Solution" in France. The outcome of these efforts were the trials of Paul Touvier in 1994, Maurice Papon in 1997–1998, and the short-circuited prosecution of René Bousquet, legally and historically the most significant of the three men. (The fourth individual, Jean Leguay, died of natural causes in July 1989 before charges could be brought.) Bousquet would have been tried for crimes against humanity had he not been gunned down in the summer of 1993 by a crazed publicity seeker. It was Bousquet, in his capacity as secretary general of Vichy police, who in July 1942 negotiated the deportation of some 10,000 foreign Jews from the Unoccupied Zone, that is, the Zone controlled by French, and not German, authorities. It was also Bousquet, that same July, who ordered the notorious roundup by French police of some 13,000 Jews in Paris. Those arrested were incarcerated in horrific conditions in a bicycle-racing stadium known as the Vélodrome d'hiver, and many were later deported to their deaths. Ironically, in December 1943 Bousquet was forced to resign from his post under German pressure because Nazi authorities did not consider him zealous enough in the roundup and deportation of Jews.[4] Despite German dissatisfaction, by the end of 1942 alone, Bousquet's efforts as well as those of his subordinates had resulted in some 42,000 Jews being deported from France to Auschwitz.

The first Frenchman to be convicted of crimes against humanity, Paul Touvier was tried in Versailles in the spring of 1994. Unlike Bousquet, who came from a well-to-do upper-middle-class family and enjoyed a brilliant government career before the war, Touvier came from a lower-class family of rightwing Catholic provincials and was a professional failure. In autumn 1940, however, his fortunes began to change. In October Touvier joined Vichy's veteran's association and stayed on as the group evolved into the more militant Service d'Ordre Légionnaire and, finally, into Vichy's overtly fascist paramilitary police force, the Milice. Touvier climbed the hierarchy in these organizations and eventually found himself in charge of the Milice's Second Service, or intelligence branch, for the Lyons region.

As head of the Second Service, Touvier proved himself to be fanatically pro-Nazi and brutally antisemitic. He was responsible for the deaths of numerous Jews, including the January 1944 murder of Victor Basch, Sorbonne professor and president of the League of the Rights of Man, and his wife. In June 1944 Touvier ordered the execution of seven Jewish hostages at the cemetery of Rillieux—now Rillieux-la-Pape—in reprisal for the assassination by the French Resistance of Vichy's propaganda minister, Philippe Henriot. It was for this

crime, and this crime alone, that Touvier stood trial for crimes against humanity a half century later.

Maurice Papon, whose six-month trial in Bordeaux in 1997–1998 was the
longest trial in twentieth-century French history, was a different figure altogether. Neither "political rabble," as François Mitterrand once described Paul
Touvier, nor a powerful figure in the Vichy government like René Bousquet,
Papon was a successful young civil servant assigned to the Gironde prefecture
in Bordeaux in May 1942. As secretary-general of the Gironde prefecture, Papon
was responsible for "Jewish affairs," and it was in this capacity that he oversaw
the roundup and deportation of Jews from Bordeaux in a series of train convoys between 1942 and 1944.

Touvier, Papon, and Bousquet

To get a sense of why the prosecutions of these men resonated as they did in
France even a half century after their crimes were committed, it is helpful in the
first instance to consider the postwar trajectories of the three accused. Paul Touvier, unlike the other two, spent most of the several decades in hiding and on
the run from the law. He survived, in part, by relying on his skills as a con man
and thief. But to a much greater extent, he survived and also avoided prosecution thanks to the concerted efforts of powerful figures in the French Catholic
Church. From the end of the Occupation through the 1980s, Touvier benefited
materially as well as politically as a result of these connections. Members of
the Catholic clergy provided him with moral support, money, and safe havens.
In November 1971 one of Touvier's powerful allies in the church, Monsignor
Duquaire, managed to secure the presidential pardon for him from President
Georges Pompidou. When Touvier was finally arrested in 1989, he was hiding
under an assumed name, Paul Lacroix ("Paul [of] the Cross") in a monastery
in Nice.[5]

At the opposite end of the spectrum from Touvier, Maurice Papon enjoyed a
highly successful and lucrative postwar career, primarily in French government
but also in the French corporate world. Following the Liberation of Bordeaux,
he was quietly retained in his post by the new government, suffering no appar-
ent repercussions for his service to Vichy or his wartime activities. After further,
often controversial, prefectural assignments in Corsica and Algeria, in 1958 Pa-

pon was named prefect of Paris police, in which capacity he was infamous for ordering the bloody suppression of Algerian protesters in October 1961.[6] Eluding blame and responsibility for this act (which, however, became a subject of extensive controversy at the outset of his 1997–1998 trial), Papon continued his climb, occupying important political, governmental, and corporate positions, serving finally as minister of budget under President Valéry Giscard d'Estaing. Initial revelations concerning his role in the deportations of Jews from Bordeaux during the Occupation, appearing in the satirical newspaper *Le Canard enchaîné* in 1981, finally derailed his career.[7]

Although René Bousquet was briefly imprisoned after the war and tried for treason and intelligence with the enemy in 1949, he, too, ultimately thrived in the postwar period. Thwarted in his desire to resume his career in government, Bousquet became a successful and wealthy corporate figure in a variety of industries and businesses, including aviation and the press. He even succeeded in keeping his hand in politics, albeit indirectly, by activities including donating large sums to the unsuccessful 1965 presidential campaign of his friend and subsequently his protector (as is discussed below) François Mitterrand.

As these brief sketches of the postwar trajectories of Papon, Bousquet, and even Touvier confirm, during most of the postwar period all three men successfully avoided punishment for their respective roles in forwarding the genocidal aims of the Nazis and, in Touvier's case, for directly ordering the murder of Jewish hostages. Bousquet, as noted, was tried for treason in 1949, and although his involvement in organizing the deportations of Jews was mentioned, it was certainly not crucial to the prosecution's case against him, nor did it figure in the court's verdict. Under any circumstances, Bousquet was found guilty but received only a five-year sentence. Moreover, the sentence was immediately commuted because Bousquet supposedly had provided assistance to the Resistance during the war. Many journalists covering the 1949 trial were outraged by the court's decision. One journalist characterized the verdict as laughable, and another described Bousquet's sentence as "one minute of punishment for his crimes."[8] Although Bousquet's trial preceded Rousso's "repressions" phase of the memory of Vichy by a few years, it is possible to see it as a crucial event anticipating the latter's advent.

But the larger issue—even larger than the lengthy periods of relative impunity enjoyed by all three men—was that they were, in effect, aided in their avoidance of punishment by prominent figures and leaders of the very institutions that traditionally form the backbone of French society. The allies of the three men acted out of combinations of ignorance, indifference, cynicism, self-interest, or even misguided loyalty, charity, or patriotism. But they nevertheless helped, protected, and indeed repeatedly promoted the respective interests of Touvier, Papon, and Bousquet. Under these circumstances, it is no wonder that during the trials much more was at issue for the French than simply punishing old men for very old crimes. Not only was the criminality of the Vichy regime put painfully on display, but the integrity and reputations of many leaders and institutions of postwar France were at stake as well.

Moral and Legal Issues and the Duty to Remember

If these observations serve to fill in a portion of the backdrop as well as the troubled contexts of the trials of Paul Touvier and Maurice Papon and the short-circuited prosecution of René Bousquet, there were also a number of other important moral, legal, and historical concerns and dilemmas that plagued these prosecutions as well. For many individuals who believed passionately in the moral value and necessity of the trials, the primary justification for prosecuting Bousquet, Touvier, and Papon was that the French people would be paying a belated homage to the many victims of the Holocaust for whom the French nation was essentially responsible. In reminding the public of the terrible fate of these victims and in retrieving their memory from historical oblivion, the trials supposedly would help to fulfill a "duty to memory" that had been shirked for decades.

But if the prosecutions themselves accomplished moral victories of sorts in this domain, there were other, equally troubling moral, or perhaps more accurately, humane or philosophical objections to the trials that for some critics, at least, trumped their value in honoring the memory of the victims. A frequently voiced objection was that, not only were the three men in question too old to suffer the ordeal of a trial, but given the time elapsed, they were not even the same men who had committed the crimes. For those who espoused this view, forgiveness was a better, more "moral" option than prosecution.

To the argument of forgiveness, one could of course respond that the *right* to forgive belongs exclusively to the victims, and not to third parties, regardless of the latter's legal or political prerogatives. Moreover, like many Nazis and French collaborators prosecuted earlier, the three Frenchmen accused of crimes against humanity in the 1980s and 1990s did not acknowledge their crimes for what they were and, moreover, had not *asked* for forgiveness. In the case of Papon, for example, in a 1996 interview with Annette Lévy-Willard in the Parisian daily *Libération*, Papon claimed to have been just doing his job and blamed his crimes on "bigger fish" for whom he claimed to be scapegoated.[9] Under these circumstances, why forgive these men?[10]

If responses such as these served as effective counterarguments to forgiveness, in the Touvier and Papon trials, at least, the claim that the passage of time had made the accused changed men was belied by the courtroom testimonies and behavior of the defendants. Touvier, for his part, gave every indication of living entirely in the past and of nursing the same political animosities and racist hatreds that had led him to the Milice in the first place.[11] During his trial Papon revealed the same bureaucratic arrogance, coldness, and indifference that had made him an effective Vichy functionary a half century earlier. Freed from incarceration by the court for "health reasons" just before the trial got underway, Papon, in effect, "dropped in" on his own trial, as one commentator observed, like a man attending a colloquium in his own honor. He also scandalized the French public by staying in the finest hotels and eating in the most expensive restaurants during the entire proceedings.

For those concerned primarily with the moral implications of these trials, there was one final objection to the prosecutions to which there was no effective counterargument. This concerned the danger of anachronism. Stated in the form of a question, how could judges and jurors too young to have experienced the Occupation directly, and who had not in all likelihood lived through similarly dangerous and confusing times, give an informed and fair judgment of individuals who had? The judgments of these younger judges and jurors could not help but be tainted by historical ignorance as well as the dubious moral superiority of those who had never been faced with such harsh political and moral choices in their own lifetimes.

This problem was particularly acute in the Papon trial. The historian and journalist Eric Conan has pointed out that the average age of the jurors in Bordeaux was forty-two. Therefore most were born after the Liberation. The only juror, in fact, who had had direct experience of the Occupation was only an adolescent during the war. In all probability he was too young to remember much or understand what was happening around him at the time.[12]

If the broadly moral and philosophical issues just enumerated were unsettling to many, for legal experts and jurists the prosecutions of Bousquet, Touvier, and Papon produced a wholly different set of problems or controversies that, ultimately, called the legitimacy of the trials into doubt and also threatened to compromise the notion of crimes against humanity. Essentially, these problems arose when the law and the legal system were adjusted to suit the needs of the moment. During the 1980s and 1990s the definition of crimes against humanity was modified or deliberately skewed in several instances, jurisdictional matters were on occasion arbitrarily manipulated for political ends, and procedural matters were often handled on a dubious ad hoc basis. Already in the aftermath of the trial of Touvier, the French jurist Christian Guéry lamented that, as a result of these manipulations and modifications, crimes against humanity no longer had real substance or legitimacy in French law.[13]

Legal quandaries and difficulties first surfaced not with the prosecutions of Bousquet, Touvier, and Papon but with the earlier prosecution of Klaus Barbie, tried and convicted, as noted, in Lyons in 1987. When the concept of crimes against humanity was incorporated into French law in December 1964—not, it should be stressed, with the intent of prosecuting French collaborators but rather former Nazis—the law simply adopted the definition of these crimes as articulated in the United Nations Resolution of February 1946 and used at Nuremberg. When Barbie was about to be tried, this definition proved inadequate to the circumstances of the moment. Former French resisters protested vigorously that the law as defined allowed that Barbie could be prosecuted only for crimes committed against Jews, and not for those committed against the Resistance. Since Barbie was most infamous for his role in the death of Jean Moulin—the great hero, martyr, and, indeed, icon of the French Resistance—this seemed both outrageous and ludicrous to many.

Eventually the French courts caved in to the pressure of the former members of the Resistance. In December 1985 the law was changed so that Barbie's crimes against Resistance fighters could henceforth be defined as crimes against humanity and included in the indictment. While the modification satisfied some, the net effect was to "water down" the definition of crimes against humanity and blur the distinction between such crimes and war crimes.

A second, highly controversial legal development occurred during the prosecution of René Bousquet and involved jurisdictional rather than definitional matters. In 1990 President François Mitterrand attempted to derail or at least stall the prosecution of his friend Bousquet by seeking, through a combination of government channels and legal maneuvers, to have the case against Bousquet tried by the High Court of the Liberation. It was the High Court that had originally tried Bousquet in 1949 on different charges. As Mitterrand well knew, however, the court in question no longer existed, and many of its members were long since dead, so reconstituting it would be a virtual impossibility. Therefore, it would not be possible to try Bousquet. While this jurisdictional maneuver ultimately failed, it underscored the extent to which these cases were subject to political pressures. Moreover, it highlighted jurisdictional uncertainties that had already complicated, and would continue to complicate, the Papon and Touvier prosecutions as well.[14]

Of all the controversial legal decisions or maneuvers plaguing the crimes-against-humanity prosecutions in France, certainly the most spectacular and historically significant was the April 1992 decision of the criminal chamber of the Paris Court of Appeals to acquit Paul Touvier. The court's decision, which provoked an immediate firestorm of protest, was based on its interpretation of the 1985 definition of crimes against humanity, handed down in the Barbie case. In addition to making it possible to classify Barbie's crimes against Resistance fighters as crimes against humanity, the 1985 definition also stipulated that crimes against humanity could be committed only on behalf of a regime like Nazi Germany, which practiced a policy of "ideological hegemony." Claiming, first, that the Vichy regime possessed no coherent ideology but rather was motivated by an ambiguous "constellation" of "good intentions" and "political animosities," the criminal chamber then argued that under these conditions Pétain's French State could not possibly have implemented a policy of "ideological hegemony." Therefore crimes against humanity could not be committed on its behalf. Since Touvier was an agent of Vichy, his crimes, including the murders of Jews at the Rillieux cemetery, could not be considered crimes against humanity, but only war crimes. And since the statute of limitations had long since run out on war crimes, Touvier had to be acquitted.

Fortunately, in November 1992 the April decision of the criminal chamber was partially overturned by a higher court, and in 1994 Touvier was, in fact, convicted of crimes against humanity precisely for the murders at Rillieux. But the April 1992 acquittal itself points to a broader concern that still hangs over all of these prosecutions, as well as the actual trials, and that is the degree to which legal proceedings and decisions ended up distorting the historical record rather than illuminating it. Certainly among the most egregious examples of this phenomenon is the assessment of Vichy and its politics articulated by the criminal chamber in April 1992.

Blurring the Historical Record

The portrayal of Vichy offered by the court in its decision distorted and in-deed perverted historical reality in at least two ways. First, it denied the fact that Vichy was deliberately repressive and indeed "hegemonic" in its ideology. Moreover, it maintained that, despite the regime's own antisemitic statutes and its willing participation in the "Final Solution," it was not fundamentally an-tisemitic. The court made this assertion because, supposedly, none of Pétain's speeches contained antisemitic statements, an assertion belied by the historical record.

That, the arguments of the criminal chamber of the Paris Court of Appeals were clearly "slanted toward an acquittal" in April 1992, as the distinguished historian and jurist Jean-Denis Bredin put it, was disturbing enough.[15] But the fact that they revised the history of Vichy in the process posed an entirely dif-ferent set of problems whose ramifications, according to some historians, ulti-mately compromised the legitimacy of the Touvier trial two years later. When the higher court partially overturned the April decision, it declined to challenge the deeply flawed historical interpretation of Vichy that the lower court had articulated. Thus, in seeking to avoid another inappropriate revision of French history by the legal system, the higher court let stand a reading of the past that was tendentious in the extreme. Moreover, equally important, when Touvier did finally stand trial for crimes against humanity for the murders at Rilliex, this meant that according to the law he would have to have acted *not* as an agent of Vichy but of the Nazis in order to be convicted, since crimes against humanity could not have been committed on Vichy's behalf. While the young lawyer Arno Klarsfeld successfully argued before the court that this was indeed the case, his convoluted reasoning left some unconvinced.[16] The weight of the historical record (as well as courtroom testimony by the accused) suggested in fact that Rillieux was an exclusively French affair, since the murders were acts of reprisal for the assassination of Vichy propaganda minister Philippe Henriot. Moreover, numerous indications also suggested that the murders were brutal *but isolated acts* carried out on the orders of just one man. If this were the case, then they also failed to meet another criterion for crimes against humanity under French law, which is that the crimes in question must form part of a "concerted plan" and be of a systematic nature. For Henry Rousso and Éric Conan at least, the upshot of all this was that while Touvier was justly convicted of murder, the historical realities of the case suggested that he might well *not* have been guilty of crimes against humanity, as legally defined, after all.[17]

During the course of the legal proceedings against Touvier, Papon, and Bouquet, there were other specific instances in which the imperatives of history and the law ran afoul of each other, prompting critics to question the legitimacy of the prosecutions on an individual basis. But in the wake of the Papon conviction, one critic, the economist and philosopher Jean de Maillard, went a step further. He argued that the trials of Papon and Paul Touvier—and, implicitly at least, the short-circuited prosecution of René Bousquet—were all predicated on a completely specious understanding of recent history. This was so, he claimed, not merely where isolated historical events and episodes discussed during the trials were concerned, but in a broader, European, and indeed global context as well. Maillard maintained that France's greatly belated prosecutions and trials for crimes against humanity were predicated on a naive and simplistic reading of World War II that completely distorted the motivations and actions of its principal antagonists. According to this reading, to quote Maillard: "all that existed, on one side, were the Nazis and their accomplices, all of whose efforts were given over to the elimination of [the other side] the Jews and their friends. [For those living at the time], no one could escape the obligation of choosing one side or the other, with a full and complete understanding of the stakes involved, and no one could escape the consequences of his or her choice."[18] As

Maillard pointed out, this Manichean vision not only misinterpreted the larger stakes of the conflict for both sides, but it anachronistically imposed an appreciation and understanding of the Holocaust on the past that was simply not in keeping with the historical record.

If Jean de Maillard's analysis is accurate—and not itself a simplification—then it is hard to understand how the 1980s and 1990s French prosecutions for crimes against humanity served any worthwhile *historical purpose*, since, ultimately, they validated a grossly distorted vision of the past. Equally important, it is hard to imagine how, under these circumstances, they could have fulfilled a "duty to memory," since the memory or memories in question would inevitably be skewed by the fallacious historical context in which they were inserted. Finally, if history and memory were *not* served, and if, in crucial instances, violence was done to the law to the point of calling its legitimacy into doubt, what positive conclusions can one draw from the entire effort to carry out these prosecutions for crimes against humanity in fin-de-siècle France?

From a very speculative perspective, Jean de Maillard argues that their value was in signaling a new, quasi-global paradigm. According to this paradigm, today's citizen of the world, having lost faith in the traditional nation-state, seeks to ensure his or her well-being and security through direct recourse to the law and the courtroom, his or her last refuge in an increasing insecure and violent world. As part of this reading, Nazi Germany and Vichy France are less historically specific entities than symbols of the discredited nation-state in the abstract, which is the real culprit and villain. While Maillard's perspective might seem far-fetched, given the increasing importance of international criminal tribunals in dealing with the terrible crimes of individuals as well as groups on a supra-national level, it is certainly not entirely wrong-headed.

But to conclude with the more modest ambitions and dimensions of the trials of Paul Touvier and Maurice Papon and the interrupted prosecution of René Bousquet: the limitations and even the failures of these proceedings in moral, legal, and historic terms should not obscure the fact that a measure of justice was done in each case. Moreover, the misplaced and ultimately frustrated hope of having these trials serve as symbolic trials of Vichy and of French complicity in the "Final Solution" should not lead us to lose sight of the fact that men guilty of heinous crimes were convicted and punished. Finally, in punishing these men, the French trials for crimes against humanity also served the valuable purpose of reminding us once again that all trials are ultimately about the crimes of individual human beings, and not regimes. But if in exposing and punishing these crimes the French trials also succeeded in shedding even an imperfect light on terrible political abuses of the past, then certainly they have done their part as well in contributing to a better recognition and understanding of similar abuses in the present. In the terribly troubled global situation in which we now find ourselves, this contribution should not be underestimated.

Notes

1. Robert Paxton made these comments in his contribution to a "Symposium on Mitterrand's Past" in *French Politics and Society* 13:1 (Winter 1995): 19.
2. Gérard Noiriel, *Les Origines républicaines de Vichy* (Paris: Hachette, 1999), p. 11.
3. For a detailed discussion of Rousso's subdivisions of the "obsessions" phase of the Vichy Syndrome, see his *Vichy: L'événement, la mémoire, l'histoire* (Paris: Gallimard, 2001), pp. 40–49.
4. It also appears that Pierre Laval was not unhappy to see Bousquet go. Among other reasons, Laval had come to see Bousquet as too powerful and a rival to his own authority in the Vichy government.
5. For the most detailed, thorough, and balanced account available on Touvier's life up until his arrest in 1989, see René Rémond et al., *Paul Touvier et l'Église* (Paris: Fayard, 1992). This book constitutes the final report of a commission established by Cardinal Decoutray to provide an accurate history of Touvier's long and controversial relationship with figures in the Catholic Church.
6. For a thorough discussion of Papon's service in North Africa, see Van Kelly, "Papon's Transition after World War II: A Prefect's Road from Bordeaux, through Algeria, and Beyond, August 1944–October 1961," in *The Papon Affair: Memory and Justice on Trial*, ed. Richard J. Golsan, pp. 35–72 (New York: Routledge, 2000). Much has been written following Papon's trial in Bordeaux of his role in the brutal suppression of Algerian protesters on 17 October 1961. For a brief account of the events themselves and the role they played in the Bordeaux trial, see Richard J. Golsan, "Memory's Time Bombs: The Trial of Maurice Papon and the Algerian War," in *Vichy's Afterlife: History and Counterhistory in Postwar France* (Lincoln: University of Nebraska Press, 2000), pp. 156–80.
7. For a general chronology of Papon's life, see Golsan, *Papon Affair*, pp. 249–67.
8. For a detailed discussion of Bousquet's 1949 trial as well as reactions at the time, see "Memory and Justice Abused: The 1949 Trial of René Bousquet," in Golsan, *Vichy's Afterlife*, pp. 24–42.
9. Lévy-Willard's interview with Papon is included in Golsan, *Papon Affair*, pp. 162–68.
10. For an excellent and moving argument against forgiveness of Nazi crimes and the complicity of those who went along with them, see philosopher Vladimir Jankélévitch's essay "Pardonner?" originally published in 1971 and republished in Jankélévitch, *L'Imprescriptible* (Paris: Seuil, 1986), pp. 17–63.
11. During Touvier's trial, for example, it came to light that the accused had maintained

a "green notebook" containing antisemitic and anti-Zionist rants. Touvier also, apparently, was in possession of Nazi paraphernalia. To all appearances, his outlook had not changed at all over time.

12. Éric Conan, *Le Procès Papon: Un journal d'audience* (Paris: Seuil, 1998), p. 12.

13. See Christian Guéry, "Une interrogation après le procès Touvier: Le crime contre l'humanité existe-t-il?" in *Juger sous Vichy* (Paris: Seuil, 1994), pp. 119–38.

14. For these complications, see the chronologies in Richard J. Golsan, ed., *Memory, the Holocaust, and French Justice: The Bousquet and Touvier Affairs* (Hanover NH: Dartmouth/ University Press of New England, 1992), and Golsan, *Papon Affair*.

15. Jean-Denis Bredin, "The Touvier Affair: History and Justice Abused," in Golsan, *Memory, the Holocaust, and French Justice*, p. 109.

16. Arno Klarsfeld's argument before the court was published as *Touvier: Un crime français* (Paris: Fayard, 1994). Klarsfeld argued that the Rillieux murders were a French crime in a narrow context, but that since the Milice was subordinate to the Gestapo, Touvier's crime fell under the broader qualification of a crime committed under the auspices of Nazi "ideological hegemony" as well.

17. See Éric Conan and Henry Rousso, *Vichy: An Ever-Present Past*, trans. Nathan Bracher (Hanover NH: Dartmouth/University Press of New England, 1998), p. 108.

18. Jean de Maillard, "À quoi sert le procès Papon?" *Le débat 101* (September–October 1998), pp. 36–37.

Milestones and Mythologies
The Impact of Nuremberg

DONALD BLOXHAM

"Nuremberg" has experienced something of a revival in the last fifteen years. After the heavily politicized critiques of the trials of German war criminals— critiques popular in Germany in the postwar period—the decades from then to the end of the cold war were characterized by a steady but unspectacular flow of accounts about the trial of the major war criminals before the International Military Tribunal (IMT). These were penned mostly by historians or trial participants, and with the exception of stern assessments like that of Werner Maser, they tended to assess the IMT trial as a qualified success, as best encapsulated in Michael Biddiss's sensible conclusion that if "Nuremberg" were not to be awarded three cheers, then it very decidedly merited two.[1] In the aftermath of the cold war, however, jurists and political commentators have added greatly to the array of published opinion on Nuremberg and its relevance.

The reasons for this pattern are easy enough to discern. Nuremberg mattered in the "postwar decade" and matters again in the post–cold war world in a way that it did not in the interim. At points during the cold war, all of the "Nuremberg principles" were disregarded as the major protagonists fought their ideological war on the territories of smaller, weaker third parties and committed war crimes and crimes against humanity in the process. Insofar as those principles were invoked at all, it was to stigmatize the opposing ideological side for doing things that both sides were actually doing, and in a manner that disillusioned both former Nuremberg lawyers and historians of the trial.[2] With the end of communism in Eastern Europe, it became possible to talk more realistically about a single world order with a single set of governing frameworks. Alongside the vanguard organizations of free market capitalism and the apostles of a range of parliamentary democracies, Western jurists could make their mark on shaping the norms of that order, and they were hurried into action by the ethnic cleansing and murder attendant on the dissolution of the former Yugoslavia. Lawyers and activists had two key touchstones to which to refer: the 1948 United Nations Convention on the Prevention and Punishment of Genocide and the prosecution of the major German war criminals after World War II.

The first thing, therefore, to note about the "relevance," "impact," or "legacy" of Nuremberg is that the meaning of these expressions is contingent upon the time and international political circumstances of their invocation. To all intents and purposes, Nuremberg meant little for decades. When it was re-invested with symbolic power, all sorts of meanings accrued to it, some of which were intended by the Nuremberg planners, and some of which were not, some of which are truly reflective of the achievements of Nuremberg, and some of which are not. The following essay details the considerable ramifications of the historical Nuremberg, while seeking to dissect some of the representations of Nuremberg that abound in The Hague, New York, and elsewhere. Ultimately, it also considers the question of whether it matters if Nuremberg has been misrepresented.

The Perspective Gap: From "Meaning" to Policy

"Nuremberg," of course, potentially signifies much more than just the IMT trial, though that is not immediately evident from the homogeneity of so much of the scholarship on the subject. In popular comprehension, Nuremberg may symbolize all of the Allied trials of war criminals in Europe in the postwar period. Figuratively, it can evoke any trial of war criminals anywhere since 1945. Pejoratively (and sometimes nonpejoratively), it may stand for "the political trial" or "victors' justice." General comprehension has not been aided by the single most important popular representation of "Nuremberg," Abby Mann's 1961 film *Judgment at Nuremberg*. This Hollywood production spliced together with considerable artistic license episodes from both the IMT trial and some of the subsequent proceedings. To the lawyers, judges, and defendants involved, to the German public of the postwar years, and to the few latter-day scholars who have devoted any attention to them, "Nuremberg" may connote not just the IMT trial but also the twelve subsequent Nuremberg trials and, indeed, the legal aftermaths of those trials. Depending on which version of Nuremberg one studies, the lessons and legacies vary considerably.

The issue is further complicated by the differing agendas that various authorities today bring to the study of whatever they hold Nuremberg to be. The advantage the lawyer has over the historian is that he or she can pick and choose from the past, finding the most appropriate precedent and developing it, while discarding others. What matters is what is useful for contemporary practice and for the future. Thus critiques based around the use of ex post facto law, or the fact that the Allies were trying Nazis for crimes that they could not be tried for themselves, or the fact that one of the prosecuting and adjudicating powers— the USSR—was itself guilty of massive crimes against humanity and, indeed, one-time collaboration-in-aggression with Nazi Germany, may be noted and regretted, but such critiques and facts are ultimately simply discarded. None of them need be applicable to future prosecutions conducted pursuant to the legal precedent provided by the IMT and by bodies more closely approximating the "international community" in their constitution. Likewise the International Military Tribunal for the Far East (IMTFE), whose procedures and outcomes were significantly more politicized and dubious than those of the IMT, has often been ignored altogether in the search for foundation stones on which to build a modern structure of international humanitarian law.[3] What matters for the lawyer are the very definite, colossal achievements of Nuremberg in making leaders and senior servants of a regime individually culpable for acts of state to which they were party, helping to undermine the doctrine of untrammelled state sovereignty and entrenching hitherto precarious legal concepts, particularly that of "crimes against humanity."

There is nothing intrinsically problematic about this policy-oriented reading of Nuremberg; indeed, it is essential for the development of international law. Problems start to occur only when the success correctly ascribed to the Nuremberg lawgivers in the achievement of their legal aims is extended to their broader social and political goals, since success or otherwise in those spheres was largely the result of factors extrinsic to the events of the courtroom, namely the political and "psychological" state of the trials' audience. Scholars whose field of study is constrained to the law and events of the IMT trial—the narrowest and commonest interpretation of Nuremberg—are simply in no position to judge whether or not aims such as deterrence or re-education were attained. We have to refer to historians to rebut many claims about Nuremberg's political impact in the postwar period, but this is a matter of greater than purely historical interest, since such claims are also being made for ongoing crimes-against-humanity trials.

The website of the International Criminal Tribunal for the former Yugoslavia (ICTY) boasts that

> In the words of the United Nations Secretary General, ". . . In an interdependent world, the Rule of the Law must prevail." By holding individuals accountable regardless of their position, the ICTY's work has dismantled the tradition of impunity for war crimes and other serious violations of international law. . . .
>
> Thanks to the ICTY, the question is no longer whether leaders should be held accountable, but rather how can they be called to account. . . .
>
> By trying individuals on the basis of their personal responsibility, be it direct or indirect, the ICTY personalizes guilt. It accordingly shields entire communities from being labelled as collectively responsible for others' suffering. . . . This paves the way for the reconciliation process within the war-torn societies of the former Yugoslavia.[4]

These points contain a combination of verifiable truth, unsubstantiated assertion, and optimistic aspiration. Into the second and third categories fall any notions that trials educate and reform their target audience. The following section takes up this issue, with particular reference to the impact of Nuremberg in the postwar decade.

Nuremberg as "Re-Education"?

While the ICTY, like Nuremberg, may certainly be credited with creating an invaluable documentary database about the crimes of their era, one cannot extrapolate from this to the value of the evidence of those trials in re-educating the former Yugoslav or German peoples.[5] Relatedly, it is true that Nuremberg, like the ICTY, did personalize guilt, but this does not mean that the former constituencies of the guilty leaders did or will draw the desired conclusions from the trials. The evidence from the former Yugoslavia, as from Rwanda, suggests that where trials mean anything to the wider public, popular attitudes divide primarily along the same ethno-national lines that provided the cleavages for ethnic cleansing and genocide.[6] The West German people identified themselves against their former leaders when that was convenient but swiftly changed their stance, and in the process actually forced the Allies to dismantle the legal machinery to which they took such exception.

However positively the German public as a whole today views the Nuremberg trials, and however enthusiastic many German lawyers today are for innovations such as the International Criminal Court and genuinely universal jurisdiction for war crimes and crimes against humanity, at the time it mattered most, namely in the immediate aftermath of Nazi rule, both the medium and the message of trial were decisively rejected by the west German populace.[7] The influence of generational change in the Federal Republic of Germany, particularly the student movement of the 1960s that brought with it a more open approach to "the crimes of the fathers," are the key factors in understanding Germany's retrospective embracing of "Nuremberg," not the beneficent and re-educative impact of the trials themselves. In other words, cultural changes have influenced as a by-product the way the legal event is viewed in Germany (and elsewhere). The legal event did not shape the cultural change; to argue otherwise is to confuse cause and effect.

Such attention as Germans did give to the IMT trial and the wider "guilt question" was shaped on one hand by the desire for individual self-exculpation and on the other by the sense that whatever Germany had inflicted was balanced if not exceeded by the suffering inflicted on Germans. Particular reference was made to Allied area bombing, the mass rape of German women by Soviet forces in 1945, the legions of German POWs lost to Soviet prison camps, and the Allied-approved forced expulsion into Germany of perhaps 12 million ethnic Germans from eastern and central Europe.[8] Within the broader context of negative reaction to the occupation, one factor was specific to the institution of trial, however: detachment.

After the initial excitement at the introduction of legal proceedings in 1945, there was a significant ebbing of interest, just as there was even among the judges on the International Military Tribunal.[9] The pattern of attention around the IMT trial is in itself instructive, indicating more about the perceived relevance of each component part of the proceedings than its intrinsic interest value. Thus we read of interest escalating again only when the twenty-two defendants made their own concluding addresses to the court: the final act before judgment.[10] The period of the attention lapse encompassed much of the substance of the trials: the cross-examinations of the individual defendants and a significant part of the presentation of the Soviet case, which contained the most graphic and extensive evidence on crimes against humanity. Conversely, the part of U.S. chief prosecutor Robert H. Jackson's opening speech in which he differentiated between Nazis and the mass of ordinary Germans met with much enthusiasm, as did those individual defendants' closing statements that defended the German people. Indeed, there was a clamor for more substantial press coverage of the latter.[11]

It was entirely understandable that many would think, as did a columnist of the left-wing newspaper *Telegraf* in May 1946, that the eyes of the world were on Germany's reaction to the trial.[12] "Appropriate" reactions were orchestrated in the Soviet zone at the conclusion of the case, yet, consistent with Stalinist thinking, these protests were specifically aimed at the acquitted former minister of economics Hjalmar Schacht, former vice-chancellor Franz von Papen, and former propagandist Hans Fritzsche as aristocratic or bourgeois enemies of the German people. That the same negative responses to the acquittals should be demonstrated spontaneously in the West indicates the extent to which Germans as a whole conceived of the prominent Nazis as "other," or at least wished to give this impression. Thus, no matter how many criticized the IMT trial on grounds of legitimacy, at the time clear majorities always averred that their former leaders deserved punishment.[13]

The only real sympathy with any of the "major war criminals" concerned those who, it was felt, were not the highest initiators of Nazi policy. Hence amid the general satisfaction displayed by the contemporary German public at the equity of the IMT proceedings and judgment, the most often-voiced reservations concerned the fate of the service chiefs. Many did not feel that a soldier or sailor, no matter how deeply complicit, should share the sentence of the overtly political grouping that had compromised him. Thus the frequently made contrast between the IMT acquittals and the death sentences for General Alfred Jodl and Field Marshal Wilhelm Keitel. On its most basic level, the principle of differentiation suggested that a general should be executed by the bullet rather than the rope.[14] In these early responses of evasion of responsibility and identification with military servicemen lay some of the seeds that would grow within a short while to full-blown condemnation of the trials that so many Germans had recently accepted.

In the years following the IMT trial, western German attitudes toward the ongoing Allied trial programs were increasingly shaped by a revisionist German nationalism. German social and political elites, resentful of the Allied occupation, sought to undermine its moral bases and rehabilitate Germany's name by, among other things, attacking war crimes trials as morally and legally unjustified and playing ever more heavily on the theme of *German* suffering. These groups were resentful of the Allied occupation and particularly its attempts to re-educate the masses and label many of the pillars of prewar German society as inherently flawed, and they sought to undermine its foundations. Thus they tried to minimize the crimes that Germany had committed and to compare these deeds with acts of the Allies. Concomitantly in this worldview, the war crimes trials were a vindictive, arbitrary act of the oppressors, and that the Allies had had to stretch existing international law to cope with the unprecedented brutality of the Third Reich was exploited to the full.[15] Thus arose the revisionist vocabulary, which was to gain popular currency in Germany, of the "*Kriegsschuldige*" (war-guilty) and the "*Kriegsverurteilten*" (war-convicted), rather than of the "*Kriegsverbrecher*" (war criminals). And thus arose also the imperative finally to discredit the trials by overturning the verdicts, or at the very least by securing the freedom of the convicts by pressuring the Allies.

The arguments and aims now were of a different nature to the early popular excuses of ignorance and powerlessness, but they fed off their precursors. The shrewdest move made by the elites was to link the two strands in the identification of all war criminals—aside perhaps from some of the "political" IMT convicts—with the ethic of service to the state.[16] Service, or "duty," was equated at the time with obedience to senior orders, and it was the unanimous rejection by the various "war crimes" courts of this principle as a defense that underpinned much of the opposition to trials.[17] The most emotive opposition predictably occurred in the cases of high-ranking soldiers.[18] In 1952 the Institut für Demoskopie inquired of Germans in the western zones which of the following group they considered justly imprisoned, and which unjustly: Field Marshal Albert Kesselring (who had been convicted by a British court), Grand Admiral Karl

Dönitz, Albert Speer, Rudolf Hess, and Baldur von Schirach (all of whom had been convicted by the IMT). The aggregate of respondents placed the men in that order, with the greatest sympathy thus reserved for the two service chiefs.[19] A reservoir of sympathy had earlier been tapped into for Keitel and Jodl, and it was exploited more and more heavily as the new rhetoric identified all convicts with German soldiers and increasingly regardless of their crime or the organization to which they belonged.[20]

Toward the Nazi past, these contentions underpinned the policy that was ultimately adopted by most West German political parties. The revisionist line was much more palatable for the majority of the population too, and as in the formation or re-formation of all national communities, a mythologizing rewrite of the past was perhaps inevitable—Nazi genocide could certainly not fit any "optimistic theory" about the present or future.[21] By 1947 the general impulse in West German society to "draw a final line" under the recent past—or at least on the suffering that they had caused, if not that which they felt as losers in the war—was increasing.[22]

By the second half of 1947 the second-largest-selling newspaper in the British zone, the Christian Democrat *Westfalenpost*, said of the defendants in the Nuremberg "Doctor's Trial" that they were murderers and "public torturers," but that "doubtless the interest of the German people in the trial would have been greater if an objective professional German judge had sat on the bench."[23] By the end of 1949, on the announcement of the eighteen-year prison term handed down by a British court to the prominent field marshal Erich von Manstein, August Haussleiter of the Bavarian section of the Christian Democratic Union reflected the further development of popular understandings of "justice" and victimhood. He suggested that such trials struck the public as "witchcraft trials" if there was no possibility of punishing under international jurisdiction crimes committed on the invasion of Germany and during the expulsion of Germans from eastern Europe.[24] The discourse was shifted from the subject matter of the war criminals cases to the legitimacy of the trials themselves: from the actions of Germany to the actions of the Allies and, by extension, to German victimhood. This concerted assault on the very idea of trial even succeeded in retrospectively influencing German opinion on the IMT trial. In October 1950 the reactions analysis staff of the U.S. High Commission encountered the greatest shift in German societal attitudes ever recorded to that time. Only 38 percent of a sample of 2,000 people regarded the IMT trial as having been conducted fairly, compared to the 78 percent registered with that view four years earlier.[25]

The German elites were presented a potent lever against Allied trial and re-education policy with the onset of the cold war. The need to placate these leading Germans, and with them broader national sentiment, in the interests of German allegiance in the burgeoning political conflict with the USSR, led first to a winding-down of the war crimes trials programs in all Western occupation zones in the context of a general easing of occupation policy. Later it resulted in a series of more or less politicized "sentence reviews" for convicted war criminals—an approach that sought to "solve" the "war criminals question" by the simple expedient of releasing them all, most prematurely.[26] Far from the legacy of Nuremberg being that of a history and morality lesson to the German public, by the 1950s the trials were increasingly being seen by the former prosecuting powers as an embarrassment and an obstacle to be removed.

The titanic efforts of the Nuremberg prosecutors in continuing until 1950 with an increasingly controversial legal venture were greatly compromised by the subsequent collapse of the American legal machinery. The final four war criminals in U.S. custody were released by 1958: the number still incarcerated in mid-1953 had been 312, and at the beginning of 1955, 41. Jails in the former British zone were empty by 1957 after similar rates of reduction. Those imprisoned in the IMT trial were held under quadripartite authority in Spandau jail and thus could not be released because of the need for Soviet agreement.[27] Included in the number released after serving only a few years of life sentences and commuted death sentences were commanders of the *Einsatzgruppen* and senior members of the concentration camp hierarchy. Just as telling in the sorry tale of the failed re-educational mission that was the subsequent Nuremberg trial program is the fact that the edited volume highlights of the twelve trials, known after their 1949–1953 Washington DC publication as the "Green Series," were never published in Germany. Finally, as Peter Maguire and Jörg Friedrich discovered, rejection of the legal validity of the trials was subtly built into articles 6 and 7 of the 1952 Bonn Treaty ending the Allied occupation statute.[28]

Treatments of the Nuremberg trials by legal scholars have generally been silent on these issues, focusing instead on the achievements of the courtroom itself, but not to the world beyond, except to the legacies created in law. Yet divorcing the trial from any broader political context is to undermine one of the most important rationales for the trial, which was, to paraphrase Jackson's opening address, to impose the rule of law on naked power relations. In other words, the collapse of much of the Nuremberg edifice in the 1950s (along with that of the IMTFE illustrates that law may influence the exercise of might, but the process also works in reverse, and thus it calls into question the universal potential of international law, which is reliant for enforcement on the most powerful members of the international community. The particular problem with the Nuremberg case is that much of its importance rested on the fact that it punished a major world power, but the enduring geopolitical significance of Germany effectively placed a limit on the extent of this reckoning. In the *political* sense, Nuremberg was an early victim of the cold war, and its fate as enshrined in the premature liberation of mass murderers foretold the transgressions of the "Nuremberg principles," transgressions that would be replicated elsewhere in that new conflict.

Forgotten Legacies, Inflated Memories: Nuremberg, Aggressive War, and Genocide

If enforced amnesia and denial about Nazi atrocities was one of the prices to be paid during the cold war, another historic Nuremberg aspect, elided from the 1950s to this day, has still to be resurrected: the matter of the prosecution of aggressive war. Gaining a positive legal judgment on the illegality of aggressive war to reinforce all of the interwar pronouncements on the issue was at the forefront of the design of the dominant American Nuremberg prosecution. The American prosecution plan has been dubbed the "conspiracy-criminal organization plan" and was based on the notion that all of the brutalities of Nazism could be connected to the drive for international dominance through warfare.[29] Jackson depicted warfare as the supreme crime because it facilitated and stimulated further atrocities.[30]

This purported link between warfare (and conspiracy to wage aggressive war) and crimes against humanity was later severed in the UN Genocide Convention. Thereafter, it became possible to prosecute such crimes without reference to warfare per se. Over and above this fact, the difficulty of defining aggression in a court of law is certainly one of the reasons that it has been marginalized as a subject of prosecution and discussion.[31] The IMT and the subsequent Nuremberg tribunals were suspicious of the conspiracy idea and closely circumscribed it, and they were not prepared to pass the most severe sentences for convictions on that or the aggressive war count alone. In general, assessing the matter is made difficult by the sheer complexity of international diplomacy and the perceptions and deceptions involved in the origin of any war. For instance, the Japanese entry into World War II was by no means as straightforward a case of unjustified aggression as the IMTFE presented it; conversely, statesmen finding self-serving, "self-defensive" pretexts for interstate conflict is as old as recorded history itself. Here we may be getting to the political nub of the matter, since overt and covert warfare remain among the most effective ways of projecting power, in the post–cold war world just as at the height of the cold war outside the European theater, and just as in the pre-1939 world. The very states that are powerful enough to meaningfully pronounce crimes against humanity as intolerable may themselves reserve the right to use aggressive war as an instrument of foreign policy.

Whatever the reason, as far as the practice of contemporary international law is concerned, the aggressive war legacy of Nuremberg is irrelevant. The legacy that matters for policy purposes is that other innovation of the postwar period, the crime against humanity. Consistent with the divergent fortunes of these two legacies, the importance of the Nuremberg precedent for the prosecution of mass murderers and ethnic cleansers at The Hague, Arusha, and other tribunals also appears to have led some authorities to believe in circular fashion that genocide must have provided the central impetus and rationale for the Nuremberg venture, too. The program notes for one of the opening panels at a 2005 conference hosted in the Nuremberg courtroom by Touro Law School, for instance, tell us that the trials "aimed to restore justice both to the defendants and to the history and memory of the Holocaust." Thus, too, Justice Richard Goldstone states: "Prior to World War II, the subjects of international law were not individuals but nations. . . . But the Holocaust changed that." Or Geoffrey Robertson: "It dawned on no political leader, even after the carnage of the First World War, that international institutions might tell states how to treat their nationals. . . . The Holocaust was a revelation that was to change this forever. It crystallized the Allied war aims and called forth an international tribunal—the court at Nuremberg—to punish individual Nazis for the barbarities they had authorized against German citizens."[32]

Each passage tells us more about the place of the Holocaust in contemporary consciousness than at Nuremberg. Each applies, unmediated by the time and perspective gap, current perspectives on the murder of Europe's Jews, and both ascribe to that putative awareness a motive force it never had. For the Soviet and the French prosecution teams at the IMT trial, charting the innumerable crimes of racism and exploitation in eastern and western Europe, respectively, were the main goals, but the fate of the Jews was often deliberately marginalized in their presentations in the interests of emphasizing national rather than ethnic losses, and creating very particular narratives of suffering appropriate to their own ideologies and national constituencies. As for the Anglo-American liberal democracies, far from "crystallizing" Allied war aims, the wartime pronouncements of London and Washington on punishment *in the future* for murderers of Jews—alongside perpetrators of many other crimes—were actually part of a pattern of avoiding rescue and other ameliorative measures in *the present*, lest they be seen to be fighting a war on behalf of Jews and thus irritate their domestic constituencies.[33] This feature of trials, not as a complement to intervention but as a palliative for the absence of intervention, would be repeated in the mid-1990s in Rwanda and, in the first instance at least, the former Yugoslavia. For the dominant U.S. prosecution in the IMT case we know that the chief trial target was the conspiracy to aggressive war; the immediate wartime catalyst in the American determination to prosecute leading Nazis had not been the "Final Solution" but rather the massacre of American POWs by a Waffen-SS formation at Malmédy in December 1944.

The quality of the Nuremberg representation of the murder of the Jews is a matter of scholarly debate.[34] As with so much in the historiography of this area, the picture would be enhanced by full study of the subsequent proceedings. These trials addressed many aspects of Nazi criminality in much greater depth than did the IMT trial, and unlike the IMT, some of them—though notably not the most important Holocaust-related subsequent Nuremberg trial, the prosecution of *Einsatzgruppen* leaders—also used victim witness testimony to good effect, thus both broadening and thickening depictions of the crime. Overall, however, a combination of the political-cultural imperative not to accord too much attention to the Jewish fate and the legal-strategic considerations around prosecuting particular individuals and groupings associated with the conspiracy to aggressive war consigned what we now know as the Holocaust to a subordinate position at Nuremberg. Meanwhile, the Nazi murder of the "Gypsies" (Roma and Sinti) was utterly ignored, marginalized then as now in legal proceedings as in the public sphere as a whole.

It is possible to argue, by piecing together disparate pieces of evidence marshaled at various points in the courtroom, that the IMT trial presented a more or less representative, if rudimentary, outline of the "Final Solution." This, however, is a different matter to ascribing intent and success to the Allied prosecutors: for instance, left to his own devices Jackson would not have had *Einsatzgruppe* leader Otto Ohlendorf testify at Nuremberg, while the other Nazi witness particularly prominent in animating the "Final Solution," former Auschwitz commandant Rudolf Höß, was actually brought to the stand by the defense rather than the prosecution.[35] It is also to fall into the trap of finding what one wants to find in the historical record and abstracting the evidence on different parts of the genocide from the broader mass of evidence thrown at the tribunal and from a stream of circulating competing narratives of Nazi criminality. Ultimately, the "Final Solution" and contingent parts thereof were used interchangeably with other "representative examples" of atrocity selected from across the full spectrum of Nazi criminality. They were used as specific manifestations of generic crimes and, at least so far as the U.S. prosecution was concerned, as outgrowths of the conspiracy. The notion of "representative examples" actually provided for the use of some rather unrepresentative examples of atrocity, chosen according to the preconceptions and agendas of the prosecuting powers, as with the primary American and British focus on "orthodox" German concentration camps rather than extermination centers in occupied Poland, or the French promotion of former resistance fighters.[36]

When the dynamics of Jewish persecution and murder were examined in their specificity by U.S. prosecutors, this was still done in the specific discursive context of the conspiracy-criminal organization plan. One result of this was, incidentally, to help create an influential early version of the still-popular "intentionalist" interpretation of the decision-making process for the "Final Solution." Consistent with the prosecutorial idea of long-standing conspiratorial designs, the wartime murder of the Jews was depicted as a logical, planned outcome of their prewar persecution and the German machinery of destruction as a "classically" totalitarian pyramidal structure, with power and initiatives flowing only downward from a leadership clique. This was a potentially useful legal representation of the crime, but historically speaking it was simply wrong.

Few of the issues raised in this section are generic to the medium of trial as a prism of history, and many have been addressed in contemporary international courts where the main focus is on specific, concrete crimes against humanity rather than more nebulous concepts such as conspiracy. At Nuremberg, nevertheless, all affected the representation of the Holocaust. What is the significance of this? One answer is that it is not a purely constructive fiction to re-imagine Nuremberg as a "trial of the Holocaust." Re-establishing exactly what the (Anglo-) Americans tried to do and how they tried to do it at Nuremberg is a part of the general story of how the Allies responded to the Holocaust as it happened and in its immediate aftermath. Remembering that the Holocaust was not given such prominence in the courtroom as we might now think it deserves is a part of understanding why the Allies did not respond during the genocide as we might have wished them to. A second answer is that while aggressive war may not always be the supreme crime, it is, inevitably, vastly destructive of human life and can be the catalyst and cover for other even more egregious offenses. Jackson was quite right in this regard. Despite the relative failure of the American prosecutors on the aggressive war issue, we should not forget their honorable efforts, for it is impossible to ignore the ongoing relevance of their subject.

Conclusion and Coda

Nuremberg achieved much. It is unnecessary to adorn it. Nuremberg was not some sort of ex post facto act of humanitarian intervention, and it was certainly not a trial about "the Holocaust" as we understand that concept today. It was the most significant attempt to give force to a number of connected ideas about concrete legal accountability for acts of state aggression and criminality that had been in circulation for years. Far from being the exercise in crude victors' justice that its contemporary opponents portrayed, the Nuremberg venture resulted for the most part in rather conservative judgments and sensible law, though for this it owes as much to a bench with a sufficiently large number of independent-minded judges as to the procedural rules improvised for the court. Nuremberg remains a hugely significant legal milestone and, at least as important, a symbol.

The Nuremberg precedent has been improved upon in many ways. Genuinely international courts—rather than quadripartite courts or American courts with international remits—with increasing reach, and legal developments such as the severing of the supposedly necessary connection between the conduct of war and crimes against humanity are both important adaptations, likewise the discarding of the collective guilt device that was the "criminal organization" plan. More criminals from more regimes can now be tried for more crimes. But like all symbols Nuremberg can be appropriated for a variety of agendas. Parts of "Nuremberg" have been inflated, parts marginalized; both processes have been products of a combination of goodwill, ignorance, and, occasionally, manipulation.

The valuable lesson of Nuremberg overwhelmingly learned by most human rights lawyers has been that of holding leaders of state and their operatives personally responsible for the commission of crimes against humanity, including genocide. The courtroom foregrounding of such crimes, instead of their subordination as at Nuremberg, has meant that it is now also possible in the legal forum to foreground detailed, coherent narratives of the deeds, amply illustrated by relevant victim and other testimony. What has happened to the prosecution of what the Nuremberg planners considered the supreme crime of aggressive war is another question entirely.

The answer to this question has serious ramifications given that states obviously still invade others, and not infrequently in circumstances in which the cynicism of the pretext for military action is so obvious that a prosecution for aggression would theoretically, and relatively, not be difficult. Such wars tend to be initiated by comparatively powerful states, and, thus, states that are difficult to bring to courts constituted by the international community of which they are pillars. This is the fundamental problem encapsulated by the "realist" critique of international law. Genocide and related crimes have latterly been perpetrated in the main by states in a situation of internal strife—states, in other words, that are relatively weak and marginalized and that may more easily be subjected to the laws of the international community. The fact that representatives of a genuinely powerful state in Germany were at one time prosecuted both for aggressive war and crimes against humanity is evidence more of the very peculiar circumstances of 1945 than it is grounds for any general optimism about the indifferent rule of law; as circumstances changed in mid-century central Europe, so too was the "war criminals question" turned on its head.

A certain ex post facto reconfiguration of Nuremberg away from its origins in the conspiracy-aggressive war idea has occurred in tandem with exaggerated claims of what it achieved in the realms of re-education and reintegration, and this at the same time as such claims are being made of the capacities of the ICTY and other courts. As with the notion of Nuremberg as a trial of the Holocaust, this is not a purely constructive fiction. "Nuremberg," for instance, forms an intrinsic part of the logic that predicted reforming Iraqi society, after Saddam Hussein's defeat, with an occupation regime—trials of the leadership included—like that which supposedly transformed Germany into a democracy from 1945.[37] Since Germany "turned out OK" in the long run, so the argument goes, the occupation—Nuremberg included—must have "worked." Yet Nuremberg as a re-educative, democratizing success story is a misleading representation, and its deployment in the Iraq connection doubly unfortunate.

Putting aside for a moment the bitter irony of the role of "Nuremberg thinking" in Iraq policy, we must be very careful about the powers we ascribe to trials beyond their vital primary task of convicting or acquitting individual defendants for specific crimes. Let us retreat for the moment from the claims that the establishment of an international judicial machinery will act as deterrent and will aid in processes of re-education and re-integration, since both are at best unproven, irrespective of the arguments of an increasingly sophisticated scholarship on the value of "didactic legalism." At the level of psychology and ethical standards, it is entirely understandable that the international community should feel it necessary to enact criminal proceedings to make a statement about its outraged values, but the force of this statement is rather diminished if punishment is selective, and if some of the acts of punishment that do occur stand in the stead of earlier preventive or (good faith) interventionist action. What happens in the court of law may in and of itself be just, and few reasonable people can today be found to object to the punishment of war criminals and genocidaires. Yet we have to acknowledge the gap between the universalistic rhetoric of legalism and the reality of ongoing impunity for certain states and mass murderers with the right connections to other powerful states and interests. At that point, too, we may have to face the fact that one reason we find (hugely expensive, showpiece) international trials valuable is that they create a reassuring if often misleading sense of the restoration of order, a comforting illusion that the "values of the international community" are being upheld, even as they palpably are not in so many cases, and even as the greatest powers within that community continue to act as laws unto themselves.

The legalist perspective is an alluring one, and its adherents would perhaps simply respond that my skepticism is the product of a lack of nuanced understanding; that the limitations currently imposed on the genuine rule of law are matters for gradual, negotiated erosion; that the gap between what is legal and what is practiced will be narrowed in favor of the former as the very existence of an objective legal yardstick shames transgressor states and opens their actions to criticism based on universally accepted standards. The strongest evidence in support of this progressivist stance is the speed and energy with which new judicial systems have been erected in the last ten years or so. But the historian cannot be so sanguine. There are two ways to view the cold war, for instance. It can be viewed as a simple hiatus, an aberration in the teleological development of worldwide democracy and international law, a period in which bad things had to be done for the greater good. According to this view, in the post–cold war world the time of true, meaningful international criminal law and genuine sovereign accountability has now arrived, and we can just pick up where Nuremberg left off. Alternatively, the cold war can be taken as a test case of how "our" political-ethical system responds under stress and how it may respond in the future. The cold war response was, to put it mildly, not an encouraging one.

A more recent test of the resilience of "Western values" has come with the so-called war on terror. Thinking toward the future and a coming test of the strength of the international legal-moral order, and one likely to bring death and destruction to an infinitely larger number of people than has fundamentalist-informed terrorism, we might ponder the threats of wars of resource scarcity, or massive cross-border refugee movements likely to be brought on by global warming. Under such circumstances, as now in the variety of civil conflicts scarring Africa in particular, it would take a very bold commentator to predict that the law will have the remotest qualifying influence over the desperate pursuit of group and state interest.

Notes

1. Werner Maser, *Nuremberg: A Nation on Trial* (London: Allen Lane, 1979); Michael Biddiss, "The Nuremberg Trial: Two Exercises in Judgement," *Journal of Contemporary History* 16 (1981): 597–615. On the postwar period, see Donald Bloxham, *Genocide on Trial: War Crimes Trials and the Formation of Holocaust History and Memory* (Oxford: Oxford University Press, 2001), ch. 4.

2. Telford Taylor, *Nuremberg and Vietnam: An American Tragedy* (New York: Bantam, 1971); Eugene Davidson, *The Nuremberg Fallacy* (Columbia: University of Missouri Press, 1973).

3. John Dower, *Embracing Defeat: Japan in the Aftermath of World War II* (London: Allen Lane, 1999), ch. 15.

4. International Criminal Tribunal for the former Yugoslavia, "Bringing Justice to the Former Yugoslavia: The Tribunal's Core Achievements," http://www.un.org/icty/glance/index.htm.

5. Geoffrey Robertson, *Crimes against Humanity* (London: Allen Lane, 1999), pp. 202–203; Jürgen Wilke et al., *Holocaust und NS-Prozesse: Die Presseberichterstattung in Israel und Deutschland zwischen Aneignung und Abwehr* (Cologne: Böhlau, 1995); Jürgen Wilke, "Ein früher Beginn der 'Vergangenheitsbewältigung,'" *Frankfurter Allgemeine Zeitung*, 15 November 1995; Anne Applebaum, "Justice in Baghdad," *Washington Post*, 19 October 2005, A21; or Roger Cohen writing in the *New York Times*, 30 April 1995, cited in Peter Maguire, "The 'Lessons of Nuremberg,'" unpublished manuscript, note 3. See also "Saddam Hussein's Trial Should Be Televised, Says Amherst College Professor," Amherst MA, 23 August 2005 (AScribe Newswire)—Lawrence Douglas, posted at http://www.collegenews.org/x4801.xml.

6. Eric Stover and Harvey M. Weinstein, eds., *My Neighbor, My Enemy: Justice and Community in the Aftermath of Mass Atrocity* (Cambridge: Cambridge University Press, 2004); Ana Uzelac, "Hague Prosecutors Rest Their Case," *Institute for War and Peace Reporting*, 27 December 2004; relatedly, "Justice at Risk: War Crimes Trials in Croatia, Bosnia and Herzegovina, and Serbia and Montenegro," *Human Rights Watch*, 16:7 (2004): 1–31. Even one of the more positive assessments of the ICTY's impact in Bosnia concludes that its "main contribution seems to have been its utility as a political lever, rather than its utility as a tool of post-conflict reconciliation." See Rachel Kerr, "The Road from Dayton to Brussels? The International Criminal Tribunal for the Former Yugoslavia and the Politics of War Crimes in Bosnia," *European Security* 14:3 (2005): 319–37, here p. 331.

7. Douglas, "Saddam Hussein's Trial Should Be Televised."

8. Robert G. Moeller, *War Stories: The Search for a Usable Past in the Federal Republic of Germany* (Berkeley: University of California Press, 2001); Norbert Frei, *Vergangenheits-*

politik: Die Anfänge der Bundesrepublik und die NS-Vergangenheit (Munich: C. H. Beck, 1996).

9. Anna J. Merritt and Richard L. Merritt, eds., *Public Opinion in Occupied Germany: The OMGUS Surveys, 1945–1949* (Urbana: University of Illinois Press, 1970), p. 93; Gollancz papers, Modern Records Centre, Warwick University UK (hereafter, MRC), MSS.157/3/GE/1/17/6, Land Nordrhein-Westphalia reaction report, July 1946; Mass-Observation Archive, University of Sussex, Brighton UK, File Report 2424 A, 27 September 1946. H. Montgomery Hyde, *The Life of Lord Birkett of Ulverston* (London: Hamish Hamilton, 1964), p. 518; Carl Rollyson, *Rebecca West: A Saga of the Century* (London: Trafalgar Square, 1995), pp. 214–15.

10. *The OMGUS Surveys*, 121–22. This report revealed a particular decline from February 1946 onward. OMGUS also recorded a diminution (within the general decline in attention) in the numbers of people reading trial reports in their entirety. See *OMGUS Surveys*, 34. For the beginning of the decline, see *New York Times*, 16 December 1945, 2 January 1946.

11. *New York Times*, 2 January 1946; MRC, MSS. 157/3/GE/1/17/6, Land Nordrhein-Westphalia reaction report, September 1946, pp. 6–7, 22–23.

12. *Telegraf*, 4 May 1946.

13. Eugen Kogon and Walter Dirks, "Nürnberg und die Geschichte," *Frankfurter Hefte* 1 (April 1946): 3–5, here p. 3. Polls in *New York Times*, 2 January, 10 November 1946.

14. A plea supported in the case of Jodl by the American and French judges. British National Archives, Kew, London (hereafter NA) FO 945/ 332, CCG-COGA, 10 October 1946. Also NA, FO 946/43, "German Reactions to the Nuremberg Sentences."

15. Frank M. Buscher, *The U.S. War Crimes Trial Program in Germany, 1946–1955* (Westport CT: Greenwood Press, 1989), pp. 92, 100–101, 109–10, 162–63; Frei, *Vergangenheitspolitik*, passim. See also Alfred Streim, "Saubere Wehrmacht?" in *Vernichtungskrieg: Verbrechen der Wehrmacht 1941 bis 1944*, ed. Hannes Heer and Klaus Naumann, pp. 569–97, here p. 575 on some of the spurious *tu quoque* arguments (Hamburg: Hamburger Edition, 1995).

16. Buscher, *U.S. War Crimes Trial Program*, pp. 126, 163.

17. Bodleian Library, Oxford UK, Goodhart papers, reel 21, Wright to Goodhart, 5 August 1952. See also Peter Steinbach, "Nationalsozialistische Gewaltverbrechen in der deutschen Öffentlichkeit nach 1945," in *Vergangenheitsbewältigung durch Strafverfahren? NS-Prozesse in der Bundesrepublik Deutschland*, ed. Jürgen Weber and Peter Steinbach, pp. 13–39, here pp. 17–18, 21 (Munich: Olzog, 1984).

18. E.g., James F. Tent, *Mission on the Rhine* (Chicago: University of Chicago Press, 1982), p. 92.

19. Elisabeth Noelle and Erich Peter Neumann, eds., *The Germans: Public Opinion Polls, 1947–1966* (Westport CT: Greenwood Press, 1981), p. 202. Six percent of interviewees thought Kesselring justly imprisoned, 65 percent thought not. The corresponding figures for Hess were 22 percent and 43 percent.

20. Bernd Boll, "Wehrmacht vor Gericht: Kriegsverbrecherprozesse der Vier Mächte nach 1945," *Geschichte und Gesellschaft* 24 (1998): 570–94, here pp. 592–93; Frei, *Vergangenheitspolitik*, pp. 268–96.

21. Ulrich Brochhagen, "Vergangene Vergangenheitsbewältigung," *Mittelweg* 36 (1992/1993): 145–54, especially p. 149; Jeffrey Herf, *Divided Memory: The Nazi Past in the Two Germanys* (Cambridge MA: Harvard University Press, 1997), p. 392.

22. Frei, *Vergangenheitspolitik*, p. 14.

23. NA, FO 1056/239, German press review, 15 August–15 September 1947.

24. E.g., *Frankfurter Allgemeine Zeitung* 20 and esp. 21 December 1949.

25. Anna J. Merritt and Richard L. Merritt, eds., *Public Opinion in Semisovereign Germany: The HICOG Surveys, 1949–1955* (Urbana: University of Illinois Press, 1980), p. 101.

26. Bloxham, *Genocide on Trial*, ch. 5; Buscher, *U.S. War Crimes Trial Program*; Thomas Alan Schwartz, "Die Begnadigung deutscher Kriegsverbrecher: John J. McCloy und die Häftlinge von Landsberg," *Vierteljahrshefte für Zeitgeschichte* 38 (1990): 375–414; Peter Maguire, *Law and War: An American Story* (New York: Columbia University Press, 2001). On German rearmament, David Clay Large, *Germans to the Front: West German Rearmament in the Adenauer Era* (Chapel Hill: University of North Carolina Press, 1996).

27. Figures from Maguire, *Law and War*, p. 256.

28. Maguire, *Law and War*, p. 229.

29. Bradley F. Smith, *The Road to Nuremberg* (London: André Deutsch, 1982).

30. Ann Tusa and John Tusa, *The Nuremberg Trial* (London: Atheneum, 1983), p. 73.

31. Michael P. Scharf and William A. Schabas, *Slobodan Milosevic on Trial: A Companion* (New York: Continuum, 2002), pp. 143–45.

32. Richard Goldstone, *For Humanity: Reflections of a War Crimes Investigator* (New Haven CT: Yale University Press, 2000), p. 75; Robertson, *Crimes against Humanity*, pp. xiii–xiv.

33. Tony Kushner, *The Holocaust and the Liberal Imagination: A Social and Cultural History* (Oxford: Blackwell, 1994).

34. Bloxham, *Genocide on Trial*, chs. 2, 3, 5; Erich Haberer, "History and Justice: Paradigms of the Prosecution of Nazi Crimes," *Holocaust and Genocide Studies*, 19:3 (2005): 487-519, here pp. 491–94; Michael Marrus, "The Holocaust at Nuremberg," *Yad Vashem Studies* 26 (1998): 5-41; and, with more nuance, Lawrence Douglas, *The Memory of Judgment: Making Law and History in the Trials of the Holocaust* (New Haven CT: Yale University Press, 2001), part 1.

35. Bloxham, *Genocide on Trial*, pp. 62, 105–7.

36. Bloxham, *Genocide on Trial*, pp. 62–63, 101–9.

37. Jeffrey Herf, "Condi Rice Is Wrong about Germany's Werewolves But Right about Iraq," *History News Network*, 1 September 2003, at http://hnn.us/articles/1655.html; Applebaum, "Justice in Baghdad."

Prosecution, Condemnation, and Punishment
Ethical Implications of Atrocities on Trial

JOHN K. ROTH

> *The wrongs which we seek to condemn and pun-*
> *ish have been so calculated, so malignant, and so*
> *devastating that civilization cannot tolerate their*
> *being ignored because it cannot survive their being*
> *repeated.*
>
> Justice Robert H. Jackson

Not always but usually, atrocities—especially war crimes, crimes against humanity, genocide, and other human rights abuses—involve murder and often
mass murder. When one considers the politics of prosecuting war crimes in
historical perspective, the focal point of *Atrocities on Trial*, it is important to
probe ethical assumptions and implications that stand at the center of those
issues. None is more fundamental than the widespread human conviction that
murder is wrong. This chapter focuses attention in that direction. Its thesis is
that advances in prosecution, condemnation, and punishment of atrocities of
the kind discussed in this book depend on nothing less than a robust and international recommitment to that quintessential ethical truth.

Atrocities experienced by human beings—especially war crimes, crimes
against humanity, genocide, and other human rights abuses—require at least
two intermingling conditions. First, something must *happen*, for such disas-
ters are scarcely possible without activity. Second, feeling, remembering, and
reasoning loom large. No feeling implies no pain or suffering. No remembering entails no continuity of experience. No reasoning means no concepts, no
distinctions between right and wrong. Absent those ingredients, there can be
no atrocities and no trials to prosecute, condemn, and punish them. Far from
being absent, however, those ingredients are very much present. In particular,

human rationality is characterized by its capacity to differentiate between right and wrong. That function is reason's heart. Human beings repeatedly make judgments between right and wrong and about good and evil—to such an extent that we face a tortuous gap between what is and what ought to be. The Holocaust makes that point with a vengeance.

Losses That Will Not Go Away

As a snowstorm gathered on a late November day in 1946, a Jewish woman named Gerda Weissmann Klein headed home after finishing her grocery shopping in Buffalo, New York.[1] Grocery shopping was important to her. Words and pictures on product labels were helping her to learn English. Shelves stocked with food reassured her; their apparently unending abundance meant that she would never again be consumed by hunger. Nevertheless, after unpacking her groceries on that day, Klein took the bread she had purchased, sat by a window in her living room, and, as she watched the storm swirl, began to eat the loaf. Fresh though it was, the bread seemed salty and soggy. Those sensations combined with feelings of sadness that made her wonder what was wrong.

Holocaust survivor Gerda Klein, whose remarkable story became the subject of an Academy Award–winning documentary called *One Survivor Remembers*, recounts this episode in her memoir, *All but My Life*. As she ate, memory told her what was wrong. "During the long years of deprivation," she recalled, "I had dreamed of eating my fill in a warm place, in peace, but I never thought that I would eat my bread alone."[2] Married to Kurt Klein, a former U.S. Army lieutenant, Gerda was not alone in late November 1946—and yet she was. Born in 1924, Gerda Weissmann had witnessed the German occupation of her hometown, Bielitz, Poland, in 1939, spent years in Nazi forced labor camps—Bolkenhain, Märzdorf, Landshut, and Grünberg among them—and endured brutal Nazi death marches in 1945 before American troops, among them Kurt Klein, liberated her in early May at Volary, Czechoslovakia.

Kurt Klein and his siblings had escaped Nazi Germany by emigrating to the United States before the war. Valiantly they tried to rescue their parents, but long-delayed U.S. immigration clearance came too late. Kurt's parents had already been gassed at Auschwitz. After Kurt and Gerda met in Volary and fell in love, they married, came to Buffalo in September 1946, and began a long and successful life together. Nevertheless, what Gerda calls "a stabbing memory" or, in particular, "a pervasive loneliness" still inflicted "pains that will not go away," for she lost most of her family and many friends in the Holocaust, too.[3]

Stabbing memories, pervasive loneliness, pains and losses that will not go away—while Gerda Klein did her grocery shopping in the late autumn of 1946, aspects of those realities also focused the attention of U.S. Brigadier General Telford Taylor.[4] A skilled lawyer, Taylor had been part of the legal team assembled the year before by Robert H. Jackson, the U.S. Supreme Court justice who served as the chief American prosecutor at the International Military Tribunal (IMT). Including representatives from France, Great Britain, and the Soviet Union as well as the United States, the IMT had spent twelve months pursuing justice against twenty-four of the most significant Nazi leaders.

The pursuit of justice at Nuremberg did not end when the IMT concluded its work in the autumn of 1946. Among thousands of Nazi war crimes trials that took place in numerous countries before and after those conducted by the IMT, the Subsequent Nuremberg Proceedings began in December 1946. Lasting until April 1949, they consisted of twelve trials under American jurisdiction. Now chief counsel for the prosecution, Telford Taylor played a key part in these proceedings, which ultimately focused on 177 Nazi doctors, jurists, industrialists, military and SS leaders (including *Einsatzgruppen* personnel), and other professionals and government officials whose indictments specified crimes ranging from abusive medical experimentation and participation in Nazi Germany's "euthanasia" program to exploitation of slave labor, the administration of concentration camps, and mass murder. Among the 142 defendants who were found guilty, 25 received death sentences, but only 12 were carried out.

Even if all of the sentences meted out to Nazi war criminals had been fully carried out, the pursuit of justice through legal proceedings could not begin to prosecute and punish all those who were responsible for the stabbing memories, pervasive loneliness, and pains and losses that will not go away for survivors such as Gerda Weissmann Klein. Nor could the pursuit of justice do anything to bring back the millions of defenseless people—Jews and non-Jews—who were murdered during the Holocaust. Nevertheless, the trials that took place in 1946 and thereafter remain significant for reasons that Telford Taylor emphasized on 9 December of that year when he made the prosecution's opening statement in the Doctors' Trial, the first of the Subsequent Nuremberg Proceedings: "It is our deep obligation to all peoples of the world," he said, "to show why and how these things happened. It is incumbent upon us to set forth with conspicuous clarity the ideas and motives which moved these defendants to treat their fellow men as less than beasts. The perverse thoughts and distorted concepts which brought about these savageries," Taylor continued, "are not dead. They cannot be killed by force of arms. They must not become a spreading cancer in the breast of humanity. They must be cut out and exposed, for the reason so well stated by Mr. Justice Jackson in this courtroom a year ago: 'The wrongs which we seek to condemn and punish have been so calculated, so malignant, and so devastating, that civilization cannot tolerate their being ignored because it cannot survive their being repeated.'"[5]

Melancholy More Than Celebration

Fifty years after the eloquent statements made by Taylor and Jackson, more international trials, akin to those at Nuremberg, have been under way. Although opposed by the United States, the International Criminal Court (ICC), the world's first permanent tribunal of its kind, came into existence on 1 July 2002. Seated in The Hague, Netherlands, and empowered to act only when appropriate national court systems are unwilling or unable to do so, the ICC can try individuals who have been indicted for genocide, crimes against humanity, and war crimes that have taken place since that date. A 1998 treaty, the Rome Statute, called for the ICC's creation. It was signed by 139 countries, the United States among them, after post-Holocaust era genocides took place in the Balkans and Rwanda.[6] Sixty governments had to ratify the treaty to establish the ICC. With the approval of 10 countries—Bosnia, Bulgaria, Cambodia, the Democratic Republic of the Congo, Ireland, Jordan, Mongolia, Niger, Romania, and Slovakia—the number of ratifications rose to 66 on 11 April 2002. The ceremony at UN headquarters to celebrate this accomplishment was boycotted by the United States, for the administration of President George W. Bush has feared, as other American administrations have done as well, that American forces committed to peacekeeping or other overseas missions could be targeted for inappropriate indictments and unfair trials. By March 2005, 98 countries had ratified the Rome Statute and become participants in the ICC. Most of the world's democracies are ICC members—among them Australia, Canada, France, Germany, and the United Kingdom. The United States, however, has continued to hold out.

It remains to be seen whether the ICC or other international tribunals can effectively prosecute mass atrocities, including genocide, let alone deter them. That point is illustrated by the proceedings of the International Criminal Tribunal for the Former Yugoslavia (ICTY) against Slobodan Milosevic, the first head of state to be put on trial for genocidal atrocities—specifically the ones that took place during the 1992–1995 Bosnian War. In 2006 the Milosevic trial in The Hague entered its fourth year, but no verdict was reached before the defendant died on 11 March of that year. Meanwhile, another trial involving charges of mass atrocities limped on. In a Baghdad courtroom where the American-sponsored proceedings against Saddam Hussein began on 19 October 2005, numerous chaotic interruptions called into question whether Saddam's trial for crimes against humanity could provide the convincing justice that was hoped for it. Two members of the defense team had been murdered. Some important witnesses had failed to appear. Owing to the resignation of the chief judge and the departure of other justices, at least one of them for reasons of conflicting interest, only two of the original five judges remained to hear the case in early 2006. The appearance, if not the reality, of political interference undermined confidence that the trial could be fair, a suspicion exacerbated by criticism that the trial should be taking place in an international court rather than in American-controlled Iraq. Neither Saddam's conviction nor his execution by hanging on 30 December 2006 removed the clouds surrounding these trial proceedings.

The human rights abuses that continued in the Darfur region of Sudan added to the early twenty-first century's jurisprudential burdens.[7] The methods employed in that onslaught by Arab militias against the Aranga, Fur, Jebel, Masalit, and Zaghawa, the key black African tribes in western Sudan, have included lethal dehydration as wells and water supplies in the arid environment have been ruined, rape, starvation, forced relocation, and outright shootings and bombings. Despite these genocidal signs, a UN commission of inquiry found on 31 January 2005 that the evidence did not lead to the conclusion that the Sudanese government has committed genocide. Sufficient evidence of genocidal intent was lacking. According to the UN report, "Generally speaking, the policy of attacking, killing, and forcibly displacing members of some tribes does not evince a specific intent to annihilate, in whole or in part, a group distinguished on racial, ethnic, national or religious grounds."[8] The UN study, however, did find that the Sudanese government and the Janjaweed militias had committed human rights abuses and war crimes that warranted prosecution in the ICC, which might also determine that that those acts took place "with genocidal intent." On 5 April 2005 UN Secretary General Kofi Annan handed the International Criminal Court a confidential list of fifty-one persons, including Sudanese government officials, who are key suspects in the mass killing and devastation that have taken place in Darfur. That step opened the door for Darfur-related war crimes trials in The Hague. What will happen in that regard remains in suspense.

Since the IMT did its work at Nuremberg fifty years ago, the history of international trials regarding human rights abuses, crimes against humanity, and genocide creates melancholy more than celebration. As illustrated by the UN's 1948 Universal Declaration of Human Rights and Convention of the Prevention and Punishment of the Crime of Genocide, those proceedings have supported attention to humanitarian causes. Such trials have documented much that has happened, and that documentation informs historical awareness and bears a distinctive moral witness. In addition, the international trials have established important principles: for example, political leaders can be held legally responsible for crimes committed in carrying out their government's policies, and individuals cannot successfully defend themselves by simply claiming that they had only obeyed orders. Nevertheless, those who perpetrate genocide and other crimes against humanity still enjoy crucial advantages because intervention and prosecution usually arrive too late. The horror unleashed by human hands makes it unclear that justice can be maintained. The repetition of atrocity makes it difficult to claim that lasting prevention will be ensured.

Injustice has inflicted deep wounds on justice. Disrespect for ethics has done immense harm to ethics. With due respect to the sentiment of Telford Taylor, the problems that remain are not as simple as exposing and cutting out cancer. Events may defy even the rhetoric of Justice Jackson, for civilization continues to survive, at least after a fashion, in spite of the repetition of atrocity. No one should be sanguine that such a pattern can continue indefinitely, but the situation has proved to be more complicated than Jackson's dichotomy between repeated atrocity and the demise of civilization suggested. It may be that humankind is just civilized enough not to succumb completely to atrocity but not to keep it in check either.

Change for the Better

What would have to happen for that situation to change for the better? The deepest responses to that question are not to be found simply in arguments for more extensive, thorough, and credible prosecution, condemnation, and punishment of atrocities, including crimes against humanity and genocide. Of course, those elements are important, but for them to be implemented more effectively, a renewal and revitalization of ethics itself is needed. In that regard, nothing is more important than paying attention to one of the oldest and most important of humankind's moral imperatives, namely, the injunction against murder. That injunction has found long-standing expression in the biblical Decalogue or Ten Commandments, whose teachings and traditions have informed, but not adequately enough, much of the Western civilization that has contained crimes against humanity and the need to prosecute, condemn, and punish them. While recognizing that the injunction against murder can and does have multiple sources, not all of which are explicitly religious, it is instructive to explore some of the significant ways in which religion, ethics, and politics are intertwined as one considers prosecution, condemnation, and punishment in response to murderous atrocities.

Some versions of the Decalogue's sixth commandment substitute *kill* for *murder*. In either case those key words require definition if the commandment is to make sense, but how much difference does it make if the Sixth Commandment contains one of those words rather than the other? The answer is *a great deal*. That response and the question that prompts it make an apt place to engage the imperative that is the most necessary, although not sufficient, condition for human civilization.[9]

More specifically, consideration of four questions can advance reflection on the injunction against murder in the context of the issues focused in *Atrocities on Trial*: (1) How has the Sixth Commandment functioned and fared in history? (2) What does this commandment reveal about humankind? (3) What does the Sixth Commandment suggest about God? (4) What place does this commandment have in humanity's future? The struggles involved with those issues are, quite literally, matters of life and death.

Definitions

As preludes to addressing the four questions above, two further steps need to be taken. The first involves definitions that inform this essay's wrestling. According to the most reliable biblical scholarship, *murder*, not *kill*, is the best English term to use in translating the original Hebrew text. That decision is significant, for the meanings of *murder* and *kill*, although closely related, are not identical.

All murder is killing, but not all killing is murder. To kill means to inflict or cause death, which also happens in murder, but distinctions exist because killing acts can be accidental and unintentional. Killing acts of that kind are not murder, which typically requires an intention, often including premeditation and careful planning, to inflict or cause death. In addition, murderous intentions are usually inflamed by anger, malice, envy, greed, fear, hate, revenge, or some other violence-inciting emotion. Not all killing actions fit that description, but typically murderous ones do.

Historically, the Sixth Commandment, along with others in the Decalogue, has been understood to be addressed to human beings—to Jews, to Christians, and indeed to all persons and communities—whose distinctiveness includes a capacity for murder that is not found in any other part of the natural world. Various interpretations of its meaning can be found, but they all share and depend upon the understanding that the imperative applies to human beings who are commanded not to do certain things that are within their power. Obvious though this point may be, awareness of it helps to underscore other crucial differences between *kill* and *murder*.

The Sixth Commandment is unequivocal and absolute. Allowing no exceptions, it does not say, "Murder is wrong in situation X, but it may be permissible in situation Y." Murder, the commandment entails, is wrong—period. Killing, however, is not so easily interpreted that way, unless one stipulates that *killing* means *murder*. In fact, unless killing is qualified in that way, or in some other way that restricts the meaning of that term to forms of killing that are intentional but unjustifiable or inexcusable, a commandment that said "You shall not kill" would be so ambiguous, even nonsensical, that it would be impossible for human beings to obey it no matter how good they might be or how hard they might try.

To see why that situation holds, notice that human life depends on killing. That statement, of course, is as problematic as it is evident, as much in need of qualification as it is bold. Therefore, to avoid misunderstanding, I need to clarify what I do and do not mean by it. I do not mean, for example, that human life depends on war; it does not, although sometimes war is unavoidable and even necessary to defend human life. Nor do I mean that human civilization depends on capital punishment; it does not, although there may be times and places where justifiable reasons for executions can be found. What I do mean is that human life and civilization cannot exist, let alone thrive, unless people eat, quench their thirst, obtain shelter, raise and educate their young, and, in short, take the actions that are necessary to sustain human life. Unfortunately, those actions cannot be taken without killing. As the philosopher Philip Hallie cogently put the point, "We are in the food web. We are killers, if only of plants."[10]

In addition, if human life, in the biblical words of Genesis, is to be "fruitful and multiply," it unavoidably becomes even more lethal than Hallie said. Human beings are thinkers and doers; they are political, social, and also religious creatures who plan, strive, and build. Scarcely any of humankind's initiatives can be pursued without dislocations and destructions of one kind or another. Even the most environmentally conscious projects that men and women carry out have lethal consequences for living creatures somewhere.

An absolute and unequivocal prohibition against killing is not what the Sixth Commandment can mean if it is coherent. With due qualification, human life depends on killing, but a corollary of that truth is that human existence and especially its *quality* also depend on careful discrimination between killing that is justifiable or excusable and killing that is not. Absent such discrimination, including laws and sanctions to implement the difference socially and politically, it is hard to imagine that human civilization could long endure. Instead, to use Thomas Hobbes's bleak description from 1651, human existence would likely be in "that condition which is called war, and such a war as is of every man against every man. . . . In such condition there is . . . continual fear and danger of violent death; and the life of man solitary, poor, nasty, brutish, and short."[11]

Not even the most thorough, rigorous, and truthful interpretation of the Sixth Commandment, however, may be able to provide a complete analysis of killing that is justifiable or excusable and killing that is not. After acknowledging that some kinds of killing are necessary for basic sustenance of human life, the category of killing may still remain larger than the category of murder. At least in many cases, if not ordinarily, murder is not the category into which one places killing in self-defense, for example, or killing to prevent the murder of another person or to combat warring aggression. Even when unjust war unleashes killing that is met with armed resistance, a gray zone of moral classification may exist, and it will be debatable whether all the killing done by the warring aggressor, wrong though it surely is, should be called murder. In short, there remain cases of killing, justifiable or unjustifiable, that are not necessarily cases of murder or at least not clearly so. That realization, however, does not cut slack for killing; at least it should not, because most killing can and should be found wrong and condemned without inevitably and always being classified as murder.

Perspectives

Much killing, but not all, is murder, but now two more questions must be addressed for the Sixth Commandment to make sense: When is killing murder? What constitutes murder? My response to those questions emerges from the perspectives that inform my thinking about the Sixth Commandment. My perspectives are those of a Protestant Christian philosopher/theologian whose work has concentrated for more than thirty years on the Holocaust, Nazi Germany's attempt to destroy the Jewish people, and on other genocides as well. This outlook reminds me, again and again, of an unmistakable instance of murder, namely, the murder that the Hebrew Bible identifies as the first one. Genesis 4 tells that story, which depicts Cain's slaying of his brother Abel.

When God favored Abel's offering but "had no regard" for Cain's, the latter's anger got the best of him. "Let us go out to the field," said Cain to the apparently unsuspecting Abel. "And when they were in the field," the biblical narrative continues, "Cain rose up against his brother Abel, and killed him." The story reports that God responded: "What have you done? Listen; your brother's blood is crying out to me from the ground!" Cain's killing made him "a fugitive and a wanderer on the earth," one who "went away from the presence of the Lord," but God spared Cain's life, marking him "so that no one who came upon him would kill him."

At rock bottom, murder takes place when one person kills another intentionally, deliberately, and unjustifiably. (Much hinges on the latter term in particular, a point to which we will return in due course.) Cain's killing of Abel was murder—*homicide*—or nothing could be. Moreover, like the Sixth Commandment, the Genesis narrative leaves no doubt that murder is wrong. That same account, however, raises as many questions as it answers. For instance, was Cain's killing of Abel clearly premeditated? Genesis does not say so explicitly, although far from being excluded, the text definitely invites such an inference. Furthermore, when Cain "rose up against his brother," was that action murderous from the outset? Again, the text allows for the possibility that it might not have been that way, although Cain's "rising up" resulted in killing that was unlikely to have been accidental. Otherwise, Cain probably would not have tried to fend off God's question—"Where is your brother Abel?"—by denial and evasion: "I do not know; am I my brother's keeper?"

The ambiguities do not end there. When Cain questioned whether he should be held accountable as his brother's keeper, was he implying that creation did not yet have a moral structure that condemned murder as the Sixth Commandment would do explicitly later on? Cain's defense might have been that he unfairly received an ex post facto judgment from God. Who says, and where and when was it said, Cain might have protested, that I am to be Abel's keeper? However, if Cain made a legalistic move of this kind, Genesis shows that God had none of it. Prior to Cain's murdering Abel, the biblical account in Genesis brims with language about what is good, about the knowledge of good and evil, about obedience and disobedience. The Genesis tradition, moreover, makes clear not only that God "created humankind in his image, in the image of God he created them; male and female he created them" but also that "God blessed them." Could it make any good sense for God to create human beings in God's image, bless them, and then permit them with impunity to slaughter one another intentionally? At the end of the day, ambiguity notwithstanding, no credible reading could interpret Genesis as doing less than defining murder quintessentially or as doing anything other than finding murder wrong—period.

The clarity notwithstanding, a troubling darkness lurks in the questions and responses above. It will need revisiting, but the basic point is maintained within Jewish tradition, which, among other things, holds that when God gave Moses the Ten Commandments at Sinai, they were etched on two stone tablets, five commandments on each. The first five identified human duties to God; the second five underscored obligations that persons have to one another. Tradition holds further that there are parallels between the two sets of five commandments. Thus, the Sixth Commandment "You shall not murder" is especially linked to the First Commandment "I am the Lord your God, who brought you out of the land of Egypt, out of the house of slavery; you shall have no other gods before me." Murder—the intentional, deliberate, and unjustifiable killing of one human being by another—is wrong for reasons that go deep down because they violate the First Commandment.

God created human life in God's image. In God's sight, and surely in ours, that act was good. It was also awesome, even sacred, for in the ultimate sense, no human being has the power to create human life, not even the wonders of twenty-first-century science contradict that fact, and murder destroys human life in ways that are beyond our repair and recovery. God may or may not resurrect the dead, but human beings utterly lack the power to do so. The result is that no human act rivals murder in defying, disrespecting, and denying God. The Christian philosopher Stephen Davis succinctly sums up the primary point: "Murder, then, is a crime both against the victim and his family and friends, and also (and most importantly) against God."[12]

Here it is worth noting that, according to the biblical scholar David Flusser, the Christian New Testament "does not use the term 'Ten Commandments' even once," but the injunction against murder is emphasized in multiple instances, and especially by Jesus in ways that are thoroughly consistent with the Jewish tradition that he observed.[13] In Matthew 19:16–22, Mark 10:17–22, and Luke 18:18–23, for example, Jesus stresses the importance of obeying God's commandments and explicitly condemns murder. Paul does the same in Romans 13:9, adding that the Sixth Commandment, along with those prohibiting adultery and theft, "are summed up in this word, 'Love your neighbor as yourself'" (Romans 13:10).

Meanwhile, for one reason or another, and here lurks another troubling problem related to the Sixth Commandment, Cain, who did not have the advantage of reading Genesis or Exodus, let alone the New Testament, may not have known as clearly as the readers of those texts that killing Abel was wrong. Genesis says little about the moral upbringing that Cain and Abel received from Adam and Eve, their biblical parents. Nor does it indicate much about what the brothers knew about God and God's expectations, except that they understood enough "in the course of time" to bring offerings to God. Abel, apparently, knew better than Cain what would please God. Whether Cain's misjudgment resulted from ignorance or from a disrespectful holding back of what he should have given to God, the result was the introduction of murder, which ever since has bloodied and scarred creation almost beyond belief. To illustrate the latter point, consider two further episodes. Linked to Cain's murder of Abel even though they are millennia removed from that act, these examples also help to shape significant perspectives on the Sixth Commandment.

Two Episodes

Richard Rhodes's *Masters of Death: The SS-Einsatzgruppen and the Invention of the Holocaust* details how Nazi Germany's mobile killing units murdered more than 1.3 million Jews in Eastern Europe during World War II. "Maps in Jewish museums from Riga to Odessa," writes Rhodes, "confirm that almost every village and town in the entire sweep of the Eastern territories has a killing site nearby."[14] Gratuitous and sadistic violence accompanied the slaughter. Rhodes describes one instance as follows: "A woman in a small town near Minsk saw a young German soldier walking down the street with a year-old baby impaled on his bayonet. 'The baby was still crying weakly,' she would remember. 'And the German was singing. He was so engrossed in what he was doing that he did not notice me.'"[15]

Although such brutal murder should rightly leave one speechless, there are many things that ought to be said about it. One of them is that if such action is not an example of unjustifiable killing, nothing could be. Of course, the young German and his Nazi superiors, SS leader Heinrich Himmler and Adolf Hitler himself first and foremost among them, would have argued differently. In their Nazi eyes, the mass killing of Jews was not only justifiable but also imperative. To them, Jews were such an unrelenting, pestilential threat to the "superior"

German *Volk* that Jewish life—including, significantly, the Jewish tradition that emphasized the Sixth Commandment—must be eradicated root and branch. Himmler was not, however, an advocate of gratuitous and sadistic violence. He would have disapproved of young Germans who found joy in impaling infants on their bayonets. He wanted "decent" killers instead.

Hitler, Himmler, and the young German soldier in Rhodes's account were neither insane nor completely irrational. They had a worldview that made sense to them, and they acted on it.[16] Nevertheless, rational and ethical scrutiny far better and deeper than theirs underscores how much the Nazis' reasoning, planning, and acting were misguided and immoral. For no matter how sincerely Hitler and his followers held their beliefs or how valid they took them to be, those convictions and the mass murder that flowed from them were based on error and terror, on deceit and delusion, on theft and tyranny, on falsehood and aggression, on hate and disrespect for human life other than their own. That catalog does not exhaust the criteria that brand killing unjustifiable, but no killing arising from those conditions, dispositions, or motivations can reasonably be justified.

Unjustified and unjustifiable, so much of the killing done by Nazi Germany and its collaborators was not only murder but also *mass murder*. In 1944, Raphael Lemkin, a Jewish lawyer who fled from Poland during the Holocaust, named such crimes when he coined the term *genocide*, which derives from the Greek word *genos* (race) and the Latin suffix *cide* (killing). It refers to instances of mass murder, such as Nazi Germany's assault on the Jews, that do not target individuals alone but aim at the murder of entire groups. Owing considerably to Lemkin's dogged persistence, the United Nations adopted the 1948 Convention on the Prevention and Punishment of the Crime of Genocide, which defined that crime in terms of "acts committed with intent to destroy, in whole or in part, a national, ethnical, racial, or religious group, as such."[17]

Cain committed homicide and fratricide but not genocide. The United Nations' definition indicates that genocide can take place without direct murder, but typically genocide is no less an occasion for murder than is the case with homicide and fratricide. Granting some genocidal exceptions, all three are instances of murder; all three involve the intended, deliberate, but unjustifiable taking of individual lives. In genocide, however, the murderous aim is immensely escalated, and a person's life is at risk not for anything in particular that he or she has done but simply because one exists at all as a member of a targeted group. The fact that the group is targeted is crucial, because all human individuals are fundamentally defined by factors of group identity of one kind or another. Indeed there can be no individual human life without such identities. Unfortunately, not even genocide is the end of the matter where mass murder is concerned, and thus we come to the second episode that influences my wrestling with the Sixth Commandment. It involves calculations of time and distance.

In 1994 the political scientist R. J. Rummel, a demographer of what he calls *democide*, published an important book called *Death by Government*. Writing before he could have taken account of the late twentieth-century genocidal atrocities in Bosnia, Rwanda, and Kosovo or the twenty-first-century genocide that remained under way in the Darfur region of Sudan at the time of this writing, Rummel estimated that "the human cost of war and democide"—he defined *democide* as "the murder of any person or people by a government, including genocide, politicide, and mass murder"—is more than "203 million people in [the twentieth] century."[18] (What the precise figure would be today, God only knows.)

"If one were to sit at a table," Rummel went on to say, "and have this many people come in one door, walk at three miles per hour across the room with three feet between them (assume generously that each person is also one foot thick, navel to spine), and exit an opposite door, it would take over *five years and nine months* for them all to pass, twenty-four hours a day, 365 days a year. If the dead were laid out head to toe, assuming each to be an average of 5 feet tall, they would reach from Honolulu, Hawaii, across the vast Pacific and then the huge continental United States to Washington DC on the East coast, *and then back again almost twenty times*."[19]

While Rummel may have thought that such calculations would make the abstraction of huge numbers more concrete, it is not clear that he even convinced himself, for he placed an endnote number at his calculation's conclusion. Note 14 reads as follows: "Back and forth, over 4,838 miles one way, near twenty times? This is so incredible that I would not believe the calculation and had to redo it several times."[20]

The Slaughter Bench of History

Turning now to the first of the four questions that I identified above, consider that the philosopher G. W. F. Hegel called history a slaughter bench.[21] Although he may not have acknowledged the point explicitly, he did so largely because the Sixth Commandment has neither functioned nor fared nearly as well as God and humankind should desire. Things could always be worse, even to the point of *omnicide*, the total extinction of life that may now be within the willful killing and murderous prowess of human beings, but humanity's murderous ways lend all too much credence to the point made by the Holocaust survivor Elie Wiesel when he said, "At Auschwitz, not only man died, but also the idea of man. . . . It was its own heart the world incinerated at Auschwitz."[22]

Meanwhile, the Sixth Commandment has had normative status, and it probably has had some braking effect on humankind's propensity for violence. Arguably, however, an honest historical appraisal leads to the conclusion that the most distinctive quality about the Sixth Commandment is the extent to which it has been violated—disregarded, dismissed, and disrespected. Coupled with those characteristics, one must add that the Sixth Commandment has never been backed sufficiently by credible sanctions, divine or human, that would ensure full respect for and obedience to it.[23]

"What have you done?" God asked Cain after he murdered Abel. The slaughter-bench history of homicide, genocide, and democide, plus the potential of omnicide, call into question the functional status of the Sixth Commandment. A commandment that is not obeyed may still be a commandment, but its functional status depends on obedience and credible sanctions against disobedience. An injunction that is not heeded lacks credibility. When Nazi Germany unleashed the Holocaust, the force of the injunction "You shall not murder" was impugned to the degree that millions of Jews were slaughtered. It took the violence of a massive world war, which left tens of millions more corpses in its wake, before the Third Reich was crushed and the Holocaust's genocidal killing centers were shut down. At least in biblical terms and in the Jewish and Christian traditions, God is the source and the ultimate vindicator of the Sixth Commandment. If God is not acknowledged and obeyed, God's existence is not necessarily eliminated, but God's authority is curtailed. And if God's authority lacks credibility, then the nature of God's existence is affected, too. How has the

Sixth Commandment functioned and fared in history? Two of the words that must be used in response to that question are *poorly* and *badly*.

Disagreement

What does the Sixth Commandment reveal about humankind? Beyond the fact that human beings have often been what Richard Rhodes called "masters of death" who flagrantly and repeatedly disobey the prohibition against murder, this commandment also shows how contentious, confident, and confused the commandment against murder can make us. Those three qualities make an ill-fitting package.

In late May 2005 I drove across the United States from Washington DC to my home in California. I had spent the 2004–2005 academic year at the United States Holocaust Memorial Museum, where I wrote a book about ethics during and after the Holocaust.[24] On my way west, somewhere outside of Little Rock, Arkansas, a billboard caught my attention. Not the only one of its kind in the United States, it said: "You call it abortion. God calls it murder."

What about abortion? Few issues are more vexed than whether God calls abortion murder and how human beings know God's mind on that matter. More than once in this area, violence has eclipsed dialogue. What about euthanasia, another issue that pitted Americans, families even, against one another in the 2005 media-hyped, "right to die" case involving Terri Schiavo? Absent the Sixth Commandment and the contentious ways in which the Decalogue, including wrangles over the relationship between civic displays of Exodus 20:1–17 and American constitutional requirements about the separation of church and state, it is hard to imagine that the Schiavo case would have riveted and ripped the American republic as it did.[25]

The Sixth Commandment creates confidence, although not necessarily confidence that is warranted and wise, when people think they know exactly what it means and precisely to what it applies. But such claims, including their assumptions about "God's will," rarely produce more agreement than disagreement. Whether intended or unintended, one consequence of confidence about the meaning of the Sixth Commandment is often disagreement, frequently contentious disagreement. Typically, confusion—recognized and acknowledged or not—accompanies disagreement of that kind. It remains to be seen whether even the most careful inquiry can produce the clarity and insight that are needed, but such wrestling should be one of the Sixth Commandment's most critical byproducts. Among other things, the quality of that wrestling is bound to have consequences for the ways in which prosecution, condemnation, and punishment of atrocities go forward.

Unmistakably, the Sixth Commandment declares that homicide is wrong. It requires us to find genocide and democide wrong as well. How it applies in other acts that take life away—along with war and capital punishment, abortion and euthanasia are two of the most crucial examples in our time—may not be as clear, but at the very least, respect for the Sixth Commandment should make us deliberate thoughtfully and humbly as we wrestle with the silence, and therefore the need for interpretation, that is embedded in its unmistakable clarity that murder is forbidden.

What Has God Done?

In wrestling with the Sixth Commandment, God's question to Cain—"What have you done?"—can be put to God as well. God's prohibition of murder is clear, but arguably not clear enough because the commandment's meaning is neither completely self-evident nor as thoroughly detailed as it might be. Even if the taking of any life is in some sense wrong, and such a case can be made, God's specific positions—to the extent that they exist—on war, capital punishment, abortion, and euthanasia appear not to be entirely free of ambiguity, leaving men and women to contend for and about the interpretations that make the best sense. The complications, however, are not restricted to matters of interpretation. They also involve God's relation to murder, which is made the more troublesome because of the Sixth Commandment.

Could it be that the Sixth Commandment is violated by God, the very one who established it? That question does not imply, God forbid, that God is a murderer, but it does raise the possibility that God can be found wanting for failing to intervene against murderers and, to that extent, for being a bystander if not an accomplice when murder takes place.

When that possibility is raised, theology usually offers justifications or excuses for God in an exercise called *theodicy*. Where murder is concerned, theodicy typically gives God a pass by arguing that human beings, and they alone, are responsible for their actions because God gave them freedom to choose. Freedom's defense for God, however, is more problematic than it seems.[26] As homicide, genocide, and democide make clear, God's gift of freedom has taken an immensely murderous toll. History shows that human beings can and will use their freedom to murder wantonly and to a large extent with impunity because the murdering is never stopped soon enough. Auschwitz makes us ask, "Where was humanity?" Auschwitz can also make us ask, "Where is God?" and it does so because of the Sixth Commandment.

"You shall not murder"—this commandment reveals much about God. The revelation is awesome, but not only because God's commanding moral voice resounds within it. The revelation is also awesome because God's refusal or inability to prevent human beings from murdering one another ramps up humankind's responsibility for itself. The Sixth Commandment contains an awesome challenge, for it reveals God to be one who takes human accountability far more seriously than men and women are likely to do. Only if human beings rise to the occasion, taking their accountability as seriously as they need to do, will the prosecution, condemnation, and punishment of atrocity possess the credibility that they ought to have.

The Sixth Commandment and the Future

The Sixth Commandment will continue to be the imperative that is the most necessary, although not sufficient, condition for human civilization. No less clear is the fact that this commandment will continue to be violated, often immensely and with a large measure of impunity. Furthermore, the God who prohibits murder is also the one who will do relatively little, if anything, to stop human beings from committing homicide, genocide, democide, and perhaps even omnicide.

The Jewish philosopher Emmanuel Levinas, who lost much of his family in the Holocaust, insisted that "You shall not murder" means nothing less than "you shall defend the life of the other."[27] The Sixth Commandment and the task that Levinas rightly identifies as following from it show that nothing human, natural, or divine guarantees respect for either of those imperatives, but nothing is more important than making them our key responsibility, for they remain as fundamental as they are in jeopardy, as vitally important as they are threatened by humankind's murderous destructiveness and indifference. Effective prosecution, condemnation, and punishment against murderous atrocities depend on keen understanding of those truths and on sound and sustained ethical responses to them.

Notes

1. The discussion about Gerda Klein and Telford Taylor in this section is adapted from my contributions to *The Holocaust Chronicle* (Lincolnwood IL: Publications International, 2000).
2. Gerda Weissman Klein, *All But My Life*, expanded ed. (New York: Hill and Wang, 1995), pp. 249–50.
3. Klein, *All But My Life*, pp. 252–53.
4. Insight about Telford Taylor's role at Nuremberg is provided by Joseph E. Persico, *Nuremberg: Infamy on Trial* (New York: Penguin Books, 1994), esp. pp. 204–6, 309–10.
5. Quoted in Michael Berenbaum, ed., *Witness to the Holocaust* (New York: HarperCollins, 1997), pp. 345–46. For more detail on Jackson's opening address at the IMT, 21 November 1945, see Michael R. Marrus, *The Nuremberg War Crimes Trial, 1945–46: A Documentary History* (New York: Bedford/St. Martin's, 1997), pp. 79–85.
6. Helpful discussions of these genocides can be found in Samuel Totten, William S. Parsons, and Israel W. Charny, eds., *A Century of Genocide: Critical Essays and Eyewitness Accounts*, 2d ed. (New York: Routledge, 2004). For Rwanda in particular, see also Jean Hatzfeld, *Machete Season: The Killers in Rwanda Speak*, trans. Linda Coverdale (New York: Farrar, Straus and Giroux, 2005) and Gérard Prunier, *The Rwanda Crisis: History of a Genocide* (New York: Columbia University Press, 1995).
7. Background on the humanitarian crisis in Darfur is provided by Gérard Prunier, *Darfur: The Ambiguous Genocide* (Ithaca NY: Cornell University Press, 2005).
8. See Colum Lynch, "UN Panel Finds No Genocide in Darfur but Urges Tribunals," *Washington Post*, 1 February 2005, p. A1.
9. Among the sources that have been most helpful in my thinking about the Decalogue, I want to mention especially William P. Brown, ed., *The Ten Commandments: The Reciprocity of Faithfulness* (Louisville KY: Westminster John Knox Press, 2004).
10. Philip Paul Hallie, "Cruelty: The Empirical Evil," in *Facing Evil: Light at the Core of Darkness*, ed. Paul Woodruff and Harry A. Wilmer (LaSalle IL: Open Court, 1988), p. 128.
11. Thomas Hobbes, *Leviathan* (Indianapolis: Bobbs-Merrill, 1958), pp. 106–7. To a considerable degree, human existence is perpetually in the state of war that Hobbes identified. The reason has much to do with humankind's repeated and escalating violations of the Sixth Commandment.
12. Stephen T. Davis, "Genocide, Despair, and Religious Hope: An Essay on Human Nature," in *Genocide and Human Rights: A Philosophical Guide*, ed. John K. Roth (New York: Palgrave Macmillan, 2005), p. 38.
13. David Flusser, "The Decalogue in the New Testament," in *The Ten Commandments in History and Tradition*, ed. Ben-Zion Segal and Gershon Levi (Jerusalem: Magnes Press, Hebrew University of Jerusalem: 1990), p. 221.
14. Richard Rhodes, *Masters of Death: The SS-Einsatzgruppen and the Invention of the Holo-*

caust (New York: Alfred A. Knopf, 2002), p. 121.

15. Rhodes, *Masters of Death*, p. 140.

16. On this point, see Claudia Koonz, *The Nazi Conscience* (Cambridge MA: Harvard University Press, 2003).

17. For more detail on these matters, see Carol Rittner, John K. Roth, and James M. Smith, eds., *Will Genocide Ever End?* (St. Paul MN: Paragon House, 2002).

18. R. J. Rummel, *Death by Government* (New Brunswick NJ: Transaction, 1997), pp. 13, 31. Observations about Rummel's data by the Holocaust historian Yehuda Bauer are worth noting: "Rummel has been criticized for exaggerating the losses. Even if the criticisms were valid, a figure lower by 10 or 20 or even 30 percent would make absolutely no difference to the general conclusions that Rummel draws." See Yehuda Bauer, *Rethinking the Holocaust* (New Haven CT: Yale University Press, 2001), pp. 12–13, 277 n.17.

19. Rummel, *Death by Government*, pp. 13, 31.

20. Rummel, *Death by Government*, p. 28.

21. See G. W. F. Hegel, *Introduction to the Philosophy of History*, trans. Leo Rauch (Indianapolis: Hackett, 1988), p. 24.

22. Elie Wiesel, *Legends of Our Time* (New York: Avon Books, 1972), p. 230.

23. If there is life beyond death, God's judgment may provide sanctions that condemn murder beyond all doubt and without remainder. Unfortunately, that outcome comes too late to be effective in history, for neither the murdered nor their murderers have returned to tell what God may have done with them. Nor has God made that situation crystal clear. Meanwhile, within history, murder is sometimes punished but not with sufficiently credible deterring impact. History's mounds of murdered dead grow larger and larger.

24. See John K. Roth, *Ethics during and after the Holocaust: In the Shadow of Birkenau* (New York: Palgrave Macmillan, 2005).

25. It is not even clear that the disputes about the Schiavo case have been entirely laid to rest by the autopsy report that was released on 15 June 2005, which found that her collapse in 1990 had not been caused by physical abuse or poison but had left her with irreversible brain damage and in a condition that could properly be described as a persistent vegetative state. See, for example, Timothy Williams, "Schiavo's Brain Was Severely Deteriorated, Autopsy Says," *New York Times*, 15 June 2005.

26. For elaborations of my views on these matters, see, for example, my contributions to Stephen T. Davis, ed., *Encountering Evil: Live Options in Theodicy*, rev. ed. (Louisville KY: Westminster John Knox Press, 2001).

27. Emmanuel Levinas, "In the Name of the Other," trans. Maureen V. Gedney, in *Is It Righteous to Be? Interviews with Emmanuel Levinas*, ed. Jill Robbins (Stanford CA: Stanford University Press, 2001), p. 192.

Selected Bibliography

Bartov, Omer, Atina Grossmann, and Mary Nolan, eds. *Crimes of War: Guilt and Denial in the Twentieth Century*. New York: New Press, 2002.

Bass, Gary Jonathan. *Stay the Hand of Vengeance: The Politics of War Crimes Tribunals*. Princeton: Princeton University Press, 2000.

Bassiouni, Cherif M. *Crimes against Humanity in International Criminal Law*. The Hague: Kluwer Law International, 1999.

Bessmann, Alyn, and Marc Buggeln. "Befehlsgeber und Direkttäter vor dem Militärgericht: Die britische Strafverfolgung der Verbrechen im KZ Neuengamme und seinen Außenlagern." *Zeitschrift für Geschichtswissenschaft* 6 (2005): 522–42.

Biddiss, Michael. "The Nuremberg Trial: Two Exercises in Judgement." *Journal of Contemporary History* 16 (1981): 597–615.

———. "Victors' Justice? The Nuremberg Tribunal." *History Today* 49 (October 1993): 40–46.

Bloxham, Donald. "From Streicher to Sawoniuk: The Holocaust in the Courtroom." In *The Historiography of the Holocaust*, ed. Dan Stone, pp. 397–419. Houndmills/Basingstoke: Palgrave Macmillan, 2004.

———. *Genocide on Trial: War Crimes Trials in the Formation of Holocaust History and Memory*. Oxford: Oxford University Press, 2001.

Buruma, Ian. *The Wages of Guilt: Memories of War in Germany and Japan*. New York: Farrar, Straus and Giroux, 1994.

Buscher, Frank. *The U.S. War Crimes Trial Program in Germany, 1946–1955*. Westport CT: Greenwood, 1989.

Byers, Michael. *War Law: Understanding International Law and Armed Conflict*. New York: Grove Press, 2006.

Conan, Éric. *Le Procès Papon: Un journal d'audience*. Paris: Seuil, 1998.

Davenport, John. *The Nuremberg Trials*. San Diego CA: Lucent Books, 2006.

Douglas, Lawrence. *The Memory of Judgment: Making Law and History in the Trials of the Holocaust*. New Haven: Yale University Press, 2001.

Fraser, David. *Law after Auschwitz: A Jurisprudence towards the Holocaust*. Durham NC: Carolina Academic Press, 2005.

Freudiger, Kerstin. *Die juristische Aufarbeitung von NS-Verbrechen: Versuch einer Bilanz*. Tübingen: Mohr Siebeck, 2002.

Freyhofer, Horst H. *The Nuremberg Medical Trial: The Holocaust and the Origin of the Nuremberg Medical Code*. New York: Peter Lang, 2004.

Friedlander, Henry. "The Judiciary and Nazi Crimes in Postwar Germany." *The Simon Wiesenthal Center Annual*, pp. 27–44. Chappaqua NY: Rossel Books, 1984.

Gellately, Robert, ed. *The Nuremberg Interviews*. New York: Vintage Books, 2005.

Gerlach, Christian. "The Eichmann Interrogations in Holocaust Historiography." *Holocaust and Genocide Studies* 15 (2001): 428–52.

Goldensohn, Leon. *Les entretiens de Nuremberg*. Paris: Flammarion, 2005.

Golsan, Richard J., ed. *Memory, the Holocaust, and French Justice: The Bousquet and Touvier Affairs*. Hanover NH: University Press of New England, 1996.

———. *The Papon Affair: Memory and Justice on Trial*. New York: Routledge, 2000.

Hankel, Gerd. *Die Leipziger Prozesse: Deutsche Kriegsverbrechen und ihre strafrechtliche Verfolgung nach dem Ersten Weltkrieg*. Hamburg: Hamburger Edition, 2003.

Harris, Whitney R. *Tyranny on Trial*. Dallas: Southern Methodist University Press, 1954; rev. ed., 1999.

Horne, John, and Alan Kramer. *German Atrocities, 1914: A History of Denial*. New Haven: Yale University Press, 2001.

International Military Tribunal. *Trial of the Major War Criminals before the International Military Tribunal: Nuremberg, 14 November 1945–1 October 1946*. 42 vols. Nuremberg, 1947–1949; reprint, Buffalo NY: William S. Hein, 1995.

Jones, Adam. *Genocide: A Comprehensive Introduction*. New York: Routledge, 2006.

Kochavi, Arieh J. *Prelude to Nuremberg: Allied War Crimes Policy and the Question of Punishment*. Chapel Hill: University of North Carolina Press, 1998.

Maguire, Peter. *Law and War: An American Story*. New York: Columbia University Press, 2001.

Marrus, Michael. "The Holocaust at Nuremberg." *Yad Vashem Studies* 26 (1998): 5–41.

———. *The Nuremberg War Crimes Trial, 1945–46: A Documentary History*. Boston: Bedford Books, 1997.

Maser, Werner. *Nuremberg: A Nation on Trial*. London: Allen Lane, 1979.

Mendelsohn, John. "Trial by Document: The Problem of Due Process for War Criminals at Nuremberg," *Prologue* 8 (Winter 1975): 227–34.

Mildt, Dick de. *In the Name of the People: Perpetrators of Genocide in the Reflection of Their Post-War Prosecution in West Germany: The "Euthanasia" and "Aktion Reinhard" Trial Cases*. The Hague: Martinus Nijhoff, 1996.

Minow, Martha. *Between Vengeance and Forgiveness: Facing History after Genocide and Mass Violence*. Boston: Beacon Press, 1998.

Miquel, Marc von. *Ahnden oder amnestieren? Westdeutsche Justiz und Vergangenheitspolitik in den sechziger Jahren*. Göttingen: Wallstein Verlag, 2004.

Müller, Ingo. *Hitler's Justice: The Courts of the Third Reich*. Trans. Deborah Lucas Schneider. Cambridge MA: Harvard University Press, 1991.

Nino, Carlos S. *Radical Evil on Trial*. New Haven: Yale University Press, 1996.

Osiel, Mark. *Mass Atrocity, Collective Memory, and the Law*. New Brunswick NJ: Transaction Books, 1997.

Pendas, Devin O. *The Frankfurt Auschwitz Trial, 1963–65*. Cambridge: Cambridge University Press, 2005.

Perels, Joachim. *Das juristische Erbe des "Dritten Reiches": Beschädigungen der demokratischen Rechtsordnung*. Frankfurt am Main: Campus, 1999.

Reginbogin, Herbert, and Christoph Safferling, eds. *Die Nürnberger Prozesse: Völkerstrafrecht seit 1945 / The Nuremberg Trials: International Criminal Law since 1945*. Frankfurt am Main: Saur Verlag, 2006.

Robertson, Geoffrey. *Crimes against Humanity*. London: Allen Lane, 1999.

Rogers, A. P. V. "War Crimes Trials under the Royal Warrant: British Practice, 1945–1949," *International and Comparative Law Quarterly* 39 (1990): 780–800.

Rückerl, Adalbert. *The Investigation of Nazi Crimes, 1945-1978: A Documentation*. Hamden CT: Archon Books, 1979.

Rüter, C. F., and D. W. de Mildt. *Justiz und NS-Verbrechen: Sammlung deutscher Strafurteile wegen nationalsozialistischer Tötungsverbrechen*. 35 vols. Amsterdam/Munich: Amsterdam University Press/K. G. Saur Verlag, 2005.

Schabas, William. *Genocide in International Law: The Crimes of Crimes*. Cambridge: Cambridge University Press, 2000.

Schmidt, Ulf. *Karl Brandt, The Nazi Doctor: Medicine and Power in the Third Reich*. London: Continuum, 2007.

Shelton, Dinah, ed., *Encyclopedia of Genocide and Crimes against Humanity*. Farmington Hills MI: Macmillan Reference, 2004.

Sieber, Ulrich, ed. *The Punishment of Serious Crimes: A Comparative Analysis of Sentencing Law and Practice*. Freiburg: Edition Iuscrim, 2004.

Stover, Eric, and Harvey M. Weinstein, eds. *My Neighbor, My Enemy: Justice and Community in the Aftermath of Mass Atrocity*. Cambridge: Cambridge University Press, 2004.

Taylor, Telford. *Nuremberg and Vietnam: An American Tragedy*. New York: Bantam, 1971.

Trials of War Criminals before the Nuremberg Military Tribunals under Control Council Law No. 10. 15 vols. Reprint, Buffalo NY: William S. Hein, 1995.

Tusa, Ann, and John Tusa. *The Nuremberg Trial*. London: Atheneum, 1983.

Ueberschär, Gerd R., ed. *Der Nationalsozialismus vor Gericht: Die alliierten Prozesse gegen Kriegsverbrecher und Soldaten, 1943–1952*. Darmstadt: Primus Verlag, 1999.

Valentino, Benjamin A. *Final Solutions: Mass Killing and Genocide in the 20th Century*. Ithaca NY: Cornell University Press, 2005.

Weber, Jürgen, and Peter Steinbach, eds. *Vergangenheitsbewältigung durch Strafverfahren? NS-Prozesse in der Bundesrepublik Deutschland*. Munich: Olzog, 1984.

Weinke, Annette. *Die Nürnberger Prozesse.* Munich: C. H. Beck, 2006.

———. *Die Verfolgung von NS-Tätern im geteilten Deutschland: Vergangenheitsbewälti- gungen, 1949–1969, oder: Eine deutsch-deutsche Beziehungsgeschichte im Kalten Krieg.* Paderborn: Schöningh, 2002.

Wette, Wolfram, and Gerd R. Ueberschär, eds. *Kriegsverbrechen im 20. Jahrhundert,* pp. 72–84. Darmstadt: Wissenschaftliche Buchgesellschaft, 2001.

Wilke, Jürgen, Birgit Schenk, Akiba A. Cohen, and Tami Zemach, eds. *Holocaust und NS-Prozesse: Die Presseberichterstattung in Israel und Deutschland zwischen Aneignung und Abwehr.* Cologne: Böhlau, 1995.

Wittmann, Rebecca E. *Beyond Justice: The Auschwitz Trial.* Cambridge MA: Harvard Uni- versity Press, 2005.

———. "The Wheels of Justice Turn Slowly: The Pretrial Investigations of the Frankfurt Auschwitz Trial 1963–65." *Central European History* 35 (2002): 345–78.

Donald Bloxham is Reader in History at the University of Edinburgh. He is author of *The Great Game of Genocide: Imperialism, Nationalism, and the Destruction of the Ottoman Armenians* (Oxford: Oxford University Press, 2005); *The Holocaust: Critical Historical Approaches* (Manchester: Manchester University Press, 2005, with Tony Kushner), and *Genocide on Trial: War Crimes Trials and the Formation of Holocaust History and Memory* (Oxford: Oxford University Press, 2001). He is editor, with Mark Levene, of the Oxford University Press monograph series *Zones of Violence*.

Jonathan C. Friedman is Director of Holocaust and Genocide Studies and Associate Professor of History at West Chester University in West Chester, Pennsylvania. He received his Ph.D. in 1996 in modern German and modern Jewish history from the University of Maryland, College Park, and is the author of four books: *The Lion and the Star: Gentile-Jewish Relations in Three Hessian Communities, 1919–1945* (Lexington: University Press of Kentucky, 1998); *Speaking the Unspeakable: Essays on Gender, Sexuality, and Holocaust Survivor Memory* (Lanham MD: University Press of America, 2002); *The Literary, Cultural, and Historical Significance of the 1937 Biblical Stage Play The Eternal Road* (Lewiston NY: Mellen Press, 2004); and *Rainbow Jews: Gay and Jewish Identity in the Performing Arts* (Lanham MD: Rowman and Littlefield, 2008).

Richard J. Golsan is Professor of French and head of the Department of European and Classical Languages at Texas A&M University. In 2001 he was a visiting professor at the Université Paris III–Sorbonne Nouvelle. He is a specialist of the Vichy period and its cultural and political legacies. He is the author of *French Writers and the Politics of Complicity: Crises of Democracy in the 1940s and 1990s* (Baltimore: Johns Hopkins University Press, 2006) and *Vichy's After-*

life: History and Counterhistory in Postwar France (Lincoln: University of Nebraska Press, 2000). He has edited several books on Fascism and the trials for crimes against humanity of former Vichy collaborators René Bousquet, Paul Touvier, and Maurice Papon. He is editor of *South Central Review* (Johns Hopkins University Press).

Patricia Heberer is a historian with the Center for Advanced Holocaust Studies at the United States Holocaust Memorial Museum. There she functions as the museum's in-house specialist on medical crimes and eugenics policies in Nazi Germany. A contributor and consultant historian for two United States Holocaust Memorial Museum publications, *1945: The Year of Liberation* and *In Pursuit of Justice: Examining Evidence of the Holocaust*, she has written and spoken widely on issues of postwar adjudication of war crimes, the Nazi "euthanasia" program, and medical and racial hygiene policies in Nazi Germany.

Michael R. Marrus is the Chancellor Rose and Ray Wolfe Professor of Holocaust Studies at the University of Toronto. A Fellow of the Royal Society of Canada, he has been a visiting fellow of St. Antony's College, Oxford, and the Institute for Advanced Studies of the Hebrew University of Jerusalem. He has taught as a visiting professor at the University of California, Los Angeles, and the University of Cape Town, South Africa. He is the author of numerous books, including *Vichy France and the Jews* (with Robert O. Paxton); *The Unwanted: European Refugees in the Twentieth Century*; *The Holocaust in History*; and *The Nuremberg War Crimes Trial, 1945–46*.

Jürgen Matthäus is a historian and currently Director for Applied Research at the Center for Advanced Holocaust Studies, a wing of the United States Holocaust Memorial Museum. His recent publications include *Deutsche, Juden, Völkermord: Der Holocaust als Gegenwart und Vergangenheit* (ed. with K.-M. Mallmann; Darmstadt: Wissenschaftliche Buchgesellschaft, 2006); and *Contemporary Responses to the Holocaust* (ed. with K. Kwiet; New York: Praeger/Greenwood 2004). He is a contributor to C. Browning, *The Origins of the Final Solution: The Evolution of Nazi Jewish Policy, September 1939–March 1942* (Lincoln: University of Nebraska Press; Jerusalem: Yad Vashem 2004).

John K. Roth is the Edward J. Sexton Professor Emeritus of Philosophy and the founding Director of the Center for the Study of the Holocaust, Genocide, and Human Rights at Claremont McKenna College, where he had taught since 1966. His most recent books include *Genocide and Human Rights: A Philosophical Guide* and *Ethics during and after the Holocaust: In the Shadow of Birkenau*. His Holocaust-related research appointments have included a 2001 Koerner Visiting Fellowship at the Oxford Centre for Hebrew and Jewish Studies in England and a 2004–2005 appointment as the Ina Levine Invitational Scholar at the Center for Advanced Holocaust Studies, United States Holocaust Memorial Museum, Washington DC.

Ulf Schmidt is Senior Lecturer in Modern History at the University of Kent, Canterbury, and a fellow of the Royal Historical Society. His expertise is in the area of the history of modern medical ethics and policy in twentieth-century Europe and America. He has recently been awarded a major Wellcome Trust project grant to write the history of Britain's biological and chemical warfare experiments on humans during the cold war. He is the author of numerous articles, chapters in books, and book reviews, and three books: *Medical Films, Ethics and Euthanasia in Germany, 1933–1945* (Husum: Matthiesen, 2002); *Justice at Nuremberg: Leo Alexander and the Nazi Doctors' Trial* (Basingstoke: Macmillan/Palgrave, 2004, 2006); and *Karl Brandt, the Nazi Doctor: Medicine and Power in the Third Reich* (London: Continuum, 2007).

Rebecca Wittmann is Assistant Professor of History at the University of Toronto. Her research focuses on the Holocaust, postwar German trials of Nazi perpetrators, and German legal history. She has received fellowships from the United States Holocaust Memorial Museum, the DAAD (or German Academic Exchange Service), and the Holocaust Educational Foundation in Chicago. She has published articles in *Central European History, German History*, and *Lessons and Legacies*. Her book *Beyond Justice: The Auschwitz Trial* was published in 2005 with Harvard University Press. She is currently working on her next project: "Nazism and Terrorism: The Madjanek and Stammheim Trials in 1975 West Germany."

Lisa Yavnai is Director of the Visiting Scholars Programs at the Center for Advanced Holocaust Studies at the United States Holocaust Memorial Museum.

She earned a Ph.D. in International History from the London School of Economics and Political Science and a J.D. from Northeastern University. Prior to joining the museum, Dr. Yavnai worked as a research associate for the Presidential Advisory Commission on Holocaust Assets in the United States and served in the Israeli Army. She has written and presented papers on topics including war crimes trials, Nazi-looted Jewish property, and the postwar fate of concentration camp Kapos.

Index